"The voice of Michael Rhodes is fresh, clear, and strong. With a deep foundation in theology and a strong grasp of biblical scholarship, he skillfully brings texts from across the scriptural canon to bear on contemporary issues of racial and economic justice. Writing in an accessible style with plentiful examples, Rhodes issues a timely challenge to the church to become just people in a deeply unjust world. I recommend this book highly: it is a creative and provocative invitation to embark on a journey of change."
John Barclay, Lightfoot Professor of Divinity at Durham University

"Jesus says that the kingdom is not for all who say 'Lord, Lord,' but for those 'who do the will of my Father.' *Just Discipleship* takes seriously Jesus' call to heed the Father's will by tapping into the justice-rich lodes that fill Scripture's pages. Rhodes's study is deeply personal, rigorously exegetical, and inspiring. Rather than leaving readers depleted and disheartened by the insurmountable problems of injustice, *Just Discipleship* will leave readers captivated by the gospel's scope and vision for holistic discipleship. I pray that churches—especially those with privileged legacies—take up the challenges and opportunities that this book offers."
Matthew Lynch, associate professor of Old Testament at Regent College

"It is rare to find scholars with expertise and experience in biblical studies, theology and ethics, and practical theology. Michael Rhodes is among them, and in *Just Discipleship* he demonstrates how all these disciplines contribute to our understanding of what it means to follow Jesus. Rhodes models how Scripture is to be read theologically and missionally, and in doing so he provides clear direction for those on the path of discipleship today. All followers of Jesus will benefit from this book."
Bo H. Lim, Seattle Pacific University

"This timely volume is born out of personal involvement in race relations, grounded in insightful readings of passages across the breadth of Scripture, and concrete in its applications. The topic is discipleship, which Rhodes convincingly defines as the formation of the people of God around the virtue of justice. This is a clarion call to faithfully, wisely, and courageously embody God's justice within the socioeconomic and political realities of life. A necessary and supremely helpful book!"
M. Daniel Carroll R. (Rodas), Scripture Press Ministries Professor of Biblical Studies and Pedagogy at Wheaton College and Graduate School

"The church today urgently needs to be discipled by the Scripture's vision for justice. Michael Rhodes illuminates passages across the Old and New Testaments to show how the call to justice is central to God's vision for the community of faith. It will challenge pastors, seminary students, and many others to discover a costly but rewarding vocation."
Carmen Imes, associate professor of Old Testament at Talbot School of Theology, Biola University, and author of *Bearing God's Name* and *Being God's Image*

"One of the things that most impressed me about *Just Discipleship* is the diversity of voices that Michael Rhodes engages with to both inform and challenge readers. The author engages in rigorous biblical, theological, and missiological analysis without being pedantic. Rhodes is a wise, compassionate guide for any and all who desire clarity on what the notion of justice can mean for contemporary Bible readers."

Dennis R. Edwards, dean of North Park Theological Seminary

"With admirable clarity, wide learning, and practical conviction, *Just Discipleship* narrates justice as a biblical story, one located in the rich details of Scripture, the deep history of Israel and the church, and the virtuous lives of ordinary people. At once powerfully convicting and unfailingly gracious, this book invites readers to encounter a conversation with God as clear-eyed prophet and gentle teacher."

Jonathan Tran, author of *Asian Americans and the Spirit of Racial Capitalism*

"True to one of his dominant passions, Michael Rhodes has provided another feast of applied biblical insight on what it means to live out the justice of God in our fallen world. There are some whose handling of Scripture is creative but unconvincing. This book is not only freshly creative in exploring the formative power of a wide range of texts, but also challengingly convincing in applying their ethical and missional demands. Rhodes combines faithfulness to the centrality of the gospel, thorough biblical scholarship, and the courage of prophetic critique."

Christopher J. H. Wright, Langham Partnership, author of *"Here Are Your Gods"*

"Michael Rhodes's exploration of justice is real and insightful, born out of hard-learned lessons, careful theological inquiry, and humility. He speaks concretely from his life and work—giving his book clarity and power—without straying from the conspicuous and unyielding call of Scripture to embrace 'justice and righteousness.' *Just Discipleship* sounds its own clarion call for those who have neglected justice as an essential category of discipleship and welcomes them into a conversation about how God's people might be more faithful disciples in an unjust world."

Michelle Knight, assistant professor of Old Testament and Semitic languages at Trinity Evangelical Divinity School

"Upon reading this book, my first thought was, *My elders, deacons, and congregation must read this!* Any Christian who does not understand that the Scriptures call them to deep relationships of economic solidarity will understand by the end of their reading of Michael Rhodes's excellent text. Bringing together Scriptural texts not often looked to for ethical guidance, such as Job, the Psalms, and Deuteronomy, Rhodes reminds us that the people of God are a people, and the way of comprehensive salvation requires a deeper understanding of justice and community than is currently broadly on offer."

Malcolm Foley, pastor of Mosaic Waco and director of Black church studies at Truett Seminary

MICHAEL J. RHODES

DISCIPLESHIP

BIBLICAL JUSTICE IN AN UNJUST WORLD

FOREWORD BY BRENT A. STRAWN

Academic
An imprint of InterVarsity Press
Downers Grove, Illinois

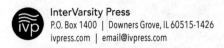

InterVarsity Press
P.O. Box 1400 | Downers Grove, IL 60515-1426
ivpress.com | email@ivpress.com

InterVarsity Press® is the publishing division of InterVarsity Christian Fellowship/USA®. For more information, visit intervarsity.org.

Scripture quotations, unless otherwise noted, are from the New Revised Standard Version Bible, copyright © 1989 National Council of the Churches of Christ in the United States of America. Used by permission. All rights reserved worldwide.

While any stories in this book are true, some names and identifying information may have been changed to protect the privacy of individuals.

The publisher cannot verify the accuracy or functionality of website URLs used in this book beyond the date of publication.

Cover design: David Fassett
Interior design: Daniel van Loon

ISBN 978-1-5140-0600-9 (print) | ISBN 978-1-5140-0601-6- (digital)

Printed in the United States of America ♾

Library of Congress Cataloging-in-Publication Data
Title: Just discipleship : biblical justice in an unjust world / Michael J. Rhodes ; foreword by Brent A. Strawn.
Description: Downers Grove, IL : IVP Academic, [2023] | Includes bibliographical references and index.
Identifiers: LCCN 2023001696 (print) | LCCN 2023001697 (ebook) | ISBN 9781514006009 (print) |
    ISBN 9781514006016 (digital)
Subjects: LCSH: Justice. | Christian life--Biblical teaching.
Classification: LCC JC578 .R53 2023 (print) | LCC JC578 (ebook) | DDC 320.01/1--dc23/eng/20230504
LC record available at https://lccn.loc.gov/2023001696
LC ebook record available at https://lccn.loc.gov/2023001697

30 29 28 27 26 25 24 23 | 13 12 11 10 9 8 7 6 5 4 3 2

FOR MIKE AND GAY RHODES:

For teaching me to love Jesus and trust his Word

AND FOR ISAIAH, AMOS, NOVA, AND JUBILEE:

May you experience the joy of a life lived in love with the Just King

CONTENTS

FOREWORD

Brent A. Strawn

CHRISTIANITY IS A BOOK RELIGION. It may well be more than that, but it is certainly not less than that. Holy Scripture is simply *indispensable* to any version of Christianity worthy of the name.

The "bookishness" of Christianity brings with it a number of benefits and not a few difficulties. On the plus side, the centrality of Scripture offers the church a lodestar. The church knows (or should know) where its most careful and reverent attention must be paid, where it must look to find supreme insight into the God the church confesses as triune. On the difficult side is the fact that the book in question is, to put it mildly, *complex*. Few, even among the truly pious, have the patience to sit with it for very long any more: the world is fast and information is cheaply gathered. (Of course, cheap information is typically worth the asking price.) Adding to this complexity, if not lying at its root, is the Bible's *antiquity*: few, even among professionals, can long stomach its ancient and diverse literature, let alone read it in its original languages in order to conduct an informed conversation about it, especially about its meaning(s).

Unfortunately, there is a third sticky spot: for a book that is supposed to be "useful for life," the Bible's given form seems singularly unsuitable for the job. Policy is not written, at least not easily, on the basis of a Hebrew psalm or a Greek parable. The parts of the Bible that seem most conducive to "life application" (whatever that means—and that remains a question) are, ironically, the ones that many Christians have little knowledge of: namely, the first five books of the Old Testament known as the Pentateuch or Torah. To be sure, there are plenty of "preachy," ethically rich parts elsewhere in Scripture, especially in the prophetic and Wisdom books, but these texts, too, are increasingly off the beaten track. Yes, Isaiah has a role to play in the Advent season, but many churches these days know little of the Christian calendar let alone the lectionary. As for the Wisdom literature, it is often robbed of its long-form shaping of the moral self and thinned down to "Bible promise" one-liners, at best, or, at worst, to simplistic justification for corporal punishment of children or some other stupidity that makes Christians look like they still live in the Stone Age. Unfortunately, even the parts of Scripture that are most familiar to Christians are seldom straightforward. How, exactly, does one *practice* "the kingdom of heaven is like yeast, which a woman took and hid in a bushel of wheat flour until the yeast had worked its way through all the dough" (Mt 13:33; CEB)? Again, policy (polity, too) is not usually based on aphorisms and psalms. The translation process from these genres to "actionable intel" is tricky to say the least.

This conundrum—the Bible as sine qua non for Christianity but manifesting difficulties that lead Christians increasingly away from it to other, more seductive resources—is a real problem but not one without recourse. In fact, *recourse* is exactly the issue: clearly, what we need now is help. Not unlike Israel at Sinai, who called on Moses as intermediary, or the Ethiopian eunuch, who asked for Philip's assistance in Acts, the average Christian needs an interpreter from *back then* in "Bibleland" to help *here and now* in our world. As was the case with Moses and Philip, such an interpreter should be a figure with knowledge and experience, one who is close to God and to God's ways in the world—someone, to borrow a phrase from John Wesley, who is a *real Christian*.[1]

At this point we come to the current book and its author, Michael J. Rhodes. I first met Michael in England and in Idaho: he was in England defending his dissertation, I was in Idaho examining his dissertation (via video conferencing). I was surprised to learn at that time that the author of the Trinity College Bristol/University of Aberdeen dissertation under discussion that day was not British at all, but an American from Memphis, Tennessee. To backtrack a wee bit, I admit that when Michael's dissertation arrived several months earlier, I felt sucker-punched. The initial invitation to serve as Michael's external examiner indicated that the dissertation was about Deuteronomy, something I know a little bit about, but when the dissertation showed up in the mail, it was clearly *not* about Deuteronomy—at least not primarily—but about

---

[1]See Kenneth J. Collins, *A Real Christian: The Life of John Wesley* (Nashville: Abingdon, 2000).

community formation especially around shared meals. Deuteronomy figured in the discussion, as did the eucharistic practices reflected in 1 Corinthians, but these were exegetical case studies in a much larger, far-reaching argument. Indeed, the first hundred pages or so were an extensive discussion of virtue ethics. That is *not* my expertise, but there was nothing to do in the face of this bait-and-switch than to roll up my sleeves and start reading…

…and learning. I found Michael's dissertation educational, as all theses ought to be, but his hit that standard at a more existential level than any others I had read. Here was not merely (!) new knowledge that made a distinctive contribution to a scholarly subfield. Here was a thesis that argued for *a better way in the world*, that showed how Scripture, from Torah to Epistle—despite its complex, ancient, and odd form—could affect real change in real communities and in real lives, even over something as simple as a shared meal. I was informed and also profoundly moved. Needless to say, the thesis passed with flying colors.[2]

A few weeks after the dissertation examination, Providence had me traveling through Memphis, with Michael back home, and so it was that he picked me up on a downtown street early one summer morning and we had breakfast in a delicious hole-in-the-wall dive. There I learned more about Michael the person, not just Michael the biblical scholar and theologian. I heard of his upbringing in the still-segregated city of Memphis. I learned of his missionary work in Africa and his family's decision to live in impoverished communities in Memphis on their return. Michael did not brag about this; it was simply a matter of fact, just what he and his wife Rebecca and their kids did as part of their everyday lives. The life of faithfulness, the poet Robert Bly once wrote, "goes by like a river, / With no one noticing it."[3] Saintliness, in other words, is baked into the saintly life: a river doesn't have to *try* to flow downstream. What I read from Rhodes the scholar, in the theoretical mode of his dissertation, and what I heard from Rhodes the person, that day over scrambled eggs and hash browns, matched. Together they testified to a saintly life, as regular as a trustworthy river—one that was making a difference in Memphis, a difference based on, rooted in, and shaped by nothing less than the odd, complex collection of texts we call Holy Scripture.

---

[2]It is now published as Michael J. Rhodes, *Formative Feasting: Practices and Virtue Ethics in Deuteronomy's Tithe Meal and the Corinthian Lord's Supper*, Studies in Biblical Literature 176 (New York: Peter Lang, 2022).

[3]Robert Bly, "An Evening When the Full Moon Rose as the Sun Set," in *Eating the Honey of Words: New and Selected Poems* (New York: HarperCollins, 2000), 134.

Once again I found myself deeply moved. I, not unlike Michael, have devoted my life to the study of Scripture because I am convinced that it matters above all else: that it is the church's only "sure thing." But I also admit to feeling my fair share of despair over the actual place of Scripture in Christian experience, where the sure thing is often the last thing on anyone's mind, let alone on their mobile devices (these are increasingly identical entities).[4] *Michael's work* gave me hope; *Michael's life* gave me more of the same. And what gave me the greatest hope of all was that Michael's biblically rooted work and Michael's real-Christian life were integrated, connected, ultimately of a piece.

I could say more about all that, but what I most want to say is this: here is an author you can trust. What Michael and his family have attempted to live out in Memphis to the best of their ability, they are now replicating in New Zealand in his teaching post there. And what Michael tried to do in his thesis he does even more broadly and accessibly in the present book. Michael has real experience and real expertise. He also has real integrity; he is a real Christian. And that means that he is precisely the kind of person we need: one who can offer assistance as a helper and guide from the back-then Bible to life here and now. Let me put it even stronger: I think Michael is one of the best guides we presently have on offer for this kind of work. People talk a lot about justice and discipleship. *Sometimes* they define those things. (Oftentimes they don't.) Michael has studied these things, and can define them, but, most important of all, he *lives* them. In the present book he shows the rest of us how to do the same: how, for example, Deuteronomy's tithe and feast legislation cultivate dispositions of solidarity that lead directly to the contemporary practice known as *relocation* (something that the Rhodes family has done more than once on three different continents); or how Job's transformation, which moved him from all-sufficient giver to one who gives-and-receives from all members of his community, can transform our own present-day structures that facilitate oppression. With gritty and insightful exegesis-into-practice engagements like these, Rhodes shows all of us how to *become* just, and how to do that precisely *as disciples*—how to become, as he puts it "militants of reconciling love and justice." That is the type of militancy even the strictest Christian pacifists could get behind, lest the discipling and justice-loving ways of Scripture fade from a Christianity increasingly adrift from its true center.

---

[4]See, e.g., Brent A. Strawn, *The Old Testament Is Dying: A Diagnosis and Recommended Treatment* (Grand Rapids: Baker Academic, 2017).

In one of the liturgies for baptism in my own Methodist tradition, there is a charge to the parents that reads as follows:

> Do you therefore accept as your bounden duty and privilege
> to live before *these children (persons)*
>   a life that becomes the Gospel?[5]

The verb "becomes" here is used in a sense that is now mostly obsolete: "to accord with, agree with, be suitable to; to befit."[6] The derived adjective, "becoming," signifies the same: "befitting, suitable, having graceful fitness," as in the sentence "the clothing is becoming on you."[7] The baptismal charge is thus urging the parents of the child awaiting baptism to live in a way that befits the gospel, that suits it and corresponds to it. Such living will make a difference, the liturgy assumes, in the life of the baptized child.

I have loved this liturgy for a long time, in part because its increasingly archaic use of "become" allows it to be reinterpreted. Nowadays, "becomes" usually means simply "to come into being or existence."[8] In modern parlance, therefore, this baptismal charge conveys the remarkable idea that the life to be lived before the baptized child is to *turn into* the gospel. What would it mean for a life to *become* the gospel in this way—not only to be suitable to or befit the gospel but to *actually* turn into the gospel? Michael Rhodes has written a book that tells us about that, that points us on the way, that gives us an example—no, that gives us *many* examples on how we might do precisely that, and do so justly, as faithful disciples on The Way. And so, no less than during that online dissertation examination a few years back, I stand in his debt: deeply grateful and profoundly instructed; moved, astonished, and amazed. I am confident all who read this book will experience the same.

---

[5] Baptismal Covenant II-B in *The United Methodist Book of Worship* (Nashville: The United Methodist Publishing House, 1992), 103-4.

[6] *Oxford English Dictionary* (revised September 2022; online; accessed December 4, 2022), s.v. "become, *v.*".

[7] *Oxford English Dictionary* (revised December 2021; online; accessed December 4, 2022), s.v. "becoming, *adj.*".

[8] *Oxford English Dictionary* (revised September 2022; online; accessed December 4, 2022), s.v. "become, *v.*".

ACKNOWLEDGMENTS

GIVEN THE TOPIC OF THIS BOOK, it's alarming to discover my inability to do justice to the people who've made it possible. My thinking has been deeply shaped by conversations with and feedback from colleagues, including Arthur Keefer, Stephen Haynes, Mark Glanville, Peter Altmann, Brian Fikkert, Chris Wright, Mark Catlin, Drew Hart, Will Kynes, David Firth, Lisa Bowens, Jamie Davies, Justin Stratis, Greg Thompson, Michael Barram, Gimbiya Kettering, Justin Stratis, Jon Coutts, Kelly Kapic, Justin Lonas, Michael Davis, Matt Lynch, Matthew Kaemingk, Tim Meadowcroft, John Barclay, the Kirby Laing Centre's Theology and Economics group, and participants in the Society of Biblical Literature's Missional Hermeneutics group, who allowed me to present on this material at several annual meetings. My former colleagues and students at MCUTS shaped me in ways that seep through every sentence of this book; I am particularly grateful to Ashley Chabot, Caroline Benny, Carter Mackie, Darriel Neely, Jake Wiig, Tyler Forney, and Victoria Fuentes for providing extensive feedback to early chapters as part of our course on community development. At Carey Baptist College, my colleagues offered enormous encouragement and numerous opportunities to present this material; students in my Wisdom and Worship class helped me with the chapters on Psalms and Proverbs (thanks especially to Liz Caughey, Caroline Bennie, Rebecca Hooper, and Ashely Bird for providing written feedback); and Siong Ng's librarian wizardry saved the day on several occasions. I am overwhelmed by the friendship and mentoring I've received from Craig Bartholomew and D. Stephen Long, both of whom advocated for this book. I am beyond grateful to Brent Strawn for his conversation, guidance, and friendship, as well as his generosity in writing the foreword. Special thanks also go to Rev. Melvin

Watkins for letting me hash out my ideas over lunches; to Daniel Warner for our ongoing dialogue about politics and feedback on chapter 11; to Duke Kwon for an extremely important conversation that first got me thinking about reparations from a biblical perspective; to Ryan O'Dowd for offering the kind of detailed, incisive feedback you usually have to pay for; and to Robby Holt and Danny Carroll, who met me in Birmingham for an epic day and a half dialogue on *Just Discipleship*.

Proverbs tells us there's wisdom in many counselors. My experience now suggests the same is true for editors. I'm grateful to Jon Boyd, Anna Gissing, and Rachel Hastings for all believing in, and serving as editors for, *Just Discipleship*.

This book owes much to the communities that have loved and cared for me on my justice journey. Those communities include the pastors and congregations of 2PC, New City Fellowship Nairobi, and Downtown Church; the Advance Memphis family and our South Memphis neighbors; the fourth of the fifth families; and the Option 105 (including Jonathan and Collins for their feedback on the reparations chapter). I am especially grateful to Marshall Teague, who read every word of my first draft, and whose feedback dramatically transformed it. I owe you one, brother.

I would never have had the experiences that drove me to write this book, nor ever finished researching and writing it, without the partnership, love, support, encouragement, and friendship of my bride, Rebecca. Words cannot express my gratitude to you, love.

Finally, this book is dedicated to my beloved parents, Mike and Gay Rhodes, and my children, Isaiah, Amos, Nova, and Jubilee. My parents planted the seeds of this book by teaching me to love Jesus with all my heart, and to follow him wherever his Word led me. My children lit a fire in my heart to finish it, in the hope that they, too, would fall in love with Jesus . . . and then leave us all in the dust as they run further and faster down the path to just discipleship.

PART 1

JUST DISCIPLESHIP

MAPPING
THE TERRAIN

THE STORY BEHIND
(AND THE STORY OF) THIS BOOK

JUST DISCIPLESHIP EXPLORES what Scripture says about how disciples of Jesus become just. Before diving in, it may help to know a bit of the story behind this book. I was raised by a family that loved Jesus, and in a church that taught me to follow Jesus with all my heart, soul, mind, and strength. They also taught me that the Bible was an authoritative, fully reliable guide to understanding what following Jesus meant in every area of life. These convictions remain central to what it means for me to live as a disciple of Jesus.

I was also raised in Memphis, a majority Black southern city with a legacy of racism and poverty. To take but one example, Dr. King was assassinated here while supporting the Memphis Sanitation Workers strike. Like many American Christians, our family and church shared in that long, problematic legacy in various ways, some of which I explore in the chapters that follow. One result of that legacy during my growing up years in the '80s and '90s was that while nearly 65 percent of Memphians are Black and nearly 25 percent fall below the poverty line, my church, neighborhood, Christian school, and overall upbringing was almost exclusively white and upper-middle class.[1]

I remember very little explicitly racist talk in my growing up years. I was raised in a segregated community, but we would never have identified ourselves as segregationists. Living a life of white, middle-class affluence in a city filled with Black poverty just seemed natural. Nor did the dynamics of being white, middle class, and affluent seem to have much to do with discipleship.

---

[1]Although all such decisions are debated, I have chosen to capitalize *Black* but not *white* in referring to racial designations. See Nancy Coleman, "Why We're Capitalizing Black," *New York Times* (July 5, 2020), www.nytimes.com/2020/07/05/insider/capitalized-black.html.

And then, at some point, our church invited Dr. John Perkins to speak. The moment he opened his mouth, you knew Perkins loved Jesus and loved his Word. He was just like us!

But he pointed out all this stuff in Scripture I'd never paid attention to, stuff that had never crossed my discipleship radar. Stuff like God's overwhelming love for the poor, his care for the ethnic outsider, his passionate commitment to justice. Perkins showed us that to be serious about Scripture, to be serious about *discipleship*, we had to be serious about poverty, racism, and injustice. Not because of some liberal agenda or to "keep up with the times." Because "the Bible tells us so"!

This changed my life. Our youth group visited Baltimore and met with white Presbyterians like me who had taken Perkins's challenge seriously. They'd moved into an economically depressed community, and seen the Spirit move powerfully.[2] I went to Covenant College and studied community development, and my wife, Rebecca, and I spent our first two years together working on agricultural development projects in Kenya. In 2011, we came home to the United States, and moved into South Memphis, the economically poorest urban neighborhood in our state. We joined a church plant in the community; Rebecca went to work as a schoolteacher, and I worked for Advance Memphis, a nonprofit in our neighborhood. All along the way, we saw ourselves as simply responding to Jesus' invitation in Scripture; the Bible told us so!

The Lord has been so kind to us on this journey, bringing joy into our lives that we could not have imagined. But along the way, we've been struck again and again with our failures. I have been shocked by how hard we find it to love our neighbors as ourselves. God has called us "to do justice, and to love kindness, and to walk humbly" with our God (Mic 6:8). Why is it that even when we agree this is central to our mission, we struggle so much to live it out?

I believe part of the answer comes down to this: *knowing that* Jesus wants us to do justice isn't enough. Disciples don't just know what Jesus wants us to do. Disciples are on a journey of *becoming* people who *follow* Jesus in *doing* what he wants us to do. Discipleship, in other words, is all about *formation*. And if the discipleship of my childhood often forgot that God cares about justice, the discipleship of my adulthood has often been shallow in knowing how to *become* people who embody God's justice.

---

[2]See Mark Gornik, *To Live in Peace: Biblical Faith and the Changing Inner City* (Grand Rapids, MI: Eerdmans, 2002).

This book asks the question, What does Scripture say about how the people of God become just disciples, and what does that mean for just discipleship today? In trying to answer this two-part question, I do three things.

1. **Carefully read biblical texts related to justice.** Most chapters of *Just Discipleship* focus on close readings of specific biblical texts. Discipleship is about following Jesus, and Scripture offers us authoritative guidance on how to do that.

2. **Bring biblical texts into dialogue with what theologians say about ethical discipleship.** Theologians have spent thousands of years investigating moral formation, or what I will often call "moral discipleship."[3] Theological accounts of character, virtue, ritual, and liturgy offer us resources for understanding how God intends for us to become who he created us to be, and I draw on these resources in my exploration of justice in Scripture.

3. **Imagine what moral discipleship might look like today.** The biblical texts I explore do not give us a blueprint for doing justice today. But, as Chris Wright suggests, they do offer us *paradigms*—models that, in all their messiness and materiality, inspire us to imagine what it might look like to live out just discipleship in the messy material realities of our world. Because of this, chapters 4 through 12 of this book each:
   a. begin with a contemporary justice issue,
   b. wrestle with specific biblical texts related to just discipleship, and
   c. consider how these specific texts inspire us to live as just disciples in relation to that contemporary justice issue.

How did I pick the contemporary justice questions I explore? I have drawn from my own context and experience, beginning with some of the issues that I've wrestled with as an upper-middle class white male seeking to follow Jesus in an almost exclusively Black, economically poor neighborhood. Because of this, let me state as clearly as possible: *issues of poverty and race are not the only justice issues facing Christians in our world*—not by a long shot. Modern day slavery and sex trafficking, the plight of the unborn, religious persecution, the marginalization of people with disabilities, the refugee crisis, global hunger, climate change, the suffering of women, war, and more demand the

---

[3]For my in-depth treatment of moral formation through practice, see Michael J. Rhodes, *Formative Feasting: Practices and Virtue Ethics in the Deuteronomic Tithe Meal and Corinthian Lord's Supper*, Studies in Biblical Literature 176 (New York: Peter Lang, 2022).

attention of God's people and could be explored in a book like this. My focus on racial injustice by white Americans against Black Americans is not intended to downplay the importance of the suffering of other groups, nor to explain that suffering by buying into a problematic Black/white binary.[4] This book focuses on the issues it does because it emerges from my personal experience reading Scripture within my context, for the sake of following Jesus on the road toward just discipleship in that context.

Your context may be different from mine, but the Bible's invitation to just discipleship is universal. I hope that my exploration of what it might look like to receive that invitation in one time and place will help you imagine how you could receive that same invitation in yours. Indeed, our family currently finds itself in precisely this kind of recontextualizing. While this book emerged out of our time in Memphis, during the final stages of editing, our family moved to Aotearoa/New Zealand. Our new context requires us to reimagine what the timeless biblical call to just discipleship looks like in *this* time and place.

Even if you occasionally disagree with what I argue just discipleship looks like in *my* context, I hope you'll allow the biblical interpretation to inspire you to think about what just discipleship might require in *your* context. Because, at the end of the day, Scripture declares that seeking justice is the path to *joy*. Or, as the psalmist would say, "*Happy* are those who observe justice" (Ps 106:3, emphasis added).

THE ROAD AHEAD: THE STORY OF THIS BOOK

Speaking of disagreement, some may already wonder whether I am overemphasizing the role justice plays in the Bible and discipleship, or perhaps slipping in a definition of justice contrary to the Bible's own. These are legitimate concerns! To address them, in chapter two, I summarize the justice story in Scripture as it unfolds from Genesis to Revelation. I also explore several ways biblical scholars and philosophers have defined justice before making a case for John Goldingay's definition of "justice and righteousness" as "the faithful exercise of power in community" as our most reliable shorthand summary of what the Bible's justice language means.[5]

In chapter three, I offer a theological model designed to help us understand the process of moral discipleship. I particularly draw on theologians exploring

---

[4]See Jonathan Tran, *Asian Americans and the Spirit of Racial Capitalism* (New York: Oxford University Press, 2022).

[5]John Goldingay, *The Theology of the Book of Isaiah* (Downers Grove, IL: IVP Academic, 2014), 21.

questions of virtue and character. This chapter concludes part one, "Just Discipleship: Mapping the Terrain."

In part two, "Becoming Just Disciples," I explore the way the feasts of Deuteronomy (chapter four), the justice songs of the Psalms (chapter five), the wisdom teaching of Proverbs (chapter six), and the imitation of Jesus in 1 John (chapter seven) all intend to help God's people *become* just. Along the way, we'll consider how these texts might shape us to do justice in relation to economic segregation in American neighborhoods, the way we sing and pray in church, the plight of low-wage workers, and the persistence of racism and classism in American life. And for readers already wondering where the *grace* is in all this justice talk, in chapter seven I explore how these practices of just discipleship are both received as God's gracious gifts and embraced as God-ordained tasks.

In part three, "Becoming a Just People," I consider how Scripture shapes the whole people of God for the work of justice. The texts I draw on address the people of God as a political community in the sense that the *church itself* is an outpost of God's kingdom. Moreover, these texts call that outpost community to organize its life in ways that align with the divine king's just rule.

In chapter eight, I do a deep dive on the year of Jubilee in Leviticus 25. While many may be familiar with this text, I suggest there's far more going on here than we realize. In chapter nine, I explore how later biblical authors drew on the Jubilee even when their situations and circumstances were quite different from those envisioned in Leviticus. I suggest we follow in their footsteps, not least in seeking a robustly Christian response to a particularly controversial justice question: the case for reparations for Black Americans.

I conclude part three with an example from the New Testament, drawing on Paul's words to the Corinthian church regarding the Lord's Supper (chapter ten). I explore the relevance of Paul's teaching for the way contemporary churches organize their common life, and draw special attention to possible implications for multiethnic churches in the United States.

In part four, "Discipling Politics: Just Discipleship amid the Nations," I consider how just disciples should relate to the political communities within which we find ourselves. I take a close look at two of the few characters in the Bible who find themselves wielding significant political power within Gentile political communities: Joseph (chapter eleven) and Daniel (chapter twelve). Their stories illuminate some of the pitfalls of contemporary Christian approaches to politics in the United States, as well as offer an invitation to just discipleship in our political lives.

In the final chapter, I summarize the key arguments of the book and offer some final reflections on what it might look like for the church to begin embracing God's program for just discipleship today.

Hopefully you now have a sense of where this book comes from and where it's going. For some, the journey may sound familiar and exciting. For others, it may seem strange and threatening. Regardless, I hope you'll keep reading, bring your questions along, and join me in exploring just discipleship in God's Word and in God's world.

"JUSTICE TO VICTORY"

Reclaiming the Old, Old Story

WHEN A WHITE COLLEGE STUDENT named Jim Bullock and a Black college student named Joe Purdy tried to attend Memphis's Second Presbyterian Church on Palm Sunday in 1964, it was the church's commitment to *segregation* that inspired church leaders to physically block their way. Bullock and Purdy's commitment to *justice* inspired them to kneel on the front steps and pray in response.

That same commitment to justice inspired dozens of Christians to join them over fourteen Sundays in the civil rights movement's longest sustained "kneel-in" campaign. The kneel-ins took aim at church segregation by drawing on the lessons of the sit-ins that desegregated restaurants, buses, and other public spaces across the South. "We really were very concerned about segregation not being just," Purdy recalls. "And the churches should have been the last places on earth to be segregated, in our minds."[1]

The line separating praying protestors outside and praying worshipers inside was a dividing line between a Christianity committed to justice and a Christianity in which concern for justice was conspicuously absent, at least in relation to American racism. Of course, many Christians at Second Presbyterian claimed that Bullock, Purdy, and others like him were not "true worshipers," but simply angsty agitators who wanted to make a scene at church.[2] But historian Stephen Haynes's extensive study demonstrates that the majority of the protestors at Second Presbyterian were devout Christians.

---

[1]Stephen R. Haynes, *The Last Segregated Hour: The Memphis Kneel-Ins and the Campaign for Southern Church Desegregation* (New York: Oxford University Press, 2012), 126.
[2]Haynes, *Last Segregated Hour*, 5.

They genuinely believed the church was both uniquely positioned to address and uniquely complicit with the injustice of racism.[3] At least for Christian activists whose commitment to justice grew out of their theological convictions, praying on the steps of a segregated church was itself—in the words of one protestor—"an act of worship."[4]

What about those praying worshipers *inside* the church? Although many of the members and pastors of Second Presbyterian were *against* the hardline segregationist stance of the elders, this majority failed to end the rampant racism on display outside their church for many months. This silent majority found it "extremely difficult . . . to openly defy men whom they regarded as pillars of the local community, generous supporters of the church and its ministries, and paragons of personal piety."[5] The church had a reputation among its members and many in the city for its commitment to "evangelism, foreign missions, education, and benevolence."[6] The members of Second Presbyterian saw themselves as—and by all accounts were—deeply committed Christians. But their theology embodied a *justice*-less Christianity, at least in relation to racism.

In 2014, on the fiftieth anniversary of the Memphis Kneel-Ins, I walked into the sanctuary at Second Presbyterian Church, the church in which I was baptized, confirmed, catechized, and sent out as a missionary; which I continue to visit regularly, and which planted my family's home church. I greeted the Black woman next to me on a pew in a sanctuary where I'd spent a lifetime of Sundays worshiping, and asked her how she was doing.

"I'm okay," she replied. "It's been fifty years since I visited this church, and my memories from the last time aren't so great."

That was the first time I got to thank one of the protestors whose courageous commitment to justice helped integrate the church I grew up in.[7] If it had not been for them, the church that raised me might have remained openly committed to racism for much longer. Thanks to their activism, the church I grew up in was a congregation in recovery from racism. Like alcoholics still working on the first of the Twelve Steps, we—and I mean *we*—had then and have now a long way to go. But the acknowledgment that our Christian lives

[3]Haynes, *Last Segregated Hour*, 13-14.
[4]Haynes, *Last Segregated Hour*, 15.
[5]Haynes, *Last Segregated Hour*, 121.
[6]Haynes, *Last Segregated Hour*, 73.
[7]Audio from this commemoration service available at www.2pc.org/steps-a-remembrance-of-the-1964-kneel-ins.

had become unmanageable came about, in part, because of the just activism nurtured primarily in Black pulpits and pews across the country and that showed up at our sanctuary door for fourteen Sundays in the mid-'60s.

The story of white Christians worshiping inside a church while another group of Christians protested their segregation on the steps outside might sound extreme. The failures of just discipleship explored in this book, however, suggest that this seemingly extreme story offers us a glimpse of the way many Christians and churches, in a variety of ways, have offered the world a justice-less, or at least, justice-light, version of our faith.

THE STORY OF JUSTICE IN SCRIPTURE

Justice-light Christianity stands in stark contrast to Scripture's own witness. Indeed, when the Gospel of Matthew declares that Jesus fulfilled Isaiah's prophesy that the Messiah would lead "justice to victory," that "in his name the Gentiles" would "hope," he placed Jesus at the turning point of a justice story that stretches across the entire Bible (see Mt 12:17-21).

There are many good, faithful, and indeed complementary ways to summarize the story of Scripture. Attempts to summarize Scripture's story around any one theme fail to capture the full range and complexity of the Bible's witness. But Matthew's language of Jesus bringing "justice to victory" gives us ample reason to explore the story of Scripture as a justice story. Before going further, we need to reclaim this way of telling the "old, old story."

Royal priestly family members: It's who we are and what we do. Scripture's justice story begins at the beginning, with God creating women and men in his image (Gen 1:27-28). The description of humans as made in God's image suggests both an *identity* and a *job description* as God's royal priestly family members.[8]

Early readers of Genesis would have heard royal overtones in the description of God making humans in his image.[9] In the ancient Near East, kings could be understood as made in God's image,[10] and Genesis 1:26 may

---

[8]The image of God should not be reduced to either the functional or the ontological aspect. See Gordon McConville, *Being Human in God's World: An Old Testament Theology of Humanity* (Grand Rapids, MI: Baker Academic, 2016), 21.

[9]See Walter Brueggemann, *Theology of the Old Testament: Testimony, Dispute, Advocacy* (Minneapolis: Fortress, 2012), 451-52; Catherine L. McDowell, *The Image of God in the Garden of Eden: The Creation of Humankind in Genesis 2:5–3:24 in Light of the Mīs Pî, Pīt Pî, and Wpt-r Rituals of Mesopotamia and Ancient Egypt* (Winona Lake, IN: Eisenbrauns, 2015), 130.

[10]See Jon D. Levenson, *Creation and the Persistence of Evil: The Jewish Drama of Divine Omnipotence* (Princeton, NJ: Princeton University Press, 1994), 114-17.

best be translated, "Let us make [humanity] in our image, according to our likeness, *that they may rule*" over the rest of creation.[11]

At the same time, priests were also sometimes described as the "image of God," not least because ancient Near Eastern ideology often thought of rulers as priest-kings.[12] Many scholars argue that Genesis's first readers would have recognized the creation narrative as the story of the building of a cosmic sanctuary, with the man and woman placed in that garden-sanctuary as the world's first priests,[13] or perhaps even as living idols.[14] In either case, humanity is being called to mediate God's presence to creation. Genesis thus summons humanity to a royal priestly familial identity and job description in God's world.

However, Catherine McDowell may be right that, at its heart, "image and likeness" language is the language of kinship. Thus, in the closest parallel in the Old Testament to Genesis 1:26-27, Genesis 5:3 declares that Adam and Eve had a child in Adam's "own likeness and after his image."[15] Image language suggests that humanity, in some mysterious, metaphorical sense, shares a "family resemblance" with God. As members of the divine king's family, we are crowned priests and rulers and commissioned for work in his world.[16]

Yahweh's creation of humanity in his image gives us an *identity* and a *job description* as Yahweh's royal priestly family members. That's who we are and that's what we do. Such royal, priestly family members mediate God's "power and presence" throughout the cosmos.[17]

Rebellious image bearers and what to do with them. Genesis 3 introduces into the biblical story the tale of two image bearers who want out. The first man and woman reject their identity and vocation. Yahweh's response to this rejection, and the broader violence, sin, and devastation that follows, is shocking. Yahweh does not give up on his plan to rule his world through his royal priestly family members; he graciously invites Abraham to become the head of a new family that will become Yahweh's "priestly kingdom" (Ex 19:6) and his "firstborn son" (Ex 4:22-23). Yahweh thus calls Israel into existence

---

[11]Translation by Gordon Wenham, quoted in McConville, *Being Human*, 17.

[12]J. Richard Middleton, *A New Heaven and a New Earth: Reclaiming Biblical Eschatology* (Grand Rapids, MI: Baker Academic, 2014), 44.

[13]G. K. Beale, *The Temple and the Church's Mission: A Biblical Theology of the Dwelling Place of God*, NSBT (Downers Grove, IL: IVP Academic, 2004), 29-80; McDowell, *Image of God*, 207.

[14]John Barton, *Ethics in Ancient Israel* (New York: Oxford University Press, 2017), 65; McDowell, *Image of God*, 207.

[15]See McDowell, *Image of God*, 125-26; 132.

[16]McConville, *Being Human*, 21-29.

[17]Middleton, *New Heavens*, 46.

so that they may take up the job description and identity that all humanity had rejected.

Israel is uniquely chosen to live out Yahweh's intentions for humanity.[18] But Yahweh makes equally clear that he has called Israel into this unique existence in order to bless all the nations of the earth *through* Israel (Gen 12:3).[19] Indeed, blessing for the nations is the ultimate goal of God's covenant promises to Abraham; God calls this particular people in order to rescue humanity.[20] Deuteronomy 4:5-8 suggests that one way blessing will flow through Israel to the nations is as Israel's life mediates God's "power and presence" by publicly living out God's way in the world.[21] In other words, Yahweh will use Israel's restoration to their identity and job description to restore humanity to that same vocation and identity.[22]

But what does image bearing have to do with justice? This summons to live as God's royal priestly family members who mediate God's "power and presence" reveals the centrality of *justice* to Israel and humanity's identity and job description. Why? Because "righteousness and justice are the foundation of [God's] throne" (Ps 89:14[15]).[23] Indeed, Yahweh "*loves* righteousness and justice" (Ps 33:5; cf. Is 61:8). In one vivid image, the psalmist Asaph envisions Yahweh calling the gods of the nations to court, judging them and casting them down because they fail to do justice and righteousness for the marginalized (Ps 82:1-8). Justice and righteousness not only characterize the heart of the divine king, but are the very measuring rod for what it means to truly *be* God.[24] The testimony of Israel is that every other pretender god is found wanting when weighed in the scales of justice and righteousness.[25] "Justice on earth," if any is to be found, "flows from justice in heaven,"[26] and the just character of Yahweh is the only such heavenly source.

If Israel wants to embrace their vocation to mediate Yahweh's power and presence, they will have to learn to mediate the power and presence of

---

[18]N. T. Wright, *The New Testament and the People of God* (London: SPCK, 1992), 262.
[19]See M. Daniel Carroll R., "Blessing the Nations: Toward a Biblical Theology of Mission from Genesis," *BBR* 10, no. 1 (2000): 17-34; Middleton, *New Heaven*, 61-62.
[20]Wright, *Mission of God*, 194.
[21]Middleton, *New Heaven*, 46.
[22]Middleton, *New Heaven*, 62.
[23]Hebrew verse numbers have been placed in brackets where they differ from English verse numbers.
[24]See Brueggemann, *Theology of the Old Testament*, 144.
[25]Bruce C. Birch, *Let Justice Roll Down* (Louisville, KY: Westminster John Knox, 1991), 157.
[26]Christopher J. H. Wright, *Old Testament Ethics for the People of God* (Downers Grove, IL: IVP Academic, 2011), 254.

Yahweh's justice and righteousness. Because doing justice and righteousness is at the heart of Yahweh's character and the top of Yahweh's job description, it will have to be at the heart of Israel's character and the top of their job description as well.

Perhaps nowhere is this clearer than in Genesis 18:18-19. In this passage, the narrator allows us to overhear Yahweh asking himself whether he should share with Abraham his plan to bring judgment on Sodom and Gomorrah, given that Abraham will become a "great and mighty nation," one in whom "all the nations of the earth will be blessed."[27] Then Yahweh continues:

> For I have chosen him, in order that he may command his children and his household after him to keep the way of Yahweh *by doing justice and righteousness*, in order that Yahweh may bring on Abraham what he has spoken concerning him (Gen 18:19 AT).[28]

Incredibly, the Lord declares that he will use his people's just and righteous character to enable them to become a vehicle of God's blessing to all the nations of the earth.[29] In other words,

Yahweh calls into existence a royal priestly family (Israel)
in order that
they will become a family characterized by justice and righteousness
in order that
they might participate with Yahweh in his mission of blessing
to all the nations.

One major feature of this mission of blessing is the restoration of all the families of the earth to their royal priestly familial identity and job description.[30]

Genesis 18:18-19 summarizes Israel's vocation to do justice and righteousness in God's world; the rest of the Old Testament unpacks it. In the Torah, Moses boldly declares that Israel's laws are superior to the nations when judged against the standard of justice, asking, "And what other great nation has statutes and ordinances as *just* as this entire law that I am setting before you today?" (Deut 4:8). Indeed, Israel maintains (uniquely in the

---

[27]For a discussion, see Wright, *Mission of God*, 263-64.

[28]The author will indicate his own translation with "AT."

[29]See Wright, *Mission of God*, 368.

[30]See Walter Brueggemann, *Genesis*, Interpretation (Louisville, KY: Westminster John Knox, 2010), 169; Moshe Weinfeld, *Social Justice in Ancient Israel and in the Ancient Near East* (Minneapolis: Fortress, 2000), 7.

ancient Near East) that God himself created these laws and assigned the *entire people* the task of doing justice by obeying them.[31]

This does not mean that the community's *rulers* are off the hook, of course. No, leaders at all levels "were charged with the primary function of maintaining or restoring righteousness and justice."[32] Consider, for instance, Israel's monarchy. At first sight, the Old Testament's ambiguous and varied testimony concerning the king borders on the bewildering. Some passages seem to see the king as the *source* of Israel's problems (see 1 Sam 8:11-22), while others seem to see the king as the *solution* (see 2 Sam 8:15; Ps 72).[33] One key to understanding this variation is to recognize that both critics and defenders of the monarchy evaluate the king's job performance on the shared conviction that the king's primary task is to "do justice and righteousness" and "judge the cause of the poor and needy" (Jer 22:15-16).[34]

Ultimately, however, justice is everyone's responsibility. The prophets summarize "what the LORD requires" from his people as nothing less than to "do justice and to love kindness, and to walk humbly with your God" (Mic 6:8). Doing justice and righteousness simply *is* what it means to know Yahweh (Jer 22:15-16). Proverbs places "righteousness, justice, and equity" (Prov 1:3) at the center of Israel's program of moral education. Indeed, doing justice and righteousness is even more important than sacrifice (Prov 21:3).

But righteousness and justice are the standards that Israel, like all humanity before her, fell far short of. "The vineyard of Yahweh is the house of Israel, and the men of Judah are the garden of his delight," Isaiah declares. "And he looked for justice, but behold, bloodshed! For righteousness, but behold, an outcry of distress!" (Is 5:7 AT). This passage reads like Genesis 18:18-19 in reverse; righteousness and justice are *the fruit* that God was after when he planted his people as a garden for his delight. Yet when he went looking for justice, he found injustice; when he went looking for righteousness, he found the outcry of the oppressed. According to Isaiah 5:8-30, these failures elicit God's devastating judgment, ultimately culminating in the exile.

While that may strike us as harsh, Isaiah's vineyard song poses the right question: What good is a garden that produces no fruit? The answer is

---

[31]Jeremiah Unterman, *Justice for All: How the Jewish Bible Revolutionized Ethics* (Lincoln, NE: University of Nebraska Press, 2017), 21-25.

[32]Wright, *Mission of God*, 269.

[33]See also 1 Kings 10:9; 2 Chron 9:8.

[34]Walter J. Houston, *Contending for Justice: Ideologies and Theologies of Social Justice in the Old Testament* (New York: T&T Clark, 2006), 136.

obvious. A fruitless vineyard is good for nothing. *God sees a people that fail to produce the justice and righteousness for which they were planted the same way: they have become good for nothing.*

Considering Yahweh's response to Israel's failure to live up to their just and righteous vocation will take us out of the Old Testament and into the New. But before we get there, we need to pause and consider a working definition for the two words that have dominated our discussion thus far: *righteousness* and *justice.*

"You keep using those words . . . " In one of my favorite scenes from the film *The Princess Bride,* the sword-fighting Spaniard Inigo Montoya has had enough. Over and over again, the events his boss Vizzini has declared to be "inconceivable" have nevertheless occurred. After the final such outburst from Vizzini, Montoya looks at him and says, "You keep using that word. I do not think it means what you think it means."

Before going further, we need to pause and ask ourselves if the words *justice* and *righteousness* mean what we think they mean. Our first associations with the word *righteousness* are often limited to issues of personal piety. Old (chauvinist) maxims like "don't smoke, drink or chew, or go with girls who do" come to mind. The immediate image provoked by the word *justice* may be a blind Lady Justice carved into the ceiling of a local courthouse. While personal piety and impartial courts are good, biblical things, it's unlikely that they stand at the center of Yahweh's purposes for humanity. So what *do* these words mean?

We could proceed by an in-depth word study of occurrences of *tsedeq/tsedeqah* ("righteousness"[35]) and *mishpat* ("justice"[36]), both individually and together as a word-pair. Such a study would suggest that *tsedeq/tsedeqah* point primarily to that which is "right," either relationally or in conformity to a norm.[37] *Mishpat*—more directly derived from judicial contexts—points to the idea of "putting things right."[38] A word study might also suggest that when

---

[35]BDB, 842. There is probably no significant difference between the forms *tsedeq* and *tsedeqah*. See Wright, *Old Testament Ethics*, 255.

[36]BDB, 1048.

[37]For discussion, see HALOT, 1005-6; TWOT, 1879c; Wright, *Old Testament Ethics*, 255; Enrique Nardoni, *Rise Up, O Judge: A Study of Justice in the Biblical World*, trans. Sean Charles Martin (Grand Rapids, MI: Baker Academic, 2001), 102; John Goldingay, "Justice and Salvation for Israel and Canaan," in *Reading the Hebrew Bible for a New Millennium*, ed. W. Kim et al. (Harrisburg, PA: Trinity, 2000), 175; B. Johnson, "צדק," *TDOT* 12:243-4.

[38]For variations, see HALOT, 652; Wright, *Old Testament Ethics*, 256; Birch, *Justice*, 155-56, 260; B. Johnson, "צדק," *TDOT* 12:239-64; Nicholas Wolterstorff, *Justice: Rights and Wrongs* (Princeton, NJ: Princeton University Press, 2008), 69-75.

paired together, *tsedeq/tsedeqah* and *mishpat* describe something like certain accounts of "social justice" or "social equity."[39]

Another option for proceeding would be with philosophical treatments of justice. Many Christians take for their starting point a sixth-century Roman definition: justice is a "steady and enduring will to render to each their *ius*," their "right" or "due."[40] Alternatively, we could consider philosopher John Rawls's description of justice as the way "major social institutions distribute fundamental rights and duties and determine the division of advantage from social cooperation."[41] We could examine Nicholas Wolterstorff's magisterial argument that justice names a social condition in which the members of a society "enjoy the goods to which they have a right."[42]

Despite the strengths of these approaches, I suggest a different entry point altogether. Let's listen to how one blameless, upright God-fearer describes the sorts of things he did when he clothed himself with *tsedeq* and *mishpat* in Job 29:12-17.

Job 29 begins with Job's longing for a return to the days when he richly experienced God's presence (Job 29:1-6). This grounds everything he goes on to say about his own character and conduct in his prior relationship with God. His just and righteous behavior are a response to God's kindness.[43] Job 29:7-11 makes clear that his character nevertheless won him extreme honor within the entire community. Then, in Job 29:12-17 (AT), he explains the heart and substance of this God-grounded character that elicited such communal respect:

> For I rescued the poor who cried out for help, and the fatherless who had no helper. The blessing of the dying person came upon me, and I caused the heart of the widow to shout for joy. Righteousness (*tsedeq*) I put on, and it clothed me; my justice (*mishpat*) was like a robe and a turban. I was eyes for the blind and I was feet for the lame. I was a father for the needy, and I investigated the court case of the one I did not know. I smashed the fangs of the unrighteous and made them drop their prey from their teeth.

---

[39]See Moshe Weinfeld, "'Justice and Righteousness'—משפט וצדקה: The Expression and Its Meaning," in *Justice and Righteousness: Biblical Themes and Their Influence*, ed. Henning Graf Reventlow and Yair Hoffman (Sheffield: Sheffield Academic Press, 1992), 235; Wright, *Old Testament Ethics*, 257. I say "certain accounts" because biblical teaching would reject some of the ways social justice language gets used in contemporary debates.

[40]Quoted in Wolterstorff, *Justice*, 22.

[41]John Rawls, *A Theory of Justice* (Cambridge, MA: Harvard University Press, 2009), 6.

[42]Wolterstorff, *Justice*, 35.

[43]William Brown, *Wisdom's Wonder: Character, Creation, and Crisis in the Bible's Wisdom Literature* (Grand Rapids, MI: Eerdmans, 2014), 99.

By embracing and embodying justice and righteousness, Job exercises his substantial social power on behalf of a long list of society's sufferers. He lifts up the downcast, liberates the poor, brings both support and joy into the lives of the vulnerable, goes to court on behalf of the stranger,[44] and actively de-fangs the oppressor.[45] Job's metaphor of clothing himself in justice and right-eousness suggests a whole-life orientation that leads Job to go far beyond what the law required and indeed beyond what any law *could* require on behalf of the vulnerable and oppressed.[46]

The justice with which Job clothes himself *includes* personal piety and the kind of fair treatment suggested by Lady Justice with her scales but is not *reduced* to these dynamics. Standing at the white-hot center of the justice Job embodies is the active, intervening, rescuing, liberating, laboring justice loved and practiced by Yahweh himself (see Ps 33:5; 146:7-9).

This is why typical summary definitions of justice won't do, at least not as our primary shorthand. This is not because the language of social justice and social equity, the virtue of rendering each their due, or the description of a society that ensures members enjoy their rights, fail to accurately describe aspects of Scripture's treatment of *tsedeq/tsedeqah* and *mishpat*. Properly defined, all such language helpfully contributes to our understanding of the biblical idiom.

The problem is that such language does not *sing*. Job's poetry in praise of justice and righteousness reminds me of Cornel West's famous line: "Justice is what love looks like in public. . . . Not simply an abstract concept to reg-ulate institutions, but also a fire in the bones to promote the well-being of all."[47] In a similar vein, John Goldingay summarizes *tsedeq* and *mishpat* as the "faithful exercise of power in community."[48] While perhaps no simple sentence can ever capture the full breadth and depth of what Scripture means by justice and righteousness, West and Goldingay capture something of the bright hot center of the concept. So with biblical justice summarized as "what love looks like in public" and "the faithful exercise of power in community," we can identify four significant features of Job's just character before returning to our overview of the justice story in Scripture.

---

[44]See Houston, *Contending*, 128; Patricia L. Vesely, "Virtue and the 'Good Life' in the Book of Job," *Horizons in Biblical Theology* 41, no. 1 (2019): 9.

[45]See Gustavo Gutierrez, *On Job: God-Talk and the Suffering of the Innocent*, trans. Matthew J. O'Connell (Maryknoll, NY: Orbis, 1988), 42-43.

[46]Carol A. Newsom, *The Book of Job: A Contest of Moral Imaginations* (New York: Oxford University Press, 2009), 194-95; Barton, *Ethics*, 234-35.

[47]Cornel West, *Brother West: Living and Loving Out Loud* (New York: Smiley Books, 2010), 23.

[48]John Goldingay, *The Theology of the Book of Isaiah* (Downers Grove, IL: IVP Academic, 2014), 21.

First, Job's faithful exercise of power includes actions that we recognize as acts of justice, like standing against oppressors or going to court on behalf of the vulnerable. But Job's justice also includes actions that we tend to think of as mercy or charity *rather than* justice. For that matter, it also includes actions that we more typically associate with upright behavior or piety.[49] Indeed, while we sometimes draw a stark distinction between charity, justice, and piety,

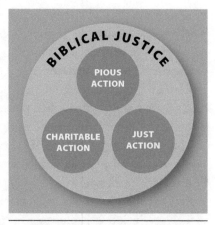

Figure 2.1. Some dimensions of biblical justice

Scripture's use of justice and righteousness language often includes all three.[50] Biblical justice is more than merciful, charitable, or pious action, but it is not less. While I focus primarily on what we might call "public justice" in this book, we need to keep the broader vision for "righteousness and justice" in the Bible in view.

Second, Job's actions make clear why the saints in Scripture *love* and *long for* God's justice. Who *doesn't* want the world to be filled with orphan-adopting, immigrant-welcoming, community-creating justice? By contrast, sometimes Christians talk about God's justice as a sort of bad thing that must be overcome by God's love or grace. The partial truth here, of course, is that God's justice does include judgment. But it's worth pointing out that the people of God *celebrate, rejoice over,* and *long for* God's justice. Seeing God's justice at work in Job's life makes it a bit easier to understand why they do so!

Third, the biblical authors don't talk about justice in the abstract for very long. Scripture most often speaks of justice and righteousness by speaking of the victims of *injustice* and *unrighteousness,* by bearing witness "to the inhuman situation in which orphans, widows, and strangers live."[51] Job's use of no less than *nine different descriptors* for marginalized groups is a particularly dense example of this biblical pattern.

This is not to say that biblical justice has nothing to do with equal treatment under the law. Exodus 23:3 specifically forbids showing partiality toward the

---

[49]On which, see Job 31.
[50]See Levenson, *Creation and the Persistence of Evil,* 104.
[51]Gutierrez, *On Job,* 40.

poor in court. As Wolterstorff recognizes, "The prophets do not approve bur-
glarizing the wealthy or assaulting the powerful."[52] What Roman Catholic
theologians have often referred to as God's "preferential option for the poor"
is not some abstract preference by God for one group over the other, but
rather Yahweh's realistic recognition that "injustice is not equally distributed."[53]
God's justice and righteousness prefers the vulnerable because they are the
primary victims of injustice and unrighteousness.[54]

Fourth, and more subtly, the text hints that Job exercises justice precisely as a royal priestly family member of the God who loves justice.
Psalm 132:9's invocation that Zion's priests "be clothed with righteousness"
closely parallels Job 29:14. Most references to being clothed in a robe or a
turban (as in Job 29) refer to either priestly or royal garments.[55] Job describes himself as one "like a king" in Job 29:25, and the passage overall
may allude to the portrait of the Just King in Psalm 72.[56] Job's royal priestly
practice of justice reflects the royal priestly work to which all human image
bearers are called.

Moreover, in his royal priestly exercise of justice and righteousness, Job
imitates Yahweh.[57] Because Yahweh is a "father of orphans and protector of
widows" (Ps 68:5[6]), Job is a father to the orphan and the needy, and he
causes the widow's heart to shout for joy. Because Yahweh loves immigrants
and outsiders (Deut 10:18), Job defends their rights in court. And whereas
elsewhere in Scripture smashing the teeth of the oppressor is *God's* work, here
Job participates in God's justice by defanging the oppressor and forcing them
to drop their prey from their teeth.[58] By exercising power on behalf of
the oppressed in line with his royal priestly familial job description, Job
imitates God.

Of course, we may have questions about this powerful patriarch doing
justice *on behalf of* those several steps down the social ladder, especially given
that the existence of a socially stratified ladder does not seem to be addressed.[59]
In chapter four of this book, we will see that the book of Job itself identifies

---

[52]Wolterstorff, *Justice*, 78.
[53]Wolterstorff, *Justice*, 79.
[54]See Gutierrez, *On Job*, 94.
[55]See John E. Hartley, *The Book of Job*, NICOT (Grand Rapids, MI: Eerdmans, 2007), 391.
[56]Houston, *Contending*, 128-29.
[57]Gutierrez, *On Job*, 40.
[58]Cf. Ps 3:7[8]; 58:6[7]; Job 4:8-10.
[59]See, for instance, Vesely, "Virtue," 12-14. On the patronage paradigm more generally, see Houston, *Contending*, 99-102; Newsom, *Job*, 187-98.

this issue and portrays Job's just character as both vindicated and transformed over the course of Job's story. But in my view, Job gives us a glimpse of what, for the authors of the Bible, "love looks like in public."

Picking up the pieces: Yahweh responds to his people's justice failures. Returning to the story of justice in Scripture, we've seen that Yahweh created image bearers tasked with doing justice as his royal priestly family members. Tragically, both humanity in general and Israel in particular failed to deliver. When Yahweh comes looking for justice, he finds injustice instead (Is 5:7).

Miraculously, the prophets declare that in response, Yahweh would clothe *himself* in righteousness (Is 59:16-17) and "faithfully bring forth justice" through the work of his Spirit-anointed servant (Is 42:1-4). This divine justice-bringing would not constitute an abandonment of God's plan to rule his world through his image bearers. No, the charismatic ministry of the servant would both liberate the oppressed and *establish them* as Yahweh's "oaks of righteousness" who would rebuild long-devastated communities (Is 61:3).

But for God's people to participate in Yahweh's mission of justice and righteousness, they would need the kind of just and righteous character that had perennially eluded them. Here too Yahweh offers incredible promises:

> "This is the covenant I will make with the people of Israel
>   after that time," declares the LORD.
> "I will put my law in their minds
>   and write it on their hearts.
> I will be their God,
>   and they will be my people." (Jer 31:33, NIV).[60]

Yahweh promises to *transform his peoples' hearts* so that they may follow the just and righteous way of life embodied in the laws he has given them.

It is the testimony of the New Testament that Yahweh accomplishes all of this through the incarnation, the sending of Emmanuel, God-with-us. As depicted in figure 2.2, when all humanity failed in their vocation to live as Yahweh's royal priestly family members, God sent Israel as his "firstborn son" and his "royal priesthood." But when *Israel* failed, Yahweh sent a faithful Israelite, *the* King, *the* High Priest, *the* Son, the true and full image of God, the "radiance of [his] glory and the exact representation of his being" (Heb 1:3 NIV). God brings justice to victory in Jesus.

---

[60]See also Ezek 36:26.

Figure 2.2. God brings justice to victory in Jesus

Jesus prioritizes justice and righteousness in his embodiment of humanity's royal priestly familial job description. In his first sermon, Jesus identifies himself as the just, liberating king who declares good news to the poor and proclaims the year of the Lord's favor (Lk 4:16-21). He brings justice to victory by healing the sick, gently caring for the "bruised reeds" and "smoldering wicks," offering hope to the nations, restoring those with physical disabilities, casting out demons (Mt 12:13-21), and prophetically confronting the religious establishment for neglecting justice (Mt 23:23; cf. Lk 11:42). Jesus embodies and enacts what love looks like in public in his generous solidarity with and welcome of the powerless, poor, oppressed, and ostracized. Jesus arrives as the Just King who inaugurates the long-expected reign of God.

Against every expectation, this Just King dies on a cross as a victim of religious and political injustice. At the cross, God sides with the victims of injustice by becoming one of them. At the resurrection, Jesus vindicates the justice of God and ensures the ultimate defeat of injustice and oppression.[61] Death, the "ultimate weapon of the tyrant," is overthrown forever.[62] Jesus' resurrection is the down payment toward the final justice that will be fulfilled in the new creation at his return. In all of this, Jesus, as the divine Word-made-flesh, fulfills the Father's plan to rule the world through his royal priestly familial image bearers by living, dying, rising, and ruling as *the* King, *the* High Priest, *the* Son, and *the* perfect Image of the living God.

Much more could be said, but for the purposes of our sketch of Scripture's justice story, there remains but one final point. In Genesis 18:18-19, Yahweh

---

[61]Joshua Jipp, *Christ Is King: Paul's Royal Ideology* (Minneapolis: Fortress, 2015), 211-72; N. T. Wright, *Paul and the Faithfulness of God*, Christian Origins and the Question of God (London: SPCK, 2013), 942.

[62]N. T. Wright, *The Resurrection and the Son of God*, Christian Origins and the Question of God (London: SPCK, 2003), 730.

declared that Abraham would be the father of a family who practiced justice and righteousness; when Zacchaeus enacts justice by repaying those he defrauded and sacrificially giving to the poor, Jesus declares him a "true son of Abraham" (Lk 19:9). Jesus does justice himself and, in fulfillment of God's promises to Abraham, *creates a just family who will join him in his mission of blessing to the world.*

The triumph of the justice of God in Christ does not signal the end of Yahweh's plan to rule his world through his image bearers. The triumph of the justice of God in Christ reestablishes that plan. In other words, as depicted in figure 2.3, one way Jesus brings justice to victory is by establishing a people who live out their human vocation to do justice. Indeed, through his rescued and restored people, Jesus offers all humanity an invitation to become the royal priestly family members they were always meant to be, *through him.*

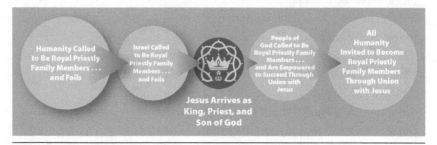

Figure 2.3. Jesus brings justice to victory by establishing a people who do justice

This new human community is launched into the world by Jesus' death and resurrection, as a reading of Paul makes clear. In Romans 3:10, Paul declares that all humanity stands under the judgment that "there is no one who is righteous [*dikaios*], not even one." Paul's description of unrighteousness includes injustice,[63] as can be seen in the frequent connection between the word *adikia* (unrighteousness/injustice) and violence (see Rom 1:29-32; 3:10-18).[64] Indeed, no "vice" listed in Romans 1:18-32 is "highlighted as strenuously as injustice or the refusal to honor God's righteousness."[65]

Humanity's injustice is more than just a behavioral problem because, for Paul, universal injustice is a result of humanity's enslavement to sin,

---

[63]On the centrality of justice to Romans, see Douglas K. Harink, *Resurrecting Justice: Reading Romans for the Life of the Word* (Downers Grove, IL: IVP Academic, 2020), 2-12.

[64]Michael Gorman, *Becoming the Gospel: Paul, Participation, and Mission* (Grand Rapids, MI: Eerdmans, 2015), 225.

[65]Jipp, *Christ Is King*, 237.

understood as a hostile alien power (Rom 6:17).[66] Enslavement to sin leads to human guilt because any human enslaved to sin inevitably ends up offering their bodies as "instruments of unrighteousness"—a phrase that could just as well be translated "weapons of injustice" (Rom 6:13). Because all are "under the power of sin," "there is no one righteous, not even one," "since *all* have sinned and fall short of the glory of God" (Rom 3:9, 10, 23). In Romans 1:18 Paul declares that "the wrath of God is revealed from heaven against" such injustice. Throughout the passage that follows, "Paul portrays God as the righteous judge who brings God's just contention against all of humanity for its injustice."[67]

Humanity finds itself fighting a losing battle with sin and injustice, failing in their vocation as image bearers of God, and justly standing under God's wrath because of their willing acts of disobedience. Paul understands the cross and resurrection of Christ as the turning of the tide. In the Christ event, the only truly just and righteous human was crucified by unjust humans. But—miracle of miracles!—by his death on the cross, Jesus became a "sacrifice of atonement" for our sins (Rom 3:25). As Peter puts it, Jesus died in our place, suffering on our behalf, the "just for the unjust," that he might bring us to God (1 Pet 3:18 KJV).

Moreover, the Father vindicated Jesus by raising him from the dead. This resurrection-vindication is both the triumph of the Son over *human* injustice, *and* the disarming and defeat of sin, death, the devil, and any other "power" or "authority" that stands against the reign of God (Col 2:15).[68] Moreover, because humans can now be *united to Christ by his Spirit through faith,* we who are in Christ are also *justified,* declared to be in the "right" (*dikaioō*; see Rom 5:19), despite our sin.[69] "There is therefore now no condemnation for those who are in Christ Jesus" because sin has been condemned in the flesh of the Crucified One (Rom 8:1-3).

---

[66]See, for instance, Philip Ziegler, *Militant Grace: The Apocalyptic Turn and the Future of Christian Theology* (Grand Rapids, MI: Baker Academic, 2018), 45.

[67]Jipp, *Christ Is King,* 234.

[68]Wright, *Paul and the Faithfulness of God,* 943.

[69]The account I have presented does not address the question whether justification itself includes both the declaration of righteousness and actual transformation (Gorman, *Becoming the Gospel,* 225-37), or whether justification refers specifically to the declaration but is bound intimately and inseparably to transformation through justification's relationship to union with Christ and the indwelling of the Spirit (Wright, *Paul and the Faithfulness of God,* 956-60). I favor the latter position, while admiring and respecting the former position's attempt to tie the forensic and transformative elements of salvation closely together.

By virtue of this same union with Christ in his resurrection (see Rom 6:4-5), believers are both acquitted and empowered, even re-created, to live lives of love, mercy, holiness, and, yes, *justice* in God's world. Christ-followers have been liberated from "service to 'sin' and its 'injustice'"[70] *for* service to God. They offer this service to God through the presentation of their bodies as "instruments of righteousness," or perhaps better, as "weapons of justice" (*hopla dikaiosynēs*) under the generous reign of God's grace (Rom 6:13).[71] Unjust, broken image bearers are being re-formed to the image of God in Christ (see Col 1:15; 3:10) and restored to their vocation as God's royal priestly family members (see Rev 5:10; 1 Pet 2:9).

The result is more than a collection of just individuals, but rather the establishment of a new family, a new community that *becomes* the good news of God's justice in the world.[72] In Jesus, who is our wisdom, justice, holiness, and redemption (1 Cor 1:30), we become "the justice of God" (2 Cor 5:21 AT).[73] The end goal is the final establishment of the just kingdom of God under the lordship of the Just King in a resurrected, new creation. Incredibly, even when Christ returns, when his just kingdom comes and his just will is done on earth as it is in heaven, *even then*, the Triune God will not abandon his plan to rule his world through his royal priestly family members. No, indeed. The one who "loves us and freed us from our sins by his blood, and made us to be a kingdom, priests serving his God and Father" (Rev 1:5-6) has an eternal intention: "The throne of God and of the Lamb will be in the city, and his servants will serve him. They will see his face, and his name will be on their foreheads. . . . *And they will reign for ever and ever*" (Rev 22:3-5 NIV; emphasis added).

ENTERING THE STORY

Scripture isn't just a story. But it is a *just* story, the story of a Just King who does whatever it takes to co-rule his good world through humans who bear his image and embody his just and righteous way. As such, it's a *justice* story that invites any who would follow Jesus as disciples to enter it and to receive it as their own.

---

[70]Nardoni, *Rise Up*, 269.

[71]See Gorman, *Becoming the Gospel*, 225; Harink, *Resurrecting Justice*, 88-96.

[72]See Richard B. Hays, *The Moral Vision of the New Testament: Community, Cross, New Creation* (New York: Harper Collins, 1996), 24; Gorman, *Becoming the Gospel*, 236-39.

[73]See Gorman, *Becoming the Gospel*, 223-25.

But what if you, like me, are part of a Christian community with a history of trying to follow Jesus *without* fully entering his justice story? What if, having heard the justice story, we don't know how to become the just disciples of the living Lord who offers it to us? Perhaps we need a map or model that can help us imagine what it might look like for Christian communities to *become* just.

BECOMING JUST

Mapping Moral Discipleship

THE PHOTOGRAPHIC EXHIBIT "This Light of Ours" presents black-and-white images of the civil rights movement of the 1950s and '60s. In one image, a group of young people can be seen sitting in the grass in a circle. Two individuals in the middle of the circle are curled up into a fetal position. The caption identifies this as a session of the Student Nonviolent Coordinating Committee training volunteers to protect themselves and others if attacked by violent white supremacists during their participation in nonviolent direct action.[1]

Cheryl Sanders argues that Christian participation in the civil rights movement then and now depends in part on a "militant reconciling love" that gets lived out through a "militant reconciling ethics."[2] The photograph of young people training for nonviolent action brilliantly captures one task of such an ethics: the task of moral formation or moral discipleship.

To clarify, it may be helpful to summarize three major approaches to ethics. What ethicists call *deontological* approaches focus on moral obligations, laws, or commands. Christians exploring justice from this perspective try to answer the question, What are the rules or obligations that help me understand what justice demands? Doing justice is understood as taking action that conforms to one's just duty.

---

[1] The photograph was taken by Herbert Randall in Oxford, Ohio, in 1964, and can be viewed online along with a brief description at www.thestoryoftexas.com/visit/exhibits/this-light-of-ours/voices-of-activist-photographers.

[2] Cheryl Sanders, presentation delivered in September 2017 as part of a teach-in held by the Memphis Center for Urban and Theological Studies in commemoration of the fiftieth anniversary of Dr. King's assassination.

Teleological or *consequentialist* approaches focus on the moral outcomes of our actions in specific situations. Christians exploring justice from this perspective try to answer the question, What would a just result look like in this context, and how do we get there? Doing justice is understood as taking the sort of actions that would lead to that just outcome in a particular time and place.

Scripture operates in both modes at various points. Both deontological and teleological elements would be included in Sanders's militant reconciling ethics. But neither ethical approach answers the question with which this book is primarily concerned and which I think the photograph of the students training for nonviolent action captures so powerfully: How do we *become* just?[3] What training do we need in order to give ourselves wholeheartedly to the work of pursuing justice, even and especially in ever-changing, complex situations?

Questions of moral formation are central to the third approach to ethics: *character ethics*. Character ethics has experienced something of a comeback in recent scholarship. Drawing on ancient accounts of the virtues and their role in character formation, philosophers such as Alasdair MacIntyre and theologians such as Stanley Hauerwas argue that Christianity must recover an ethic of character. Character ethics highlights the way that moral formation occurs as a community

- learns to tell its shared stories,

- celebrates certain virtues and condemns specific vices,

- engages in formative practices aimed at the cultivation of virtuous character, and

- embraces the community's structures, norms, and policies.

Christians exploring justice from this perspective try to answer the question, How do we become just? Answers will focus on what I call *moral formation* or *moral discipleship*, the journey of individuals and communities toward becoming just disciples. Since character ethics often focuses on the role of community in character formation, Christian character ethics often emphasizes the unique role of the church in moral discipleship.

Scripture reflects all three approaches to ethics. Indeed, as figure 3.1 makes clear, at its best, Christian ethics seeks to hold all three approaches together. *God's just way*, embodied in laws, norms, and commands (the deontological

---

[3]Sanders herself speaks to the issue of moral formation in Cheryl J. Sanders, *Empowerment Ethics for a Liberated People: A Path to African American Social Transformation* (Minneapolis: Fortress, 1995), 104-13.

focus) must be embraced and embodied by *just disciples* (the character
focus) who find creative ways to *seek
justice in particular situations* (the teleological focus).[4] Each corner of the
triangle is connected to all the others.

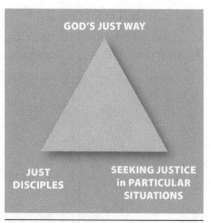

In practice, though, ethicists tend
to enter ethical conversations through
the doorway of one of these approaches. Beginning with a character
ethics approach, we can glimpse just
discipleship in that powerful image of
those young student activists. They

Figure 3.1. A threefold approach to Christian
ethics

are not simply learning what just, rec-
onciling love requires or would look like when it arrived—they are practicing
to *become* militants of reconciling love and justice, to *become* disciples who
"take Jesus seriously" by prophetically and sacrificially pursuing justice for
others.[5] Indeed, this moral discipleship included training in how to take a
beating in the quest for a more just society. The moral formation required to
become a just disciple was serious business.[6]

In contrast, moral formation in many other streams of American
Christianity, including my own, has often been anything *but* serious, at least
when it comes to becoming just. Many American Christians have grown more
vocal about the need to "let justice roll down like waters." But many of us have
too often failed to ask how Christians with a history of injustice might
become just.

Scripture's justice story shows us that justice—the faithful exercise of power
in community—is central to our job description as God's royal priestly family
members. But does Scripture give us guidance as to how to become people
who faithfully exercise power in community? And if so, could character ethics
help us hear and respond to this biblical invitation to just discipleship? To
answer these questions, we need to dig a bit more deeply into what character
ethics teaches about the *mechanics* of moral discipleship.

---

[4]My thanks to Robby Holt for the idea behind this diagram.
[5]This language comes from James Hudson, quoted in Larry O. Rivers, "'Militant Reconciling Love':
Howard University's Rankin Network and Martin Luther King, Jr.," *Journal of African American
History* 99 (2014): 223.
[6]Rivers, "Militant Reconciling Love," 155.

MAPPING THE MECHANICS OF MORAL DISCIPLESHIP

We all know that communities *shape us*. Every community offers its members a path of discipleship that leads toward a certain way of life. But how does this

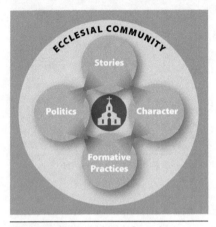

transformation happen? What are the mechanics of formation at work in community life?

My desire to consider these questions led me to explore the writings of ethicists and theologians interested in virtue, character, ritual, and liturgy. In figure 3.2, I offer a visual model of what I see as character ethics' best answers to the question of how moral formation happens. Let's unpack each of the four central elements of the diagram.

Figure 3.2. The mechanics of moral discipleship

Stories, character, formative practices, and politics. First, character ethics claims that a community's *stories* shape the individual and corporate character of that community. Grounding narratives provide each member with a sense of identity: who they are, and where they are headed. These stories identify the grand goals that every member seeks, both individually and collectively. They also offer the community stories of people who embody the kind of character to which every member ought to aspire. For instance, the way the Bible tells Job's story helps us imagine what it would mean to put on righteousness and justice like clothing.

Stories do not simply shape our thinking. Stories shape our desires, our affections, and our gut-level sense of what the world is like and what our role is in it. A community disciples its members, in part, by telling and retelling their stories.

Second, character ethics recognizes that formation occurs through the way the community promotes a certain type of *character*. Communities disciple their members, in other words, by celebrating certain virtues as central to their life together and condemning certain vices as threatening to that common life.

Drawing primarily on Aristotle and Aquinas, character ethicists describe virtues as habits or dispositions that empower a person to work effectively toward a particular telos, or goal.[7] The goals themselves are specific goods

---

[7] See for instance, Aristotle, *Eth. nic.* I.i.1-5; Aquinas, *ST* I-II q. 49, a. 3-4; q. 50, a. 1; q. 52, a. 1; q. 55, a. 4; q. 65, a. 1-2.

such as love, courage, or justice, which the virtuous person has learned both to long for and seek with their actions.[8] A person who has acquired the virtue of justice, for instance, is both driven by a deep desire for justice and proactively aims their actions toward it.

At the same time, acquiring the virtue of justice requires gaining the habits necessary to make progress toward justice in a complicated world. This is another reason character ethics understands the virtues as habits: they involve "*precognitive* tendencies to act in certain ways and toward certain ends."[9] Virtues, like the skills of a craft, give us "the ability to respond creatively to the always unanticipated difficulties involved" with our ever-changing situations.[10] Like an athlete who acts intuitively to score the next goal, the virtuous person carries an embodied, intuitive disposition toward the practice of the virtue in question.

Having a particular virtue, then, means that we have a sort of constant disposition to recognize, desire, and act effectively in pursuit of a particular virtuous goal in a variety of circumstances. Communities disciple their members in part by teaching and celebrating certain accounts of these virtues and condemning their corresponding vices.

Third, character ethics recognizes that one way community members acquire these virtues is through *formative practices*.[11] Because the virtues are habits, we develop them by "doing the things that we shall have to do when we have learnt [them]."[12] Virtuous *habits*, in other words, require *habituation*. Through repeated actions aimed at a particular virtuous goal,[13] we acquire virtuous habits or dispositions. Such repeated actions include imitating virtuous characters from our community's stories or embracing the rituals and liturgies that shape our community's rhythms.

If a virtuous person's instinctive ability to act virtuously is a bit like the way an athlete can instinctively avoid the defender and score the goal, then formative practices are a bit like that athlete's training program. Or to use a musical example, formative practices are like the scales a guitar player

---

[8]*ST* I-II q. 28, a. 6.

[9]James K. A. Smith, *Desiring the Kingdom: Worship, Worldview, and Cultural Formation,* Cultural Liturgies, vol. 1 (Grand Rapids, MI: Baker Academic, 2009), 55-57, emphasis added.

[10]Stanley Hauerwas, *A Community of Character: Toward a Constructive Christian Social Ethic* (Notre Dame, IN: University of Notre Dame Press, 1991), 115.

[11]For a much more in-depth account of formative practices, see my book *Formative Feasting: Practices and Virtue Ethics in the Deuteronomic Tithe Meal and Corinthian Lord's Supper,* Studies in Biblical Literature 176 (New York: Peter Lang, 2022), especially pages 7-86.

[12]Aristotle, *Nicomachean Ethics,* translated by H. Rackham, LCL (Cambridge, MA: Harvard University Press, 1934), II.i.4-7.

[13]Aristotle, *Eth. nic.* I.i.1-5.

practices to gain the *virtue* of guitar playing; practicing the scales shapes them for the day when they'll be able to improvise freely and fully with others.

Sometimes this work is particularly hard because we've already acquired bad habits by practicing *vicious* actions, or even simply because we do the right thing half-heartedly. Perhaps we practiced the scales with poor technique under the influence of an inadequate guitar teacher. Perhaps we did not practice our scales frequently enough, or simply practiced them without much energy. Regardless, the point is this: what we *do*, or *fail to do*, shapes who we *are*.

Finally, a community disciples its members through corporate structures and policies. Character ethicists often refer to this as the community's *politics*. Although it may strike us as a bit strange, when character ethicists talk about politics, they are not referring to the community's participation in government. Instead, they use the language of politics to describe the way that every community has structures, norms, policies, ways of making decisions, processes for initiating new members, and other social arrangements that shape its life. The politics of the church, in this sense, would include the church's structures for receiving members, deliberating over important decisions, organizing corporate gatherings, caring for the poor, and much more. Character ethics recognizes that living within the politics of a community shapes the character of community members.[14]

The overlap between these four elements in figure 3.2, and the arrows between them, capture further insights about moral discipleship. Each element works in concert with the others to shape the members of the community. When people participate in the life of a community, they enter a morally formative feedback loop composed of the community's stories, character, practices, and politics. For instance, a community's core stories determine what they see as virtue and vice, become memorialized through rituals and practices, and shape the community's politics. At the same time, a community's ability to tell their story or faithfully participate in their community's politics and practices depends in part on their having become a community of character.

To take another example, when we adopt a particular role within our community's politics, fulfilling that role will require us to embrace certain practices and relate to others in particular ways. These often taken-for-granted

---

[14]See Luke Bretherton, *Christ and the Common Life: Political Theology and the Case for Democracy* (Grand Rapids, MI: Eerdmans, 2022), 35-36.

norms within the community's politics create "smooth pathways to certain kinds of activities and produce barriers to others." Over time, this will "encourage the acquisition of certain character traits and discourage others."[15] Life in the community creates a kind of soil in which it is extremely likely, though not quite inevitable, that members will acquire certain virtues, and, more concerningly perhaps, acquire similar vices.

The stories, practices, account of character, and politics of a particular community are interdependent and mutually influential. Moral discipleship happens as people engage in this formative feedback loop within community.

While this model seeks to capture truth about how formation occurs in any community, *Christian* character ethics is particularly concerned with how it illuminates the way moral discipleship happens within ecclesial communities. By ecclesial communities I refer to the shared life of local Christian communities as they

1. Gather weekly to worship God, confess sins, give of their resources, hear the Word preached and taught, celebrate the Lord's Supper, baptize new members, and more.

2. Participate in shared lives of love and service beyond such gatherings by sharing resources, working together to welcome children, loving and serving neighbors, seeking justice together, and much more (fig. 3.2).

Moral discipleship in competition and collaboration with the alternatives. Of course, no community is as isolated as figure 3.2 suggests. Ecclesial communities pursue moral discipleship within various cultural contexts in which they participate in all sorts of ways (see fig. 3.3). We aren't just members of a church. We're also members of neighborhoods, workplaces, local and national governments, and more. Each of these has their own stories, accounts of character, formative practices, and politics. These communities disciple us too.

The dotted lines between the circle representing the ecclesial community and the circle representing the cultural contexts in figure 3.3 remind us that *every aspect of our discipleship* within the ecclesial community occurs in implicit dialogue with and under some influence by the formation occurring in the broader cultural environment. What difference does this make for how we understand the mechanics of moral discipleship?

---

[15]Daniel J. Daly, "Critical Realism, Virtue Ethics, and Moral Agency," in *Moral Agency Within Social Structures and Culture: A Primer on Critical Realism for Christian Ethics*, ed. Daniel K. Finn (Washington, DC: Georgetown University Press, 2020), 95.

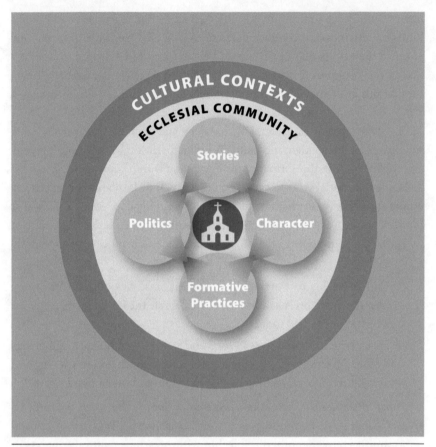

Figure 3.3. Moral discipleship in context

First, the way ecclesial communities practice moral discipleship influences and is influenced by practices of moral discipleship in their broader cultural contexts. Christian discipleship doesn't take place in some rarefied space perfectly sealed off from the rest of "the culture."[16] The boundary between the church and the broader context is less like a solid concrete wall than it is like the sides of a porous sponge.[17] For that matter, we as individuals are porous like sponges as well; our character is deeply influenced by both the ecclesial community *and* the broader cultures around us, for better *and* for worse.[18] We

---

[16]Even talk of "*the* culture" is misleading since there is no singular culture at work in any one context.

[17]See Katie Walker Grimes, *Christ Divided: Antiblackness as Corporate Vice* (Minneapolis: Fortress, 2017), 208-24.

[18]See Christina McRorie, "Moral Reasoning in 'the World," *Theological Studies* 82, no. 2 (2021): 215; Kate Ward, "Virtue and Human Fragility" *Theological Studies* 81, no. 1 (2020): 152.

bring who we've learned to be in other cultural spaces into the church, and we take who we're becoming in the church out into the cultures of which the church itself is a part.

Second, this isn't just the way it *is*. It's also the way it *should be*. The broader cultural context is part of the arena of God's mission and the mission of God's people. This is true not only because God calls us to share the good news with those currently outside the church, but also because Christians are called to bear witness to God's reign over all of creation. Indeed, Christian engagement with the broader cultural context can even help transform the church itself.

The fact that moral discipleship occurs within the church *and* within the broader cultural context presents us with both problems and opportunities. To understand these dynamics further, we can identify a continuum of engagement between ecclesial communities and their cultural contexts (fig. 3.4).

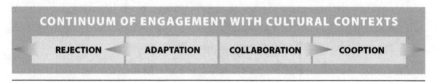

Figure 3.4. Continuum of engagement with cultural contexts

On the one hand, the church's moral discipleship will sometimes require us to completely reject stories, practices, accounts of character, or political formations embraced elsewhere. For instance, when the New Testament authors celebrated humility as a virtue, they rejected the Greco-Roman culture's idea that pride was a virtue and humility a vice.[19]

Other times, ecclesial discipleship will shape us to adapt cultural discipleship, bending it toward God's purposes. Meals in the ancient world had tremendous power to shape the character of those who ate them. Both the Old Testament and New Testament give us depictions of God's people drawing on food's formative power, while dramatically adapting cultural food practices for a discipleship quite distinctive from that on offer in their broader cultural environment.

Sometimes, the ecclesial community collaborates with the broader culture. As we will see in a later chapter, Daniel worked to promote certain virtues in

---

[19]James Thompson, *Moral Formation According to Paul: The Context and Coherence of Pauline Ethics* (Grand Rapids, MI: Baker Academic, 2011), 106-7.

the political community of Babylon that he had learned as a member of God's people. But at other times, the culture's stories, accounts of character, formative practices, and politics co-opt and corrupt the moral discipleship of the ecclesial community, luring the people of God into *de*-forming discipleship.

This suggests that moral discipleship occurs both within the ecclesial community *and* beyond it, and that discipleship requires learning to navigate this dynamic faithfully. At the same time, by placing the ecclesial community at the center of these circles, I am claiming that

- to be a member of the church of Jesus is to give primary allegiance to Jesus and his kingdom,
- moral formation in line with such allegiance puts a strong emphasis on life in the local body of believers as the primary place where we experience transformation, and
- such ecclesial formation is always influenced by the formation occurring within our broader cultural context, both because the church exists within that context, and because the church's mission draws God's people into creative engagement with it.[20]

Mapping moral discipleship in God's good world and under his generous reign. Ultimately, Christian character ethics recognizes that moral discipleship finally occurs in God's good creation and under the active reign of the triune God (see fig. 3.5). "Whether they acknowledge it or not, churches and cultures only exist in the real world: created good by God, under the ever-encroaching reign of Christ, and pervaded by the Spirit."[21]

On the one hand, then, Christian character ethics must grapple with the fact that all ecclesial communities and every human culture have participated in humanity's rebellion against God's reign. We have refused to live in ways that "go with the grain" of God's good world. "All have sinned and fall short of the glory of God" (Rom 3:23), and all our stories, accounts of character, practices, and politics likewise fall short. Indeed, because of sin, the church's formative discipleship often proves frail, faulty, and even de-forming.

On the other hand, the good news is that "the world-as-it-truly-exists" nevertheless remains "the world with God on the throne as the creating, sustaining, reconciling, and ruling King."[22] The hope of *ecclesial* formation is that

---

[20]See Rhodes, *Formative Feasting*, 66.
[21]Rhodes, *Formative Feasting*, 69.
[22]Rhodes, *Formative Feasting*, 69.

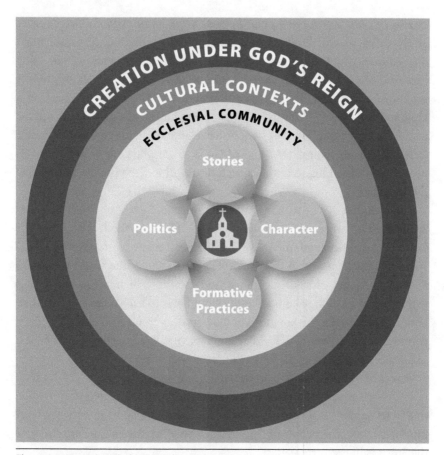

Figure 3.5. Moral discipleship in God's good creation

by God's grace we can truly (albeit imperfectly) begin to embody narratives, practices, politics, and character that reflect God's reign and "go with the grain" of God's universe.

This means that we cannot finally or fully talk about moral discipleship without talking about *grace*. Our existence as disciples is God's *gift* to us before it is ever our *task*. As the late John Webster reminds us, we can only talk about the church's acts of moral discipleship by constantly talking about *God* and *God's* acts.[23] Even and especially when we strenuously pursue moral formation, we discover that the Lord's own powerful work hems us in, behind and before, and that the Lord himself lays his hands on us in our journey of discipleship.

---

[23]John Webster, *God Without Measure: Working Papers in Christian Theology*, vol. II, *Virtue and Intellect* (New York: Bloomsbury T&T Clark, 2015), 188-89.

The difference grace makes for how we think about church. Grace makes all the difference for how we think about moral formation. It helps explain, for instance, why the ecclesial community stands at the center of our "map" of moral discipleship. The church's unique identity and job description is grounded entirely in God's grace poured out into the life of this particular community.[24] The church exists as a "a movement launched *into* the life of the world" by God and given the gift of bearing "in its own life God's gift of peace *for* the life of the world." Because of God's grace, the church not only tells people *about* the kingdom; the church bears "in its own life the presence of the kingdom."[25]

This dynamic can be seen in Paul's references to the church as a temple (see 2 Cor 6:16) or his summons to little groups of believers to live out their citizenship to God's kingdom amid the kingdoms of the world (see Phil 1:27). These images suggest that the church is a prototype of the world to come.[26] Paul believed that when the people of God embraced their allegiance to Jesus within the church, they embodied the good news to such an extent that their communities made the kingdom of God *encounterable* in the world.[27] Such congregations served as a "form of down payment, a guarantee that the age of justice, peace, and joy is not a pipe dream but a future reality."[28]

This is all grace! It is only because God unites his people to the body of Jesus that his people offer the world a glimpse of the resurrected new creation that is to come.[29] But because God does so, participation in ecclesial communities allows the people of God to learn how "to trace out where and how the Spirit is liberating creation."[30]

The difference grace makes for how we think about character. The fact that Christian moral discipleship is God's gift before it is our task radically re-shapes the way we think about the virtues. Consider, for instance, the difference between Aristotle's account of the virtues and Thomas Aquinas's attempt to transform that account in light of the good news about Jesus. Both Aristotle and Aquinas believe that the virtues are habits that empower us to

---

[24]John Webster, *God Without Measure*, 188-89.

[25]Leslie Newbigin, *The Open Secret: An Introduction to the Theology of Mission* (Grand Rapids, MI: Eerdmans, 1995), 48-49, emphasis added.

[26]See Wright, *Paul and the Faithfulness of God*, 1493-4; also Webster, *God Without Measure*, 138.

[27]See Stanley Hauerwas, *With the Grain of the Universe* (Grand Rapids, MI: Brazos Press, 2001), 214.

[28]Gorman, *Becoming the Gospel*, 47.

[29]Jonathan Tran, *Asian Americans and the Spirit of Racial Capitalism* (New York: Oxford University Press, 2022), 283.

[30]Tran, *Asian Americans*, 283.

know, desire, and effectively work toward particular goods. Both recognize that what we do shapes who we are. But while Aristotle thinks that good teaching and practice are enough to make at least some people truly virtuous, Aquinas disagrees. True, perfect virtue is always God's *gift*. We can only live out the virtuous law of love if God writes it on our hearts through the indwelling work of the Holy Spirit.

But doesn't this put an end to our entire discussion of moral *formation*? If God gives us the gift of a transformed character, can't we just expect to automatically and passively live just and righteous lives as a natural response to that gift? By no means! Aquinas argues that the virtues God graciously gives us involve our active effort. When we practice them, they take greater root in our hearts. Moreover, discipleship requires us to exercise the character God has given us to uproot the bad habits we accrue from our lives apart from Jesus. In all of this, Aquinas seeks to offer a model of virtue formation that is faithful to Scripture's twofold claim that we both receive transformed lives as a gift and pursue transformed lives as a task.

This theological account of the virtues is by no means peculiar to Aquinas or Roman Catholic theologians. Within my own Reformed tradition, Calvin's ethical theology stands in significant continuity with Aquinas "in regarding [good works] as a pathway of transformation along which the goal of steady growth in sanctity throughout the Christian life is sought."[31] The authors of the Westminster Confession of Faith believed that sanctification was "the work of the Holy Spirit infusing a habit of holiness in the believer," so that "sanctification" included the "human pursuit of holiness subsequent to justification."[32] Both Calvin and the Confession identify the "divine law" as a "summons" intended to "elicit character-forming practices of obedience,"[33] a point that is particularly relevant to my exploration of Leviticus and Deuteronomy in the chapters that follow. While there are substantial disagreements in the details, Reformed virtue ethicists, like Aquinas and much of the Christian theological tradition more generally, understand the Christian's virtuous character as a *gift* from God that elicits and enables our own efforts in the *task* of moral formation.[34]

---

[31]Stephen J. Chester, *Reading Paul with the Reformers: Reconciling Old and New Perspectives* (Grand Rapids, MI: Eerdmans, 2017), 265.

[32]David B. Hunsicker, "Westminster Standards and the Possibility of a Reformed Virtue Ethic," *SJT* 71, no. 2 (2018): 182, 184.

[33]Rhodes, *Formative Feasting*, 30.

[34]See further Rhodes, *Formative Feasting*, 26-35.

EVALUATING THE CHARACTER ETHICS MODEL

Can this model of moral discipleship inspired by character ethics help the people of God hear Scripture's invitation to *become just*? Does it fit the Scripture-shaped life of just discipleship to which we've been called? I believe the answer to these questions is yes. I will make that case by bringing sustained readings of the Bible's teaching about justice into dialogue with the model of moral discipleship presented here.[35]

We have already begun to see how this might work. We started our journey by exploring Scripture as the story of God bringing "justice to victory" (Mt 12:20) through the establishment of a just kingdom under the reign of the Just King and in collaboration with human image bearers. It is precisely this kind of grand narrative that definitively shapes our community's moral discipleship. Moreover, hearing that story required us to place it in contrast to the way many white churches in America have embraced a justice-light version of Scripture's story. Again and again, we will discover ways that Scripture's justice narrative spills over into stories, practices, accounts of character, and communal politics that shape the people of God for just discipleship in the real, messy world you and I live in today.

ANTICIPATING, ACKNOWLEDGING, AND BEGINNING TO ADDRESS THE OBJECTIONS

This book draws on character ethics to explore justice primarily as a virtue, *a holistic disposition to faithfully exercise power in community*. But focusing on justice as a virtue has its weaknesses. Wolterstorff is right that the language of virtue must be supplemented by some account of rights. Otherwise, exploring justice as a virtue risks overemphasizing "our" need to become just, without giving adequate attention to the moral reality of those who have been wronged by injustice.[36]

Even more importantly, many American Christian churches and traditions, including my own, have been notoriously, shamefully weak in assessing injustice at a structural level. We have tended to believe that if you focus on converting individuals, their individual transformed lives will eventually

---

[35]Methodologically, I see this as a version of theological interpretation, in which theological ethics provides the theological dialogue partner. This methodology bears some affinity with the Society of Biblical Literature's now-ended consultation on "Character Ethics and Biblical Interpretation," especially William Brown and M. Daniel Carroll R.'s application of virtue ethics to OT exegesis.

[36]Nicholas Wolterstorff, *Justice: Rights and Wrongs* (Princeton, NJ: Princeton University Press, 2008), 8-10.

solve any and every social problem.[37] Given this history, my focus on justice as a virtue could risk downplaying the systemic, structural reforms toward justice that the Bible demands.

To avoid these dangers, let me state clearly that Scripture speaks of justice as both a human virtue and a characteristic of institutions and social systems. The Bible not only speaks about just people like Job, it also speaks of just laws in society (see Is 10:1-2) and just weights and measures in the marketplace (see Prov 11:1). The many texts that call on judges and kings to do justice speak to these figures as representatives of broader legal and political institutions. The very existence of the law speaks not only to the need for just individuals, but for a society to be ordered in line with justice. Indeed, as we will see, the virtue of justice both demands and depends on just social systems and structures.[38] Such structures create the space for human flourishing, not least by providing the possibility for all God's image bearers to exercise justice in their own lives through the faithful exercise of power.

At an even deeper level, the Bible claims that the world was created and is sustained by a God who loves righteousness and justice. Justice, understood as the faithful exercise of power, stands at the heart of God's character and is woven into the very fabric of God's world. Biblical justice encompasses all these dynamics, and my focus on justice as a virtue is not intended to reject accounts of virtue that focus on its systemic or cosmic aspects.

Why focus on justice as a virtue at all, then? The first answer, of course, is simply that Scripture does often speak of justice as something that individuals and groups do through their

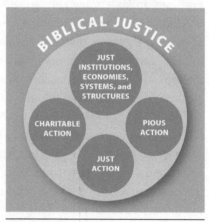

Figure 3.6. Justice woven into the fabric of God's world

own agency and effort. However abused, the idea of justice as a virtuous disposition toward living just and righteous lives runs deep in the Bible.

---

[37]See Michael O. Emerson and Christian Smith, *Divided by Faith: Evangelical Religion and the Problem of Race in America* (New York: Oxford University Press, 2000), 115-33.
[38]See Bretherton, *Christ and the Common Life*, 35.

Ultimately, however, my focus on justice as a virtue is strategic. Many churches in America have woken up to the biblical concern for justice, at least theoretically. We have spent much less time investing in the kind of *discipleship* that would help us become just. Addressing this gap is the focus of this book. While I focus on justice as a virtue, understood as the habituated disposition to faithfully exercise power in community, doing so will nevertheless require us to think about the ways that the triune God brings "justice to victory" through systems, structures, and indeed a renewed creation that bears witness to God's own just way.

Others may raise theological concerns about the extent to which I rely on virtue ethics in my model of moral discipleship. Some critics argue that virtue ethics veers toward works righteousness, is overly dependent on Aristotle, and posits far too stable and progressive an account of Christian character development. For these critics, in other words, character ethics places far too much emphasis on *human* agency, on what humans do. Some argue that the whole approach runs roughshod over Scripture itself.[39] Others argue that character ethics does not adequately account for formation *failure*—and may even contribute to it. My interest in character ethics was originally driven by my desire to *understand* and *respond* to our failure to embody God's justice in relation to economic and racial injustice. But Willie James Jennings makes a powerful argument that traditional models of moral formation *contributed* to racial and economic oppression, both in the colonial era and today. Some versions of virtue ethics, at least, have perpetuated the problem of unjust, vicious, *de*-forming discipleship.

These critiques will be considered in greater depth in the chapters that follow. What we need, and I hope to offer in this book, is a model for moral discipleship that builds on the insights offered by character ethics, while also embracing the important truths raised by these criticisms. The test of whether it has done so will be whether it helps us understand Scripture's *own* invitation to the journey of just discipleship.

LOOKING AHEAD

In this fairly technical exploration on the nature of moral formation, ethics, and theology, it's important not to lose sight of where we're headed. The brave protestors we met in the photograph at the beginning of this chapter knew

---

[39]See Brian Brock, *Singing the Ethos of God: On the Place of Christian Ethics in Scripture* (Grand Rapids, MI: Eerdmans, 2007), 241.

that if they wanted to do justice, they had to practice for it. Their hearts, minds, and bodies had been trained to do justice, to faithfully exercise what power they had in their community. Likewise, our goal in understanding the mechanics of moral formation is to relentlessly ask how we too might hear in Scripture God's invitation to become just through our relationship with the Just King who brings justice to victory.

PART 2

BECOMING
JUST DISCIPLES

CONSUMING CHARACTER

Justice Begins at the Feast

THE PROTESTORS OF THE CIVIL RIGHTS ERA challenged white Christians to wake up to the racial and economic injustices of their day. Despite the significant success of these protestors, Christians still live in a world rife with racially influenced economic injustice. In 2021, "median household income for African American households" was less than 60 percent of that of white households,[1] while Black households held a mere one-tenth the net worth of white households.[2] Similar indicators of economic disparity could be cited in relation to health care, education, home ownership, and more.[3]

Perhaps an equally important reality to consider, though, is the attendant racial and economic *segregation* of society. Residential segregation by income has been on the rise for thirty years,[4] while many metropolitan areas are still substantially segregated by race. Schools across the country have witnessed

---

[1]Dedrick Asante-Muhammad and Joshua Devine, "Closing the Racial Wealth Divide: A Plan to Boost Black Homeownership," *Nonprofit Quarterly* (September 29, 2021), available at: https://non profitquarterly.org/closing-the-racial-wealth-divide-a-plan-to-boost-black-homeownership/.

[2]William Darity Jr. and Kirsten Mullen, *From Here to Equality: Reparations for Black Americans in the Twenty-First Century* (Chapel Hill: University of North Carolina Press, 2020), 31.

[3]See "CDC Health Disparities and Inequities Report—U.S. 2013," available at: https://www.cdc.gov /minorityhealth/CHDIReport.html; Liz Sablich, "7 Findings That Illustrate Racial Disparities in Education," Brookings Institute, June 6, 2016, www.brookings.edu/blog/brown-center-chalk board/2016/06/06/7-findings-that-illustrate-racial-disparities-in-education; Jason Stauffer, "The Black Homeownership Gap Is Larger Than It Was 60 Years Ago. COVID-19 Made It Worse," Next Advisor, April 21, 2022, www.time.com/nextadvisor/mortgages/what-is-black-homeownership -gap.

[4]Richard Fry and Paul Taylor, "The Rise of Residential Segregation by Income," Pew Research Center, August 1, 2021, www.pewsocialtrends.org/2012/08/01/the-rise-of-residential-segregation -by-income.

ongoing racial segregation and increasing income segregation.[5] Racial segregation in the workplace is "greater today than it was in the '70s,"[6] and in terms of economic segregation, "high-wage workers are increasingly likely to work with each other, while low-wage workers are clustered in different firms and workplaces altogether."[7] In nearly every area of public life, "rich and poor Americans today are less likely to know one another and to share the same social spaces" than they were even fifty years ago.[8]

Churches largely mimic or even exacerbate these trends. They are often divided along class lines,[9] and when it comes to race the story is much worse: "Religious congregations are *ten times less diverse* than the neighborhoods in which they reside and *twenty times less diverse* than the nation's schools."[10]

Jesus famously told his disciples, "The poor you will always have with you" (Mt 26:11 NIV). But the data we've been exploring suggests that, for middle- and upper-class American Christians at least, at home, at work, and at church, the poor are *no longer with us* in any meaningful sense.[11] How does this impact the people of God's pursuit of just discipleship?

Jesus' line about the poor always being with us is a quote from Deuteronomy 15:11. While some Christians treat it as an excuse for apathy in relation to economic poverty, Deuteronomy offers a stunning portrayal of God's heart for the poor. Exploring Deuteronomy helps us see how our contemporary class-segregated society gets in the way of God's vision for justice, and inspires us to imagine what just discipleship might look like in our class-segregated world.

---

[5]See Jonathan J. B. Mijs and Elizabeth L. Roe, "Is America Coming Apart? Socioeconomic Segregation in Neighborhoods, Schools, Workplaces, and Social Networks, 1970–2020," *Sociology Compass* 15, no. 6 (2021): 7-9, compass.onlinelibrary.wiley.com/doi/epdf/10.1111/soc4.12884.

[6]Dana Wilkie, "Across the Economy, Workplaces are More Segregated Than 40 Years Ago," SHRM, March 6, 2018, www.shrm.org/resourcesandtools/hr-topics/employee-relations/pages/workplace -diversity-.aspx.

[7]Mijs and Roe, "Coming Apart," 9. See also Judith K. Hellerstein and David Neumark, "Workplace Segregation in the United States: Race, Ethnicity, and Skill," *The Review of Economics and Statistics* 90, no. 3 (2008): 467.

[8]Mij and Roe, "Coming Apart," 1.

[9]See Christian Smith and Robert Farris, "Socioeconomic Inequality in the American Religious System: An Update and Assessment," in *Religion and Class in America: Culture History and Politics*, ed. Sean McCloud and Bill Mirola (Leiden: Brill, 2008), 29-39; Sam Reimer, "Class and Congregations: Class and Religious Affiliations at the Congregational Level of Analysis," *Journal for the Society of Religion* 46, no. 4 (2007): 583-92.

[10]Michael O. Emerson, William A. Mirola, and Susanne C. Monahan, *Religion Matters: What Sociology Teaches Us About Religion in Our World* (London: Routledge, 2010), 161.

[11]Mark Gornik, *To Live in Peace: Biblical Faith and the Changing Inner City* (Grand Rapids, MI: Eerdmans, 2002). 2.

JUST DISCIPLESHIP AND DEUTERONOMY

Deuteronomy claims that one way Israel participates in God's mission is by obeying Yahweh's just and righteous law. This is just what we'd expect given Scripture's overarching justice story. Through their faithful obedience to God's good law, Israel will become a countercultural community that embodies God's character and participates in God's purposes.

And the world will take notice! Deuteronomy 4:6-8 envisions the nations looking over Israel's proverbial fence and declaring, *Surely this great nation is a wise and understanding people. . . . What great nation is there, that has statues and rules as just as this law?* By embodying God's justice and righteousness, God's people become a vehicle of God's blessings to the world.

Against this background, Deuteronomy's laws on tithing, debt forgiveness, and debt slavery provide some of the most radical socioeconomic legislation found in the entire ancient world (Deut 14:28–15:18). These laws form a crucial part of the just politics of the community of faith envisioned by Deuteronomy as a whole. As we saw in the previous chapter, a community's politics foster moral discipleship, not least as the community's political practices reject, adapt, collaborate with, or are coopted by the broader culture's politics (see fig. 4.1).

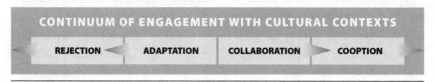

Figure 4.1. Continuum of engagement with cultural contexts

The explosive nature of Deuteronomy's laws becomes clearer when we compare them to the political and economic alternatives among Israel's neighbors. Take the tithe laws, for instance. Among Israel's neighbors, tithes were taxes collected for a king or temple. By contrast, Deuteronomy 14:28-29 tells the Israelites to store up their tithes every third year in their village gates. These offerings would be used to provide emergency food aid for orphans, widows, and immigrants.[12] This "triennial tithe" represents "the first known tax instituted for the purpose of social welfare" in human history.[13]

---

[12]See David Baker, *Tight Fists or Open Hands? Wealth and Poverty in Old Testament Law* (Grand Rapids, MI: Eerdmans, 2009), 248.
[13]Baker, *Tight Fists*, 248.

The laws around debt forgiveness that immediately follow are equally striking.[14] Every seventh year "Yahweh's release" is declared. In this sabbatical year, anyone who holds a debt against "his neighbor and his brother" (Deut 15:2) must forgive it. While other cultures practiced debt forgiveness through royal edicts, these occurred sporadically and at the whim of a human ruler.[15] By establishing debt forgiveness as a fixed pattern declared by Yahweh, Deuteronomy moves toward a permanent "reform."[16] Such a reform sought to prevent households overwhelmed with debt from becoming a "permanent underclass."[17]

Similarly, Deuteronomy 15:12-18 declares that if a fellow Israelite becomes so impoverished that they must sell themselves or their family members into debt bondage, these debt slaves must be set free after seven years. When the debt slave is released, they must be sent off lavishly provided for from the flock, threshing floor, and wine vat of the household in which they had been indentured. Not only does this serve as at least partial compensation for previously unpaid work, the law also seeks to prevent the released debt slave from falling back into poverty and servitude.[18] As with the legislation concerning the sabbatical year, this law seeks to interrupt the debt cycle and prevent multigenerational poverty among Israelite families.[19]

What do these laws tell us about the socioeconomic structure of the community? What kind of socioeconomic structures do these economic laws envision? In the Old Testament, Israel found herself surrounded by monarchies and empires with powerful rulers and highly stratified societies. Israel eventually sought to emulate that kind of system. Such political economies are filled with bureaucrats, professional soldiers, priestly classes, and—down at the bottom of the social pyramid—peasants. The peasants, of course, must provide food for the ever-increasing classes of non-food-producers.

But the society required and cultivated by the economic laws of Deuteronomy 14:27–15:18 appears to be more in line with the "village

---

[14]Walter Brueggemann, *Deuteronomy* (Nashville: Abingdon Press, 2001), 163.

[15]These royal edicts are referred to as *andurārum* and *mišarum* in the literature. For more on ancient Near Eastern debt relief, see Peter Altmann, *Economics in Persian Period Biblical Texts: Their Interactions with Economic Developments in the Persian Period and Earlier Biblical Traditions* (Tubingen: Mohr Seibeck, 2016), 43-44.

[16]For discussion, see J. J. Finkelstein, "Ammisaduqa's Edict and the Babylonian 'Law Codes,'" *Journal of Cuneiform Studies* 15, no. 3 (1961): 100.

[17]Walter J. Houston, *Contending for Justice: Ideologies and Theologies of Social Justice in the Old Testament* (New York: T&T Clark, 2006), 181.

[18]Baker, *Tight Fists*, 145.

[19]See Georg Braulik, "Deuteronomy and Human Rights," *Verbum et Ecclesia* 19, no. 2 (1998): 209-24.

economy."[20] In a village-based economy, small villages composed of several extended-family households worked together to perform nearly all the essential political and economic functions of the community.[21]

The legislation we've explored so far addresses two major socioeconomic threats facing such village economies. On the one hand, the limits in Deuteronomy 15:1-18 on debts and debt servitude protect the economic viability of each household, ensuring that struggling families could remain intact socially and economically. Indeed, by preventing any one household from becoming permanently indebted to or having its members permanently absorbed by another, these laws sought a relative equity among the households within the village.[22] On the other hand, those community members most likely to fall through the cracks *between* households—orphans, widows, vulnerable outsiders, and Levites—receive emergency food aid through the triennial tithe.

These economic laws make clear that when Deuteronomy says "there will always be poor people in the land" (Deut 15:11 NIV) it does *not* mean that God's people ought to be unconcerned about poverty.[23] After all, just seven verses earlier Yahweh had told the people "there will be *no* poor among you" (Deut 15:4 AT)! Against the socioeconomic background we've been exploring, one way of understanding the tension between verse 4 and verse 11 is that while there will always be temporary poverty due to natural disaster, injustice, or human error, there *need be no permanently poor class* in Israel *if* the people will follow God's just instruction. Indeed, the temporary poor in Israel will be able to remain "with you" in the community through laws aimed at ending permanent poverty for all. These laws seek to shape Israel's structures and systems in line with God's vision of justice.

Laws too good to be true? But not everyone is convinced. Knight complains that these Deuteronomic laws have "no teeth, no provisions for enforcement and no remedies for violations."[24] Westbrook argues that a law

---

[20]Boer calls it the subsistence regime (Roland Boer, *The Sacred Economy of Ancient Israel*, Library of Ancient Israel [Louisville, KY: Westminster John Knox, 2015], 3).

[21]See Boer, *The Sacred Economy*; Norman K. Gottwald, *Social Justice and the Hebrew Bible*, vol. 1 (Eugene, OR: Wipf & Stock, 2016), 21, 24-6; Christopher J. H. Wright, *Old Testament Ethics for the People of God* (Downers Grove, IL: IVP Academic, 2011), 55, 89; Sandra Lynn Richter, "The Question of Provenance and the Economics of Deuteronomy," *JSOT* 42, no. 1 (2017): 23-50.

[22]See Braulik, "Deuteronomy and Human Rights," 209-24; Richard D. Nelson, *Deuteronomy: A Commentary* (Louisville, KY: Westminster John Knox, 2002), 192.

[23]We ought to assume that this isn't what Jesus intended either!

[24]Douglas A. Knight, "Whose Agony? Whose Ecstasy? The Politics of Deuteronomic Law," in *Shall Not the Judge of All the Earth Do What Is Right?: Studies on the Nature of God in Tribute to James L. Crenshaw*, ed. David Penchansky and Paul L. Redditt (Winona Lake, IN: Eisenbrauns, 2000), 111.

requiring debt forgiveness at fixed intervals would simply dry up sources of credit for struggling households; if the lender can't guarantee they will get repaid, they will simply refuse to lend to their neighbor in the first place.[25] Such a law is either utopian rhetoric or an actual legal practice that does more harm than good.

It isn't skeptical scholars who first voiced these concerns, though; *the text itself* raises precisely these questions. Deuteronomy 15:7 addresses the potential credit shortage these laws might create, declaring that if there is a poor person in one of the towns "you must not harden your heart and you must not close up your hand" from your brother,[26] but instead "open wide your hand and lend him enough for his need" (AT). Deuteronomy 15:9 sounds a similar warning: "Guard yourself, lest there be a wicked thought in your heart, saying 'the seventh year, the year of release is near,' and your eye be evil against your brother who is poor" (AT).

Texts like these, which directly address each household in the community, make clear that the people of God must pursue the virtue of justice if they're ever going to be able to obey God's just economic laws. Within the book of Deuteronomy, the "heart" represents the center of a person's thoughts, intentions, and feelings.[27] The language of "not hardening your heart" points both to the importance of one's moral dispositions toward one's neighbors, and to the need for individuals to pursue such dispositions. The Israelites must proactively seek a just and generous heart if these just and generous laws are going to work. They need more than knowledge about what justice looks like; they need to *become* just.

Deuteronomy's response to critics who complain that the book's laws are unenforceable or could inadvertently do more harm than good is simple: law alone is never enough. Just laws depend on the formation of a just community made up of just persons.[28]

But where do such just communities and individuals come from? How do people gain and grow in the virtue of justice? To address this question, Deuteronomy offers a breathtaking vision of discipleship, one capable of inspiring us to reimagine what it would mean to *become* just in the

---

[25]Raymond Westbrook, *Law from the Tigris to the Tiber: The Writings of Raymond Westbrook*, ed. F. Rachel Magdalene and Bruce Wells (Winona Lake, IN: Eisenbrauns, 2009), 158-9.

[26]The familial language of "brother" is morally significant; I have preserved the gendered language here because the most likely socioeconomic transaction envisioned is one taking place between male heads of Israelite households.

[27]Jeffrey H. Tigay, *Deuteronomy: The Traditional Hebrew Text with the New JPS Translation, Commentary by Jeffrey H. Tigay* (Philadelphia: JPS, 1996), 77. See also TWOT, 1071a; BDB, 523.

[28]See Altmann, *Economics in Persian Period Biblical Texts*, 73.

class-segregated context we explored earlier. But be warned: Deuteronomy's answer is a surprising one. For Deuteronomy, just discipleship begins at a feast.

BECOMING JUST GOD-FEARERS AT THE FEAST

If we turn to look at what comes immediately before the economic legislation we've been exploring, we read this:

> You will surely tithe all the produce of your seed that comes from the field year by year. And you will eat before Yahweh your God, in the place that he will choose to establish his name there, the tithe of your grain, your new wine, and your olive oil, as well as the firstborn of your cattle and your flocks, in order that you will learn to fear Yahweh your God always. But if the way is so far for you that you are not able to carry your tithe, because the place Yahweh your God will choose to put his name there is far from you, because Yahweh your God blesses you, then you will exchange your tithe for money. And you will take the money in your hand and you will walk to the place that Yahweh your God will choose with it. And you will use the money to buy all that you deeply desire—in cattle and in flocks and in wine and in strong drink and in all that your deep desires ask of you. And you shall eat there before Yahweh your God and you will rejoice, you and your household. (Deut 14:22-26 AT)

The text commands Israelite households to bring their tithes and the firstborn of their livestock to the sanctuary in order to feast on those offerings together before the Lord. The explicit goal of this feast is that they "learn to fear Yahweh" always (Deut 14:23). But that explanation raises more questions than it answers: How do you *learn* an emotion by *eating*?

The learning that occurs at the feast is *learning by doing,* or, to be more precise, *learning by eating.*[29] Deuteronomy 14:22-27 makes no mention of teaching, reading, or instruction. Instead, the text emphasizes the *repetitive* and *bodily* nature of the meal.[30] In the language of our map of moral formation, the tithe feast is a *formative practice.*

What is formed through the feast is the "fear of Yahweh." Scholars have often argued that such fear refers *either* to the literal emotion of fear *or* to acts of covenant obedience.[31] One problem facing interpreters who embrace this

---

[29]See Peter Altmann, *Festive Meals in Ancient Israel,* BZAW (Berlin: De Gruyter, 2011), 227-28; Suee Yan Yu, "Tithes and Firstlings in Deuteronomy" (PhD diss., Union Theological Seminary, 1997), 69.

[30]This does not preclude the Deuteronomic feasts from including corporate practices like hearing and reciting the law, as is explicit in Deut 31:10-13.

[31]*TDOT,* 6:307; Moshe Weinfeld, *Deuteronomy and the Deuteronomistic School* (Oxford: Clarendon Press, 1972), 274-81; Stephen L. Cook, *Reading Deuteronomy: A Literary and Theological*

division is explaining how both kinds of fear show up in the same book, as they do in Deuteronomy.[32] The "fear of Yahweh" in Deuteronomy 5:24-33, for instance, is a literal fear in response to a terrifying encounter with God. Elsewhere, though, Deuteronomy places language about "fearing Yahweh" in direct parallel with the language of covenant obedience (see Deut 6:13; 10:20; 13:4).

Others argue that we should see the fear of Yahweh as a virtue or disposition that includes both emotional and active dimensions.[33] Lasater claims that, in the ancient world, both the fear of God and the fear of the king refer to an appropriate disposition or posture toward a superior.[34] Such a disposition includes both appropriate actions *and* appropriate feelings. Similarly, Brown argues that the fear of Yahweh in Proverbs is "a posture of awe and the embodiment of virtue" before the Lord.[35] This virtuous disposition of the heart comes from an awareness of one's position "in relation to God."[36]

The fear of Yahweh in Deuteronomy is best understood as a virtuous disposition, or, perhaps better, a summary description of the virtuous character that God requires of his covenant partners.[37] "This explains why some passages emphasize the feeling of fear and others the active, covenantal obedience of fear. Action and feeling are both present because to have acquired a virtuous disposition toward Yahweh is to desire, think, feel, and act rightly in relation to him."[38]

If the fear of Yahweh is best understood as a virtue, then the feast is a formative practice that fosters that virtue among those who feast. But this raises further questions for us. *How* does the feast form this virtuous fear of the Lord? And how might such fear shape the people for the just politics of

---

Commentary (Macon, GA: Smyth & Helwys Publishing, 2014), 51; Bernard Jacob Bamberger, "Fear and Love of God in the Old Testament," *Hebrew Union College Annual* (2006), 40.

[32]Some interpreters argue that the meaning of the phrase changed over time, such that the ongoing use of the same phrase with two different meanings suggest different redactional layers. For a brief discussion, see Brent Strawn, "The Iconography of Fear," in *Image, Text, Exegesis: Iconographic Interpretation and the Hebrew Bible*, ed. Joel M. LeMon and Izaak J. de Hulster (London: Bloomsbury T&T Clark, 2014), 95-97.

[33]See Strawn, "Iconography," 96-97.

[34]Philip Lasater, "Fear" in *The Oxford Encyclopedia of Bible and Theology*, ed. Samuel E. Balentine, (Oxford: Oxford University Press, 2015), 2:346, 348.

[35]William Brown, *Wisdom's Wonder: Character, Creation, and Crisis in the Bible's Wisdom Literature* (Grand Rapids, MI: Eerdmans, 2014), 89.

[36]Brown, *Wisdom's Wonder*, 37; *NIDOTTE*, 2:530.

[37]As I argue in detail in my *Formative Feasting: Practices and Virtue Ethics in the Deuteronomic Tithe Meal and Corinthian Lord's Supper*, Studies in Biblical Literature 176 (New York: Peter Lang, 2022), 90-95.

[38]Rhodes, *Formative Feasting*, 93-94.

the triennial tithe, debt forgiveness, and slave liberation legislated in Deuteronomy 14:28–15:18?

The mechanics of Deuteronomic meal formation. First, the tithe feast shapes the community to relate to Yahweh as the generous king who is present among his people. Deuteronomy takes a tax for temple or palace and turns it into the food budget for a community-wide feast. While every citizen in the ancient world would be prepared for the powerful to demand that they bring tithe-taxes to the central sanctuary (Deut 14:22), they would *not* be prepared for these tithe-taxes to be returned to them as funds for a community-wide festival (Deut 14:23)![39]

Second, the formative power of Yahweh's innovative tithe goes far beyond the fact that taxes won't be so steep this year. The feast invites God's people to taste, see, and smell—quite literally—the lavish generosity of their divine king. That's why the text highlights the feast's lavish portions—10 percent of a household's total crop harvest and the firstborn of all their herds—and offers a mouthwatering description of the menu: grain, new wine, olive oil, cattle, sheep, wine, "strong drink," and the twice-repeated catchall "whatever you deeply desire" (Deut 14:26).

Third, the description of this lavish feast must be read in light of the reality that, in the ancient world, feasts, like tithes, were tools the elite used to consolidate power and reinforce the social hierarchy. Royal feasts served to display the ruler's power, put attendees in his debt, and even gather tribute.[40] In Israel's larger world, you couldn't take it for granted that big meals would foster the virtue of justice; they might well be tools for shoring up *injustice*. Deuteronomy's feast, by contrast, invites Israel to encounter a divine king who generously gives back to his people the tax that is his by rights and invites them to a party of royal proportions.

This royal feast depends in no way on any human king, priestly class, or emerging elite. Instead, Yahweh alone presides over a joyful festival, inviting each guest to feast on whatever their hearts desire. This meal would foster the fear of Yahweh by shaping those who ate it to relate to Yahweh as the generous king who is present among his people.

Fourth, such feasting would also foster certain virtuous dispositions toward one's fellow-Israelites. In ancient Near Eastern festivals, where you sat at the

---

[39] Altmann, *Festive Meals*, 243.

[40] See Altmann, *Festive Meals*, 231; Denise Schmandt-Besserat, "Feasting in the Ancient Near East," in *Feasts: Archaeological and Ethnographic Perspectives on Food, Politics, and Power*, ed. Michael Dietler and Brian Hayden (Tuscaloosa, AL: University of Alabama Press, 2010), 392-401.

feast, what you wore, when you entered, and what portions of food you received could all communicate and solidify where you belonged within a complex hierarchy.[41] The tithe festival mentions no such behavior. Instead, the text merely states that the feast is to be celebrated by household. Such feasting would shore up in the central place and at the sacred festival the sort of relatively egalitarian relationships between households that characterized life back in the village.

Moreover, households in the ancient world included both extended family and non-relatives such as Levites, hired workers, debt servants, dependent strangers, and others who became attached to the household as "fictive kin." These groups are explicitly included in the household at the feasts in Deuteronomy (see Deut 12:7-12; 16:11, 14; 26:11). This emphasis on feasting by household, then, is morally significant. "While God is not hung up on the details of festival party planning, he's deeply committed to an inclusive guest list."[42] The lavish feast to which Yahweh invites his people is one in which all are welcomed and provided for.

At Yahweh's table, just generosity flows through communal ties, and the shared cup of wine and passed plate both *solidify* such ties and *create* new ones.[43] "Because of this, orphans, widows, Levites, debt slaves, and dependent strangers received far more at the feast than food, drink, and an occasional vacation; this feast provided for the *inclusion* of the vulnerable as *kin*."[44] This is true because "to be able to eat together, one must *be* kin or one *becomes* kin."[45]

Indeed, while Yahweh is the ultimate provider of the feast, the household itself is the proximate means for funding it. What the household feasts on, in other words, is the result of the collective labor of the households who celebrate it.[46] This dynamic becomes even clearer when we consider just how much work this kind of feast would require. The planting, harvesting, storing, and preparing of the food required for the feast would have begun months beforehand. That time horizon expands to more than a year when it comes to the alcoholic beverages that this text goes on and on about! Because the entire household would have been engaged in this work, if at one level the tithe meal

[41]Brian Hayden and Michael Dietler, "Digesting the Feast—Good to Eat, Good to Drink, Good to Think: An Introduction," in Dietler and Hayden, *Feasts*, 10.

[42]Rhodes, *Formative Feasting*, 104.

[43]A. J. Culp, *Memoir of Moses: The Literary Creation of Covenantal Memory in Deuteronomy* (Minneapolis: Fortress Academic, 2019), 150.

[44]Rhodes, *Formative Feasting*, 104.

[45]Georg Braulik, *The Theology of Deuteronomy: Collected Essays of George Braulik*, trans. Ulrika Lindblad (North Richland Hills, TX: D & F Scott Publishing, 1998), 61.

[46]Braulik, *Theology*, 44.

is hosted by the divine king, at another level, the people would experience it as a highly participatory potluck, a meal to which the entire household and village had contributed.[47]

In short, learning to fear Yahweh through the feast includes acquiring a virtuous disposition toward Yahweh as the generous and present king *and* a virtuous disposition of generous mutuality and solidarity toward the vulnerable. Incredibly, the justice-working fear the Israelites learn at the feast has everything to do with *joy*. Yahweh's program of God-fearing, just discipleship includes an invitation for all to attend the community's most over-the-top, extravagant, destination festival: "You shall eat there before Yahweh your God and you will rejoice, you and your household" (Deut 14:26 AT).

Just formation begins at the feast, but it doesn't stay there. Deuteronomy suggests that the legislation of the triennial tithe, debt forgiveness, and slave liberation we explored earlier *depends on* this formative practice of feasting. In other words, learning to fear Yahweh through feasting is part and parcel of developing the individual and corporate virtue of justice that will help the people follow the just legislation of Deuteronomy 14:28–15:18. This can be seen in four ways.

First, acquiring the virtues of generous welcome and solidarity with the vulnerable by feasting together would make the Israelites more likely to do the costlier work required by the triennial tithe. Feasts require subsistence farmers to practice a kind of fasting, because one foregoes on the front end to indulge on the back end.[48] But this same self-sacrifice would be required in the third year, when the Israelites would fast, not to feast, but to fund the social safety net for the vulnerable. If we imagine a family skipping their big Christmas dinner and expensive gift giving so that they can cut a big check to the food bank, we might get a *glimpse* of what this practice would mean. But that glimpse pales in comparison to the reality of vulnerable farmers giving up their community's harvest feast in order to make sure everyone eats all year round. Having become the family of God at the annual feast, the Israelites have fostered a virtuous commitment to make sure their newfound family members are fed every day of the year.

Second, the laws around debt forgiveness and slave liberation depend on the lender seeing the borrower as an equal within the community. This

---

[47]Brian Hayden, "Fabulous Feasts: A Prolegomenon to the Importance of Feasting," in Dietler and Hayden, *Feasts*, 47-50.

[48]Mark R. Glanville, *Adopting the Stranger as Kindred in Deuteronomy*, Ancient Israel and Its Literature 33 (Atlanta: SBL Press, 2018), 200-1.

explains why Deuteronomy 15:1-18 contains the first seven of twenty-nine instances in Deuteronomy's law code of the language of "brother" to define a "fellow Israelite."[49] Such language "encourages listeners to see the neighbor as a member of a family in which they are 'linked by kinship.'"[50]

But it is at the feast that one learns to treat potential needy borrowers as brothers and neighbors with an equal stake in the community. Solidarity between the heads of households would have been strengthened through the pilgrimage feast, as they presumably made the long journey to the central location as a village. This would make any one "brother" or "neighbor" more likely to open wide their hands in generous lending toward any other "brother" or "neighbor" who had become poor. Moreover, the feasting that occurred by household would include debt slaves waiting for release, thus building solidarity and generosity between the lender and the indentured worker.

Third, the tithe feast forms Israelite character in relation to both food and money, because distant pilgrims might have to sell their tithes in the village and then buy ingredients for the feast once they arrived at the central sanctuary. The laws of Deuteronomy 14:28–15:18 depend on the Israelites acquiring virtuous dispositions toward these same material goods. On the one hand, the triennial tithe requires the generous donation of a tenth of their harvest. On the other hand, the law concerning debt forgiveness depends on community members having a habituated willingness to "open wide" their hands in lending, and Deuteronomy 23:19-20 makes clear that both food and money would have been lent. The same agricultural goods that one learns to share with debt slaves attached to one's household at the feast must also be provided to the debt slave on their release (Deut 15:13-14).

Summarizing these first three points together, we might say that Deuteronomy 14:28–15:18 depends on the Israelites acquiring the economic virtues of generosity and solidarity, and that the Israelites acquire such virtues through a joyful, indulgent feast in Yahweh's presence and alongside the full community. This feast forms them for the practice of justice by training them to exercise power faithfully in community.

A strange solution? Before turning to a fourth way the moral formation of the feast spills over into the economic legislation of Deuteronomy 14:28–15:18, we ought to acknowledge that Deuteronomy's depiction of indulgent feasting as a

---

[49]Norbert Lohfink, "Poverty in the Laws of the Ancient Near East and of the Bible," *Theological Studies* 52, no. 1 (1991): 46.

[50]Houston, *Contending*, 183; see also Nelson, *Deuteronomy*, 199.

morally formative practice that encourages economic justice is surprising. This is especially true given the deep suspicion of indulgent eating and economic prosperity elsewhere in the book. Deuteronomy 8:1-20, for instance, moves seamlessly from a vivid portrayal of the Promised Land to a stern warning that, *when they have eaten their fill,* the people guard themselves against the danger of allowing economic abundance to lead them to idolatry and the self-aggrandizing declaration "My strength and the power of my hand have made for me this wealth" (Deut 8:11, 14, 17 AT).[51]

Such idolatrous self-aggrandizement is bound up with the oppression and neglect of the neighbor who is poor. The language of "guarding oneself" from economic vice is repeated in the exhortation to guard oneself from a vicious disposition to ignore a brother's need because the year for debt forgiveness is near (Deut 15:9). Deuteronomy recognizes that the very economic abundance that would enable a wealthier Israelite to "open wide" their hands to their poor brother might tempt them to refuse that brother in their hour of need. Prosperity presents a perennial temptation toward the disordered economic desire of greed, and toward neglect or outright oppression of the poor driven by that greed.

What is so startling is that Deuteronomy's solution to the danger presented by economic prosperity is not *fasting,* but *feasting.* Deuteronomy does not seek to squash vicious economic desire through self-imposed deprivation, but to encourage and reorient economic desire toward joy together with God and the vulnerable.

Learning to look to God. Fourth and finally, feasting year in and year out shapes God's people to trust Yahweh as the present and generous king who provides generously to those who obey him. The need to trust God is alluded to in Yahweh's promise to bless the people's work if they follow the triennial tithe (Deut 14:29) and in his promise to make them the lenders to nations if they embrace the costly practice of debt forgiveness (Deut 15:6, 10).

Truly believing that God was both present and able to deliver the goods for obedience would be particularly crucial given that the "haves" imagined by these texts are not wealthy individuals with disposable income, but subsistence farmers in a climate where an estimated three out of every ten years would produce crop failure.[52] Deuteronomy calls vulnerable farmers, often

---

[51]George McConville, *Deuteronomy,* AOTC (Downers Grove, IL: IVP Academic), 170.

[52]Albino Barrera, *Biblical Economic Ethics: Sacred Scripture's Teachings on Economic Life* (Lanham, MD: Lexington Books, 2013), 31.

themselves victims of various injustices, to do justice by exercising what power they have on behalf of the poor. For such people, obeying these laws would entail genuine risk, and might be unwise, unless their risky, vulnerable, generosity would be noticed by a king who would provide abundantly for his obedient people.

Deuteronomy 14:22–15:18 seeks to create a community characterized by just laws and made up of just people. At the feast, the community learns to fear Yahweh by joyfully fostering a habituated disposition toward him as the generous king who is present among his people and by a disposition of generous solidarity toward the vulnerable. In a world where both political systems and communal feasts could contribute to injustice, Israel's feasts serve as a central practice that enable the people of God to *become* just.

FEASTING FOR JUSTICE TODAY?

What does it mean to hear Deuteronomy 14:22-15:18 as God's address to us today? How might these texts inspire us to pursue just discipleship in communities facing the economic injustice and segregation we explored at the beginning of this chapter?

First, by tying laws about emergency food relief and debt forgiveness to the feast, Deuteronomy demonstrates that economic justice requires the formation of just character. As a corporate practice of hospitality, generosity, solidarity, and worship, the feast plays an essential role in fostering that just character. This highlights the way contemporary economic *segregation* fundamentally undermines the quest for economic *justice*. If the poor are "no longer with us" in middle-class spaces, then true justice is impossible, at least according to Deuteronomy. One cannot feast with people who are not present, and feasting fosters the virtue of justice on which systems of justice depend.

The second point is the opposite of the first: the formation of virtuous character alone is also not enough. Some American Christians respond to calls for systemic change in relation to race and class by claiming that these are "heart" issues that must be dealt with at the level of the heart *rather than* at the systemic level.[53] But God calls us to pursue *both* just character *and* just systems. Indeed, just systems make just discipleship more likely. In Deuteronomy, the

---

[53]Michael O. Emerson and Christian Smith, *Divided by Faith: Evangelical Religion and the Problem of Race in America* (New York: Oxford University Press, 2000), 117-19, 130-32; Chanequa Walker-Barnes, *I Bring the Voices of My People: A Womanist Vision for Racial Reconciliation* (Grand Rapids, MI: Eerdmans, 2019), 7-9, 113, 215-20.

limitations on indebtedness and the care for the vulnerable in the villages sought to make it more likely that all would find a place at the community's table. In our world, economic injustice at the structural level makes interpersonal relationships across lines of race and class, and by extension the kind of solidarity shaped by feasting that Deuteronomy imagines, far less likely.[54]

What, then, might it look like for ecclesial communities inspired by Deuteronomy's feasts to pursue justice in relation to economic segregation, in terms of both structures and moral character, both within the church and beyond?

Practicing feast-like formation through relocation. Willie James Jennings describes the early church's sharing of possessions similarly to the way I have described the feast. "Money here will be used," he writes, "to destroy what money normally is used to create: distance and boundaries between people." The early church's possessions and property, like the Deuteronomic feasts, become the tools that God uses in his miraculous work of joining former enemies in the community of faith.[55] In imaginatively considering what it would look like to respond to Scripture's invitation today, Jennings calls Christians to "transgress the boundaries of real estate, [buying] where we should not and living where we must not, by living together where we supposedly cannot, and being identified with those whom we should not."[56]

No contemporary Christian has done more to put flesh on this biblical vision than Dr. John Perkins. Perkins fought for structural change throughout his career and was tortured for leading a strike targeting segregated businesses. In his neighborhood-level work, though, he realized that the young people they had helped gain skills, education, and opportunity used those gifts to leave the impoverished communities in which they had grown up behind. The result of this "brain drain" was that the individual was better off, but the neighborhood worse so, not least because this "up and out" dynamic contributed to economic segregation.

And so, in addition to protesting systemic injustice, Dr. Perkins began practicing and preaching the principle of relocation. The relocation principle

---

[54]For further theological reflection on this theme, see Daniel J. Daly, "Critical Realism, Virtue Ethics, and Moral Agency," in *Moral Agency Within Social Structures and Culture: A Primer on Critical Realism for Christian Ethics*, ed. Daniel K. Finn (Washington, DC: Georgetown University Press, 2020), 95.

[55]Willie James Jennings, *Acts*, Belief (Louisville, KY: Westminster John Knox, 2017), 50.

[56]William James Jennings, *The Christian Imagination: Theology and the Origins of Race* (New Haven, CT: Yale University Press, 2010), 287.

invites historic residents of poor communities to choose to stay in those communities or return to them if they've left them. It also invites some middle-class Christians to choose to live in impoverished neighborhoods as an act of Christian solidarity. Decades later, Perkins's organization, the Christian Community Development Association (CCDA), still promotes this kind of intentional neighboring in publications, an annual gathering, and a national network.

The practice of relocation works similarly to the practice of Deuteronomy's feast. Relocation, Perkins writes, changes "'they, them, and theirs' to 'we, us, and ours.'"[57] As such, it is a meta-practice of generous solidarity. Those of us who have sought to practice relocation have discovered that it leads to a wide host of other practices that form neighbors who would otherwise be divided along lines of race and class for solidarity, mutuality, generosity, and trust.[58] Recent research demonstrating that cross-class friendships significantly increase the income potential of poor children demonstrates what both Perkins and Deuteronomy predicted: justice demands that we pursue communities that bring people together across lines of class.[59]

But in American society as in Deuteronomy, economic success often degenerates into little more than idolatrous self-obsession: "My might and the power of my hand have bought for me real estate in this suburban gated community or hipster urban apartment next door to my favorite brewery." Because rising income inequality is one primary driver in economic segregation, such deformed economic desire drives the "haves" and "have nots" further and further apart.[60] As in Isaiah 5:8, our economic desire too often leads us to add "house to house" until we dwell alone in the land, whether in affluent suburbs or unjustly gentrified urban neighborhoods.

Such economically segregated spaces threaten to disciple us in all the wrong ways. Families living in affluent enclaves give a smaller percentage of their wealth "to charity than do the rich who live in more economically mixed

[57]John M. Perkins, ed., *Restoring At-Risk Communities: Doing It Together & Doing It Right* (Grand Rapids, MI: Baker, 1996), 22.

[58]For a story of a church founded in line with Perkins's vision of relocation, see Gornik, *To Live in Peace*. See also the description of Redeemer Community Church in Jonathan Tran, *Asian Americans and the Spirit of Racial Capitalism* (New York: Oxford University Press, 2022), 152-292.

[59]See Claire Miller, Josh Katz, Francessa Paris, and Aatish Bhatia, "Vast New Study Shows a Key to Reducing Poverty: More Friendships Between Rich and Poor," *New York Times*, August 1, 2022, www.nytimes.com/interactive/2022/08/01/upshot/rich-poor-friendships.html.

[60]Cf. Bischoff and Reardon, "Residential Segregation," 209; Mary Hirschfield, *Aquinas and the Market: Toward a Humane Economy* (Cambridge, MA: Harvard University Press, 2018), 185-86.

neighborhoods."[61] Segregated lives lead to hearts segregated from the needs of our neighbors. Unjust structures generate the vice of apathy toward injustice that sustains those structures.[62]

The tithe feast sought to address this problem by forming the individual Israelite's economic desire *toward God and neighbor* through indulgent, joyful celebration together with God and the vulnerable. When Deuteronomy talks about eating one's fill, it's usually talking about the way affluence tempts the people to faithlessness. In Deuteronomy 14:29, however, the goal of the triennial tithe is for the *vulnerable* to "eat their fill." The only safe way to pursue and experience economic abundance, Deuteronomy suggests, is in the context of a community that seeks to ensure *all* eat their fill *together*.

The relocation principle works similarly, drawing diverse members of disenfranchised communities together in generous celebration and joy. In the process, relocators learn that their joy, prosperity, and delight is bound up in the joy, prosperity, and delight of their neighborhood as a whole, and especially the neighborhood's most vulnerable residents.

The practice of relocation and the politics of advocacy. Similar to the way Israel's feasts shaped the community to practice the triennial tithe and debt relief, the morally formative practice of relocation also shapes people to seek structural change. By moving into struggling neighborhoods, relocators discover structural forces at work in housing, private enterprise, real estate, city planning, and more that make economic segregation and exploitation almost inevitable, either through disinvestment or gentrification. On the river of such systems, we naturally drift downstream toward greater separation from one another.

Tran clarifies how this works in relation to both racism and economic exploitation. He argues that the economic conditions created by outright white supremacy (slavery, Jim Crow laws, etc.) outlived our society's explicit commitment to white supremacy. Most of us do not subscribe to those white supremacist commitments anymore, but we live in an economic world strongly shaped by them. As such, we live and work amid what he calls the "aftermarkets" of racism. Such aftermarkets create opportunities for people with no explicit racist commitments to profit off conditions created through explicitly racist policies. In such a world, you can either "seek to redress and repair [the] legacy, or [you] can, wittingly or unwittingly, take advantage of the opportunities it presents."[63]

---

[61]Mijs and Roe, "Coming Apart," 11.
[62]McRorie, "Moral Reasoning," 221.
[63]Tran, *Asian Americans*, 194.

Consider one "aftermarket" from my own experience seeking to live out Perkins's principle of relocation in our South Memphis neighborhood. Both local government and the private sector worked systematically to turn what was a "stable, racially mixed neighborhood" in 1910 into a community both racially segregated and economically poor by 1953.[64] Mayor Crump used federal "slum clearance" dollars to destroy a "stable, middle-class, Black neighborhood" and turn it into a 900-unit public housing complex. Through redlining, the banks then systematically denied FHA-backed mortgages to would-be homeowners in the neighborhood.

But this explicit racist exploitation also created a racist "aftermarket." Because Black people could not qualify for the legitimate home loans white Americans were able to obtain, they had to look elsewhere for loans to buy homes. Predatory lending practices emerged to fill that gap. And they still do. In 2012, Wells Fargo "settled for $432.5 million for targeting Memphis's minority neighborhoods with predatory loans."[65]

But Tran reminds us that we should not simply picture shady, cigar-smoking bankers scheming in back rooms over how to profit off South Memphis's white supremacist "aftermarket." White supremacy drove property values into the tank; according to Zillow, average home values in this neighborhood between 2013 and 2019 ranged from roughly $28,000 to $40,000. With property values so low, building new homes or even investing in repairs on existing homes makes little economic sense. Black households in our community are once again denied any real opportunity to build stability through home ownership.

But you know who *can* build wealth in, and as a result of, this racist "aftermarket"? Investors looking for passive income through low-income rental properties, a practice on the rise nationally and in Memphis specifically.[66] While there are many difficult issues related to affordable housing, and while some investors provide much needed, quality affordable housing, others are exploitative. Investors looking for passive income in economically impoverished communities face endless opportunities and have every incentive to

---

[64]See Preston Lauterbach, "Memphis Burning," *Places Journal*, March 2016, https://placesjournal.org/article/memphis-burning.

[65]Cole Bradley, "Seeing Red I: Mapping 90 Years of Redlining in Memphis," High Ground, March 31, 2019, www.highgroundnews.com/features/SeeingRedlining.aspx.

[66]Melvin Burgess, "Memphis Must Come Together to Address Looming Affordable Housing Crisis," Commercial Appeal, October 28, 2021, www.commercialappeal.com/story/opinion/2021/10/28/memphis-depletion-affordable-housing-has-become-major-issue/8572402002.

delay repairs and upkeep. Why invest in improving a home if those invest-ments will not increase the economic value of the property, especially when you can find plenty of renters willing to pay for substandard living conditions anyway? The logic of the market encourages property owners whose under-lying asset isn't worth very much to get as much as they can from their tenants while spending as little as possible on their property. And if the economy ever shifts dramatically, sending housing prices skyrocketing, the dreaded process of gentrification will simultaneously displace historic neighbors of our com-munity and create enormous wealth for property owners.[67]

Semuels tells grim stories of tenants living in properties owned by institu-tional investors in Georgia. Describing one management company, Semuels writes: "At one point, a mandate came down from a field manager that the [company] was going to do everything it could not to return security deposits to tenants. 'It wasn't a company policy, and you will never find it in writing, but it was a verbal thing passed down to field project managers.'"[68]

Tenants face an uphill battle getting any redress against their landlords, because doing so requires the costly, complicated, time-consuming process of going to court. Even if they do get their day in court, they may find the laws stacked against them. I once helped a neighbor take her landlord to court because she was paying rent in a house that had no heat and only two func-tioning electrical outlets. We lost.

Again, this is not a "them" problem. It's an "us" problem; I've seen slum houses owned by large, shadowy, institutional investors, and I've seen slum houses owned by local, middle-class people, both Black and white. I myself am a landlord in our neighborhood, and can testify to the ample opportunity to prioritize my own economic desires over those of my tenants. Given the extent of Wall Street investment in rental properties, many of us may be profiting off these aftermarkets without knowing it, and all of us who buy homes participate in a housing market bound to this history and its after-market results.

---

[67]The aftermarket opportunities of gentrification in San Francisco play a major role in Tran's account (see Tran, *Asian Americans*, 151-243). On the other hand, some research suggests that poor com-munities are more likely to stay stuck in long-term poverty than they are to gentrify (see John Buntin, "The Myth of Gentrification: It's Extremely Rare and Not as Bad for the Poor as You Think," Slate, January 14, 2015, https://slate.com/news-and-politics/2015/01/the-gentrification-myth-its-rare-and-not-as-bad-for-the-poor-as-people-think.html).

[68]Alana Semuels, "When Wall Street Is Your Landlord," *The Atlantic* (February 14, 2019), available at: https://www.theatlantic.com/technology/archive/2019/02/single-family-landlords-wall-street/582394/

On top of all this, it is genuinely difficult for the private sector to provide good opportunities for home ownership or high-quality rentals when divestment has driven property values so low. The economic conditions of our neighborhood, created through explicit racism, create an economic environment where it is very *difficult* for the market to provide affordable housing and opportunities for our neighbors to build wealth through home ownership, and *much easier* for outsiders to profit off this difficulty.

Relocation amid the aftermarkets. All of this lies under the surface for most of us, but relocators discover these dynamics in the very process of relocating. As with the tithe feast, relocation shapes them to see their flourishing and joy as bound up with neighborhoods characterized by such aftermarkets and neighbors who suffer from them. But it also shapes relocators to imagine what it would look like to embrace God's economy within such aftermarkets.

Relocators have advocated for legislation and created private sector entities that promote mixed-income neighborhoods. They have fought for and created both greater opportunities for home ownership *and* better, more affordable rental housing. Sometimes they have done so through nonprofits. At other times they have created businesses that seek to generate modest revenue while creating affordable, wealth-building opportunities for their neighbors.[69] In either case, just as the tithe feast flowed into the triennial tithe and debt forgiveness systems, the virtue-forming practices associated with the relocation principle have led individuals and communities to seek more just systems that promote more prosperous and less segregated neighborhoods.

In all of this, both the tithe feast and relocation require practitioners to simultaneously subvert *and* collaborate with existing political and economic practices on offer in the broader culture. Israel would have been well aware that feasts were often used to generate social stratification rather than solve it. They could have decided that feasts were far too complicit with injustice to be useful in the pursuit of justice. Instead, they sought to *reform* and *reorient* existing feast practices, leaning into the feasts and subverting their oppressive tendencies at the same time.

Relocation similarly makes it possible for practitioners both to engage *and* subvert the socioeconomic practices of America's real-estate, banking, education, and entrepreneurial systems, among others. All these tools so often

---

[69]For an example of this in housing, including my own meager efforts in this direction, see Michael Rhodes and Robby Holt, *Practicing the King's Economy: Honoring Jesus in How We Work, Earn, Spend, Save, and Give* (Grand Rapids, MI: Baker, 2018), 189-90.

used to perpetuate economically and racially segregated communities can become tools for pursuing the beloved community together.[70]

This is a risk, of course. Justly navigating how to engage and subvert these practices requires wisdom—the subject of a later chapter—especially because relocation sometimes simply replaces economic-segregation-through-disinvestment with economic-segregation-through-gentrification. In our broken world, it also requires a posture of repentance, a willingness to identify when even our best efforts have fallen short.[71] But from the perspective of Deuteronomy and the principle of relocation, this is a risk that justice demands we take.

RELOCATED FEASTING

Perkins's practice of relocation functions analogously to Deuteronomy's tithe feast. But the resonances go even deeper, because, as any relocator knows, when it comes to building solidarity and seeking justice in community, food is nearly always involved. My friend Marlon Foster, a pastor and nonprofit founder who has lived out Perkins's principle of relocation by staying in the South Memphis community he grew up in, learned quickly that food would play a key role in the church he planted. Their congregation hosts a community breakfast before every service, often welcoming the homeless and the very poor. After every celebration of the Lord's Supper, they have a potluck feast where all are welcome.

Not everyone is called to relocation. But in line with Deuteronomy's vision of the feast, everyone can find ways to practice greater proximity with the economically poor and marginalized. We can resist racial and economic segregation in other social spaces, not least by changing where and how we work, play, worship, or educate our children. We can develop rich partnerships with churches and organizations embedded in poor communities. We can look for ways to feast with God's people across the lines that so often separate us.

As in Deuteronomy, so also today: seeking to create just structures and seeking to foster just character are two sides of the same coin. The good news is that the path to such just discipleship is paved with joy. We become just disciples by learning the fear of Yahweh through practices of communal

---

[70]For a similar, albeit broader argument about our economic life, see Luke Bretherton, *Christ and the Common Life: Political Theology and the Case for Democracy* (Grand Rapids, MI: Eerdmans, 2022), 353.

[71]Tran, *Asian Americans*, 289-90.

celebration and solidarity before God and alongside all our neighbors. Communities that pursue such just discipleship find themselves inevitably engaged in the hard work of seeking a just politics, both within the community of faith and beyond. They find themselves feasting on the road to justice.

VIRTUE WRECKED AND REGAINED

As we have seen, Deuteronomy 14:28–15:18 offers a set of laws designed to

1. maintain relatively equitable relationships between households and

2. provide for the members of the community most likely to fall through the cracks within and between households.

Maintaining this system requires the community to cultivate the virtues of generosity and solidarity through feasting.

Yet contemporary readers may still have questions about this. While Israel's ideal village economy aimed at a more equitable society than the monarchies and empires around Israel, much still depends on the good will of the (relatively) prosperous. The implicit reliance on what Houston calls a "benevolent hierarchy" haunts us.[72] Will these virtues and practices provide the community with the character to sustain genuine *solidarity,* rather than simply charitable giving across classes? Will such virtues enable the community to continue improving the economic system at large, or will it tempt them to settle for that system?

With these questions ringing in our ears, I want to return briefly to the story of Job clothing himself with justice and righteousness. I hinted previously that while Job does embody justice, contemporary readers notice that his virtuous action on behalf of those further down the social ladder does not seem to question the existence of a socially stratified community in the first place.

Indeed, in Job 29–31, Job subtly situates himself at the center of the social spheres within which he practices virtue and receives honor.[73] Job moved from tent to village gate, distributing wisdom and material aid, and receiving honor and praise.[74] Job is, from Job's own perspective, the central hub point

---

[72]Houston, *Contending,* 133.

[73]Carol A. Newsom, *The Book of Job: A Contest of Moral Imaginations* (New York: Oxford University Press, 2009), 188.

[74]See Patricia L. Vesely, *Friendship and Virtue Ethics in the Book of Job* (Cambridge, MA: Cambridge University Press, 2019), 204.

for all of those around him;[75] he "thrives on the esteem of his colleagues and glides on the gratitude of the indigent."[76] But, concerningly, besides giving him praise or crying for help, the marginalized remain mostly silent.[77]

In Job 24, Job describes the poor as wild animals expelled into the wasteland. This comparison presents the poor as objects of pity. In Job 30:29, he laments his own relocation to these wasteland margins. He has joined the outcasts, and now dwells in a wilderness with wild creatures as his siblings and companions.[78] Job's desire, of course, is for the "days of old" (Job 29:1), for a "relocation . . . back to the center."[79] Just under the surface of all this is Job's apparent belief in creation as a stable, well-ordered, predictable world, with clear centers and peripheries. Job's understanding of virtue, and not least the virtue of *justice,* works well within such a world.

Job's assumptions about the connection between *virtue, power,* a *stable world,* and the pursuit of *honor* resonate with some of the most problematic aspects of the virtue tradition. Consider Aristotle's description of the virtue of "greatness of soul." For Aristotle, the "great-souled" person claims great honors because they deserve them. Indeed, when the great-souled person receives such honors

> he will feel he is receiving only what belongs to him, or even less, for no honor can be adequate to the merits of perfect virtue, yet all the same he will deign to accept their honors, because they have no greater tribute to offer him.[80]

This "great-souled man" is "justified in despising other people," because he has estimated their worth correctly.[81] While the great-souled person "is fond of conferring benefits," he is "ashamed of receiving them, because the former is a mark of superiority and the latter of inferiority."[82]

Jennings calls this vision of the "self-sufficient man" the "greatest temptation for Christian formation."[83] Indeed, he argues that an allegedly

---

[75]Vesely, *Friendship and Virtue Ethics,* 204.

[76]William P. Brown, *The Ethos of the Cosmos: The Genesis of Moral Imagination in the Bible* (Grand Rapids, MI: Eerdmans, 1999), 335.

[77]Patricia L. Vesely, "Virtue and the 'Good Life' in the Book of Job," *Horizons in Biblical Theology* 41, no. 1 (2019): 12-13.

[78]On which see Brown, *Ethos,* 333-36.

[79]Vesely, "Virtue and the 'Good Life,'" 14.

[80]Aristotle, *Eth. nic.,* trans. H. Rackham, LCL (Cambridge, MA: Harvard University Press, 1926), IV.iii.17.

[81]Aristotle, *Eth. nic.,* IV.iii.22 [Rackham].

[82]Aristotle, *Eth. nic.,* IV.iii.24 [Rackham].

[83]Willie James Jennings, *After Whiteness: An Education in Belonging* (Grand Rapids, MI: Eerdmans, 202), 29.

Christian version of such moral formation became demonically bound to the colonialist project.[84] Moral formation became the attempt to form every human into the image of "white self-sufficient masculinity."[85] Those who master "white self-sufficient masculinity" become *masters*: "first and always teachers,"[86] permanent and perfect instructors, advisers, and evaluators of all who fall short of such mastery. The modern person who has been formed in the image of this "white self-sufficient masculinity"—Jennings is quick to point out that neither skin color nor gender prevent a person from striving to be so formed—has become like Aristotle's great-souled man. They deserve to despise others.

This is a serious critique of the virtue tradition in at least some ancient and modern versions. Does it indict Job?

Job at the center. I do not think we should accuse Job of despising the poor per se.[87] But his moral world certainly places him in the center as a unilateral giver of gifts and the poor on the margins as unilateral recipients of his virtuous action. Those of us who have attempted to practice relocation have often bought into this deeply problematic vision of ourselves as at the center, always giving and never receiving. Contemporary readers concerned about justice are right to raise questions about Job's moral vision on this account.

What may surprise us is that the book of Job itself also raises this very issue. Indeed, while Job 1:1 describes Job as a genuinely virtuous person, the book as a whole recognizes that Job's justice requires further *transformation*.

Into the wild. This transformation takes place in large part through Yahweh's speeches to Job from the whirlwind. These speeches take Job on a round-the-cosmos-tour, from the well-laid foundations of the earth to the deep recesses of the dangerous sea (Job 38:1-17), from the desolate wastelands unfit for habitation but well-watered by God to the constellations of the heavens that cross the sky in their seasons (Job 38:25-33). The effect of this journey is to *de-center* Job and *deconstruct* his vision of the cosmos as a tidy, predictable place where the righteous occupy obvious centers and the less important dwell on clearly defined peripheries.[88] This divine tour draws his

---

[84]Jennings, *Christian Imagination*, 65-118. Jennings specifically refers to Aquinas's deployment of virtue ethics as problematic in Jennings, *After Whiteness*, 30-32, and the title of that book is a (critical) reference to Alasdair MacIntyre's *After Virtue*.

[85]Jennings, *After Whiteness*, 32.

[86]Willie James Jennings, "Overcoming Racial Faith," *Divinity* (Spring 2015): 9.

[87]For discussion, see Vesely, "Virtue and the 'Good Life,'" 14; Houston, *Contending*, 129.

[88]Brown, *Ethos*, 342.

gaze beyond the limits of the carefully cultivated hierarchies he had previously known and which he had previously assumed provided the only context for the formation and practice of virtue.

The creatures that populate the wild wastelands also force Job to reimagine the world he lives in and the way he lives in it. The lion, often associated with royal power and independence in the ancient world, becomes a creature completely dependent on Yahweh for its food (Job 38:39-40).[89] While Job had seen the wild donkey as an empathy-eliciting symbol of the landless poor, Yahweh draws Job's attention to that same wild donkey and implies that it is God who has set this magnificent creature free to find a genuine home in the wastelands, unbound by the "tumult of the city" or the "shouts of the driver" (Job 39:5-8).[90] While Job had nothing but pity for the wild donkey, Yahweh expresses deep admiration for its wild freedom.[91]

Indeed, Vesely suggests these creatures are specifically designed to show Job that the world does not revolve around him. Whereas Job had issued directives and commands in kingly fashion (Job 29:21-25), out in the wilderness he finds eagles who fly at no human's command (Job 39:27), donkeys that pay no attention to human rules (Job 39:5-8), and Behemoth and Leviathan, mythological creatures of cosmic proportions, who "would not yield their place to Job" as the citizens of his previous life had (Job 29:7-10).[92]

Taken together, Job's journey "beyond the margins" of the world he knows takes this patriarchal paragon of the virtues to places that "humans often consider barren, lifeless, and lacking any value."[93] What he finds is that where he expected nothing but waste lies a world of wonder.[94] Job discovers that, as Gutierrez puts it, "gratuitousness is the hinge on which the world turns and the definitive seal set upon it."[95]

---

[89]Brown, *Ethos*, 361.

[90]Brown, *Ethos*, 363.

[91]William P. Brown, "Virtue and Its Limits in the Wisdom Corpus: Character Formation, Disruption, and Transformation," *The Oxford Handbook of Wisdom and the Bible*, ed. Will Kynes (New York: Oxford University Press, 2021), 18.

[92]Vesely, "Virtue and the 'Good Life,'" 18. This is not to say that Job is maligned or put down by God's words. After all, in the epilogue, Yahweh *vindicates* Job's wild words throughout the poetic debates between Job and his friends. It is Job with his raging, rather than the friends with their conventional piety, who has spoken rightly (Job 42:7; see Elaine Phillips, "Speaking Truthfully: Job's Friends and Job," *BBR* 18, no. 1 [2008]: 31-43).

[93]Vesely, "Virtue and the 'Good life,'" 16.

[94]Vesely, "Virtue and the 'Good life,'" 16.

[95]Gustavo Gutierrez, *On Job: God-Talk and the Suffering of the Innocent*, trans. Matthew J. O'Connell (Maryknoll, NY: Orbis, 1988), 88.

We must remember that both in the Bible and in the ancient Near East, to describe creation is, at the same time, to describe *culture*. The ancients assumed that there was a "seamless connection" between the created universe and society.[96] When Yahweh shatters Job's view of creation, then, he is simultaneously challenging Job's implicit moral map of society, with the virtuous helpers at the center; the silent, powerless poor in need of assistance on the margins; and the worthless outcasts in the wastes beyond. During his world tour, Job's virtue gets wrecked on the rough edges of Yahweh's wild world.

There and back again. But the story does not end there. The book of Job makes the ultimate insider an "outsider" who then returns as a "transformed insider."[97] In this journey, God does not so much reject Job's prior just and righteous character as supplement and thus transform it. God *sanctifies* "righteous Job," taking him further up and further into the love and justice in which God delights. As Vesely summarizes so well:

> Having encountered the far-off places and creatures of God's cosmic display, Job is poised to cultivate certain virtues that reflect his new understanding of the world: *humility* and *awe* before other life, in recognition of the value and mystery of each created being; *openness* and *receptivity* to the voices and opinions of those who differ from him, particularly with respect to what constitutes notions of "flourishing;" *respect* and *honor* for those who share his world, regardless of their status or place in the community; and a sense of *solidarity* and *interdependence* with all inhabitants of the cosmos—human and non-human, drawn from the realization that his well-being is intimately linked with their own.[98]

In his re-entry to the community in the epilogue of the book, we encounter the virtue of justice *reborn* in Job's life. While we are quick to notice Yahweh's doubling of all that Job had lost, we often miss that this process begins with Job *receiving* comfort, consolation, and financial support from his brothers, sisters, and "all who had known him before" (Job 42:11). If we are to understand verse 11 as the first sign to Job himself that Yahweh is beginning to restore his fortunes, a restoration which would inevitably take time,[99] then Job's community is an integral part of the solution to the problem of evil in Job's life. Indeed, the community's care becomes one way Yahweh restores Job

[96]Brown, *Ethos*, 2.
[97]William P. Brown, *Sacred Sense: Discovering the Wonder of God's Word and World* (Grand Rapids, MI: Eerdmans, 2015), 77.
[98]Vesely, "Virtue and the 'Good Life,'" 20.
[99]David J. A. Clines, *Job 39–42*, WBC (Grand Rapids, MI: Zondervan, 2011), 1235.

after his suffering.[100] And just as we might expect from our discussion of the tithe feast in Deuteronomy, Job's transformation from giver alone to giver-and-receiver takes place at a meal: "and they ate bread with him in his house" (Job 42:11).

If we take that inauspicious phrase "all who had known him before" seriously, we have to imagine that this meal at which everyone brings support to their friend Job included at least some of the orphans, widows, outsiders, and poor that Job boldly declared he had treated as kin in chapters 29–31. Whereas previously Job had seen these vulnerable people as kin who de-pended on *him,* he now sees that they are also kin that he himself depends on in real ways. This meal on the other side of Job's transformation is not a pa-triarchal soup kitchen of generous provision, but a potluck where everyone brings a contribution to a feast designed to help Job get back on his feet.[101]

Deuteronomy 14:22-27 claims that we learn to fear Yahweh by feasting with God and alongside the entire community. Job, as one of the chief paradigms of Yahweh-fearing in Scripture, reminds us that the feast forms our fear best when it compels each to acknowledge their interdependence with all the others, as well as their final dependence on God. Indeed, Job has begun to learn those dispositions that could never have been acknowledged as virtues by Aristotle, the virtues of "acknowledged dependence."[102] God has provided Job with the necessary education to begin to learn both "uncalculated giving *and* graceful receiving."[103]

Justice reborn? Is there evidence that these lessons transform Job's con-ception and practice of justice? Indeed, there is. In his remarkable book *On Job,* Gutierrez argues that Job's experience of suffering allows him to discover the suffering of the world's poor in a new way, and to join them in solidarity and struggle.[104] In support of this, I suggest that the epilogue of the story shows us Job's just character renewed and reborn in at least two ways that now *transcend* the sociopolitical context of his world. These examples show that Job has grown deeper into the virtue of justice, learning to exercise power faithfully in new and countercultural ways.

---

[100]Brown, *Wisdom's Wonder,* 130. Contra Nathan MacDonald, *Not Bread Alone: The Uses of Food in the Old Testament* (New York: Oxford University Press, 2008), 186.

[101]Robby Holt and I use this metaphor extensively in *Practicing the King's Economy.*

[102]See Alasdair MacIntyre, *Dependent Rational Animals: Why Human Beings Need the Virtues* (Peru, IL: Open Court, 2001), 119.

[103]MacIntyre, *Dependent Rational Animals,* 121.

[104]Gutierrez, *On Job,* 31-48.

First, Job gives his daughters an inheritance alongside their brothers.[105] This is an "unprecedented move within Israel's legal traditions and unusual in the ancient Near East."[106] Thus while Job in the epilogue is in some sense once again a patriarch, he now exercises his power in ways that are deeply unpatriarchal.[107]

Second, Job 42:12 presents an exact doubling of Job's wealth in every respect but one: slaves are conspicuously absent. Thomas rightly argues this absence demonstrates that Job "has apprehended something about social hierarchy and inherent injustice"; "in a world wherein all belongs to God—even Leviathan—no [person] may belong to another."[108]

Job's character has been transformed. Within the ordered, hierarchical world Job imagined prior to his encounter with Yahweh, his justice and righteousness led him to one of the strongest statements of the human equality between slave and master in the ancient world (Job 31:15).[109] But it did not lead him to use his power to address the *structure* of slavery itself. The justice at work in Job's life after the speeches, on the other hand, goes further, ridding his household of the institution of slavery altogether.

No doubt Job continued to navigate a world in which social hierarchies and uneven distributions of power played a role. No doubt he interacted with people on various rungs of the social ladder as he experienced a restoration to wealth. The epilogue suggests, however, that the virtue of justice cannot rest content, but instead creatively seeks solidarity with the socially oppressed *and* the transformation of those structures that facilitate their oppression. At the same time, those who fear Yahweh learn not only to lead lives of just action, but also to cultivate the virtues of acknowledged dependence on both God and the most unlikely human others.

Like Jacob limping into a new day with a new name after his wrestling match with God, Job does not come away from his encounter with Yahweh unscathed. This is the model we need for virtuous character formation today: not the self-confident, overreaching, independent justice embodied by Aristotle's magnificent man, nor the confident, controlling mastery of Jennings's "white self-sufficient masculinity," but the humbled, awed,

[105]Brown, *Ethos*, 379.
[106]Brown, *Wisdom's Wonder*, 130.
[107]Brown, "Virtue and Its Limits," 19; Vesely, "Virtue and the 'Good life,'" 21.
[108]Philip Thomas, "A Theological Interpretation of Inexplicable Chaos in the Book of Job, Read Alongside the Novels of Cormac McCarthy" (PhD diss., Trinity College Bristol, 2019), 21.
[109]Houston, *Contending*, 130.

communal justice embodied in Deuteronomy's feasts and Job's post-trauma table fellowship.

A humbled, awed, communal justice is certainly the kind of justice needed for the joining that Jennings describes and that Perkins promotes through relocation. Otherwise, Christians working for justice by choosing to take up residence in places others are abandoning too often fall into the trap of imagining that "we are first and always teachers rather than being first and always learners."[110] Perhaps that's why, as activist Ed Loring put it, "justice is important, but supper is essential." Because until we learn to feast for fear of the Lord, to eat in ways that cultivate the kind of character that knows how to give and receive in community, we will fail to join with God in bringing justice to victory.

---

[110] Jennings, "Overcoming Racial Faith," 9.

SINGING OUR WAY
TOWARD JUSTICE

IN 2018, AN UNUSUAL BIBLE made national news.[1] Published in 1807, the so-called Slave Bible offered Caribbean slaves a highly edited publication of the King James Version. While the origins of the Slave Bible aren't entirely clear, it appears to have been edited to exclude texts that undermined slavery.

Many of the editors' decisions are unsurprising. They cut out the story of Yahweh's liberation of Israelite slaves in Exodus, and they drop Paul's declaration that in Christ "there is neither Jew nor Greek, neither slave nor free." What might strike us as less obvious, though, is their decision to cut out the Psalms in their entirety.[2]

Why would pro-slavery Christians find the Psalms dangerous? The snippets that tend to be well-known and well-loved aren't exactly threatening, at least on the surface. They draw our minds toward well-tended sheep and well-worn metaphors about God being an "ever present help." Comforting? Yes. Revolutionary? Not obviously.[3]

Against this knee-jerk intuition, I suggest the editors of the Slave Bible had at least two good reasons to be afraid of the Psalter. First, a careful reader quickly discovers that the Psalms are obsessed with Yahweh's *liberating justice for the oppressed*. Second, because the book of Psalms provides us with songs and prayers, it carries a unique power to form us for justice.

[1]See Michel Martin, "Slave Bible from the 1800s Omitted Key Passages That Could Incite Rebellion," *NPR*, December 9, 2018, www.npr.org/2018/12/09/674995075/slave-bible-from-the-1800s-omitted -key-passages-that-could-incite-rebellion.
[2]The Slave Bible can be seen at https://researchdata.gla.ac.uk/955.
[3]See Walter Brueggemann, *From Whom No Secrets Are Hid: Introducing the Psalms* (Louisville, KY: Westminster John Knox, 2014), 8.

THE UNIQUE CONTRIBUTION OF THE PSALMS

To understand the unique contribution Psalms makes to just discipleship, we need to consider the nature of the Psalms themselves. What exactly *are* these texts, and how do they work? Some scholars emphasize the way the Psalms give us a glimpse of what humans prayed and sang to God in the past. They allow us to "listen in" to prayers of praise and the suffering groans that the saints poured out to the Lord. Others argue the book should be understood primarily as God's address to his people.[4] While the individual psalms comprise what were undoubtedly originally human words to God, the Psalter as a whole has been intentionally shaped to allow these human words to God to *become* God's Word to humans.[5]

The true power of the Psalter can only be seen when we hold these two perspectives together. Because all Scripture has both a divine and a human author, God's Word always includes human words. What's unique about the Psalms, though, is that these God-given human words offer us scripts to help us engage with the Lord in prayer and song.[6] They offer us words *from* God that we *can only receive* by speaking and singing them *back* to God. Indeed, in the Psalms, we discover that God has learned to speak our human language in order to offer us language lessons in our "mother tongue." These language lessons are designed to help us gain fluency in the language we need for life with him.[7]

Much of Scripture tells the story of Yahweh's covenantal relationship with us. In the Psalms, it's as if the Lord sits down with us and says, *Now in this relationship of ours, you will need to learn how to relate to me. So I've given you a book to help you learn the language necessary for this relationship. In a world like this, with people like you, and a God like me, this is the sort of language you'll need to live with me as a child in my family and a citizen in my kingdom.*

These psalmic scripts play a unique role in moving us beyond knowing what justice requires to *becoming* the just people of God.[8] They offer God's

---

[4]See Gerald H. Wilson, *Psalms*, vol. 1, NIVAC (Grand Rapids, MI: Zondervan, 2014), 100; J. Clinton McCann Jr., "Hearing the Psalter," in *Hearing the Old Testament: Listening for God's Address*, ed. Craig G. Bartholomew and David J. H. Beldman (Grand Rapids, MI: Eerdmans, 2012), 280.

[5]Nancy L. deClaissee-Walford, "The Theology of the Imprecatory Psalms," in *Soundings in the Theology of the Psalms: Perspectives and Methods in Contemporary Scholarship*, ed. Rolf A. Jacobsen (Minneapolis: Fortress, 2011), 80.

[6]See Kit Barker, *Imprecation as Divine Discourse: Speech-Act Theory, Dual Authorship, and Theological Interpretation*, JTI Supp 16 (Winona Lake, IN: Eisenbrauns, 2016), 175.

[7]I owe the idea of Scripture as "like a language" to Brent A. Strawn, *The Old Testament Is Dying: A Diagnosis and Recommended Treatment* (Grand Rapids, MI: Baker Academic, 2017).

[8]See Harry Nasuti, "The Sacramental Function of the Psalms in Contemporary Scholarship and Liturgical Practice," in *Psalms and Practice: Worship, Virtue, and Authority*, ed. Stephen B. Reid (Collegeville, MN: Liturgical Press, 2001), 35.

people a critical tool for pursuing moral discipleship oriented toward the kind of just character that faithfully exercises power in community. Let's consider three aspects of the Psalms' unique contribution.

1. The Psalms Give Us Scripts to Praise the Just King and Celebrate His Just Rule

The oldest title for the book of Psalms is simply *Praises*. When we ask what these texts invite us to praise God *for*, however, Yahweh's just rule stands at the top of the list: "[The LORD] loves righteousness and justice; the earth is full of the steadfast love of the LORD (Ps 33:5).

Because the Psalms celebrate justice as fundamental to who Yahweh is, they also give him praise for the way that justice stands at the center of what Yahweh does in the world. Amid the five-psalm "crescendo of praise" that concludes the book as a whole, Psalm 146 praises Yahweh as the Creator

> who executes justice for the oppressed;
>   who gives food to the hungry.
> The LORD sets the prisoners free;
>   The LORD opens the eyes of the blind.
> The LORD lifts up those who are bowed down;
>   the LORD loves the righteous.
> The LORD watches over the strangers;
>   he upholds the orphan and the widow,
>   but the way of the wicked he brings to ruin. (Ps 146:7-9)

This psalm's celebration of Yahweh's just character and action is connected to the declaration that Yahweh is *King* (Ps 146:10), the "theological heart" of the Psalter.[9] But of course, a declaration of kingship could well be bad news; Israel knew all about tyrants. What makes Yahweh's kingship *good news,* a proclamation of the gospel, is that this divine king makes the justice and righteousness the world longs for "the fundamental platform of his royal policy."[10] Again and again, the Psalms offer prayers and songs to God as the Just King whose justice wins him exuberant praise.

2. The Psalms Give Us Scripts to Protest to, Rage at, and Plead with God over Injustice

While we might not identify justice as one of the primary grounds for worshiping God, when it comes to learning the language of faith, we are quite

---

[9]See McCann, "Hearing the Psalter," 281.
[10]McCann, "Hearing the Psalter," 286.

comfortable with the idiom of praise. Yet Scripture's psalmic language lessons regularly speak in another idiom with which many of us are deeply uncomfortable: the language of protest, lament, and angry plea to Yahweh. Astoundingly, when God gives his people scripts to train their tongues to talk to him, he gives them scripts that require them to shout at him. And when we ask *what* it is that these scripts require us to shout at God about, *injustice* stands at the top of the list.[11]

Thus while we pray confidently that Yahweh is "a stronghold in times of trouble" in Psalm 9:9, Psalm 10:1 requires us to shout,

> Why, Yahweh, do you stand far off,
> Why do you hide in *times of trouble*? (AT)

The psalmist backs up this angry accusation with evidence:

> The wicked arrogantly chase the oppressed;
> the oppressed are trapped by the schemes the wicked have dreamed up.
> (Ps 10:2 NET)

In his rage at oppression, the psalmist not only accuses God of hiding, but also decries the injustice of the wicked. They are driven by greedy desires for gain (Ps 10:3); speak from mouths filled with cursing, deceit, oppression, mischief, and iniquity; and lurk in the dark so that they can drag the poor away and devour them (Ps 10:8-10). While it's possible to interpret poverty language in some psalms as strictly spiritual, and much psalmic poverty language certainly includes spiritual dynamics,[12] Psalm 10 clearly decries experiences of concrete socioeconomic oppression.[13] While this language no doubt includes literal violence, the references to greed and crimes of the tongue suggest that the psalmist also rages at the more subtle, but equally deathly ways the powerful pursue their own desires at the expense of their neighbors in fields, marketplaces, and courtrooms.[14]

Part of what drives the intensity of the psalmist's protest is the fact that the behavior of the wicked suggests that "there is no God" (Ps 10:4), and that, at the moment, the oppressors appear to be right!

---

[11]See McCann, "Hearing the Psalter," 289.

[12]See Enrique Nardoni, *Rise Up, O Judge: A Study of Justice in the Biblical World*, trans. Sean Charles Martin (Grand Rapids, MI: Baker Academic, 2001), 129.

[13]Brueggemann, *No Secrets*, 218-20; Richard Bauckham, *The Bible in Politics: How to Read the Bible Politically* (Louisville, KY: Westminster John Knox, 2011), 53.

[14]See John Goldingay, *Psalms*, vol I: *1-41*, Baker Exegetical Commentary on the Old Testament Wisdom and Psalms (Grand Rapids, MI: Baker Academic, 2006), 1, 169; and more generally, Trevor Laurence, "Cursing with God: The Imprecatory Psalms and the Ethics of Christian Prayer" (PhD diss., University of Exeter, 2020), 200-225.

Their ways prosper all the time!
Your just judgments are high—far away from him!
All of *his* enemies? He scoffs at them! (Ps 10:5-6 AT)

Everything is upside down! the psalmist shouts. *Instead of being struck down, the wicked prosper. Instead of you bringing your just judgments to earth, God, your justice is nothing but 'pie in the sky when you die'! You promised to stand against the wicked, Lord! But the wicked scoff at all their enemies.*

This is a serious accusation. Because the Psalms praise Yahweh as the Just King, both the psalmist *and* the wicked understandably believe that *if* just judgment is not forthcoming, *then* God may be absent.[15] The wicked use this perceived absence as an opportunity to go after unjust gain.[16] The psalmist responds to Yahweh's perceived absence by shouting until Yahweh shows back up.

Far from being a sign of a lack of faith, such protest to God is an act of deep and abiding faithfulness.[17] In Psalm 10 we encounter the cry of the oppressed[18] as they enter into a genuine relationship with a just God in an unjust world.[19] When we remember that these protest psalms are given to us by God, we discover that this sort of relationship is not only what God wants, but also that he has given us these angry psalms as scripts to help us learn how to engage in such a relationship.

This is absolutely staggering. I have tried to cultivate a relationship with my loved ones where we can openly confront and challenge one another. What I have *not* done, however, is draw up an outline of grievances I think they might have about me and given it to them, saying, "Listen, I know our relationship isn't always easy. If you feel that something's off, here are some accusations you could shout at me to get you started." Yet this is precisely what the Lord has done in the Psalms.[20]

Such passionate protest to God over injustice is everywhere in the Psalter. While the protest of Psalm 10 focuses on the bad behavior of the enemies, Psalm 44 protests *God's* actions!

---

[15]Bauckham, *Politics*, 57.

[16]Brueggemann, *No Secrets*, 19.

[17]See Brent A. Strawn, "Poetic Attachment: Psychology, Psycholinguistics, and the Psalms" in *The Oxford Handbook of the Psalms*, ed. William P. Brown (New York: Oxford University Press, 2014), 412-13.

[18]See Bauckham, *Politics*, 53; Brueggemann, *No Secrets*, 19.

[19]Strawn, "Poetic Attachment," 416.

[20]See Nasuti, "God at Work," 42.

You have made us like sheep for slaughter,
    and have scattered us among the nations.
You have sold your people for a trifle,
    demanding no high price for them. (Ps 44:11-12[12-13])

While acknowledging Yahweh's right to bring judgment on the people should
they sin, the psalmist protests that in their current situation the people are
innocent (Ps 44:17-18[18-19]). This leads the psalmist to one of the most
striking calls for help in all of Scripture:

Rouse yourself! Why do you sleep, O Lord?
    Awake, do not cast us off forever!
Why do you hide your face?
    Why do you forget our affliction and oppression?
For we sink down to the dust;
    our bodies cling to the ground.
Rise up, come to our help.
    Redeem us for the sake of your steadfast love. (Psalm 44:23-26[22-25])

The suggestion that the God who "neither slumbers nor sleeps" (Ps 121:3[4])
is in fact asleep at the wheel and must be shaken awake is shocking. Apparently,
God knows that in a world like ours and with a God like him, people like us
will occasionally need to rage not only at the injustice we encounter in the
world, but also at the perceived injustice we encounter in God. While the
Psalms and Scripture as a whole deny that any such injustice truly exists in
God, praying and singing the psalms of protest requires us to press God on
this very point.

But surely not those psalms! Contemporary pray-ers find the psalmist's protests to Yahweh over injustice startling.[21] We are downright alarmed by the
psalmists' frequent calls to God to execute forceful judgment on the
perpetrators of injustice. Psalm 58 calls on Yahweh to melt his enemies like
snails into slime (Ps 58:8[9]). If we sing Psalm 139's beautiful celebration of
Yahweh's wonderful work in forming us in our mother's wombs to the end, we
find ourselves *also* singing a request to God that he would kill the wicked

---

[21]In reckoning with the psalms of imprecation, I have been particularly helped by Brent Strawn,
"Poetic Attachment"; Strawn, "Imprecation," in *Dictionary of the Old Testament: Wisdom, Poetry,
and Writings*, ed. Tremper Longman III and Peter Enns (Downers Grove, IL: IVP Academic, 2018),
315-19; Ellen F. Davis, *Getting Involved with God: Rediscovering the Old Testament* (Lanham, MD:
Cowley Publications, 2001); Laurence, "Cursing with God"; and, most of all, Erich Zenger, *A God
of Vengeance? Understanding the Psalms of Divine Wrath* (Louisville, KY: Westminster John Knox,
1994), 37.

(Ps 139:19). And in undoubtedly one of the most troubling texts in all of Scripture, Psalm 137 declares,

> O daughter Babylon, you devastator!
>   Happy shall they be who pay you back
>   what you have done to us!
> Happy shall they be who take your little ones
>   and dash them against the rock! (137:8-9)

How in the world could singing *that* shape us for anything but evil?

We need to make two preliminary points. First, these psalms of imprecation are *not* the words of people caught up in normal, everyday conflicts.[22] They are *not* the words of citizens in communities where functioning systems reliably deliver at least a minimal standard of justice. They are not the bloodthirsty words of a powerful people looking for God to justify them in battle.

Instead, they are the anguished cries of those who are suffering extreme violence, who have done "nothing to warrant the lethal threat" their enemies pose to them,[23] and whose powerless position in society means they are utterly out of options.[24] Before we judge Psalm 137's desire that somebody would cut off the Babylonians' descendants, we have to take seriously the fact that it is sung by people who have *watched* their own children get brutally murdered by the Babylonian superpower (see Ps 137:1-8).[25] They sing their desires for a brutal military victory against their enemies *not as a people who could possibly get such a victory against their enemies themselves*, but as those who have just suffered a brutal defeat at their enemies' hands.

Second, "the one thing that binds the imprecatory psalms together is the call for justice."[26] In Psalm 94, the psalmist prays amid a world of rulers who "fashion injustice by legal statute" (Ps 94:20 AT). The "decisions and deliberations" of lawgivers and courts have "become mere instruments of the wicked who control the levers of power."[27] In this context, the psalmist calls Yahweh

---

[22]deClaisse-Walford, "Theology," 86.
[23]Laurence, "Cursing," 227-28. The psalmists claim "relative innocence" rather than total innocence.
[24]See Strawn, "Imprecation," 315-16.
[25]Barker, *Imprecation*, 170.
[26]David Firth, "Cries of the Oppressed: Prayer and Violence in the Psalms" in *Wrestling with the Violence of God in the Old Testament*, BBR Supp 10, ed. M. Daniel Carroll, R. and J. Blair Wilgus (Winona Lake, IN: Eisenbrauns, 2015), 81.
[27]Nahum Sarna, *On the Book of Psalms: Exploring the Prayers of Ancient Israel* (New York: Schocken Books, 2013), 82.

to "shine forth" as the "God of Retribution"[28] because he is the only one able to end their oppression and pay back the oppressor for their violence (Ps 94:1-2).

Nor does the psalmist desire the irrational, bloodthirsty revenge we associate with the language of "vengeance,"[29] as the NRSV translates Psalm 94:1. What the psalmist demands is just retribution. The psalmist appeals to the God of Retribution (Ps 94:1) because he is the "judge of the earth" who gives to the wicked what they have genuinely earned (Ps 94:2).[30]

This dynamic characterizes the psalms of imprecation more generally.[31] Because what the psalmists demand is justice, the imprecatory psalms tend to limit their requests to God to what would be considered just within the Torah's legal traditions.[32] And while the principle that the punishment should fit the crime sets the *limits* for the kind of intervention the psalmist demands, their larger concern is simply that Yahweh's delivering justice bring an end to violence "by any just means necessary."[33]

Such just deliverance will often include force, but this does not mean the psalmist always cries for the *elimination* of their enemies. They regularly ask Yahweh simply to *disarm* them. The psalmists pray "in metaphorical language for broken teeth, excised fangs, blunted arrows (Ps 58:6-7), shattered arms (Ps 10:15), and divided tongues (Ps 55:9), petitioning God to thwart the instruments of the enemy's aggression, to render the tools of violence ineffective."[34]

Indeed, Zenger argues that Psalm 137:9's blessing on those who would dash Babylon's little ones against the rocks does not reflect a desire to see every Babylonian child murdered. It is instead a "political psalm" that longs to see the end of the "royal house, that is, of the dynasty" that has decimated God's people.[35] It is a way of expressing the desire that God would do whatever it takes to stop the violence being perpetuated by the Babylonian superpower. The issue is not infanticide, but regime change, although expressed in a deeply disturbing way.

Moreover, the psalmist makes clear that Yahweh's forceful, just intervention against the wicked might be for their own good! In the midst of rhetoric that

---

[28]Strawn, "Imprecation," 317.

[29]See Zenger, *God of Vengeance?*, 38, 71.

[30]See Van Gemeren, *Psalms*, 711; Sarna, *Psalms*, 192.

[31]See, for example, Ps 7:6-11; 35:23-24.

[32]David Firth, *Surrendering Retribution in the Psalms: Responses to Violence in Individual Complaints* (Eugene, OR: Wipf & Stock, 2005), 142.

[33]Laurence, "Cursing," 363.

[34]Laurence, "Cursing," 230.

[35]Zenger, *God of Vengeance?*, 50.

would otherwise seem to require Yahweh's utter destruction of the enemy as the only just outcome, Psalm 83 suddenly and surprisingly declares,

> Fill their faces with shame,
>> *so that* they may seek your name, O LORD! (Ps 83:16[17])

Indeed, I suggest that these imprecatory psalm scripts intend to transform those who sing and pray them, shaping them for just discipleship in the world. We can see this transformative potential in four ways.

Learning to bring anger at injustice into our relationship with God. First, the imprecatory psalms offer us scripts to "bring our own anger into the context of our relationship with God."[36] This may be one of the most precious gifts Yahweh offers those who have experienced serious injustice. As Zenger writes, these psalms "are serious about the fundamental biblical conviction that in prayer we may say everything, literally everything, if only we say it to GOD, who is our father and mother."[37] Indeed, the psalms do not merely express this conviction. They offer those who suffer scripts to *practice* expressing their anger. Such language lessons do not force us to suppress our rage at our enemies; instead, they shape us to offer that rage to the LORD.

Contemporary insights from psychology demonstrate just how important this is. Strawn draws on empirical studies to show that suppressing trauma leads to psychological suffering and even physical ailments.[38] Conversely, "empirical studies have demonstrated that disclosure plays a key role in recovery" from trauma, creating "direct and positive effects" on mental health and even the immune system of the victim.[39] It is precisely such healing disclosure that the psalmic process makes possible.

Learning to surrender our rage to God. Second, these psalmic scripts also subtly compel us to leave our rage at our enemies, and indeed our enemies themselves, in the Lord's hands.[40] This explains why the psalms of imprecation do not suggest that the psalmists go out and get retribution on their enemies. They teach us to voice our desire for retribution, and then surrender that retribution to God.[41]

---

[36]Davis, *Getting Involved*, 24-25.

[37]Zenger, *Vengeance?*, 79.

[38]Brent A. Strawn, "Trauma, Psalmic Disclosure, and Authentic Happiness," in *Bible Through the Lens of Trauma*, ed. Elizabeth Boase and Christopher G. Frechette (Atlanta: SBL Press, 2017), 145.

[39]Strawn, "Trauma," 143, 145.

[40]See Nardoni, *Rise Up*, 127.

[41]See Patrick Miller, *The Way of the Lord: Essays in Old Testament Theology* (Grand Rapids, MI: Eerdmans, 2007), 201; but Firth rightly notes that the Psalms do approve of the *king's* use of force in executing justice (Firth, "Cries of the Oppressed," 76).

This means that sometimes the psalmist may make requests of Yahweh that are, in fact, inappropriate.[42] We may pray that Yahweh melt our enemies like snails, but he may regularly refuse to do so.[43] Praying the imprecatory psalms shapes us for justice by forcing us to confront our rage—and to surrender it.

Imprecatory prayer as an act of love. Third, and much to our surprise, these imprecatory psalms also shape us for love. First and foremost, they foster love for God and God's kingdom. The psalmists demand just judgment *for the sake of God's own name.*[44] At the same time, they give us scripts to love our oppressed neighbor by calling on God to deliver them "by any just means necessary."[45] Because injustice is bad for everyone, and because God's just judgment is intended to lead oppressors to repentance (see Is 19:22), praying the imprecatory psalms can even be an act of enemy love.

Singing these songs might even be an act of self-love, confronting *us* with the horrifying question: "Is there anyone in the community of God's people who might want to say this to God *about me—or maybe, about us?*"[46] In such situations, these scripts summon us either to repent or willingly invoke Yahweh's forceful judgment to fall on our own heads! Praying the psalms of imprecation on behalf of our oppressed neighbors and in a world of oppression can thus be one way God transforms us for the task of seeking justice with them and on their behalf.[47]

Imprecatory psalms pave the way back to praise. Fourth, these psalms transform us by paving the way back to praise.[48] After angrily demanding to know why Yahweh is hiding amid the world's injustice, Psalm 10 returns to the language of trustful praise:

> The LORD is king forever and ever;
>   the nations shall perish from his land. (Ps 10:16)

---

[42]Contra Laurence and Barker, who seem to suggest that this would undermine the authority of the Psalms (see Laurence, "Cursing," 149-51; Barker, *Imprecatory*, 175). Psalm 73 demonstrates that, at least sometimes, the psalms give us scripts for expressing theological claims that are in fact false. God knows we need this sort of speech and gives us scripts to express it. Job offers a narrative model of this dynamic, in which Yahweh affirms Job's way of speaking, even as he clearly rejects some of the content of Job's speeches.

[43]See Strawn, "Poetic Attachment," 415.

[44]For example, Ps 109:21; 143:11. See Laurence, "Cursing," 240.

[45]Gordon Wenham, *Psalms as Torah: Reading Biblical Song Ethically* (Grand Rapids, MI: Baker, 2012), 178; Laurence, "Cursing," 363.

[46]Davis, *Getting Involved*, 28, emphasis added.

[47]Zenger, *God of Vengeance?*, 76, 85.

[48]Typically, although not quite universally (for example, Ps 88).

The people's journey to praising Yahweh's justice runs *through*, rather than *around*, the people's angry protest to God about the times when his apparent absence throws his justice into question. Identifying such scripts as coauthored by God reveals that the Lord knows people like us, in a world like ours, and with a God like him, need to practice such protest, not least so that we might find our way back to praise.

3. *The Psalms Give Us Scripts to Commit Ourselves to Do Justice*

Finally, however, the Psalms give us scripts to commit ourselves to justice—the faithful exercise of power in community. When we sing and pray these scripts, we practice the language of commitment.[49] This happens in part through psalms that celebrate the *just* life as the *good life*. When we sing Psalm 106:3, we declare,

> Happy is the one who keeps justice
> who enacts righteousness at all times! (AT)

Such a song serves as a kind of self-talk that stirs our hearts in the direction of justice.

Other psalms give us scripts to plead with God to *help* us practice justice and righteousness (see Ps 139:23-24). Others, somewhat alarmingly, call on God to *test* us or even *judge us* based on our adherence to Yahweh's righteousness and justice (see Ps 7:8[9]). God gives us these scripts in much the same way that a contemporary judge says to the defendant: "Repeat after me. I swear by Almighty God that the evidence I shall give will be the truth, the whole truth, and nothing but the truth." The consequences for repeating such words are serious.[50]

WHAT HAPPENS WHEN WE SING JUSTICE SONGS *TOGETHER*?

Praying and singing the Psalms fosters the virtue of justice in us. As we praise the Just King; protest to, rage at, and plead with God over injustice; and commit ourselves to do justice, we become people who exercise power more faithfully in community. The power of the Psalms to do this transforming work is only increased, however, by the fact that these scripts are intended to be prayed and sung by *communities* gathered in public worship. The Psalms offer us language lessons not only as an isolated *I*, but also as a gathered *we*.

---

[49]See Wenham, *Psalms*, 117-19.
[50]See Wenham, *Psalms*, 64; Ps 26:2, 9-11; 119:121.

Considering who is included in this *we* is illuminating. Injustice haunted ancient Israel at every stage of her history. When Amos and Isaiah rage at the oppressors in Israel, they often accuse them of combining their oppression with participation in Israel's religious life.[51] The psalmist calls out to God about the experience of betrayal at the hands of those with whom they had previously worshiped God.[52] When the people of God gathered to sing the Psalms, at least some of the time, the innocent sufferers, the oppressors causing the suffering, and everybody standing in between would all be, quite literally, *singing from the same hymnal*! How does this dynamic impact our understanding of the Psalms' transformative power?

Praising the Just King together. First, scripts that praise God for his saving justice invite the oppressed to declare with their lips the gospel news that the Lord saves his people, not least by saving them from the forces of oppression that so often dominate in our world. For those who are not themselves suffering, praising God for his justice amounts to a celebration of his work on behalf of others in the community. This might serve to draw the attention of the one praising God to the importance of those often pushed to the margins. On the other hand, when we praise God for forcefully confronting the oppressor, we effectively invite God's own forceful judgment on us if we participate in oppression![53]

Protesting to, raging at, and pleading with God together. The oppressed among the people of faith represent the *I* or the *we* that merges most naturally with the *I* or the *we* of psalms that protest to, rage at, and plead with God over injustice. Praying such psalms amid oppression is empowering, giving voice to the legitimate feelings of rage and pain provoked by the intensity of human injustice. Such scripts declare good news to the poor, not least because they vindicate the desire of the poor that Yahweh forcefully interrupt injustice "by any just means necessary."

Indeed, these scripts suggest that Yahweh himself knows that human injustice is such an affront to his claim to rule the world that people suffering unjustly must be allowed—no, more, *equipped*—to rage at him in their suffering. As Ellen Davis declares, these scripts offer those pray-ers who need them most

> First Amendment [rights] for the faithful. They guarantee us complete freedom
> of speech before God, and then (something no secular constitution would ever

---

[51]See, for example, Is 1:10-15; Amos 5.
[52]See Ps 55:12-14[13-15].
[53]Wenham, *Psalms*, 57.

do) they give [the oppressed] a detailed model of how to exercise that freedom, even up to its dangerous limits, to the very brink of rebellion.[54]

At the same time, because the imprecatory psalms surrender retribution to God, they give those who have the greatest right to unrelenting hate a way to process their anger and surrender their desires for judgment to the Lord. This, too, is good news for the oppressed. As Martin Luther King Jr. declared:

> I have seen too much hate. I've seen too much hate on the faces of sheriffs in the South. I've seen hate on the faces of too many Klansmen and too many White Citizens' Councilors in the South to want to hate, myself, because every time I see it, I know that it does something to their faces and their personalities, and I say to myself that hate is too great a burden to bear. I have decided to love.[55]

Strange as it seems at first, the psalms of imprecation offer a transformative path for the oppressed out of the crippling cycle of endless desire for vengeance. By bringing the understandably violent desires of one's heart to speech before God, flinging those desires in his face, and leaving them there for him to deal with, victims among God's people take up speech that clears the way to healing as well as praise.

When oppressors come to worship, open their hymnal, and find themselves urging God to "break the arms" of those who put their own prosperity before the well-being of the community, however, these scripts strike a different chord! Such scripts force the oppressor to celebrate their own imminent judgment at Yahweh's just hand should they choose not to repent and turn from their violent ways. For a king failing to deliver the oppressed (Ps 72; 82), a judge taking bribes in court, or a farmer exploiting their neighbor through lending at interest (Ps 15:5), such songs would prove menacing indeed.

Moreover, by forcing oppressors to not only *hear* but *recite* the anguished cries of pain emerging from their victims, these psalms may also intend to foster empathy for the oppressed among the oppressors. Those who commit injustice often do so "at arm's length," protecting themselves from having to look at the real human costs of their actions. Long before the arrival of documentaries designed to shake us up from our apathy over injustice, God forced his people to hear the cries of the suffering by singing the Psalms. Indeed, God

---

[54]Davis, *Getting Involved*, 8-9.

[55]Martin Luther King Jr., "Where Do We Go from Here?," (sermon, Southern Christian Leadership Conference, Atlanta, Georgia, August 16, 1967). A portion of the sermon is available at www.beaconbroadside.com/broadside/2017/08/martin-luther-king-jrs-where-do-we-go-from-here-sermon-50-years-later.html.

forced his people to hear the cries of the suffering coming out of their own mouths!

By requiring oppressors among the people to recite the sentence of judgment hanging over their behavior and thus their lives—a sentence that the oppressed are singing with gusto on the other end of the pew!—these psalms implicitly offer the oppressor a way out. The sing-song equivalent of a "scared straight program," they carry an implicit, urgent summons to repentance before it is too late (Ps 2:11-12). A pray-er who has participated in injustice either allows these scripts to draw them to repentance, or discovers themselves sing-signing their own sentence of judgment.

What of those who stand somewhere in between, as most readers of this book likely see themselves standing? These protest psalms force us to take sides. They offer enormous incentives to side with the oppressed who appear to be losing rather than the powerful who appear to be winning. They give us scripts for "mourning with those who mourn," for "carrying one another's burdens," for loving our suffering neighbor as ourselves.[56] As we adopt the posture of the *I* who suffers injustice in the Psalms, we embrace a form of solidarity with those who suffer and on whose behalf we pray.[57] Through these scripts, God says to those of us who are not suffering, *Your brothers and sisters are dying out there. Use these words to join them in shouting to me about their suffering.*[58]

***Committing ourselves to do justice* together.** Third, by giving us scripts to commit ourselves to the faithful exercise of whatever power we have in community, the Psalms seek to shape the oppressed, the oppressor, and everyone between for the work of justice. Psalm 37:16 gives those who suffer a prayerful pep-talk, encouraging them to cling to the "better" life of righteousness instead of turning toward a life devoted to "abundance" characterized by wickedness. Oppressors who sing "Happy are the ones who keep justice" (Ps 106:3 AT) hear themselves celebrating a good life that they're missing out on. Meanwhile, all those who stand in between, wondering like the psalmist of Psalm 73 whether the wealthy and wicked might not have the right idea after all, discover in these psalmic texts scripted opportunities to recommit themselves to the justice Yahweh desires.

---

[56]See Harry Nasuti, "The Sacramental Function of the Psalms in Contemporary Scholarship and Liturgical Practice," in *Psalms and Practice: Worship, Virtue, and Authority*, ed. Stephen B. Reid (Collegeville, MN: Liturgical Press, 2001), 83; Strawn, "Trauma," 153-58.

[57]See Wenham, *Psalms*, 60.

[58]See also Davis, *Getting Involved*, 20.

Nowhere is the so-called preferential option for the poor more clearly on display than in the Psalms. To be invited into a community that celebrates Yahweh as the Just King who stands against evil, to be given scripts for prayer that rage at Yahweh over his delay in dealing with oppression, to be invited to sing songs that commit the singer to living out Yahweh's own justice is to be forced, by the public prayers and songs of the community, to choose to side with the poor . . . or to stop singing. Such choosing involves a serious commitment to do justice by pursuing the "faithful exercise of power" wherever one has influence. If "justice is what love looks like in public,"[59] then the Psalms offer the sort of "praise [that] makes loving others possible."[60]

No wonder the editors of the Slave Bible were afraid of the Psalter! In the American South, we know too well the stories of Black worshipers forced into back rows and balconies, catechized to believe God was on the side of the master, and preached a message of subservient obedience. But imagine such an intentionally segregated church being given a hymnal for Black and white worshipers to sing together. Imagine the impact of cracking open that hymnal and discovering hymns calling on God to grind to dust the regime that had taken a people far from their native land for its own oppressive purposes, hymns celebrating God for being a Just King who "executes justice for the oppressed" and "sets the prisoners free" (Ps 146:7). Imagine white slaveholders singing, and hearing their Black slaves sing behind them, "O, that you would kill the wicked!" (Ps 139:19). And imagine Black slaves singing, in the presence of their oppressors, those same words! While the prophets make clear that worship can *fail* to shape us for justice, there can be no doubt that the Psalms intend to give the people scripts that, if taken seriously and sung genuinely, are nothing short of revolutionary.

BUT CAN WE SING JUSTICE SONGS WITH JESUS?

Some may wonder, though, whether such prayers and songs are appropriate for those who pray and sing in the wake of Jesus' life, death, and resurrection. Many believe that Jesus downplays justice in order to emphasize mercy and grace. Even those who want to emphasize justice in the New Testament may be uncomfortable with the psalms of imprecation. How can somebody follow Jesus' command to love their enemies while praying for God to melt them like snails?

---

[59]Cornel West, *Brother West: Living and Loving Out Loud* (New York: Smiley Books, 2010), 23.
[60]Brian Brock, *Singing the Ethos of God: On the Place of Christian Ethics in Scripture* (Grand Rapids, MI: Eerdmans, 2007), 232.

When we look to the New Testament, however, we discover that it quotes the Psalms more than it quotes any other Old Testament book. Indeed, the New Testament's teaching on and examples of prayer demonstrate that the early church spoke fluent "psalmese." Let's look at just two of the many examples that could be considered.

Praying for justice with the widow. Many of us know and love Jesus' parable juxtaposing the prideful, boasting Pharisee and his prayer with the tax collector's humble pleas for mercy (Lk 18:9-14). We often neglect the parable that comes just before this one, in which Jesus teaches his disciples that they "need to pray always and not to lose heart" (Lk 18:1-8). This parable clearly calls Jesus' followers to follow in the footsteps of the Psalms by pleading with God to do justice on their behalf.

In the parable, an "unjust judge" is confronted by a vulnerable widow's plea: "Grant me justice [*ekdikeō*] against my opponent" (Lk 18:3). The verb *ekdikeō* ought to be understood as an appeal for *forceful* intervention. A form of the word is used in the Septuagint to translate the title "God of Retribution" in Psalm 94:1.[61] The widow thus pleads for the judge to rise up and enact justice in court *on her behalf* and *against her adversary.*[62]

Jesus uses this parable to make an argument about how God will respond to his people's prayers. If even wicked judges will eventually do justice in the face of exhausting, constant pleas from the oppressed, then "will not God grant justice to his chosen ones *who cry to him day and night?* Will he delay long in helping them? I tell you, he will quickly grant justice to them" (Lk 18:7-8).

Jesus explicitly calls on his disciples to plead with God for just retribution "day and night" rather than to "lose heart." In the context of the teaching as a whole, "Jesus' final question" about whether the Son of Man will find faith when he comes communicates that "prayers for God's justice against believers' enemies are evidence of the faith the Son of Man desires. . . . Jesus desires his disciples' desires for divine justice."[63] It is hard to imagine our Lord offering a stronger endorsement of the Psalms' justice prayers.

Justice prayers among the departed. Perhaps the greatest example of psalm-like praying in the New Testament occurs in Revelation 6:9-11. In the passage, John sees "the souls of those who had been slaughtered for the word

---

[61]Psalm 93:1 in the LXX. LEH translates *ekdikeō* as "avenge" or "punish" (180).
[62]See Laurence, "Cursing," 343-45.
[63]Laurence, "Cursing," 345.

of God and for the testimony they had given" under the altar in the heavenly throne room. These martyrs are in the presence of the living God, freed from earthly pain, and awaiting the resurrection. Yet they are also praying a shocking prayer: "Sovereign Lord, holy and true, how long will it be before you judge and enact retribution [*ekdikeō*] for our blood on the inhabitants of the earth?" (Rev 6:10 AT).[64]

The heavenly response is not to tell them that they need to learn how to pray New Testament prayers rather than those nasty Old Testaments ones. The heavenly response is to tell them to wait just a bit longer for God to answer their prayers. The only other use of *ekdikeō* in Revelation occurs in chapter 19, when the saints offer psalm-like hallelujahs to God for exercising just judgment on "Babylon" by bringing retribution for the blood of those who had been killed by her politically and economically oppressive regime (Rev 19:2; see Rev 18:1–19:3).

But what about enemy love and surrendering vengeance? Both Jesus and the early church adopted the language of the Psalter's justice songs.[65] But how *does* this fit with the New Testament's teaching that we love and pray for our enemies? How does it fit with the New Testament's persistent claim that Christians should eschew violence and entrust the work of avenging blood to God?

First, we need to recognize that the command to love your neighbor as yourself comes from Leviticus 19:18, a passage that directly prohibits taking vengeance on one's neighbor. Old Testament law requires, and the book of Proverbs recommends, actively and sacrificially promoting the welfare of an enemy who hates you.[66] The ethic of enemy love is present in the Old Testament, and it coexists quite comfortably with the psalmist's plea that God do justice *against* their enemies when necessary.

Likewise, Jesus can teach us both to love our enemies and to pray like oppressed widows that God would grant justice *against* our adversaries.[67] Because while both the Psalms and the New Testament call the people of God to surrender retribution, they do so on the basis that God himself will one day enact just judgment. We do not leave retribution in God's hands because retribution is a bad thing, but because retribution is *God's* thing. As Miroslav

---

[64]The phrase "how long" is frequent in the Psalms.

[65]See Strawn, "Imprecation," 317.

[66]See Ex 23:4-5; Prov 20:22; 25:21.

[67]For an extensive argument concerning the relationship between imprecation and enemy love, see Barker, *Imprecation*, 137-56.

Volf puts it, "It takes the quiet of a suburban home" to believe that "human nonviolence corresponds to God's refusal to judge,"[68] that we reject forceful retribution because God himself forever does. In the face of horrific violence, the faithful surrender human retribution precisely because God can be trusted to enact it. "Retribution is mine," says the Lord.

Does this mean that there is nothing genuinely new in the Christ event? Absolutely not! In the Old Testament we hear God calling his people to love their neighbors, including those who hate them. In Jesus we see the overwhelming, unexpected, unimaginable depths to which God himself will go in loving *his* enemies—including us.

> Christ also suffered once for sins,
> *the just for the unjust,*
> to bring you to God,
> by being put to death in the flesh
> but by being made alive in the Spirit. (1 Pet 3:18 NET)

In Jesus, we see God's commitment to bring justice for the oppressed paired with his deep longing to bring all to repentance. Jesus' proclamation of judgment against those who refuse to turn from their wicked ways makes clear that the oppressed can count on Jesus to end their suffering. But his offer of forgiveness at the very brink of death reminds us that the door yet remains open for the violent to turn from their wicked ways, to "kiss the Son" and live (Ps 2:12). Indeed, the logic of the Psalms and Scripture as a whole suggests that one way the oppressor is turned to repentance is by the threat and even the experience of just judgment.[69]

Christians also stand at a different place in the story of Scripture than the psalmists do.[70] While Christians can and should pray for God to interrupt violence immediately, life in the church awaiting God's eschatological judgment places a "priority" on praying for God to do so by bringing our enemies to repentance and conversion.[71] On the other hand, the New Testament's emphasis on our supernatural enemies—Sin, Death, and the Devil—invites us to pray psalms of imprecation against supernatural evil in our battle against the "powers and principalities,"[72] even while keeping in

---

[68]Miroslav Volf, *Exclusion and Embrace* (Nashville: Abingdon Press, 1996), 303-4.
[69]Laurence, "Cursing," 248-50.
[70]Zenger, *Vengeance?*, 68; Laurence, "Cursing," 24, 281.
[71]Laurence, "Cursing," 26.
[72]Cf. Strawn, "Imprecation," 318.

sight the way such supernatural evil is often connected to the concrete human and social dynamics of our lives.

Most importantly, believers not only *see Jesus* praying for justice and loving his enemies, but we are also *united to Jesus* by the power of the Holy Spirit! We therefore pray the Psalms' justice songs *with Jesus*. When we pray for justice with Jesus, we're allowed to use the psalmic scripts to rage at God to bring an end to injustice by any just means necessary. But when we pray for justice with Jesus, we always plead that the means necessary would include bringing all, including ourselves and our most dangerous enemies, to repentance and restoration.

SINGING JUSTICE SONGS WITH JESUS TODAY

Singing and praying the Psalms stands as one of Scripture's central strategies for shaping the people of God for the work of justice. Yet just as the editors of the Slave Bible cut out the Psalms, there is ample evidence that contemporary Western congregations often cut justice out of our singing and praying.

This is particularly true in the case of psalms that give us scripts to protest to, rage at, and plead with God over injustice.[73] As Soong-Chan Rah points out,

> Lament constitutes 40 percent of all psalms, but only 13 percent of the hymnal for the Churches of Christ, 19 percent of the Presbyterian hymnal and 13 percent of the Baptist hymnal. Christian Copyright Licensing International (CCLI) licenses local churches in the use of contemporary worship songs and tracks the songs that are most frequently sung in local churches. CCLI's list of the top one hundred worship songs in August of 2012 reveals that only five of the songs would qualify as a lament.[74]

Nor is the problem restricted to what we sing. Strawn demonstrates that more than a third of the psalms have been omitted from the Revised Common Lectionary, which provides biblical texts for weekly readings across the world.[75] Equally problematic, forty-three of the ninety-nine psalms that *are* included have been excerpted.[76] And what gets cut out most often? Scripts that lament, protest, and plead with God for forceful intervention on the psalmist's behalf.[77]

---

[73]See also Zenger, *God of Vengeance?*, 13-23.
[74]Soong-Chan Rah, *Prophetic Lament: A Call for Justice in Troubled Times* (Downers Grove, IL: InterVarsity Press, 2015), 22.
[75]Strawn, *Old Testament Is Dying*, 49-51.
[76]Strawn, *Old Testament Is Dying*, 51-52.
[77]Strawn, *Old Testament Is Dying*, 52.

In September 2021, I compared the CCLI's Top 25 worship songs to the Psalms.[78] Their lyrics suggest that many contemporary congregations fail to follow in the footsteps of the psalmists in singing for justice. For example,

1. There is only one mention of justice in the Top 25. *Mishpat*—just one of the Hebrew words for justice—shows up sixty-five times in thirty-three different psalms.

2. There are zero references to "the poor" or "poverty" in the Top 25. The Psalms use varied language to describe the poor on nearly every page.

3. The widow and oppressed are regularly featured in the Psalms, but are completely absent from the Top 25.

4. "Enemies" are the third most common character in the Psalms, but they show up rarely in the Top 25. When they do, they appear to be enemies only in a spiritual sense.

5. Most devastatingly, in the Top 25, *not a single question is ever posed to God*. The Top 25 never ask God anything. Prick the Psalter and it bleeds the cries of the oppressed pleading with God to act. But such language is completely lacking in the Top 25.

Indeed, there is very little evidence that the Top 25 are ever speaking clearly about situations of social and economic harm. "Are you hurting and broken *within*?"[79] sums up the way these songs tend to reject the holistic nature of the Psalms—which speak to both spiritual *and* social suffering—in favor of scripts that celebrate spiritual or emotional transformation exclusively.

I love many of these songs, but if we rely on them to teach us how to talk to God, we will fail to praise God for his justice as he invites us to; fail to protest to, rage at, and plead with God over injustice as he instructs us to; and fail to commit ourselves to justice in worship the way he requires us to. Worship that doesn't sing like Scripture fails to relate to God the way God himself teaches us to relate to him, and cuts us off from a significant avenue of transforming power in our discipleship. Such worship, moreover, denies

---

[78]The list included "Way Maker," Build My Life," "Graves into Gardens," "Goodness of God," "Living Hope," "Great Are You Lord," "What a Beautiful Name," "Who You Say I Am," "Raise a Hallelujah," "This Is Amazing Grace," "King of Kings," "10,000 Reasons," "Great Things," "Glorious Day," "Lord, I Need You," "In Christ Alone," "The Lion and the Lamb," "How Great Is Our God," "The Blessing," "Cornerstone," "See a Victory," "Reckless Love," "King of My Heart," "O Come to the Altar," and "Amazing Grace (My Chains Are Gone)."

[79]Elevation Worship, "O Come to the Altar," by Mack Brock, Wade Joye, Chris Brown, and Steven Furtick, on *Here as in Heaven* (Provident Music, 2016), emphasis added.

the poor among us the "First Amendment rights" the Psalms offer them. Meanwhile, by refusing to sing like the Psalms do, those of us who are not poor and oppressed refuse to learn how to mourn and protest alongside them. We complain that the poor and oppressed sound too angry, *rather than discovering the angry rage in the face of injustice on nearly every page of Holy Scripture's hymnbook.* Just discipleship stands or falls, in part, on the way we worship. So how do we begin singing our way to justice today?

Pray the Psalms. Perhaps the easiest first step is simply for Christians to use the Psalms as scripts for their own daily prayer. When we read the Psalms continuously, we find ourselves forced to learn to pray justice prayers. Indeed, we often find ourselves praying scripts that do not seem to fit our situation. This gives us an incredible opportunity to ask, *Who needs this prayer today?* We can take up Scripture's justice prayers on behalf of others, mourning with our oppressed brothers and sisters in their mourning, and protesting the injustice they experience to God on their behalf.

Sing the Psalms. Another obvious step would be for churches and individual Christians to reclaim the entire Psalter as a script for singing in corporate worship. This would obviously require, in part, identifying arrangements of the Psalms that the congregation can sing. Chanting them is one option, of course, but so is looking for hymns or contemporary arrangements that celebrate God's justice, lament injustice, or commit the singer to the work of justice. Because of the tendency to play up the spiritual and cut out the psalmic emphasis on justice, it's important to evaluate whether specific arrangements reflect fully the psalmic scripts that undergird them.

Sing (and write!) psalm-like worship songs. Another possibility is to use the Psalms' justice talk as an "audit" for the non-Psalm hymns and songs we sing. After all, some singers of the Psalms are inspired to write new songs. That's good news! The question is whether the worship canon we create adequately reflects the worship canon Scripture offers us in the Psalter. Asking questions about whether the songs we sing and the songs we write give us words to praise God's justice, protest the world's injustice, and commit ourselves to just service is essential.

Justice singing and social location. This isn't just a message for song writers, though. The Top 25 CCLI songs, for instance, isn't a list of what gets written. It's a list of what large segments of the Christian church *like to sing.* We've gotten the songs we wanted, in other words, and they sound nothing like the Psalms, at least when it comes to singing for justice. Maybe that's because many American churches have placed the affluent American experience at the center of the choir, whereas in the Psalms, the poor often sing the loudest.

The middle class *we* that dominates so many of our churches doesn't like justice songs because they don't "speak to us." We middle-class folk love songs that focus on spiritual, emotional, and psychological healing—essential but far from exclusive concerns in the Psalms—*because those are our felt needs*. It is this very dynamic that makes the Psalms such an essential guide to a life of prayer and song that is not reduced to and distorted by the concerns of "people like us."

This means that our success in recovering psalm-like prayer and song will depend, in part, on addressing the questions about social location explored in our discussion of the feast in the previous chapter. Who is at the table, and who is at either end of the pew, may well determine the extent to which God's people can join with the psalmists in praying our way toward justice.

Teach the Psalms. Finally, pastors, teachers, parents, theological educators, and anybody involved in discipleship must *teach* the Psalms. Given that Christians often explicitly deny that we *should* talk to God the way the Psalms *teach us* to talk to God—"You can't question God!"—recovering the Psalter represents an enormous educational task. Moreover, because we're out of the habit of singing for justice, because middle-class congregations are ill-equipped to understand the psalmists' rage at injustice, and because the angry psalms can be dangerous if misused, we also need extensive teaching and preaching on the Psalms, and imprecatory psalms in particular.

SINGING OUR WAY TOWARD JUSTICE

For many of us, this would amount to a revolution in the way we sing and pray, a revolution driven neither by smoke machines nor by the theological flavor of the week, but by the scripts God has given us to use in our life with him. The ideas for action above represent an enormous amount of work. But if we embrace that work, we might just find ourselves singing our way toward the justice that our God loves and our world longs for.

This became real for me when Russia launched its unprovoked, vicious war on Ukraine while I was writing this chapter. I visited Ukraine twice as a teenager, and as a result, have ended up receiving a Ukrainian pastor's regular email updates. His depictions of the horror and violence happening in Ukraine were disturbing in the extreme. One morning, just before I was set to teach Sunday School at our church, I received a request from the pastor to pray for Ukraine, including a specific request to pray for Russian President Vladimir Putin's death.

So that morning in Sunday School we read the psalms of imprecation. We talked about how the Psalms invite us to plead with God to end injustice by any just means necessary. We specifically highlighted psalms that include requests for God to defang the wicked, to disarm them and remove their ability to destroy. And then we prayed.

A few days later, I received another email from that Ukrainian pastor. This is what it said:

> Friends!
>
> Yesterday I asked God for some sign of His support. I got it. I can't keep quiet about it.
>
> Last night a rocket flew into the house of my friend Pastor _____ in _____ *and did not explode*. The rocket broke through the roof and on the second floor broke up into three parts. The explosive unit fell on the first floor where [the pastor] was with deacons and brothers from the church. There were six of them.
>
> The power of this missile was so great that half of the street would be destroyed by the explosion. . . .
>
> Our great Lord saved the lives not only of the six brothers, but also of the inhabitants of many houses on the street. I praise my Lord, who has revealed His glory.

As these Ukrainian pastors helped me see, just disciples today still worship a God who "breaks the bow and shatters the spear" (Ps 46:9[10]). When we believe that, and when we take seriously the horrendous injustice of our world, we'll take up the book of Psalms and sing its justice songs at the top of our lungs.

JUSTICE WITHOUT WISDOM IS POWERLESS, WISDOM WITHOUT JUSTICE IS PREDATORY

IN DISCUSSING POVERTY IN THE UNITED STATES, scholars and citizens alike often emphasize the plight of the working poor. It's easy to see why: In 2018, there were 7 million adults who spent at least 27 weeks that year in the labor force, yet still fell below the poverty line.[1] 3.3 million of these were usually working full-time. In 2019, 44 percent of all American workers qualified as "low wage."[2] Nearly a third of these workers lived in families earning less than 150 percent of the poverty line, or roughly $30,000 "for a family of three."[3]

Advocacy by Fight for $15, the Poor People's Campaign, and others, has brought this reality to the center of national attention.[4] These activists deploy the moral language of justice to demand that workers get paid a wage that allows them to "support their families" and reflects the dignity of their employment.[5] Such a policy would give a pay raise to somewhere between 10 and 32 million Americans.

Many who oppose these efforts, however, argue that dramatic increases in the minimum wage could potentially result in serious, unintended

---

[1] US Bureau of Labor Statistics, "A Profile of the Working Poor, 2018," July 2020, www.bls.gov/opub /reports/working-poor/2018/home.htm.

[2] Martha Ross and Nicole Bateman, "Low Wage Work Is More Pervasive Than You Think, and There Aren't Enough 'Good Jobs' to Go Around," Brookings Institute, November 21, 2019, www.brook ings.edu/blog/the-avenue/2019/11/21/low-wage-work-is-more-pervasive-than-you-think-and -there-arent-enough-good-jobs-to-go-around.

[3] Ross and Bateman, "Low Wage Work."

[4] See these organizations online at fightfor15.org and poorpeoplescampaign.org.

[5] Language taken from fightfor15.org.

consequences.[6] These include potential job losses and price increases that could prove particularly damaging for low-wage workers.[7] Such responses do not argue that "we should be unconcerned about the working poor"; they argue that "out of concern for the working poor we should be cautious about adopting policies that might well result in fewer of them having jobs."[8] These arguments often respond to the moral language of *justice* by drawing on the moral language of *wisdom*.[9]

This debate brings to the surface a question that's often hiding in the background of our debates about socioeconomic ethics: What is the relationship between justice and wisdom? While this is an oversimplification, debates about economic ethics sometimes feel as if they are taking place between two camps—let's call them the "justice camp" and the "wisdom camp"—whose different moral rhetoric makes collaboration and compromise difficult, if not impossible.[10]

On the one hand, sometimes the "justice camp" speaks as if what justice requires is simply to identify what a just economy might look like, while giving less attention to the question of how, in the complicated, broken world we live in, we might make reasonable progress toward those just goals. On the other hand, the "wisdom camp" sometimes responds to any demands for a more just economy by pointing to "the way the world works," claiming that allegedly utopian efforts will create vast, unintended negative consequences.

This division between wisdom and justice would have befuddled our theological predecessors, especially those interested in the kind of character ethics I have argued is vital for understanding just discipleship. Theologians interested in the virtues often identify a unique connection between justice and wisdom, such that we might almost see these virtues as two sides of the same coin.[11] Indeed, you might summarize one key claim about their relationship

---

[6]Concerns about this dynamic increase the more dramatic the proposed increases and the more rapidly they are implemented.

[7]See William E. Even and David A. Macpherson, "California Dreamin' of Higher Wages: Evaluating the Golden State's 30-Year Minimum Wage Experiment," Employment Policy Institute, December 2017, https://epionline.org/app/uploads/2017/12/EPI_CaliforniaDreamin_final.pdf.

[8]Mary Hirschfield, *Aquinas and the Market: Toward a Humane Economy* (Cambridge, MA: Harvard University Press, 2018), 15.

[9]On the fact that underlying commitments can affect the *way* economists interpret the data, see Hirschfield, *Aquinas and the Market*, 16.

[10]These "two camps" are not to be confused with either of the primary political parties in the United States.

[11]See Alasdair MacIntyre, *Whose Justice? Which Rationality?* (Notre Dame, IN: University of Notre Dame Press, 2003), 197.

like this: justice without wisdom is *powerless*, while wisdom without justice is *predatory*.

The Deuteronomic feast and the Psalms' justice songs offer us practices to help us become people who do justice by faithfully exercising power in community. But the Bible's *moral teaching* also aims at just discipleship. To see this, we will explore what the book of Proverbs has to say about the virtues of justice and wisdom before considering how this character-ethics oriented reading of Proverbs might inspire just disciples to respond to the plight of the working poor today.

WHAT DOES PROVERBS HAVE TO DO WITH *JUSTICE*?!

Proverbs may seem a strange place to go looking for guidance on justice. Indeed, Proverbs has developed something of a reputation for being hostile to the cause of economic justice.[12] When I first started working in South Memphis, the staff read a chapter of Proverbs at the beginning of the workday. Sayings about how hard work led to prosperity and laziness led to poverty sounded all too similar to the kind of "pull yourself up by your bootstraps" "wisdom" so often wielded *against* my neighbors. Hearing those sayings in an overwhelmingly Black neighborhood, in a city whose wealth was built largely off the economic exploitation of Black people, infuriated me. Honestly, Proverbs was probably the *last* place I'd go looking for guidance on justice for the oppressed.

Returning to Proverbs after a long season of wrestling with virtue ethics, however, I'm convinced we need to give Proverbs a second chance. When we do, the first thing we discover is that Proverbs itself signals that justice stands at the center of its concerns, not least in the very structure of the book. Indeed, while Proverbs tells us that the fear of Yahweh is the beginning and end of wisdom, the structure of the book places *justice* at the beginning and end of Proverbs.

Proverbs' prologue provides a thematic introduction to the book (Prov 1:1-7).[13] This prologue piles up diverse descriptors of the wise life that the book offers its audience. Standing at the center of the prologue's aspirations, we encounter the triad: "righteousness, justice [*mishpat*], and equity"

---

[12]See J. David Pleins, *The Social Visions of the Hebrew Bible: A Theological Introduction* (Louisville, KY: Westminster John Knox, 2001), 456-73.

[13]William Brown, *Wisdom's Wonder: Character, Creation, and Crisis in the Bible's Wisdom Literature* (Grand Rapids, MI: Eerdmans, 2014), 30; See also Timothy J. Sandoval, *The Discourse of Wealth and Poverty in the Book of Proverbs*, Biblical Interpretation 77 (Leiden: Brill, 2006), 46-61.

(Prov 1:3). Structurally at least, justice stands at the center of the comprehensive character Yahweh requires, which the book refers to as the "fear of the LORD."

Recognizing the close connection between wisdom, justice, and "the fear of the LORD" is vital. As we saw in chapter 3, "the fear of the LORD" refers to a whole-life orientation toward God, an orientation that includes the comprehensive character that God requires and that *flows out of a life lived with him.* Proverbs recognizes that virtues like justice and wisdom come from God and equip us for life with God in God's world.

Justice also brings the book to a close. Both the oracle of King Lemuel's mother and the song in praise of the "valiant woman" prioritize justice. The structure of the book suggests that the kind of skillful, successful, wise living for which Proverbs is famous aims at—indeed, is for the purpose of—understanding and enacting justice. Wisdom and justice go together. What Yahweh has joined together, let no person separate!

JUSTICE AS A VIRTUE IN PROVERBS

I have argued that character ethics can help us understand and embrace the just discipleship demanded by Scripture, not least by drawing our attention to the role of the virtues in the Christian life. Character ethics understands these virtues as habitual dispositions to know, desire, delight in, and successfully pursue the specific goods related to those virtues. From this perspective, Proverbs is helpful not only because it emphasizes justice, but also because Proverbs talks about justice in ways that resonate deeply with this understanding of the virtues. Broadly speaking, Proverbs sees justice as a virtue, a habitual disposition to know, desire, delight in, and successfully pursue that which is *just.*

We can see this in the way Proverbs constantly labels characters in terms of their moral attributes (the "wise" and the "fool"; the "righteous" and the "wicked"). This suggests that Proverbs sees human character as including habitual dispositions toward certain actions, thoughts, and feelings.[14] And in Proverbs, justice is central to the habits of action, thought, and feeling that God wants his people to embrace.

---

[14]See similarly Arthur Keefer, *The Book of Proverbs and Virtue Ethics: Integrating the Biblical and Philosophical Traditions* (New York: Cambridge University Press, 2020), 217; Christopher B. Ansberry, "What Does Jerusalem Have to Do with Athens? The Moral Vision of the Book of Proverbs and Aristotle's *Nicomachean Ethics*," *Hebrew Studies* 51 (2010): 173.

On the one hand, Proverbs refers to "the righteous" (*tsaddiq*) constantly. There is substantial overlap between the language of "righteousness" (*tsedeq*) and "justice" (*mishpat*) in the Old Testament as a whole and in Proverbs specifically, beginning with its prologue, and including those passages where translators render *tsdk*-language as "justice."[15] Indeed, Proverbs identifies justice as an essential piece of the "righteous" character type.[16] The "thoughts" or "plans" of the righteous simply *are* "justice" (*mishpat*; Prov 12:5). The righteous person *knows* the "rights [*din*] of the poor" (Prov 29:7).[17] Indeed, "doing justice" is a *joy* to the righteous (Prov 21:15).

Proverbs also teaches us about the virtue of justice by describing the wicked or vicious dispositions of those who *lack* it. While the "plans of the righteous are justice," the "advice of the wicked is treacherous" (Prov 12:5 AT). Doing justice may be a delight to the righteous, but it is a "terror to evildoers" (Prov 21:15 ESV). "Evil people" simply do not *understand* justice. But Yahweh-seekers not only understand justice, they also understand everything else as well (Prov 28:5).

Reading Proverbs in dialogue with character ethics helps us see that becoming just requires us to gain a virtuous disposition to understand, desire, delight in, and successfully work toward that which is just. But this raises the question that has driven this entire book: How do we become just in the first place?

BECOMING JUST IN PROVERBS

If there's anything obvious about Proverbs, it's this: the book believes in teaching. On every page, in nearly every verse, the book offers us educational instruction as to how to gain the character the book celebrates. It's unsurprising, then, that Proverbs sees *teaching* as one essential way we gain the virtue of justice in our lives.[18]

What may be less obvious is the extent to which Proverbs' pedagogy offers teaching that seeks to transform our *desires*, not least by attempting to

---

[15]Such passages include Lady Wisdom's depiction of wise kings decreeing what is "just" (NRSV, ESV) and those who govern "justly" (ESV) in Prov 8:15-16.

[16]This makes sense, given that wisdom and righteousness can both be understood as "meta-virtues" that contain all the others. Sun Myung Lyu, *Righteousness in the Book of Proverbs* (Tubingen: Mohr Siebeck, 2012), 53; Sandoval, *Discourse of Wealth*, 47.

[17]See Lyu, *Righteousness*, 49.

[18]While Proverbs also celebrates the role of both moral formation through practice and divine enablement in just discipleship, in this chapter, I focus strictly on Proverbs' emphasis on teaching.

cultivate in us a desire for justice.[19] From Proverbs' perspective, doing justice is a joy to the righteous because they have *learned* to delight in doing justice, and to loathe and fear doing injustice.

Learning to loathe and fear injustice. Indeed, the father's very first lecture focuses on teaching the proverbial son to loathe and fear economic injustice (Prov 1:8-19). He begins by warning the son to resist the enticing invitation to join a group of criminals in seeking treasure by ambushing the innocent (Prov 1:10-13). In the course of the lecture, the father imitates these sinners' enticing speech, revealing both the moral horror of their actions and the power of their appeal.[20]

> Come with us, let us lie in wait for blood;
>> let us wantonly ambush the innocent; . . .
> We shall find all kinds of costly things;
>> we shall fill our houses with booty. (Prov 1:11, 13)

Their seductive speech aims at the son's deep desires for prosperity and community. Just as the father will later seek to prepare the son for sexual fidelity by exposing him to the seductive speech of the adulterous woman, here he exposes him to the genuine allure of fast money, costly treasure, and a certain sort of camaraderie.[21]

But while the father's pedagogy acknowledges the appeal of their invitation, it also seeks to foster a deep fear of accepting their invitation through the vivid depiction of this criminal gang lying in wait to kill *themselves,* setting an ambush *for their own lives* (Prov 1:17-18). If the son submits himself to the father's emotional education, he will not only recognize the alluring enticements of these sinners, but he will also have acquired a visceral fear of embracing them. In other words, the purpose of the father's teaching is not only that the son understands the danger, but that he *feels* it.[22]

The father's skill as a moral teacher is obvious, and this first lecture is only one example of a broader pattern. Proverbs' pedagogy regularly draws "mind, body, emotion, [and] desire" into "imaginative modes of moral reasoning."[23]

---

[19]On the formation of desire generally, see Christine R. Yoder, "The Shaping of Erotic Desire in Proverbs 1-9," in *Saving Desire: The Seduction of Christian Theology,* ed. F. LeRon Shults and Jan-Olav Henrickssen (Grand Rapids, MI: Eerdmans, 2011), 149-63.

[20]Michael V. Fox, *Proverbs 1-9: A New Translation with Introduction and Commentary,* AB (New Haven, CT: Yale University Press, 2010), 350.

[21]Fox, *Proverbs 1-9,* 349.

[22]Fox, *Proverbs 1-9,* 349; Yoder, "Shaping of Erotic Desire," 151.

[23]Anne Stewart, "Wisdom's Imagination: Moral Reasoning and the Book of Proverbs," *JSOT* 40, no. 3 (2016): 352.

One way it does this is by offering to the student's imagination vivid depictions of "alternative situations, characters, and action." These then allow the student to imaginatively *experience* the process and consequences of certain high stakes choices.[24] In Proverbs 1:8-19, the father offers the son a chance to gain wisdom through imaginative teaching that is *experience-like*, in order to be *spared* the pain of gaining that wisdom through actual—and potentially deadly!—experience.

Yet there is something much more subversive at work in this father's teaching. On the surface, his lecture condemns economic injustice of the most violent and obvious kind. The father warns the son about criminals roving the street and looking for blood. This doesn't seem to be the most obvious temptation for the young men in the courtly context many scholars identify as the likely setting for this portion of the book![25]

In fact, the father's concluding summary reveals that this first lecture works more like a parable. And like so many of Jesus' parables, this one lays a trap for its audience. The criminal in the back alley isn't the only one who sets an ambush for his own life. No, "thus are the ways of *all* who are *greedy for unjust gain*; [it] takes the life of its owner" (Prov 1:19 AT).

The first lecture's message that unjust gain kills the one who claims it is not, after all, restricted to the obvious, over-the-top violence of gangs. It also applies to other forms of "unjust gain" (*batsa*), and not least those kinds of economic injustice accessible only to the socially powerful.[26] Proverbs speaks of unjust gain on two other occasions:

> A troubler of their house is the one who is greedy for unjust gain,
>   but the one who hates gifts will live. (Prov 15:27 AT)
> Like a roaring lion or a charging bear
>   is a wicked ruler over a poor people.
> A ruler who lacks understanding is a cruel oppressor,
>   but one who hates unjust gain will enjoy a long life. (Prov 28:15-16)

---

[24]See Ryan O'Dowd, "Pain and Danger: Unpleasant Sayings and the Structure of Proverbs," *CBQ* 80, no. 4 (2019): 624; Stuart Weeks, *Instruction and Imagery in Proverbs 1-9* (Oxford: Oxford University Press, 2009), 372; Wongi Park, "Sensing Ethnic Difference: A Kinesthetic Reading of Proverbs 7.1-27," *JSOT* 44, no. 1 (2019): 57-61.

[25]See Christopher B. Ansberry, *Be Wise, My Son, and Make My Heart Glad: An Exploration of the Courtly Nature of the Book of Proverbs* (Boston: De Gruyter, 2011), 44; Michael V. Fox, *Proverbs 10-31: A New Translation with Introduction and Commentary*, AB (New Haven, CT: Yale University Press, 2009), 500-505; Pleins, *Social Visions*, 456; Bruce Waltke, *The Book of Proverbs: Chapters 1-15*, NICOT (Grand Rapids, MI: Eerdmans, 2008), 58. But see also Waltke, *Proverbs*, 63.

[26]See Sandoval, *Wealth and Poverty*, 75.

In the first lecture I ever delivered on Proverbs, I connected Proverbs 1:8-19 to the way that gangs recruited young men in our communities. I was working with a group of ministers for whom gang violence was a real issue and was excited about how relevant the text appeared to be to our context. But one of my students, Andre Manning, quickly pointed out that the "white collar" gangs of corrupt banks, businesses, real-estate agents, politicians, and others might also find themselves in the crosshairs of this text. At the time, I agreed with his sentiment, but thought Proverbs was pointing in a different direction.

Years later, I realized this veteran, urban youth worker had grasped the heart of the passage. If the implied audience of Proverbs 1:8-19 is indeed a relatively well-off son, or, for that matter, anyone likely to be rightly horrified by the wanton injustice of the muggers, then the last line of the lecture springs the parabolic trap. It may be much more socially acceptable for kings to pile on taxes or for judges to accept a "gift." Just wisdom teaches that these economic practices are just as evil and just as deadly as the gang's back-alley violence. Indeed, for readers caught up in more socially acceptable forms of unjust gain, the parable tricks them into a visceral condemnation of their own behavior. In doing so, it offers the reader an emotional education critical to developing the virtue of justice: learning to loathe and fear injustice, even and especially if one finds it in one's own life.

Learning to love and desire justice. Proverbs also shows us we need teaching that shapes our hearts to love and desire justice. This explains Proverbs' teaching that pursuing justice, righteousness, and wisdom leads to a flourishing life.

> In the house of the righteous—great wealth,
>> but the yield of the wicked will be ruined. (Prov 15:6 AT)

This proverb reiterates the father's teaching on unjust gain, while also adding its opposite: *true* treasure can be obtained by the righteous. While the proverb appears observational, it is preceded by the reminder that Yahweh's eyes keep watch on both the wicked and the good (Prov 15:3). Proverbs 15:6 is then followed by this proverb pair:

> The sacrifice of the wicked—an abomination to Yahweh
>> but the prayers of the upright—his delight!
> An abomination to Yahweh—the way of the wicked
>> but the one who chases down righteousness he loves. (Prov 15:8-9 AT)

Taken together, these proverbs invite the audience to *desire* just economic practice, not least because it leads to material prosperity and a loving relationship with the Lord.

Of course, unjust economic practice wouldn't be appealing if it *never* paid off, at least in the short run. Because of this, many of the "better than" proverbs teach that there are things in life worth more than riches, justice among them.

> Better a little with righteousness,
>> than great yield with no justice. (Prov 16:8 AT)

Wealth is only genuinely good when it is "subordinate to righteousness, justice, and wisdom."[27] Part of what just wisdom requires, then, is recognizing the difference between what is *good* and what is *better*.

Proverbs' attempt to woo its audience to justice ultimately rests on the foundation of the book's breathtaking theology of creation. For Proverbs, the just life is the good life because

> The LORD by wisdom founded the earth;
>> by understanding he established the heavens. (Prov 3:19)

God's just way is "embedded in the fabric of creation."[28] To embrace that just way is to engage in the joyful journey of a life lived with God, a life that reflects God's own character and goes "with the grain" of his universe.

Proverbs' attempt to entice our desires for justice is powerful. But we have to acknowledge that the association of righteous behavior with material prosperity is one of the dynamics in Proverbs that has drawn the most criticism. We need to take a moment to address this challenge, because the view that assumes the poor are poor because of their bad decisions and the wealthy rich because of their good ones arguably stands in the way of economic justice. What are we to make of proverbial teaching that incentivizes righteous behavior by associating it with material gain?

First, Proverbs does *not* teach that all good behavior leads to wealth nor that all wealth comes from good behavior. Neither does it teach that all bad behavior leads to poverty nor that all poverty comes from bad behavior.[29] On close inspection, Proverbs describes a morally complex world.[30] Because that complex

---

[27]Raymond C. Van Leeuwen, "Wealth and Poverty: System and Contradiction in Proverbs," *Hebrew Studies* 33 (1992): 31.

[28]Raymond C. Van Leeuwen, "Liminality and Worldview in Proverbs 1–9," *Semeia* 50 (1990): 116.

[29]See Van Leeuwen, "Wealth and Poverty."

[30]See also Stewart, "Wisdom's Imagination," 352-57; Sandoval, *Discourse of Wealth*, 205.

world is ultimately God's good creation, Proverbs *does* maintain that righteousness and justice produce genuinely good results, including economic prosperity.[31] But Proverbs describes this dynamic working, as the economists say,
"all else equal."[32] And Proverbs is well aware that often all is *not* held equal.

Second, Proverbs' description of material abundance as a (possible!)
reward for righteous, just living serves its overall pedagogical program of
shaping the character of its listeners to desire and do justice. "Wealth is a
potent symbol of the desirable,"[33] and so Proverbs uses this symbol to seduce
the desires of the simple for the wise life of righteousness, justice, and equity.
The proverbial father's depiction of wisdom's riches plays a similar role to his
depiction of the deeply satisfying sex life of the person who avoids the "strange
woman" and instead rejoices in the wife of his youth (Prov 5:1-23).[34]

Third, given the lack of "extremes of wealth and poverty" in the society
within which Proverbs developed, the relative good of riches should be understood as a "generous sufficiency,"[35] rather than the kind of hyper-affluence
often imagined by contemporary Western readers.[36]

BUT WHAT DOES JUSTICE HAVE
TO DO WITH *WISDOM*?

Proverbs gives us both a vision for justice as a virtue and a pedagogy to help
us acquire it. But what does this so-called Wisdom book say about the relationship between justice and wisdom?[37] Drawing on character ethicists'
claim that justice and wisdom are mutually dependent virtues, I suggest two
ways Proverbs clarifies for us the need for *just wisdom*. Taken together, they
demonstrate that wisdom without justice becomes *predatory*, while justice
without wisdom is *powerless*. Paying attention to these two dynamics helps us
understand how Proverbs' pedagogy can equip us to respond to the plight of
the working poor with which we began this chapter.

---

[31]On *eudaimonia* and the structures of creation in Proverbs, see Carol A. Newsom, "Positive
Psychology and Ancient Israelite Wisdom," in *The Bible and the Pursuit of Happiness: What the Old
and New Testaments Teach Us About the Good Life*, ed. Brent A. Strawn (Oxford: Oxford University
Press, 2012), 127-28.

[32]See Lyu, *Righteousness*, 76-93.

[33]Sandoval, *Wealth and Poverty*, 57.

[34]For further discussion, see Lyu, *Righteousness*, 62; Sandoval, *Discourse of Wealth*, 61; Van Leeuwen,
"Wealth and Poverty," 26.

[35]I owe this phrase to Ronald J. Sider, *Just Generosity: A New Vision for Overcoming Poverty in
America*, 2nd ed. (Grand Rapids, MI: Baker, 2007), 62.

[36]Newsom, "Positive Psychology," 123.

[37]See Lyu, *Righteousness*, 75.

Just wisdom identifies economic practices that look wise, but aren't.
Proverbs suggests that economic justice requires identifying practices that
appear wise because they work, at least in the short run, but which must nevertheless be rejected as unjust. The very language Proverbs uses alerts us to
this dynamic. The "prudence" (*mezimmah*) Proverbs offers as a major goal of
its moral pedagogy can also be understood as the skilled scheming of the
wicked.[38] If a certain street smarts is required for the wise life, that very same
disposition becomes something else entirely when not oriented toward the
just, righteous way of Yahweh.

A more complex example can be seen in Proverbs' treatment of bribery. At
first glance, Proverbs offers a bewildering diversity of perspectives on the
matter.[39] Proverbs 15:27 associates the one who loves "bribes" (*mattanah*)
with those greedy for unjust gain. But the book also includes proverbs that
seem to put bribery in a much more positive light:

> A bribe [*shokhad*] is like a magic stone in the eyes of those who give it;
> > wherever they turn they prosper. (Prov 17:8)
> Many seek the favor of the generous,
> > and everyone is a friend to a giver of gifts [*mattan*]. (Prov 19:6)

These sayings appear to identify bribery as wise! What are we to make of this
apparent contradiction? There are at least four options.

1. Proverbs may simply contradict itself. While this is possible, it's hard to
   explain why the final editors of the book would include completely
   contradictory perspectives.[40]

2. The seemingly positive evaluations of bribery may simply be observations about the way things do work, without providing any moral
   comment on that fact.[41] Proverbs does offer a fair amount of observation about the way things are. But Sandoval argues that the book's

---

[38]Prov 12:2, 14:17, 24:8-9. See Brown, "Virtue and Its Limits," 48.

[39]On ambiguity as an intentional strategy in Proverbs, see Knut M. Heim, *Poetic Imagination in Proverbs: Variant Repetitions and the Nature of Poetry*, BBR Supp 4 (Winona Lake, IN: Eisenbrauns, 2012), 641.

[40]Yoder offers a celebration of contradiction in Christine R. Yoder, "Forming 'Fearers of Yahweh': Repetition and Contradiction as Pedagogy in Proverbs," in *Seeking Out the Wisdom of the Ancients: Essays Offered to Honor Michael V. Fox on the Occasion of His Sixty-Fifth Birthday*, ed. Ronald L. Troxel, Kelvin G. Firebel, and Dennis R. Magary (University Park: Penn State University Press, 2021), 179-83. I draw on some of her helpful insights below, but it seems to me that what she's describing is not the kind of flat-footed contradiction I'm rejecting here.

[41]Knut Heim acknowledges this possibility in *Like Grapes of Gold Set in Silver: An Interpretation of Proverbial Clusters in Proverbs 10:1–22:16* (Berlin: De Gruyter, 2001), 232.

observations about "the way things work," when read together with the book's treatment of justice, morally *interpret* what the sages of Proverbs *describe*.[42] Proverbs that seem to observe "the way things are" may actually describe things that happen, but shouldn't.[43]

3. It may be the case that, as in other languages and cultures within the ancient world,[44] the same Hebrew words can refer both to legitimate gifts and the justice-corrupting and widely condemned practice of bribery.[45] Perhaps texts that look as if they offer contradictory perspectives on bribery actually address different economic practices altogether.[46] This interpretation would emphasize the way just wisdom is required to distinguish between wise gift giving and unjust bribery, even and especially when these practices appear similar on the surface.

4. Building off the second and third options, Proverbs may invite the wisdom-seeking reader to examine bribes as a practice that sometimes *works* but must nevertheless be rejected as unjust. Such an interpretation requires looking more carefully at the individual proverbs that appear to recommend bribes within their larger contexts.[47]

For instance, while Proverbs 17:8 describes a bribe as like a magic stone in the eyes of the bribe-giver, readers who continue through the end of the chapter soon encounter the most explicitly anti-bribe text in the whole book:

The wicked take a secret bribe
   to twist the paths of justice [*mishpat*]. (Prov 17:23 AT).

Proverbs 17:23 seems to categorically reject this practice—which appears associated with wisdom just a few verses previous—on the grounds of justice.

Between these two texts, Proverbs 17:15 describes those who justify the wicked or condemn the righteous as an abomination to Yahweh, decrying the actions most often associated with bribery in the strongest possible terms.

---

[42]Sandoval, *Discourse of Wealth*, 190.

[43]Sandoval, *Discourse of Wealth*, 193.

[44]See David J. Montgomery, "A Bribe Is a Charm: A Study of Proverbs 17:8," in *The Way of Wisdom: Essays in Honor of Bruce K. Waltke*, ed. J. I. Packer and Sven K. Soderlund (Grand Rapids, MI: Zondervan, 2000), 137.

[45]David Baker, *Tight Fists or Open Hands? Wealth and Poverty in Old Testament Law* (Grand Rapids, MI: Eerdmans, 2009), 216-17.

[46]For further discussion, see Montgomery, "Bribe," 139-40; Andreas Scherer, "Is the Selfish Man Wise? Considerations of Context in Proverbs 10.1–22.16 with Special Regard to Surety, Bribery, and Friendship," *JSOT* 22, no. 76 (1997): 65-66; Heim, *Grapes of Gold*, 232.

[47]See Scherer, "Selfish Man," 61.

This condemnation is reiterated in verse 26. Thus the apparently pro-bribe position of Prov 17:8 appears to be contradicted, in the strongest possible terms, three times within the same chapter.

If we allow these seemingly contradictory positions to drive us back to reexamine Proverbs 17:8, new insights emerge. The magic of the bribe exists "in the eyes of its owner." *But should we trust the bribe-giver's self-assessment?*[48] Careful readers discover that the phrase *in the eyes of* "virtually always" carries a "negative connotation" in Proverbs.[49] It describes the misguided self-perception of fools, sluggards, and the rich who are all "right, pure, or wise" *in their own eyes.*[50] Once we recognize that the proverb immediately before Proverbs 17:8 offers a "strong condemnation of treacherous lips," we can see that the proverb's observations about what bribery appears to do for the one who gives a bribe is surrounded by a moral evaluation of such behavior as deeply unjust, even if, perhaps, such bribery may be "socially acceptable."[51] Similar dynamics are at work in at least some of the other seemingly pro-bribe passages.

A combination of the second, third, and fourth options seem to me the best path forward for understanding Proverbs' overall account of bribery. But note what such a conclusion contributes to our study of just wisdom in the whole of Proverbs! The book's presentation of the texts on bribery is itself a crucial part of the book's strategy for helping us gain *just wisdom*. The text presents us with apparently common-sense, standalone depictions of the reality and effectiveness of bribery. It then surrounds these common-sense proverbs with other sayings that add moral commentary and additional complexity. Making sense of these apparent contradictions requires us to wrestle with the deeper dynamics of what's at work in the apparently common practice of bribery, and indeed perhaps to differentiate between "bribery," which is evil, and potentially similar practices that are not.

The text requires us to *work hard*, in other words, to examine and understand the moral dynamics of a common economic practice that may well have been "business as usual" for many of Proverbs' earliest readers. But the interpretive textual effort the book requires of us is similar to the hard work required for *practical wisdom*, which examines and evaluates complex cases in the mess of the real world in order to discern the wise and just path forward.

---

[48]For a similar dynamic in Proverbs 10:15 and 18:11, see Heim, *Imagination*, 235-40, 634.
[49]Heim, *Like Grapes*, 232.
[50]Montgomery, "Bribe," 139.
[51]Heim, *Like Grapes*, 232.

From the perspective of wisdom untethered from justice, bribes may appear to be simply "the way the world works." But Proverbs recognizes that becoming reconciled to the way a broken world works is "a sick wisdom."[52] Indeed, what looks like "the way the world works" may actually be an illusion! Because the wisdom by which Yahweh founded the earth (Prov 3:19) includes the justice that Yahweh loves more than sacrifice (Prov 21:3), justice is written into the fabric of the universe. The just wisdom Proverbs offers us is an invitation to live in "the world as it *is* rather than as it merely appears to be."[53] Proverbs' practical wisdom enables us to identify practices like bribery that *appear* wise because they work, but which must be rejected as foolishness because they are *unjust*. Wisdom without justice becomes predatory folly.

Just wisdom promotes the virtues of economic wisdom that make economic justice possible. Another way we see the relationship between justice and wisdom in Proverbs is in the book's celebration of virtues like diligence and thrift. According to Proverbs, these virtues make economic justice possible. Justice *needs* such wisdom to accomplish its work in the world. This explains, at least in part, Proverbs' emphasis on the virtue of wise, hard work, as well as its scathing criticism of laziness.

Of course, some scholars identify Proverbs' treatment of diligence and sloth as a sign of its bourgeois perspective. For Pleins, the sages describe the poor as a "despised and lazy lot," not least because describing them that way allows the rich to ignore their role in perpetuating injustice.[54] "Poverty can only be evaluated in this way," another scholar argues, "by someone who has never been a victim himself and who, as a result, has never felt the difficult problem."[55]

There can be no doubt that Proverbs' rhetoric has been wielded as a weapon against the poor, and I admire these scholars' attempt to speak up for them. But I suspect such statements say more about our own distance from poor communities than they do about Proverbs. In my experience, economically impoverished people are quite capable of critiquing systemic injustice in one breath and their lazy neighbor down the street in the next. When I hear a friend in my neighborhood criticizing another neighbor for being lazy, I do

---

[52]Willie James Jennings, *After Whiteness: An Education in Belonging* (Grand Rapids, MI: Eerdmans, 2020), 92.

[53]Stanley Hauerwas, *With the Grain of the Universe* (Grand Rapids, MI: Brazos Press, 2001), 183.

[54]Pleins, *Social Visions*, 469; see also John Barton, *Ethics in Ancient Israel* (New York: Oxford University Press, 2017), 180.

[55]C. Van Leeuwen (quoted in Pleins, *Social Visions*, 469).

not assume they think laziness the exclusive cause of poverty in our community. Why would we impose that criterion on Proverbs?[56]

Across the entire Old Testament period, most people survived through subsistence agriculture practiced on small, rain-dependent farms. Rain that fell too early or too late brought disaster.[57] Food shortages were common.[58] Agrarian peasants seeking to survive in such an environment would be quite comfortable with understanding hard work as an essential virtue and laziness as a deadly vice.[59]

Nor would Proverbs' audience have understood that vice individualistically.[60] The idea that any one member's laziness could negatively affect the broader community stands behind Proverbs 18:9:

> Surely one who is slack in their work,
> they are a sibling to a master of destruction! (AT)

Elsewhere, Proverbs uses this language of destruction to describe those who destroy their lives by adultery (Prov 6:32), their neighbor with their speech (Prov 11:9), and their parents through theft (Prov 28:24). In a context as communally oriented and economically precarious as that of ancient Israel, the vice of laziness is *seriously* wicked.

The diligent work Proverbs associates with just wisdom is not simply the practical wisdom necessary to avoid poverty for oneself; it's the practical wisdom necessary to ensure that the entire household (including the vulnerable) flourishes, and further, that there's something left to share with those who are suffering. Economic justice requires economic wisdom.[61]

The poem celebrating the "valiant woman"[62] offers the most vivid depiction of this aspect of just wisdom in the book. Chapter 31 begins by allowing us to overhear a mother's advice on what wise justice looks like for kings. The

---

[56]So, similarly, Enrique Nardoni, *Rise Up, O Judge: A Study of Justice in the Biblical World*, trans. Sean Charles Martin (Grand Rapids, MI: Baker Academic, 2001), 134. To be clear, I am not arguing for a particular social location for any individual portion of Proverbs, nor for the book as a whole.

[57]Barrera, *Biblical Economic Ethics*, 31-32

[58]See Peter Altmann, "Feast and Famine: Theoretical and Comparative Perspectives on Lack as a Backdrop for Plenty in the Hebrew Bible," in *Feasting in the Archaeology and the Texts of the Hebrew Bible and the Ancient Near East*, ed. Peter Altmann and Janling Fu (Winona, IN: Eisenbrauns, 2014).

[59]See Madipoane J. Masenya, "Proverbs 31:1-31 in a South African Context: A Bosadi (Womanhood) Perspective" (PhD diss., University of South Africa, 1996), 66; Nardoni, *Rise Up*, 135.

[60]See Ellen Davis, *Scripture, Culture, and Agriculture: An Agrarian Reading of the Bible* (Cambridge, MA: Cambridge University Press, 2009), 140.

[61]This resonates deeply with Hirschfield, *Aquinas and the Market*, 166-88.

[62]Indeed, perhaps we ought to label this woman the *virtuous* woman, given that *hayil* is probably the "closest Hebrew term to virtue" (Keefer, *Virtue Ethics*, 52).

chapter ends by describing what the wise, just life looks like in a household run by wisdom incarnated in a diligent agrarian matriarch.[63]

Like Lady Wisdom herself (Prov 8:11), this woman is worth far more than jewels to the wise son who marries her. Indeed, this valiant woman offers the wise son a model for imitation. She provides spoil better and more reliably than the criminals who first offered him spoil through injustice (Prov 1:13),[64] and the poem revels in her agrarian and economic acumen. Moreover, this valiant woman is also a talented teacher in Yahweh's righteous way: "Her mouth she opens in wisdom, and the faithful teaching"—literally, the *torah* of *hesed*—"is on her tongue" (Prov 31:26 AT).

This woman's wise economic efforts provide not only for her husband and children, but for her entire household and all those who make their livelihood through the flourishing agricultural activity overseen by that household (Prov 31:15). Indeed, while one of Proverbs' sages had prayed that Yahweh would provide his "daily portion," it is the economic energies of the valiant woman that provide the "portions" for those who work for her.[65] Perhaps, though, it amounts to the same thing; perhaps this valiant woman has become, through her creative economic activity, the conduit of Yahweh's provision to vulnerable workers.

Standing toward the center of the poem, Proverbs 31:19 and 20 present an artful chiasm that points poetically toward the moral goal of this woman's virtuous work.[66]

(A) her hand she sends out to the distaff
   (B) and her palms seize the spindle
   (B') her palms spread out to the poor
(A') and her hand she sends out to the needy

The same hands that are sent to the distaff are sent out with the abundance secured through the distaff to the needy. The very palms that seize the spindle

---

[63]For a description of how this valiant woman would have accrued and exercised significant economic and social power through these activities, see Carol L. Meyers, "Material Remains and Social Relations: Women's Culture in Agrarian Households of the Iron Age," in *Symbiosis, Symbolism, and the Power of the Past: Canaan, Ancient Israel, and their Neighbors from the Late Bronze Age Through Roman Palestine*, ed. William G. Dever and Seymour Gitin (University Park: Penn State University Press, 2003), 435-36.

[64]See Sandoval, *Discourse of Wealth*, 202.

[65]Yoder points out that the language could suggest either servants in the household or "young female workers," as in the book of Ruth. It could include economic relationships more akin to a workgroup or even employees. Christine Yoder, *Wisdom as a Woman of Substance: A Socioeconomic Reading of Proverbs 1–9 and 31:10-31* (Berlin: De Gruyter, 2001), 86.

[66]On the artful chiasm, see Yoder, *Wisdom as a Woman*, 88.

are opened wide to share the fruits of the labor accomplished on that spindle with the economically impoverished. Deuteronomy 15:8 and Proverbs 19:17 suggest that the virtue of justice requires God's people to faithfully exercise power by opening wide their hands to the poor. Proverbs 31:19-20 winsomely depicts the virtues of economic wisdom necessary to faithfully exercise power so that *when* these subsistence farmers open their hands, there's something in them to share.

While Proverbs' celebration of the valiant woman has been read by some as a "bourgeois fantasy," Ellen Davis is right that, in its agrarian context, it is instead a powerful poetic confrontation with the "economic status quo."[67] In a political economy in which farm families were constantly under economic assault by their own monarchs and distant imperial forces, the valiant woman's wise work perpetuates the kind of village economy Deuteronomy's law sought to establish. For Davis, this closing poem presents

> the mother of the family as a teacher, sharing fully with her husband in the work of maintaining both the household and the covenantal identity of its members. . . . In the words of a contemporary agrarian poet,
> . . . the world survives
> By the survival of
> This kindly working love.[68]

Such kindly working love depends on a community that fosters *just wisdom*, a disposition that includes the virtues of both economic justice and economic wisdom. Proverbs draws its wisdom teaching to a close by offering us a vision of this just wisdom in the life and labor of the valiant woman.

JUST WISDOM TODAY

We began this chapter by exploring how debates about minimum wage legislation sometimes seem to take place between a "justice camp" and a "wisdom camp." The claim of character ethics that wisdom and justice are deeply interrelated virtues led us on a quest to discover whether Proverbs too describes justice and wisdom as two sides of the same coin. On this quest, we've seen that

1. Proverbs sees justice as a virtue: a holistic disposition to understand, desire, and effectively pursue justice, and conversely, to loathe, fear, and avoid injustice.

---

[67]Davis, *Scripture, Culture, and Agriculture*, 149.
[68]Davis, *Scripture, Culture, and Agriculture*, 154 (quoting "The Farm" from Wendell Berry, *A Timbered Choir: The Sabbath Poems, 1979–1997* [Washington, DC: Counterpoint, 1998], 141).

2. Proverbs' toolkit for helping the people of God become just includes vivid teaching designed to shape our hearts to desire the kind of justice that characterizes God's own heart.

3. The virtue of justice depends on the virtue of wisdom to such an extent that we can refer to *just wisdom* as one primary goal of Proverbs' moral discipleship.

4. *Just wisdom* enables the people of God to identify and reject economic practices that *look* wise, but are actually unjust.

5. *Just wisdom* offers us the virtues of economic wisdom that make economic justice possible.[69]

Reading Proverbs in dialogue with character ethics gives us the beginnings of a way forward in those many contemporary economic debates that feel like stalemates between the "justice camp" and the "wisdom camp." Proverbs may yet help the people of God begin to cultivate *just wisdom* in our world today.

What might this look like in practice? I want to offer four principles derived from Proverbs' depiction of just wisdom before concluding with several examples of what those principles might look like in practice.

Principle one: The goal of economic wisdom is economic justice. Proverbs teaches us that one primary reason why we learn to be economically wise is so that we might practice economic justice. Justice, understood as the faithful exercise of power, stands at the center of the goal of wise living. In our economic lives, justice is not an abstract standard that we have to be careful not to violate while we chase down the "real" goals of economic wisdom, such as increased wealth for our families. No, we gain the virtues of hard work, diligence, thrift, and cagey practical wisdom *so that we can fulfill our job description to do justice.* Economic wisdom matters primarily, although not exclusively, because it makes justice, mercy, and neighbor love possible.

Principle two: Learning just wisdom means learning to love justice and fear injustice. Proverbs teaches us that one of the first steps on the road to wisdom is *learning to desire justice and fear injustice.* Yes, Proverbs does teach the reader the nitty gritty practicalities of economic wisdom throughout the book, including the path to material economic abundance. But Proverbs strategically chooses to focus its *first* wisdom lectures on the need to *fear* falling for temptations to *injustice,* and the need to *desire* the just wisdom that

---

[69]These arguments lend significant support to the claims of Brown, Keefer, and other OT scholars that virtue ethics can be a fruitful tool in the task of interpreting the book of Proverbs.

Yahweh offers. The very structure of the book suggests that you can't graduate safely to the lessons on wisely producing wealth until you've learned to *love* justice and *loathe* and *fear* the injustice that threatens to destroy you.

We ought to pause and note just how different Christian economic discipleship might be if we took these first two principles seriously. Christians like myself have often tried to follow Proverbs carefully when it comes to sex. Like Proverbs, we see sex as a tremendous good within the context of a marriage oriented toward God, and as enormously dangerous and destructive outside that context. But when it comes to the matter of making money, we fail to follow Proverbs' pedagogy.

We celebrate Proverbs' teaching on hard work and the goodness of enjoying the fruits of one's labors. But we separate that teaching from Proverbs' equally insistent warnings that *wealth, like sex, is a good fraught with danger.* Worse, we tend to assume that wealth is usually the result of righteous living. We treat economic injustice like some kind of aberration, a serious and obvious trap most of us probably won't fall into. If we *do* fall into economic injustice, we assume, it will be obvious to others and ourselves.

By contrast, Proverbs suggests that economic power is deadly and dangerous when pursued apart from a love and desire for justice. Indeed, the faithful exercise of power—righteousness, justice, and equity—is a primary *goal* of the wise life! Wealth earned apart from this moral goal often turns out to be predatory folly. And pedagogically, Proverbs seems to think that, to understand all of this, disciples need to spend a lot of time and energy learning to desire justice and fear injustice.

Wherever Christians talk about good work, wherever we want to foster among God's people the hard work and diligence and economic wisdom that Proverbs celebrates, Proverbs' own program suggests we need to spend *equal* (and often prior) energy helping Christians see that justice is the goal of economic success and injustice is a deceitful trap that can spring on us unawares. From Proverbs' perspective, this is all good news for disciples! Because disciples have learned that doing justice is *joy* (21:15).

If we want to apply these insights, we might take a few lessons from Proverbs' teaching style, with its vivid, affection-shaping stories, and its memorable, reflection-inspiring sayings. In our own day, we might teach and tell stories that highlight how just economic practice has *become* joy to those who have exercised it in our community. Conversely, we also need to follow in Proverbs' footsteps by drawing ugly, startling depictions of economic *injustice*, including those injustices many Christians see as simply practical wisdom in line with "the way the world works."

Principle three: Economic justice depends on economic wisdom. If Proverbs makes clear that the goal of economic wisdom is justice, it also teaches that economic justice *depends on* economic wisdom. Proverbial economic wisdom does indeed celebrate and encourage hard, diligent work, exercised with the kind of cagey economic savvy that takes into account "how the system works"—without being enslaved to it. When this economic wisdom is rightly directed, it is essential to the justice Yahweh demands and in which he delights.

Cultivating this kind of just wisdom does indeed require Christians to think about what policies, compensation structures, and discipleship practices encourage the diligent work Proverbs celebrates. Central to such economic wisdom is the learning that comes from experience. As we saw with Proverbs' complex teaching on bribes, wisdom requires us to closely examine complex realities in our quest for the best path forward. Doing so will inevitably require us to debate, disagree, and discern carefully how best to exercise economic power on behalf of one's neighbors and in faithfulness toward God. Because we gain wisdom in part through experience and debate, we would be well served by having this debate, disagreement, and close examination of specific economic practices with people who have been directly involved with the economic practices in question.

If my first two points proved most challenging for the "wisdom camp" associated with the politically conservative Christianity in which I was raised, this third point proves more challenging for the "justice camp" in which I've spent much of my adult life. We argue fiercely for greater justice for the poor, not least in the form of raised wages. But we rarely involve Christians who've been deeply involved in the marketplace in these conversations, nor do we consider carefully how, in many cases, raising wages for the poor may well require forms of economic wisdom we ourselves lack.

Don't believe me? Take a look at the example of the many nonprofits that have sought to start social enterprises, businesses specifically designed to hire people with fewer marketable skills or other obstacles to employment, and to pay them above-market wages. I love this movement, have worked for a nonprofit that practiced it well, and have promoted it to others.[70] But there

---

[70]See Michael Rhodes and Robby Holt, *Practicing the King's Economy: Honoring Jesus in How We Work, Earn, Spend, Save, and Give* (Grand Rapids, MI: Baker, 2018), 148-50.

can be no doubt that many social enterprises struggle to pay what they consider just wages and produce enough revenue to be self-sustaining. The ones that succeed either find people who, from long experience in the marketplace, bring to the nonprofit the kind of savvy economic wisdom required, or they last long enough to gain that savvy economic wisdom on their own.

Yet often "justice camp" types like me do not value adequately the amount of work it takes to figure out what economic wisdom entails when it comes to starting and growing a business in our current economy, or to identify employment practices that both do justice to the worker *and* incentivize excellent work. Without such wisdom, we often discover ourselves powerless to move toward economic justice.

Principle four: Just wisdom discerns the difference between wisdom and folly. Just wisdom evaluates practices that *look* wise because they are widespread or seem effective, and *rejects* those that actually represent unjust folly. Our exploration of bribery not only offers an example of this principle in action, but also demonstrates how it depends on the previous three.

The description of the gang's unjust gain leading to their own destruction sets the reader up to discover that bribery can also be considered just such a deadly, unjust practice (Prov 15:27). But Proverbs' complex treatment of bribery requires the reader to think hard about this, presumably because bribery was a complex, widespread phenomenon that often appeared to work. Indeed, the very complexity of Proverbs' teaching may be designed to help the reader learn to discern which economic exchanges could count as a wise use of an economic gift or even appropriate compensation,[71] and which apparently similar economic exchanges constitute the justice-twisting deeds of the wicked (see Prov 17:23). Wise thinking about bribery requires a disciple to have a godly fear of finding themselves engaged in injustice, while also requiring them to examine and understand which practices count as injustice and which do not.

This principle challenges our assumption that if we're not breaking any laws, we're in the clear. Proverbs puts the reader on alert that much that produces wealth in the short run must be rejected, even if it apparently works. After all, "better a little with righteousness, than great yield with no justice" (Prov 16:8 AT). Furthermore, because the sages recognize that Yahweh himself

---

[71]The wise use of an economic gift may be in view in Proverbs 18:16; on which see Montgomery, "Bribe," 139-42. Heim suggests the possibility of appropriate compensation in Proverbs 17:23 in *Like Grapes*, 232.

oversees the economy, they warn us that we must work hard to ensure that we have not unwittingly fallen into the false, worldly economic wisdom that Yahweh hates.

At the same time, Proverbs recognizes that it takes *work* to distinguish between wisdom and folly. As anyone who has tried to start a business, work through the best compensation package for employees, or tried to address a workplace issue with a worker who reports to them knows, figuring out what just wisdom looks like is *hard*. It may be easy to say, *Just pay fair wages!* But raising wages for workers requires the kind of cagy, experiential wisdom that knows that figuring out what just wisdom requires and figuring out how just wisdom can get there takes work.

TAKING JUST WISDOM TO WORK

How might these principles for just wisdom guide us in responding to the plight of the working poor?

Practicing just wisdom to raise wages in workplaces we influence. First, many Christians have significant influence in their workplaces, and could exercise just wisdom in those workplaces by seeking to raise the wages of the working poor. This obviously includes the many executives who are already involved in making decisions about compensation.

One of the huge privileges of my life has been meeting many members of a growing movement of Christian business folks doing just that. Years before it was industry standard in Memphis, my friend Matt Terhune decided to raise the starting wage of every employee in his plumbing company to $15.00. "For me, it's a matter of justice," Matt said. "I had been talking to friends working with the materially poor about wages, and then one day I read this quote from one of the workers in the civil rights movement here in Memphis. He said, 'We think a hard day's work should allow a man to put food on his table.' And after that, I just committed."

My friend Wes Gardner's decision to hire teen mothers in partnership with an area nonprofit led him to creatively reconsider the kind of wages they paid entry-level employees. "It has changed the whole way I think about business," Wes says. "Now, I see my payroll as profit. I look at what our company spends on compensation, and I think, '*Look how much money we've made.*'"

That phrase, "Look how much money we've made," reflects a massive paradigm shift in line with just wisdom. Just wisdom required Wes and the team to keep the company growing, to navigate myriad employment issues within the complicated corporate and legal environment that affected every aspect of the business. Raising wages is *not* simply a matter of waving a magic wand. It's a task that Wes and his team accomplished by identifying the just use of economic power as a key purpose of their company.

Or consider Dayspring Partners, a successful technology company started by Christians associated with Redeemer Community Church in San Francisco. Dayspring's founders committed themselves to a 3:1 compensation ratio so that "no employee, including the company's CEO," makes more than three times the salary of anyone else in the business, "including Dayspring's janitorial staff."[72] Such a commitment requires just, generous wisdom: "Keeping to 3:1 while also attracting talent and balancing budgets [requires] discounting executive salaries in order to compensate for above-market incoming salaries."[73]

These examples reflect a broader shift in how we think about the very purpose of business. The primary purpose of business has often been understood as maximizing shareholder profits. Indeed, this is enshrined in legislation for corporations, whose shareholders can sue managers if company decisions are *not* justifiable in terms of profit maximization. Because this makes wealth an ultimate, rather than instrumental good, both Proverbs and virtue ethics would condemn shareholder profit *maximization* within the bounds of the law as the sole driver of decision-making.[74]

Whole Foods founder John Mackey and professor Rajendra Sisodia call businesses to make maximizing value for *stakeholders* the primary goal instead.[75] This stakeholder paradigm includes company owners alongside managers, employees, customers, suppliers, and the surrounding communities in which companies operate. Such a framework places justice—understood as the faithful exercise of economic power on behalf of all stakeholders—at the center of a company's concerns. This does not require companies to reject profits! It does require them to reject *profit maximization for shareholders*, replacing that commitment with a principled practice of just generosity toward all stakeholders. But it also includes discerning how best to foster proverbial virtues like hard work, diligence, creativity, and relational IQ. Just wisdom, in other words, recognizes that wisely improving company and worker performance can serve the work of economic justice.

---

[72]Jonathan Tran, *Asian Americans and the Spirit of Racial Capitalism* (New York: Oxford University Press, 2022), 227-28.

[73]Tran, *Asian Americans*, 228.

[74]On which, see Hirschfield, *Aquinas and the Market*, 138-60.

[75]John Mackey and Raj Sisodia, *Conscious Capitalism: Liberating the Heroic Spirit of Business* (Cambridge, MA: Harvard Business Review Press, 2012).

My friend Dave Barrett shares about how the company he works for, Cascade Engineering, helped more than eight hundred employees successfully make the journey from "welfare to career." Their efforts at just wisdom included embracing a triple bottom line that includes people and profit and requiring *all* employees to attend training designed to deconstruct stereotypes about the poor (the kinds of stereotypes that Proverbs has so often been misused to perpetuate!). But it also includes working with the local government to bring a social worker on site who can help workers identify roadblocks to succeeding at work. This practice of just wisdom helped these employees make their best contributions within the company.

Other companies partner with nonprofits who help workers gain the skills they need to contribute more effectively to the company's profitability. My friend Sarah Steckel cofounded The Collective Blueprint to serve some of the forty thousand eighteen- to thirty-year-olds in the greater Memphis area who are neither working nor in school. The Collective Blueprint offers these young people a stipend, helps them enroll in and complete zero-debt, high-return vocational educational certificates, helps them gain soft-skills, and then places them in jobs with partner companies. Sarah has been a leading voice demanding that our city practically commit to raising wages for the working poor. Through the Collective Blueprint, she offers businesses a partner that can help them answer this call by hiring previously disenfranchised workers and paying them a living wage.

Another strategy for just wisdom in relationship to wages is simply to make all workers owners, either by adopting a worker-owner cooperative structure, or in the form of profit-sharing, as in Employee Stock Ownership Programs (ESOPs). Such business structures not only have a long history, but they also make a lot of sense. Given that the Bible pairs its celebration of justice as the faithful exercise of power with a deep suspicion of concentrations of power, *sharing* economic power with all workers through profit-sharing or worker-ownership seems almost obvious.[76]

This is exactly what founder Bob Mills did when he turned his 100-million-dollar company over to his employees.[77] Mills turned down lucrative offers from others to buy his business precisely because of his Christian

---

[76]See Jamin Hubner, "Production for the Common Good," *Journal of Religious Leadership* (2021): 41-2, 55-60. My thanks to Jamin Hubner for providing input on this whole section.

[77]On Bob Mill's story, see Jane Thier, "Executive Greed Is Driving the Labor Shortage," Fortune, June 17, 2022, https://fortune.com/2022/02/17/bobs-red-mill-president-on-his-employee-owned -company.

commitments: "I learned almost 70 years ago how integral hard work and kindness is to success," Mills says. "As our small business grew, I realized I had a great opportunity for generosity. My favorite bible scripture, Matthew 7:12, says do unto others what you'd want them to do unto you. That's something I think we should all live by."[78]

At the same time, studies demonstrate that the justice of worker-ownership and profit-sharing is a form of just *wisdom*. Cooperative economics *works*. Workers in firms with employee ownership earn more money, receive better benefits, and are less likely to be laid off than workers in traditional firms.[79] Moreover, cooperative ownership *promotes* proverbial virtues like hard work, diligence, creativity, and relational IQ. Studies suggest worker performance is higher in companies that practice profit-sharing, that there is less turnover, and that workers demonstrate greater investment in company performance through "self-monitoring and quality control."[80]

In other words, while business leaders often complain their employees don't take enough ownership of their work, research suggests one powerful way for company owners to help workers do so is by creating space for them to *become* owners. Just wisdom indeed!

Seeking to raise wages in public policy. As citizens with the right to vote and exercise free speech, Christians also have the opportunity to engage the current political debates about minimum wage and the working poor through the lens of just wisdom.[81] One challenge to doing so has been the long, vehement arguments about the potential impact of dramatic minimum wage increases.

Economists continue to debate the impact of a policy like a fifteen dollar federal minimum wage.[82] Some studies argue, in line with mainstream economic theory, that essentially any increase in the minimum wage will do more harm than good, killing jobs or reducing hours, especially for workers with lower education.[83] Others have found evidence suggesting

---

[78]Thier, "Executive Greed."

[79]For resources on employee ownership, see https://democracycollaborative.org/elements/employee -ownership and https://www.ownershipeconomy.org/

[80]Jamin Hubner, "Owning Up to It: Why Cooperatives Create the Humane Economy Our World Needs," *Faith & Economics* (2020): 153.

[81]We will return to a fuller exploration of just discipleship in relation to local and national politics in part four of this book.

[82]Charles C. Brown and Daniel S. Hamermesh, "Wages and Hours Laws: What Do We Know? What Can Be Done?," *Russell Sage Foundation Journal of the Social Sciences* 5, no. 5 (2019): 69, https:// muse.jhu.edu/article/742465.

[83]See, for instance, Ekaterina Jardim et al., "Minimum Wage Increases, Wages and Low-Wage Employment: Evidence from Seattle," *National Bureau of Economic Research* (2018), www.nber.org

that raising the minimum wage, at least within the ranges contemplated by lawmakers, has little negative effect on employment,[84] even on workers in low-income communities.[85] Others even suggest a positive impact on employment.

Another line of economic research suggests that the impact could vary significantly based on economic sector. Workers in low-wage jobs in sectors that comprise many companies (like food service) could suffer the worst impacts, while workers in low-wage jobs in sectors that comprise relatively few companies (like retail) might see significant benefit.[86] The non-partisan Congressional Budget Office's report on the likely impact of a fifteen dollar federal minimum wage predicted a number of impacts—some good for lower-wage workers, some bad.[87] What might our account of just wisdom contribute to our understanding of how to engage public policy in light of this complex debate?

First, if justice is about the faithful exercise of power in community, then citizens in the richest country in the history of the planet, a country where CEOs in the nation's largest companies earn on average more than three hundred times that of entry-level employees,[88] can and should exercise our economic and political power to seek increased wages for the working poor.

/system/files/working_papers/w23532/w23532.pdf; David Neumark et al., "Revisiting the Minimum Wage–Employment Debate: Throwing Out the Baby with the Bathwater?," National Bureau of Economic Research, January 2013, www.nber.org/system/files/working_papers/w18681/w18681.pdf; Qiuping Yu et al., "Research: When a Higher Minimum Wage Leads to Lower Compensation," *Harvard Business Review*, June 10, 2021, https://hbr.org/2021/06/research-when-a-higher-minimum-wage-leads-to-lower-compensation.

[84]Doruk Cengiz et al., "The Effect of Minimum Wages on Low-Wage Jobs," *Quarterly Journal of Economics* 134, no. 3 (2019): https://academic.oup.com/qje/article/134/3/1405/5484905; Arindrajit Dube et al., "Minimum Wage Effects Across State Borders: Estimates Using Contiguous Counties," Institute for Research on Labor and Employment, November 2010, https://irle.berkeley.edu/files/2010/Minimum-Wage-Effects-Across-State-Borders.pdf.

[85]Anna Godoey and Michael Reich, "Are Minimum Wage Effects Greater in Low-Wage Areas?," Institute for Research on Labor and Employment, September 25, 2020, https://irle.berkeley.edu/are-minimum-wage-effects-greater-in-low-wage-areas.

[86]See José Azar et al., "Minimum Wage Employment Effects and Labor Market Concentration," National Bureau of Economic Research, July 2019, www.nber.org/system/files/working_papers/w26101/w26101.pdf.

[87]"The Budgetary Effects of the Raise the Wage Act of 2021, Congressional Budget Office, February 2021, www.cbo.gov/system/files/2021-02/56975-Minimum-Wage.pdf

[88]Lawrence Mishel and Jori Kandra, "CEO Compensation Surged 14% in 2019 to $21.3 Million," Economic Policy Institute, August 18, 2020, https://www.epi.org/press/ceo-pay-increased-14-in-2019-and-now-make-320-times-their-typical-workers/. See also Hirschfield, *Aquinas and the Market*, 185. Of course, the realities of executive compensation vary widely among firms.

Justice requires us to put raising the wages of the working poor on our political agenda.

Moreover, as we engage economic policy in relation to low-wage workers, Proverbs offers us a stern warning that much "business as usual" in any economy may actually be unjust. Proverbs decries bribery, *even while recognizing the short-term effectiveness of bribery*. The US economy has proved enormously productive, enabling millions of Americans to attain standards of living unimaginable even a hundred years ago. At the same time, from 1979 to 2013, low-wage workers saw a real *decline* in their wages while the market grew 706% and CEO pay grew 1,007.5%.[89]

More troubling still, the dramatic difference between the growth of the market and the growth of CEO pay suggests that "CEOs are getting more because of their power to set pay, . . . not because they are increasing productivity or possess specific, high demand skills." As a result, "wage growth for the bottom 90% would have been nearly twice as fast over the 1979–2017 period had wage inequality not grown."[90]

Our system, in other words, has found ways to make ever more money without increasing the wages of many poor workers. If I'm right that biblical justice is about the faithful exercise of power, the reference to CEOs' "power to set pay" contributing to massive growth in income inequality should alarm us. Perhaps poverty wages, like bribery, appear to work in the short-term, but actually constitute a grave injustice.

Christian discipleship should foster a desire to exercise power justly on behalf of low-wage workers, fearing the ways that our economy has embraced wage practices that appear to work, but may actually be unjust. While the previous section identified companies whose executives willingly embrace the kind of just, generous wisdom required by all of this, Christians should also use our political power to advocate for systems and structures that improve the plight of low-wage workers more broadly.

At the same time, both Proverbs and the complex economic debates about the actual impact of various wage policies suggests we also need *wisdom* to discern how best to increase wages. At a bare minimum, this requires acknowledging the complexity of the problem, rather than merely shouting talking points at one another. At a maximum, just wisdom means Christians getting involved as economists, policy experts, and activists

---

[89]Tran, *Asian Americans*, 224.
[90]Mishel and Kandra, "CEO Compensation."

committed to figuring out how best to accomplish the just outcome of higher wages for low-wage workers. In a world where the working poor suffer, just wisdom requires Christians to learn how to marshal the disciplines of political science, community organizing, economics, and business to best pursue a more just world for workers at the bottom of our economic pyramid.[91]

This includes examining and debating the relative merits and trade-offs entailed by various minimum wage policy proposals in combination with and compared to other policies, including localized living wage efforts, investment in workforce education, Universal Basic Income, an expanded Earned Income Tax Credit, incentivizing and protecting the kind of employee ownership explored in the previous section, labor reform and the role of unions, investment in work programs for populations most likely to be negatively affected by minimum wage increases, and more.

Of course, this will still leave Christians disagreeing with one another about what specific path just wisdom ought to take in the public square, and it is far outside my area of expertise to make any definitive policy claims. Personally, I am enormously grateful for the way activist organizations such as the Fight for $15 have put the plight of the working poor squarely at the center of our concerns. I have occasionally participated directly in their advocacy efforts. At the same time, the complexity of the empirical data makes me cautious about seeing a fifteen dollar federal minimum wage as an unambiguous good, *unless* other steps are taken to mitigate potential negative consequences. Such steps include advocating for job creation and work opportunities for those workers most likely to be negatively impacted by an increase in minimum wage legislation, particularly young people in poor communities.

ON THE ROAD TO JUST WISDOM

Proverbs offers disciples a pedagogical path toward the virtue of just wisdom, a holistic disposition to understand, desire, and act toward that which is just, under the reign of our Just King, and in the messy world within which we find ourselves. Without such just wisdom, a wisdom inextricably bound up with the "faithful exercise of power" on behalf of others, all our efforts at justice

---

[91]For similar reflections, see Robert C. Tatum, "A Theology of Economic Reform," *Faith & Economics* 69 (2017): 63-83; Hirschfield, *Aquinas and the Market*, 191-218.

will fall short, and our efforts at wisely pursuing economic gain will often turn predatory. The good news is that Proverbs invites us to embrace the journey toward just wisdom, not least because such a journey is the road toward *joy* (Prov 21:15). After all, the just wisdom God requires is written into the very fabric of the universe.

BECOMING JUST IN
THE MEANTIME

The Gift and Task of Discipleship in 1 John

THE INJUSTICES WE HAVE EXPLORED so far can be overwhelming. For me, though, facing up to the fact that Christians have often contributed to these injustices is even harder. These difficult realities have driven us to explore Scripture's invitation to moral discipleship as a hopeful way forward. In the Bible, the living Lord offers us a program of moral formation designed to help us *become just*. Through Scripture's stories, formative practices, account of just character, and invitation to a certain "politics," or form of communal life, God invites us to embrace the journey of becoming his just and righteous people. This journey, though, is often a countercultural one, requiring us to resist alternative forms of discipleship on offer in our world. We have explored how this kind of discipleship might play out in our discussion of Deuteronomic feasts, the Psalms' justice songs, and Proverbs' justice teaching.

But many Christians may find this . . . unsatisfying. Is the mess we find ourselves in simply a result of our failure to "get with the program"? Doesn't Scripture make clear that sinful humans *can't* "get with the program"? Has my choice to draw so heavily on character and virtue ethics gotten us off on the wrong track completely?

Furthermore, how much of the story I've been telling must be thrown out once we leave the Old Testament and enter the New? What becomes of our account of "just discipleship" in dialogue with virtue ethics if what Jesus brings is not a liberation "from vice to virtue, but from vice *and* virtue to the grace of Christ"?[1] Have I not failed to capture both the depth of the problem of human sinfulness *and* the difference that Jesus makes for addressing it?

To answer these challenges, we need to bring our account of just discipleship into dialogue with John's programmatic vision in 1 John 3:1-3. Doing so will not require us to reject the vision of moral discipleship I have presented so far, but it will place that vision within a broader frame. For John, discipleship is always Jesus' *gift* before it is ever our *task*. By helping us ground the biblical task of just discipleship in God's gracious gifts, John invites us to understand both God's gifts and our actions as bound up in the good news of Jesus.[2] By reading John's invitation in dialogue with character ethics, moreover, we can begin to imagine how to move through our discipleship failures and forward into the loving justice of God today.

RECEIVING THE GIFT: THE *WHO, WHERE,* AND *WHEN* OF DISCIPLESHIP IN 1 JOHN 3:1-2

In 1 John 3:1-2, John offers us an explosive depiction of what God has done in giving us the gift of discipleship.[3] In the process, he redefines the way we answer the most basic questions of our moral lives:

- *Who* are we as disciples?
- *Where* are we as disciples?
- *When* are we as disciples?[4]

Who are we? "Look at what sort of love the Father has given to us, that we might be called the children of God! And that is what we are!" (1 Jn 3:1 AT). In this outburst of praise, John summarizes his answer to his audience's identity question: Who are we? *We are children of the Father.*

---

[1]Philip Ziegler, "Completely Within God's Doing: Soteriology as Meta-Ethics in the Theology of Dietrich Bonhoeffer" in *Christ, Church, and World: New Studies in Bonhoeffer's Theology and Ethics,* ed. Philip Ziegler and Michael G. Mawson (New York: T&T Clark, 2016), 109. Ziegler explicitly identifies this claim with Luther.

[2]For my more technical treatment of many of the themes in this chapter, see Michael J. Rhodes, "Becoming Militants of Reconciling Love: 1 John 3:1-3 and the Task of Ethical Formation," *JTI* 15, no. 1 (2021): 79-100. Portions of these ideas also appeared first in Michael J. Rhodes, "(Becoming) Lovers in a Dangerous Time: Discipleship as Gift and Task in 1 John," *Word & World* (2021) 41.1.

[3]For reasons of convenience, I refer to the author of 1 John simply as "John."

[4]These questions address what John Webster refers to as *moral ontology.* John B. Webster, *Word and Church: Essays in Christian Dogmatics* (New York: T&T Clark, 2001), 283.

Being a child of God is a deeply *moral* reality.[5] As John claims in 1 John 2:29, everyone born of God does the "righteousness" or "justice" (*dikaiosynē*) that defines God's own character. "Being a child of God and acting that way" thus stands at the heart of John's ethical discipleship.[6] But John makes clear that this identity as God's "just" children is solely the result of God's lavish love. *Look at his love,* John declares, *that we should be called children of God!* For John, we owe our just, familial identity to the lavish love of God expressed in his begetting us as his children (1 Jn 2:29). The result of such gratuitous love is no less real for all that. As John immediately reminds us, children whose existence is grounded in God's love is "what we are" (1 Jn 3:1). Our identity as disciples is a *true gift*.

Where are we? Immediately after reminding disciples of *who* they are, John reminds them of *where* they are: "Because of this the world does not know us, because it did not know him" (1 Jn 3:1 AT). The significance of John's seemingly straightforward assertion that disciples are in a world that does not know them, however, turns out to be remarkably hard to pin down.[7] This complexity comes because John uses the Greek word *kosmos*, most often translated as "world," in at least three different, yet related ways.

First, as in the Gospel prologue, John understands the *kosmos* as God's good creation, created through Jesus in the beginning (Jn 1:1-10) and saved through Jesus' willing assumption of the material world at the incarnation (1 Jn 4:2, 9, 14).[8] But second, and much more strongly stated in the letter, John tells us all is not well in God's good world: "We are from God," but "the whole world lies in the power of the evil one" (1 Jn 5:19 AT). God's good *kosmos* has become a battlefield, and all humanity is caught up in the conflict.[9]

Nor is it only individual humans who are caught up in this battle. As Wink suggests in his translation of *kosmos* as "system," we should not think of the devil's influence in a reductionist or solely spiritual sense. When John speaks of the world as lying "in the power of the evil one" (1 Jn 5:19), he includes the

---

[5] See J. G. van der Watt, "Ethics in 1 John: A Literary and Socioscientific Perspective," *CBQ* 61 (1999): 494.

[6] van der Watt, "Ethics in 1 John," 494; See also Cornelis Bennema, "Moral Transformation in the Johannine Writings," *In die Skriflig* 51 no. 3 (2017): 4.

[7] See J. G. van der Watt, "Cosmos, Reality, and God in the Letters of John," *In die Skriflig* 47, no. 2 (2013): 7.

[8] This aspect also makes sense of John's positive role for the "goods of the world" in 1 John 3:17.

[9] See Andreas J. Kostenberger, "The Cosmic Trial Motif," in *Communities in Dispute: Current Scholarship on the Johannine Epistles*, ed. R. Alan Culpepper and Paul N. Anderson (Atlanta: SBL Press, 2014), 159.

way that social, economic, cultural, and political systems are also under de-monic influence.[10] They participate in the evil one's mission to steal, kill, and destroy (Jn 10:10). This perspective on the world recognizes that the problem is not simply an aggregation of individual sinners, but rather "the systemic defiance of God's lordship over the world" and the "structural refusal by human authority"[11] to recognize Jesus as the world's rightful king (see Jn 18:28-40). Because John understands the *kosmos* as a system under the reign of the evil one, he sees desire and love for the things of the *kosmos* as antithetical to the will of God (1 Jn 2:16-17), and thus can describe the *kosmos* as that which must be overcome by faith (1 Jn 5:4-5).

John offers the sort of theological vision of moral reality that theologians sometimes describe as apocalyptic.[12] This apocalyptic understanding of *where* we are as disciples has major implications for our understanding of *who* we are as disciples. For instance, according to Martyn, we often imagine humans as living within a two-agent drama.[13] In this two-agent drama, the world is made up of people who can competently choose good or evil on the one hand, and a "self-limiting" God who makes room for them to do so on the other. But Martyn argues that the New Testament's apocalyptic vision rejects this two-agent drama in favor of a three-agent drama. The cast of characters in this story include God, morally *incompetent* humans, and the devil and other dark suprahuman forces, whose influence renders humans incompetent.[14]

John's moral vision of *who* and *where* disciples are resonates with this apocalyptic vision. For John, we don't start out in some morally neutral position and then pick a side. All humanity is always already "claimed."[15] All

---

[10]Walter Wink, *Engaging the Powers: Discernment and Resistance in a World of Domination* (Minneapolis: Fortress, 1992), 55-57.

[11]Brian K. Blount, *Then the Whisper Put on Flesh: New Testament Ethics in an African American Context* (Nashville: Abingdon, 2001), 110.

[12]On apocalyptic theology in John's Gospel, see Catrin H. Williams and Christopher Rowland, eds., *John's Gospel and Intimations of Apocalyptic* (London: T&T Clark, 2013). On the emergence of a "Union School" interested in apocalyptic theology and drawing on the work of J. Louis Martyn, see J. P. Davies, *Paul Among the Apocalypses? An Evaluation of the "Apocalyptic Paul" in the Context of Jewish and Christian Apocalyptic Literature*, Library of New Testament Studies (New York: T&T Clark, 2016), 18.

[13]J. Louis Martyn, "Epilogue: An Essay in Pauline Meta-Ethics," in *Divine and Human Agency in Paul and His Cultural Environment*, ed. John M. G. Barclay and Simon J. Gathercole (New York: T&T Clark, 2008), 175.

[14]Martyn, "Epilogue," 178.

[15]Philip Ziegler, *Militant Grace: The Apocalyptic Turn and the Future of Christian Theology* (Grand Rapids, MI: Baker Academic, 2018), 10.

who have not become children of God are children of the devil (1 Jn 3:10), an identity that John equates with being "of the world" (1 Jn 2:16; 4:5). As with the children of God, the character of this worldly family is derived from its demonic parent: unjust, unrighteous, and sinful deeds overflow from the unjust, unrighteous, and sinful character of those like Cain, "who was from the evil one" and murdered his brother (1 Jn 3:10-12).[16] Such worldly children are *powerless* to practice fully the justice and love that characterizes the Just One who *is* love (1 Jn 4:16). The just discipleship we were designed for is impossible.

This does not mean that humans caught up in this cosmic battlefield are simply passive victims, morally speaking. Life lived in the world suffering under the devil's assault habituates human agents into active *complicity* with his demonic powers through individual acts of sinful rebellion.[17] In other words, "living in homes battered by the hurricane forces of our enemy's dark power, we do not seek shelter on higher ground, but rather jump in a boat, trim the sails, and actively set off in the direction the wind wants to take us."[18] We willingly choose to walk in step with our enemy's enslaving influence.

Thus, for John, the *kosmos* comprises the good creation and its human inhabitants, invaded and overrun by the devil and his brood of dark powers and false prophets (see 1 Jn 4:1; 2 Jn 7). Life lived in such a world renders humans incapable of fully embracing just discipleship.

Yet this dark reality is not John's last word on the *kosmos*. For John, the *kosmos* is finally and fully the world that *God so loved* that he sent his only Son as the "savior of the *kosmos*" (1 Jn 4:14). In Jesus, the Creator has returned to reclaim what's his, a rescue operation that has required him to "destroy the works of the devil" (1 Jn 3:8) and offer himself as an atoning sacrifice for the whole *kosmos* (1 Jn 2:2). The incarnate Lord liberates the devil's children by forgiving them, begetting them anew, and granting them new life lived "through him" (1 Jn 4:9).

The answer to the question of who we are is deeply tied to the question of where we are. Either we remain both *in* and *of* the world that is passing away, or we are liberated from *that* world and born afresh for participation in the

[16]Ziegler, *Militant Grace*, 10.
[17]Ziegler, *Militant Grace*, 62. See also J. Louis Martyn, "Afterword: The Human Moral Drama," in *Apocalyptic Paul: Cosmos and Anthropos in Romans 5–8*, ed. Beverly R. Gaventa (Waco, TX: Baylor University Press, 2013), 163.
[18]Michael J. Rhodes, *Formative Feasting: Practices and Virtue Ethics in the Deuteronomic Tithe Meal and Corinthian Lord's Supper*, Studies in Biblical Literature 176 (New York: Peter Lang, 2022), 162.

reign of love, righteousness, and justice in the savior's reclaimed and rescued *kosmos*.[19]

When are we? John's answers to the disciples' *who* and *where* questions now raise a third question: *When* are disciples? Here again, 1 John 3:1-2 offers a programmatic answer. "Beloved, *now* we are God's children, but it has *not yet* been revealed what we will be. But we know that when he is revealed, we will be like him, for we shall see him as he is" (1 Jn 3:2 AT). While the first part of verse 2 emphatically declares that we are God's children *now*, the second line of the verse immediately complicates this temporal picture: those who are children *now* do not yet know what they *will be*. The *full* revelation of their identity is utterly bound up in the full revelation of Jesus' own identity in his second coming, because "when he is revealed, we will be like him, because we will see him as he is" (1 Jn 3:2 AT).[20] Because the goal of redeemed human life is nothing less than becoming like Jesus, who we are as disciples is not static. Humans *are* what we *are* in the light of both what we *were* and what we *will be*.[21]

John's depiction of moral reality, then, is determined by a now/not yet distinction in moral time.[22] It is only because the darkness of the world (see 1 Jn 2:8, 17) under the influence of the devil (1 Jn 5:19) is passing away and the true light that has broken in at the incarnation is already shining (1 Jn 2:8) that believers can, ought to (see 1 Jn 2:6), and indeed will (1 Jn 2:28-29) live lives of righteousness, justice, and love, walking in the light as he is in the light (1 Jn 1:6-7).

Meanwhile, 1 John 3:2 holds this "already" dimension in tension with the "not yet" reality that Christians can't even imagine the extent to which they will be transformed into the image of Jesus at his return.[23] So while discipleship is a *gift*, it is not a gift that we fully possess in the present. This

---

[19]Benjamin E. Reynolds, "The Anthropology of John and the Johannine Epistles: A Relational Anthropology," in *Anthropology and New Testament Theology*, ed. Jason Maston and Benjamin E. Reynolds (London: T&T Clark, 2018), 121.

[20]For discussion, see Stephen S. Smalley, *1, 2, 3 John*, WBC (Waco, TX: Word, 1984), 139.

[21]John Webster, *God Without Measure: Working Papers in Christian Theology*, vol. 2, *Virtue and Intellect* (New York: Bloomsbury T&T Clark, 2015), 14. See also Marianne Meye Thompson, *1-3 John* (Downers Grove, IL: InterVarsity Press), 87; Rudolf Bultmann, *The Johannine Epistles*, Hermeneia (Philadelphia, PA: Fortress Press, 1973), 48.

[22]Smalley, *John*, 137.

[23]While a final verdict on the question lies beyond the scope of this chapter, I believe this is the context within which we should understand the epistle's apparent contradiction between 1 Jn 1:8–2:2's frank claim that Christians will continue to sin and 1 Jn 3:6-8's claim that "everyone who remains in him does not sin." For a summary of options, see Reynolds, "Anthropology of John," 133.

now/not yet dynamic prevents disciples from overconfidence or illusions of autonomy and control in their moral lives. While we are already God's children, our lives remain a great distance from what they ought to be and will be when Jesus returns.

EMBRACING THE TASK: BECOMING DISCIPLES
IN THE MEANTIME

John offers disciples a programmatic answer to our *who, where,* and *when* questions. Disciples are the children of God. They have been liberated from the power of the evil one and live in the world that God loves and is reclaiming. When Jesus returns, these disciples will become like him, for they will see him as he is. For John, to become a disciple is to join a community of people totally and utterly dependent on Jesus' saving, rescuing, and transforming love. It is to embrace a way of life that is a gracious gift, a gift that includes a righteous and just character given to us by God.

All of which makes what John says next so strange: "Everyone who has this hope in him purifies themselves as he is pure" (1 Jn 3:3 AT).

Wait . . . what?

If we've been following John's argument so far, this line catches us completely off guard. Worse, it seems almost heretical. Surely it is Jesus who does the purifying! Surely all we have to do is receive the good news and watch God do his transforming work! John's suggestion that the life of discipleship includes "purifying oneself" as Jesus is pure seems to be altogether too focused on the power of human effort and the possibilities of human character. The dangers of works righteousness and self-absorption appear to be crouching at the door.

Such concerns reflect genuine dangers. But John goes on and calls us to look to Jesus and proactively purify ourselves in imitation of the character we find in him despite those dangers. Crucially, the language of purifying oneself suggests not simply that Christians who have become God's children will freely and spontaneously perform good deeds that flow out of their transformed status, nor that the sole path to sanctification is constant reflection on God's work in saving us. No, the language of purifying oneself suggests rather that self-consciously *pursuing* a continual process of moral formation is a central part of what it means to live as a liberated child of God awaiting Jesus' return. God's action in human transformation, in other words, demands and enables our own efforts at moral formation. For John, the gift of transformation that disciples receive is always also an invitation to the task of *becoming disciples in the meantime.*

How are we to understand this dynamic theologically? As the late John Webster put it, the triune God's liberating love changes our lives by "altering the conditions they exist under."[24] Discipleship is indeed a total impossibility for "children of the devil" caught up in a world system shot through with dark demonic influence.[25] But for those who have been reborn as children of God, discipleship has become a glorious possibility, indeed a God-given *responsibility.* This glorious possibility requires disciples to self-consciously *pursue* a continual process of discipleship, a "disciplined and serious laying-hold of that mode of existence which is [ours] already" in Christ.[26]

To speak this way suggests that our efforts at the task of discipleship are themselves bound up in the Triune God's ongoing gifts to us. We are never more than branches whose fruit-bearing capacity is utterly dependent on our remaining intimately united to the vine (Jn 15:1-5). The gift of God's presence and power at work in disciples is revealed by his having given his Spirit to his people (1 Jn 4:13). For John, when we embrace the task of discipleship, our action is always dependent on God's own action in us and through us. Whether practicing the feast, singing Scripture's justice songs, listening to Proverbs' teaching, imitating Jesus, or embracing any other practice of just discipleship, God's grace hems us in behind and before, and our every action is enabled by God's gracious, empowering presence on us.

JOHN AND CHARACTER ETHICS IN DIALOGUE

John's theological vision is beautiful, but what difference does it make for our daily lives? Once again, reading Scripture in dialogue with character ethics helps us understand and live into the theological reality John describes. For instance, Thomas Aquinas's account of the virtues offers us a tool for exploring what John says about the gift and task of just discipleship.[27]

---

[24]John Webster, "Eschatology, Ontology and Human Action," *Toronto Journal of Theology* 7, no. 1 (1991): 13.

[25]This does not mean that our neighbors apart from Jesus never get anything right or that they are our enemies. It *does* mean that genuine discipleship is genuinely impossible apart from Jesus.

[26]Oliver O'Donovan, *Resurrection and Moral Order: An Outline for Evangelical Ethics,* 2nd ed. (Leicester: Apollos, 1994), 260.

[27]Several recent treatments of Johannine ethics have looked to the virtue ethics of Aristotle for such dialogue. See Cornelis Bennema, "Virtue Ethics and the Johannine Writings," in *Johannine Ethics: The Moral World of the Gospel and Epistles of John,* ed. Christopher W. Skinner and Sherri Brown (Minneapolis: Fortress, 2017), 264-66; Bennema, *Mimesis in the Johannine Literature* (New

In the last chapter, we explored the way character ethics' understands the virtues as habits or dispositions that empower a person to know, desire, and pursue the goods associated with those virtues. Theologians like Aquinas basically get this understanding from Aristotle. But when it comes to explaining how people *gain* these virtues, Aquinas offers a startling innovation. While this discussion may seem unnecessarily technical, trust me, the payoff for our understanding of the Christian life is significant.

Aristotle believed that a person gained the virtues through teaching and practice. However, for Aquinas, unaided teaching or practice could never finally enable a person to obtain the virtuous character God requires. Drawing on Augustine, Aquinas argues that *true* virtues are habits "by which we live righteously, of which no one can make bad use, *which God works in us, without us*."[28] For Aquinas, as for John, when God adopts his children, he gives them a transformed character out of which they live transformed lives.[29] These true, perfect virtues are "infused" in us by God, rather than "acquired" by our own action, as with the Aristotelian virtues. For Aquinas, the virtues are God's gifts.

But here's where it gets interesting. While disciples receive these infused virtues as gifts from God, that does not mean believers are passive in the life of discipleship. For Aquinas, these gifted, virtuous habits take greater root in a person's character *when they practice them*.[30] But sinful dispositions a person has acquired through living in the fallen and rebellious *kosmos* can make living out these infused virtues difficult.[31] So believers must grow in the infused virtues by both actively seeking to live out of those virtues *and* putting to death those bad habits that might get in the way of them doing so. The virtuous character God gives his people as a gift is thus also assigned to them as a task.

York: T&T Clark, 2017), 144; Jeffrey E. Brickle, "Transacting Virtue Within a Disrupted Community: The Negotiation of Ethics in the First Epistle of John," in *Rethinking the Ethics of John: "Implicit Ethics" in the Johannine Writings*, ed. Jan G. van der Watt and Ruben Zimmermann (Tubingen: Mohr Siebeck, 2012), 340-49. I suggest Thomas Aquinas proves an even better interlocutor. For a more technical treatment, see Rhodes, "Becoming Militants," 79-100.

[28] Thomas Aquinas, *The Summa Theologica of St. Thomas Aquinas*, trans. by Fathers of the English Dominican Province, 2nd ed., 21 vols (London, UK: Burns Oates & Washbourne, 1920-1935), I-II q. 55, a. 4 (emphasis added).

[29] See Stanley Hauerwas and Charles Robert Pinches, *Christians Among the Virtues: Theological Conversations with Ancient and Modern Ethics* (Notre Dame, IN: University of Notre Dame Press, 1997), 68-9; Brickle, "Transacting Virtue," 345.

[30] Aquinas, *ST* II-II q. 24, a. 4. Although even this is the result of the Holy Spirit's work, as Aquinas makes clear in II-II q. 24, a. 5.

[31] Aquinas, *ST* I-II q. 65, a. 3.

Aquinas transforms Aristotle's insights about moral growth by reframing them within the bigger story of God's action in our lives. By calling disciples to "purify themselves as Jesus is pure" only after making it clear that his audience totally depends on God's gracious love for every aspect of their discipleship, John makes a similar move (1 Jn 3:1-3). In what follows, I explore the gift and task of just discipleship in 1 John in dialogue with Aquinas's virtue ethics.

The gift and task of imitating the beloved. The very idea of purifying oneself *as Jesus is pure* points to the importance of imitation in John's account of just discipleship.[32] Just four verses later, John calls disciples to practice *dikaiosynē* just as Jesus is *dikaios*. In Greek, these *dikaios-* words refer to the idea of both righteousness and justice. John thus summons his audience to practice righteousness and justice in line with their identity as God's children and in imitation of Jesus' own just and righteous character.

For John, *justice* or *righteousness* is also closely connected to *love*, as can be seen in his parallel use of the two terms in 1 John 3:10. Crucially, in 1 John 3:16, John calls disciples both to acknowledge the gift of love they received in Jesus' laying down his life for their sakes, and to imitate that love in laying down their own lives for their brothers and sisters.

Of course, the summons to imitate Jesus might sound to us like all *task*, calling believers to grit their teeth and work to replicate the particulars of Jesus' life. Maybe that's why many ethicists and theologians express skepticism about the role of imitation in moral formation.

Yet as John makes clear, it is the liberating love of God that renews humans so that they can imitate their loving Lord. The foundation of John's command to love as Christ loved is nothing less than the reality that disciples have passed from death into life (1 Jn 3:14). Indeed, the claim that God simply *is* love makes our *imitation* of God's love dependent on our *experience* of God's love. That is why John introduces the love command in 1 John 2:7 by referring to his audience as the *beloved* for the first time in the epistle.

The believer's imitation of Christ's righteousness and justice (*dikaiosynē*) follows the same pattern. John makes clear that such moral formation is only possible because the Just One (*dikaios*) has cleansed his people from all

---

[32]See Dirk G. van der Merwe, "'A Matter of Having Fellowship': Ethics in the Johannine Epistles," in *Identity, Ethics, and Ethos in the New Testament*, ed. Jan G. van der Watt (New York: de Gruyter, 2006), 547, 554.

injustice (*adikia*; 1 Jn 1:9). Our imitation of Jesus' justice depends on our receiving the gift of a relationship with Jesus.

Once again, virtue ethics can help us understand this dynamic. According to Aquinas, when God gives his people the virtues as gifts, he gives them the gift of a relational disposition or "stance" toward him as well.[33] Pinsent describes this gift as a second-person disposition, an I-You orientation to be moved by God in the context of a relationship.[34] Pinsent and others point to recent social cognition studies to explain Aquinas's account of these second-person dispositions, including studies on the relational aspects of imitation. For instance, studies demonstrate that infants begin imitating the facial expressions of their parents within the first hour of birth.[35] Such imitation appears to be "programmed deeply into our brains."[36] Indeed, some scientists present evidence for so-called mirror neurons that fire in the brain in the same way whether a person is performing an action or *observing* someone perform an action,[37] expressing an emotion through facial expressions or observing others "expressing their emotions."[38] These studies show that face-to-face, interpersonal imitation is one key way we humans gain new skills and habits, develop emotional empathy, and acquire similar character traits to those we imitate.[39]

They also provide an analogy for understanding how our efforts to imitate Jesus are made possible by the gift of a relationship with him. In imitation, "the movements are mine, but I am also moved" by another.[40] When we imitate Jesus, we actively embrace the *task* of discipleship through a second-person practice. But this task is only possible because of the prior and ongoing *gift* of a second-person relationship with Jesus.

John highlights the deeply relational nature of the disciple's imitation of Jesus. In 1 John 3:1, John calls his audience to *look* at what great love the Father

---

[33]Andrew Pinsent, "Aquinas: Infused Virtues," in *The Routledge Companion to Virtue Ethics*, ed. Lorraine Besser and Michael Slote (New York: Routledge, 2015), 149.

[34]Andrew Pinsent, *The Second-Person Perspective in Aquinas's Ethics: Virtues and Gifts*, Routledge Studies in Ethics and Moral Theory (New York: Routledge, 2012), 42.

[35]Istan Czachesz, "From Mirror Neurons to Morality: Cognitive and Evolutionary Foundations of Early Christian Ethics," in *Metapher-Narratio-Mimesis-Doxologie: Begründungsformen fruhchristlicher und antiker Ethik* (Tubingen: Mohr Siebeck, 2016), 274.

[36]Czachesz, "Mirror Neurons," 273.

[37]Czachesz, "Mirror Neurons," 274.

[38]Czachesz, "Mirror Neurons," 274.

[39]Czachesz, "Mirror Neurons," 274-75.

[40]Susan Eastman, *Paul and the Person: Reframing Paul's Anthropology* (Grand Rapids, MI: Eerdmans, 2017), 68.

has given us. While sometimes lost in translation, the imperatival form of this Greek verb nearly always refers to actual sight.[41] Thus John's summons to *look* at the love of God embodied in Christ's example and to long for the final transforming *vision* of Christ at his royal return is intended to inspire his audience both to gaze on Christ and to embrace the imitation of their beloved that such contemplation inspires. One way we purify ourselves as Jesus is pure, then, is to fix our gaze on him and exercise our renewed agency in imitating the purity we behold there.

The fact that our vision of Jesus is currently imperfect—that we do not yet see him fully as he truly is—is crucial.[42] This reality introduces a deep sense of humility and dependence in our attempt to imitate Jesus, as well as the recognition that any growth that occurs through our own efforts is nevertheless at the same time a divine gift. When we imitate Jesus, the movements are ours, but we are also moved by our relationship with the Lord. In such imitative action, "Jesus' love for [us] is not only the model but also the enabling force of [our] love."[43] The imitation that John calls us to is "far deeper and more self-involving than a 'free individual choice' to follow another's example."[44] When disciples imitate Jesus, they "participate in the very life of God."[45]

Nevertheless, imitating Jesus requires our active effort. Purifying ourselves as Jesus himself is pure is hard work. Aquinas warns us that the bad habits and moral dispositions that remain in us can make it painful to imitate Jesus in line with our transformed character. Virtue ethics recognizes that the journey of sanctification requires us to actively put these sinful dispositions to death, and to stir up the virtues we have received in our daily lives. Similarly, John makes clear that imitating Jesus requires us to proactively put to death those habits and tendencies that linger from life lived under the devil's dark influence, and to actively stir up the gift of love God has given us in our relationship with others. Crucially for our understanding of justice-oriented discipleship, John fleshes this process out in his command that disciples imitate Jesus in relation to their poor brothers and sisters in Christ.

---

[41]See Raymond E. Brown, *The Epistles of John*, ABC (New Haven, CT: Yale University Press, 2007), 387; Smalley, *1, 2, 3 John*, 133.

[42]O'Donovan, *Resurrection and Moral Order*, 347.

[43]Volker Rabens, "Johannine Perspectives on Ethical Enabling in the Context of Stoic and Philonic Ethics," in *Rethinking the Ethics of John*, 120.

[44]Eastman, *Paul and the Person*, 144-45.

[45]Rabens, "Johannine Perspectives," 125.

Putting to death, stirring to life. In 1 John 2:12-14, John declares that disciples already "know the Father," have had their sins forgiven, and have even "overcome the evil one" (AT). Disciples of Jesus have received the gift of a powerful new birth. They are now children, and they have received Jesus' Spirit to such an extent that they need no one to teach them (1 Jn 2:27).

Nevertheless, work remains! In 1 John 2:15, John declares with equal vehemence that those who have received the gift of discipleship are still in danger of continuing in the habits and disordered desires associated with their old life lived in the *kosmos* that is passing away.

> Do not love the *kosmos*, nor the things in the *kosmos*. If anyone loves the *kosmos*, the love of the Father is not in them. Because everything that is in the *kosmos*, the craving of the flesh and the craving of the eyes and the pride of possessions,[46] is not from the Father, but is from the *kosmos*. And the *kosmos* is passing away along with its cravings, but the one who does the will of God remains forever (1 Jn 2:15-17 AT).

The challenge is for those who have received the gift of discipleship to embrace the task of discipleship by *putting to death* their disordered, "worldly" loves.

How familiar we are with these particular disordered loves! It's easy to see why scholars believe John's "mini-catalog of vices" would have been understood by his audience as the greedy, gluttonous, and sexually depraved lifestyles especially available to the wealthier members of the congregation.[47] The language of the "pride of possessions" may even suggest that these wealthier members of the community were rather proud of the higher status they had managed to attain by pursuing their desires.[48]

Such habits and tendencies are, for John, unjust vices associated with the devil. They get in the way of a disciple's imitation of Jesus' sacrificial love. In a world of grinding poverty and social vulnerability,[49] worldly obsession with power and status easily become a kind of hatred for the poor that aligns us with Cain, "who was of the evil one, and murdered his brother" (1 Jn 3:12 AT).

---

[46]While the Greek word *bios* is often translated life, I have translated it as "possessions" here to highlight the close connection between John's words in this passage and the only other use of *bios* in the Johannine corpus (1 Jn 3:17), where the reference is clearly to possessions.

[47]William R. G. Loader, "The Significance of 2:15-17 for Understanding the Ethics of 1 John," in *Communities in Dispute*, 224-33.

[48]Jörg Frey, "'Ethical' Traditions, Family Ethos, and Love in the Johannine Literature," in *Early Christian Ethics in Interaction with Jewish and Greco-Roman Contexts*, Jan Willem van Henten and Joseph Verheyden (Leiden: Brill, 2013), 178-80.

[49]Frey, "'Ethical' Traditions," 178-80.

Such addictive, vicious desires must be put to death if we are ever to imitate Jesus' sacrificial love. John makes it clear that this is particularly true when it comes to the sort of self-sacrificial imitation that includes sharing our economic resources with the poor, the only concrete example of a disciple's sacrificial love he offers in the entire letter.

> In this we know love, that he laid down his life for us. And we ought to lay down our lives for our siblings. Whoever has the world's possessions, and sees their sibling who has need, and shuts up their heart from them—how can the love of God remain in them? Children, let us not love in word nor in tongue but in deed and truth. (1 Jn 3:16-18 AT)

John thus summons his audience to imitate the love of Jesus demonstrated at the cross by creatively and contextually applying that same love to the socio-economic realities within the community. Because they are called to imitate Jesus who died for them, they must embrace a practice of costly economic self-sacrifice within the community of faith.

Note that such virtuous imitation requires a certain kind of seeing and feeling as well. Virtues and vices include our moral vision, desires, and affections. John demands we put to death precisely those desires and affections we have so often invested time and energy in cultivating: habituated desires and affections dedicated to our own upwardly mobile self-interest and a cultivated distance from the poor and the oppressed.

That's why John brilliantly draws our attention to the moment of *seeing* one of our siblings in need, and the temptation to actively "close our hearts," to shut down our affections, to guard our emotional life from being moved by the suffering of our brothers and sisters in Christ, lest we be so moved that we open wide our hands in sacrificial generosity. Indeed, John not only draws our attention to the role of our affections, but to our active *agency* in relation to our affections. What is forbidden is *closing* one's emotional life from one's siblings.[50]

The obvious implication is that disciples should actively seek to *stir up* the affection of love so they can imitate Jesus by loving their siblings through concrete acts of economic self-sacrifice. To love in "deed and truth" (1 Jn 3:18) will require disciples to embrace a different kind of seeing and feeling. We will strive to see in the destitute another child of God for whom Christ died, and actively seek to stir up a loving affection for those who are suffering. Imitating

---

[50]There is a strong, if subtle connection between this passage and Deuteronomy 15:9-11.

Jesus requires us to open the new eyes and hearts we've received as children of the Father, so that we might lay down our lives for one another, and particularly for the poor.

The gift and task of community. Reading John in dialogue with character ethics also helps us see that imitation isn't something you can do alone. In the ongoing battle with the defeated-but-still-active-devil, the "antidote to the encroaching *kosmos*"[51] is a community which is itself a foretaste of the *kosmos* that is on the way in Christ. In other words, the community is the place where one "jettisons [one's] socialization" into the hostile "world," and instead experiences a resocialization by the Spirit in the community of faith.[52] For John, this happens very practically as one turns from the vices associated with greed in1 John 2:15-17 and instead embraces the communal sharing required by the imitation of Jesus (see 1 Jn 3:17).

Moral formation is truly a team sport, one that occurs in part through the community's *corporate* practice of imitation. When we imitate Jesus together in this way, we willingly live into the dawning reality given to us in Christ.[53] The result of such imitation is not navel-gazing self-obsession, but rather the formation of a community that bears witness to the justice, love, and liberating power of God amid a world system whose demonic domination is being overturned by the power of Jesus. We might even say that by imitating Jesus' love in the space opened up by Jesus' life, death, and resurrection, the community *participates* in Jesus' destruction of the devil's work (1 Jn 3:8) and stands as a declaration of his victory over the evil one (1 Jn 2:13).[54] Such a community will itself, in some sense, "be the gospel," offering the world "the alternative of eschatological life, begun *now* in communion with the one who is the resurrection and the life."[55]

This dynamic is on display in John's bold declaration that "no one has ever seen God" (1 Jn 4:12). This declaration replicates precisely the first half of the final line of the prologue of John's Gospel: "No one has ever seen God. It is God the only Son, who is close to the Father's heart, who has made him known" (Jn 1:18).

---

[51]Brickle, "Transacting Virtue," 346.

[52]Wink, *Engaging the Powers*, 55-56.

[53]K. R. Harriman, "Take Heart, We Have Overcome the World: Participatory Victory in the Theological-Ethical Framework of 1 John," *Evangelical Quarterly* 88, no. 4 (2016): 311.

[54]Harriman, "Take Heart," 103. See also Kostenberger, "Cosmic Trial," 162.

[55]David K. Rensberger, *Johannine Faith and Liberating Community* (Philadelphia: Westminster, 1988), 150. See also Richard B. Hays, *The Moral Vision of the New Testament: Community, Cross, New Creation* (New York: Harper Collins, 1996), 147.

In 1 John 4:12, the premise is the same, but the conclusion is different: "If we love one another, God abides in us and his love *en hēmin teteleiōmenē estin.*" While most English versions render the quoted Greek along the lines of "his love is perfected in us" (RSV) or "his love is made complete in us" (NIV), Rensberger translates it as "his love has been brought to its completion in us."[56] Such a translation captures the sense of God's love attaining its end in the community of faith. The Gospel prologue emphasizes the invisibility of God as a way to call attention to the incarnate Son as the one who makes God visible. John's epistle identifies the community that practices the love of God in imitation of the incarnate Son as the tangible place that makes the love of the Triune God visible.

John's love ethic is, as Blount puts it, an "ethics of active resistance. . . . It advocates the creation of a visible community whose intramural love sets it apart and makes it a viable, recognizable alternative to the traditional ways of being and living in the world."[57] Indeed, to paraphrase Cornel West's definition of justice, for John, "justice is what love looks like" in the public that is the community of faith.[58]

Because such communal love is a response to and imitation of the self-sacrifice of Christ for his enemies, it is also intrinsically missional.[59] The love of God for the world fueled the Father's sending of the incarnate Son on a mission of salvific love. The community's embodiment of that divine love in the world participates in the Triune God's ongoing mission of redemption. Indeed, it is one of the primary ways the community receives the risen Lord's commission: "As the Father has sent me, even so I send you" (Jn 20:21 AT).

EMBRACING JOHN'S VISION OF JUST DISCIPLESHIP TODAY

How does John's programmatic description of discipleship in 1 John 3:1-3 shed light on the question of the contemporary church's failures of just discipleship? How has John's account revealed the depths of the human predicament and the difference that Jesus makes for addressing it?

---

[56]David K. Rensberger, "Completed Love: 1 John 4:11-18 and the Mission of the New Testament Church," in *Communities in Dispute*, 249.

[57]Blount, *Whisper*, 112.

[58]Cornel West, *Brother West: Living and Loving Out Loud* (New York: Smiley Books, 2010), 23.

[59]Contra that tradition of scholarship that sees the Johannine literature as entirely sectarian and unconcerned with the world.

First, John's vision of the world as God's good creation now overrun by the evil one offers insights into why, theologically speaking, injustice is such an intractable problem. It is not simply that humans are tempted by the opportunity to occasionally and individually misuse our power. It is that we have a hostile enemy who seeks to "steal, kill, and destroy" both individual humans *and* the cultures, structures, and institutions that we corporately create as part of our vocation as God's image bearers. "The Devil has a far-reaching undertaking. He enslaves not just individuals but all humanity, including authorities and institutions."[60]

It's worth pointing out that this view of humanity as under the enslaving influence of hostile powers is by no means limited to John. John's depiction of the evil one has significant overlap with the way Paul talks about both Sin and Death as *characters*, enslaving agents that exert hostile power over humanity. For instance, Paul's account of sin includes both individual acts of transgressions—"sins"—*and* the story of Sin with a capital S, Sin as an enemy, a taskmaster that desires to "reign" in our mortal bodies and dominate our lives (see Rom 6:12-14).

Moreover, just as John's depiction of the *kosmos* includes the idea that human cultures, institutions, structures, and systems have come under the destructive influence of the evil one, Paul's references to "powers and principalities" seem to include both spiritual powers *and* human systems created good, but deeply distorted and life-destroying due to sin. For both Paul and John, part of the reason injustice is so prevalent and powerful is that our battle against injustice is not simply against "flesh and blood" (Eph 6:12), but against a demonic anti-trinity: Sin, Death, and the Devil.

Their corrupting influence impacts every aspect of human life. Even worse, John makes clear that as we live our lives in this world under the evil one's hostile influence, we conform our character to it. Life lived in a world under the influence of the evil one initiates us into practices of de-forming discipleship oriented toward injustice.

Second, if John deepens our appreciation of the problems facing discipleship, he does so only to expand our understanding of the depth and breadth of what Jesus has done as the *Savior* of the world. John tells us the truth of our dark world only to dazzle us with the unimaginable goodness and glory of God's salvation. Our Savior's rescue operation is cosmic in scope.

---

[60]Enrique Nardoni, *Rise Up, O Judge: A Study of Justice in the Biblical World*, trans. Sean Charles Martin (Grand Rapids, MI: Baker Academic, 2001), 296.

Jesus loves the *kosmos,* and it is the *kosmos* that he rescues. Jesus is the Word-made-flesh, the One by whom all things were created, and the Just King who will reclaim all of creation when he returns. That creation includes the human cultures and structures that, in their brokenness, so often contribute to human suffering and injustice. They, too, shall be restored. Jesus is making *all things new.* This is hallelujah territory!

Our discipleship is utterly dependent on this same cosmic rescue operation. Jesus not only defeats the devil, he also offers himself as a sacrifice in response to the sins we have committed in our willing enslavement to the evil one. God's people receive full atonement for their sins. At the same time, Jesus also *liberates* us for the work of discipleship, "altering the conditions we exist under," making a life of just, loving discipleship possible. We are God's children *now.* We have been relocated out of the world dominated by the devil and into the realm of God's love and justice. We stand in the sure hope of full transformation into the image of Jesus when he returns.

John deepens our appreciation for the powers of injustice at work in our world, but only to reveal the infinitely greater power for love and justice that God has unleashed in the world and in his people's hearts through Jesus' life, death, and resurrection. If John gives us resources for understanding the power of injustice, he also gives us reasons to look for the just power of God unleashed in the world through his people.

Why then do we continue to fail? On the one hand, John's reminder that we will not fully be what God has given us to become until Jesus returns reminds us that injustice will never be fully overcome, in our hearts, churches, or world, until Jesus returns. But on the other hand, John makes clear that *often the people of God simply fail to embrace the task of discipleship, refusing to avail themselves of the righteousness, justice, and love that God gives to them as his children.*

Christians have received the virtues that are our birthright as members of God's family. But we have also been invited into a journey of discipleship, a journey of purifying ourselves in imitation of Jesus. We are called to grow into the love and justice God has given us, and to strive against the unjust, vicious dispositions that are the remnants of the evil one's reign in our lives. Too often, however, we willingly cling to "the craving of the flesh and the craving of the eyes and the pride of possessions," actively shutting down our affections toward our siblings who are in need.

John's vision, especially when read in dialogue with character ethics, can help us gain a deeper understanding of the racial and economic injustice we have been exploring in this book. Our economic systems, for instance, are part of that good *kosmos* now lying under the influence of the evil one. This is brilliantly captured by a conversation between bankers and poor tenant farmers whose farms are being foreclosed on by the bank in Steinbeck's novel *The Grapes of Wrath*:

> "We're sorry. It's not us. It's the monster. The bank isn't like a man."
>
> "Yes, but the bank is only made of men."
>
> "No, you're wrong there—quite wrong there. The bank is something else than men. It happens that every man in a bank hates what the bank does, and yet the bank does it. The bank is something more than men, I tell you. It's the monster. Men made it, but they can't control it."[61]

This conversation captures the sense we so often have that structural dysfunction in our economy is somehow more than the sum of our individual dysfunctional economic practices. There is indeed "something more."[62] John and Paul help us see that this "something more" includes the action of the rebellious, supernatural enemies of God and God's good world.[63]

Similarly, theologians have recently argued that this understanding of powers, principalities, and the *kosmos* can help us understand the intractability of racism and white supremacy in our society.[64] Chanequa Walker-Barnes argues that the "powers of evil can co-opt everyone and everything—every individual, community, and culture; every social structure, policy, and practice."[65] Based on this idea, she argues that white supremacy, in all of its cultural, historical, institutional, and individual complexity, is "a manifestation of the powers and principalities."[66]

---

[61]John Steinbeck, *Grapes of Wrath* (New York: Penguin, 2006), 33-34 (Walter Wink also quotes this exchange in his *Engaging the Powers*).

[62]For a brilliant summary of the way critical realist sociology offers us tools for understanding and analyzing the reality of this "something more," see the helpful essays in Daniel Finn, ed., *Moral Agency Within Social Structures and Culture: A Primer on Critical Realism for Christian Ethics* (Washington, DC: Georgetown University Press, 2020).

[63]Wink, *Engaging the Powers*, 50.

[64]Willie James Jennings calls whiteness a "power" in "Willie Jennings: To Be a Christian Intellectual," Yale Divinity School News, October 30, 2015, https://divinity.yale.edu/news/willie-jennings-be -christian-intellectual. For an extensive argument about the "relationship between racist domination and political economic exploitation" that places economic exploitation at the center, see in its entirety Jonathan Tran, *Asian Americans and the Spirit of Racial Capitalism* (New York: Oxford University Press, 2022).

[65]Chanequa Walker-Barnes, *I Bring the Voices of My People: A Womanist Vision for Racial Reconciliation* (Grand Rapids, MI: Eerdmans, 2019), 47.

[66]Walker-Barnes, *I Bring the Voices of My People*, 192.

For Americans, then, there is something literally demonic about our long history of injustice against Black people, injustice that has created a set of overlapping systems and structures that we currently inhabit. But when we live our lives within these structures—and all of us do—we are shaped by them. As Eddie Glaude puts it, Americans acquire a whole host of racial habits by which we "live the belief that white people are valued more than others." And we acquire these

> not by way of overt racism but through the details of daily life, like when we experience the differences in the quality of the schools we attend, the different nature of our interactions with the police, the different ways we navigate where we work, our different neighborhoods, and the daily barrage of signals and cues about race that all Americans get through television and news reports.[67]

But our reading of John in dialogue with Aquinas helps us see that we are not passive, innocent participants in our relationship to our broken economic system or our sinful racist culture. In terms of our economic lives, recall the structural forces driving racial and economic segregation in the housing market that we considered in chapter 4. These forces make it easy to participate in that economic segregation by creating "smooth pathways" toward decisions in line with that segregation.[68] Our housing market, for instance, offers the rewards of a quickly appreciating financial asset and proximity to the best schools to those who make living in the "best" neighborhoods their top priority. That same housing market imposes serious penalties on those who choose to buy a home in a low-income community where house values are not appreciating and schools often struggle.[69] But while these forces put pressure on us, *they do not force our actions.* We willingly choose to act—or to resist—the forces we encounter within the structure of the housing market.[70]

Or consider what John's theological vision offers in relation to recent social scientific studies of implicit or unconscious racism in our society today. Such studies demonstrate structural injustice against Black people in a variety of areas.[71] The exact same resume gets twice as many callbacks from an employer

[67]Eddie S. Glaude Jr., *Democracy in Black: How Race Still Enslaves the American Soul* (New York: Crown, 2017), 56.
[68]Daniel J. Daly, "Critical Realism, Virtue Ethics, and Moral Agency," in *Moral Agency Within Social Structures and Culture*, 95.
[69]See Daniel K. Finn, "Social Structures," in *Moral Agency Within Social Structures and Culture*, 36-40.
[70]See Tran, *Asian Americans*, 194.
[71]Much of the remainder of this paragraph first appeared in Michael Rhodes, "Should We Repent of Our Grandparents' Racism? Scripture on Intergenerational Sin," Center for Hebraic Thought,

if the name at the top is Brendan rather than Jemal. Doctors given statistically identical patient histories were significantly less likely to recommend helpful heart procedures to Black patients than to white patients. One study showed that police demonstrated racial bias in video-game style simulations in which they had to decide whether a person was armed and dangerous or an innocent bystander. In that same study, civilians performed even worse.[72] After describing the way our vision of beauty is deeply shaped by a preference for body shapes, colors, and types associated with white norms, Walker-Barnes points to

> a large body of literature [demonstrating] that people perceived as physically attractive are considered more intelligent by their teachers, are more popular among their classmates, are more likely to be hired, have higher earnings, receive better performance evaluations, are promoted more often, and receive less severe punishments in criminal justice proceedings.[73]

All of these studies identify situations where Black people suffer because of racial bias. But there aren't enough Klansmen on the planet to explain all this injustice. Without downplaying the persistence of explicitly racist perspectives and policies, some social scientists argue that that many of those perpetuating these racial inequities do so *unintentionally.* This phenomenon is often referred to as "implicit" or "unconscious" bias.[74] Though we may have worked quite hard to address our *consciously held* racial stereotypes, our *subconscious* has been warped and twisted by racist ideology and a life lived in institutions and structures historically shaped by racism. And sometimes, particularly when we make decisions at speed, that implicit racism overrules our conscious convictions.

Social scientists help explain how broken, racist structures shape humans toward racist decisions and behaviors at a level beneath their conscious

June 19, 2020, https://hebraicthought.org/repenting-intergenerational-racist-ideology-scripture-intergenerational-sin.

[72]Sendhil Mullainathan, "Racial Bias, Even When We Have Good Intentions," *New York Times,* January 3, 2015, www.nytimes.com/2015/01/04/upshot/the-measuring-sticks-of-racial-bias-.html.

[73]Walker-Barnes, *Voices of My People,* 88-97.

[74]The claim that we can measure implicit bias, especially using Harvard's Implicit Association Test, is enormously controversial. For a lengthy summary of that test's failures, see Jesse Singal, "Psychology's Favorite Tool for Measuring Racism Isn't Up to the Job," *New York* (2017), available at: https://www.thecut.com/2017/01/psychologys-racism-measuring-tool-isnt-up-to-the-job.html?utm_source=pocket_mylist. Such criticisms do not contradict the enormous evidence for the existence of implicit bias. They do suggest that measuring such bias is difficult, and maybe even impossible. See the helpful comments in Keith Payne et al, "How to Think About 'Implicit Bias,'" (March 27, 2018), available at: https://www.scientificamerican.com/article/how-to-think-about-implicit-bias/.

awareness. John helps us see the deeper, darker reality: the infectious disease of racial and economic injustice is part of the devil's demonic power, corrupting both individuals and structures. That demonic power has been broken by Jesus, yet somehow continues to infect the still disordered loves of his disciples. Too often, Jesus' followers refuse to embrace the task of discipling these disordered desires. But dealing with them is part of what it means to purify ourselves as Jesus is pure (1 Jn 3:3). When Christians fail to do so, we not only fail to do battle with one outpost of Sin, Death, and the Devil in our world, we also end up partnering with and benefiting from our demonic enemies.[75]

But the good news John offers us is that Jesus has given us all that we need to repent of this partnership and embrace the journey of just discipleship. That journey is grounded in the explosive reality that Jesus has indeed come to destroy the works of the devil, liberate human lives, and transform his people into his own glorious image.

What might it look like to receive the *gift* and embrace the *task* of just discipleship in light of John's vision? John reframes all that we have said about just discipleship so far in this book by reminding us that the power to pursue moral discipleship is grounded in God's past, present, and future action. When Christians practice relocation, cry out for justice alongside the poor in prayer, seek the virtue of just wisdom, or imitate Jesus' sacrificial love by sharing with the economically impoverished, we do so as God's children, rescued from the evil one's hostile influence and empowered for the journey of becoming the just people of God. All our efforts flow out of and depend on God's past, present, and future grace to us in Jesus. We are merely growing by grace into the character that God has already given to us as his children.

More specifically, however, in a *kosmos* whose economic and racial systems have been so deeply distorted, I propose that we return to 1 John 3:17's warning about the dangers of having distorted eyes and hearts toward our siblings in need. "Whoever has the world's possessions, and sees their sibling who has need, and shuts up their heart from them, how can the love of God remain in them?" (AT). Easy words to say, but immensely difficult words to apply "in truth and deed" (1 Jn 3:18). After all, when those of us who are white and wealthy are exposed to the sufferings of our Black, brown, or poor brothers and sisters, how easy is it in a society like ours to look the other way! How easy it is for us to allow those biases we have acquired to cause us to "shut up our hearts,"

---

[75]Walker-Barnes, *Voices of My People*, 192; Tran, *Asian Americans*, 194.

endlessly offering defenses of the status quo or questioning the integrity of those who call our attention to our siblings' sufferings!

Might this dynamic explain, at least partially, the enormous gaps between the way white evangelical Christians like me tend to *see* the world when compared to Black Americans?[76] Consider the following findings from the Institute for Advanced Studies in Culture:

- 90% of all Black Americans *agree* that "our founding fathers were part of a racist and sexist culture that gave important roles to White men while harming minorities and women." 77% of white evangelicals *disagree.*[77]

- While 86% of Black people "regard racism as a very or extremely serious threat" to America's future, only about a third of white evangelical Protestants do,[78] with nearly the exact same responses given to the question of whether inequality and poverty are "very or extremely serious" threats.

- 91% of Black people *agree* that there is racial injustice in policing and law enforcement, while 83% of white evangelicals *reject* this claim.[79]

Crucially, white evangelicals' views on these matters make them outliers not only to most other Americans, but also to *other Black and brown evangelicals.* In other words, these different views of the world divide evangelicals otherwise united by belief along racial lines.[80]

As an evangelical by belief, I have no desire to vilify the movement of which I am a part. Describing the role that racism plays in our society is complicated, and rigorous debate about the role of racism in society is important and should not be shut down.[81] But behind each of these statistics lies a claim made by Black and brown brothers and sisters: we are hurting, we are suffering, the systems and structures of our society are broken. And

---

[76]The language of *evangelical* can be controversial, and casting aspersion on evangelicals is common. For the most part, I have tried to limit my references to evangelicals to sections of the book where I draw on research that uses the category "evangelical" as part of qualitative research.

[77]James Davison Hunter and Carl Desportes Bowman with Kyle Puetz, *Democracy in Dark Times: The 2020 IASC Survey of American Political Culture* (New York: Finstock & Tew Publishers, 2020), 58. A PDF is available at https://s3.amazonaws.com/iasc-prod/uploads/pdf/sapch.pdf.

[78]Hunter and Bowman, *Democracy in Dark Times,* 59-60.

[79]Hunter and Bowman, *Democracy in Dark Times,* 60.

[80]The dynamics of Christian nationalism explored in chapter 11 of this book surely drive some of these differences, but here I want to focus on another aspect.

[81]For an important attempt at Christian antiracism that offers a sustained argument with what he takes to be "antiracist orthodoxy," see Tran, *Asian Americans,* in its entirety.

behind each of these statistics lies a set of responses by many white evangelicals: it's not that bad, quit complaining, the system basically works. Is this not an example of white Christians seeing and hearing our brothers and sisters in need, and actively shutting up our hearts toward them? And if so, do we not need to hear John's devastating challenge: *How can the love of God remain in us?*

John makes clear that stirring up an open, loving heart toward our suffering siblings is one way we participate in the just discipleship to which we have been called. Having opened our hearts toward our suffering siblings, we can embrace a life imitating Jesus' self-sacrificial love empowered by Jesus' work in the world. The *joy* of discipleship is the discovery that Jesus has made it possible for us to begin to live the life for which he created us. Because justice—the faithful exercise of power—stands at the center of that God-given, God-empowered life, John invites us to receive the *gift* of just discipleship and embrace the *task* of just discipleship today.

In our efforts to do so, perhaps we may once again draw inspiration from that branch of the civil rights movement characterized by "militant reconciling love." For Martin Luther King Jr., Rosa Parks, James Lawson, and many of those protestors who kneeled on the steps of Second Presbyterian Church early one Palm Sunday, the civil rights movement represented a "struggle between an already completed divine event—the promise of deliverance signed and sealed on the Cross—and the promise's fulfillment in history—the divine event crashing onto the streets of" our world.[82] Like John, they understood the moral reality of the universe as ultimately "on the side of justice" because of the "great epic" of the cross that "split history into A.D. and B.C." That understanding empowered these nonviolent resisters to "suffer and not retaliate" in the course of nonviolent direct action.[83]

Like John, they recognized that God's world-altering actions in Jesus had opened the way for a life of discipleship oriented toward justice. Like John, they saw imitating Jesus as an important piece of that just discipleship. Both the theology of enemy love and the pragmatic tactics of nonviolent resistance were often framed as acts of imitation, as "[following] in the footsteps of

---

[82]Charles Marsh, "The Civil Rights Movement as Theological Drama—Interpretation and Application," *Modern Theology* 18, no. 2 (2002): 234.

[83]Martin Luther King Jr., "Non-Aggression Procedures to Interracial Harmony," Address Delivered at the American Baptist Assembly and American Home Mission Agencies Conference, July 23, 1956. Annotated transcript available at https://kinginstitute.stanford.edu/king-papers/documents/non-aggression-procedures-interracial-harmony-address-delivered-american.

Jesus."[84] Such imitation depended on and was itself an act of moral discipleship, part of the process of *becoming* militants of reconciling love. As James Lawson argued in 2019,[85] the task of overcoming "racism, sexism, militarism, and plantation capitalism" begins with ridding these evils from our own hearts.[86] Such a call resonates strongly with John's summons to purify ourselves as Jesus is pure, not least by practicing justice in imitation of the justice we see in Jesus' own life.

In his final public speech, Dr. King challenged his audience to embrace "a kind of dangerous unselfishness" modeled on Jesus' Good Samaritan story. To live such unselfishness, King argued, required his audience to stop asking what would happen to them if they stood with the sanitation workers in their strike, and start asking "If I do *not* stop to help the sanitation workers, what will happen to *them*?"[87]

King knew this practical summons could cost him his life. He was murdered the very next day. But in the final lines of his final public speech, he declared: "I'm not worried about anything; I'm not fearing any man. Mine eyes have seen the glory of the coming of the Lord!"[88] Standing within a world transformed by the death and resurrection of Jesus, empowered by God to imitate Jesus in his self-giving love in anticipation of God's final victory, and practically discipled and formed in the Black church, King gave testimony to the power of God's justice and love in action. Perhaps today, 1 John may yet continue to guide disciples following in his footsteps as we seek to *become* just disciples, for the glory of God and the good of our neighbors.

---

[84]James M. Lawson Jr., ed., *Nonviolence and Social Movements: The Teachings of Rev. James M. Lawson Jr.* (Los Angeles: UCLA Press, 2016), 37.

[85]Lawson, *Nonviolence and Social Movements*, 6.

[86]James M. Lawson, Jr., speech given at Clayborn Temple, April 5, 2019.

[87]Martin Luther King Jr., "Mountain Top Address" (1968). Available at https://www.afscme.org/about/history/mlk/mountaintop#:~:text=Dr.-,Martin%20Luther%20King%2C%20Jr.,day%20before%20he%20was%20assassinated.

[88]King, "Mountain Top Address."

PART 3

BECOMING A JUST PEOPLE

A (JUBILEE) CASE FOR
(ECCLESIAL) REPARATIONS?

IN MAY 1969, James Forman brought the case for reparations home to the church. Taking over the pulpit of Riverside Church to read aloud his Black Manifesto, Forman argued that white congregations had profited tremendously from the past and present exploitation of Black people.[1] Because of their role in America's racism, Forman demanded that white congregations acknowledge their guilt and pay 500 million dollars in reparations.[2] The Black Manifesto explained that these funds would pay for a variety of projects, including helping Black farmers retain and acquire land;[3] creating training centers, media and publishing companies; and establishing a fund "charged with producing more capital for the establishment of cooperative businesses."[4] These reparations payments would thus be used to address both economic disparity and what Forman saw as an oppressive imbalance of power in American life.

Forman was not the first advocate for reparations for Black people in the United States. Such advocacy goes at least as far back as the federal government's failure to give emancipated slaves the promised "forty acres and a mule."[5] Because of this failure, at the end of the Civil War

> four million newly liberated slaves found themselves with no bread to eat, no land to cultivate, no shelter to cover their heads . . . [they] were given abstract

---

[1]James Foreman, "The Black Manifesto," in *Black Theology: A Documentary History*, vol. 1: *1966–1979*, ed. James H. Cone and Gayraud S. Wilmore (Maryknoll, NY: Orbis Books, 1993), 30-31.

[2]Foreman, "Black Manifesto," 31-32.

[3]Foreman, "Black Manifesto," 31-32.

[4]Foreman, "Black Manifesto," 31-32.

[5]William Darity Jr. and Kirsten Mullen, *From Here to Equality: Reparations for Black Americans in the Twenty-First Century* (Chapel Hill: University of North Carolina Press, 2020), 9.

freedom expressed in luminous rhetoric. But in an agrarian economy [they were] given no land to make liberation concrete.[6]

Nor did white theft of Black wealth end in the nineteenth century. In some ways, then, the Black Manifesto was just the latest in a long history of Black Americans demanding compensation for the horrors of slavery and its aftermath.[7] Nevertheless, the Manifesto's demand for *ecclesial* reparations was somewhat unique in claiming that the church itself should pay reparations for its role in "aiding and abetting" the "exploitation of colored peoples around the world."[8]

Black Christians who endorsed the Manifesto highlighted this aspect.[9] "The white churches and synagogues," the National Council of Black Churchmen wrote in their endorsement, "undeniably have been the *moral cement of the structure of racism in this nation, and the vast majority of them continue to play that role today.*"[10] Gayraud Wilmore wrote, "The White religious establishment cannot evade the fact of its special burden of guilt. That is the message of the Black Manifesto."[11] Indeed, Wilmore interpreted the Manifesto's demand for an acknowledgment of injustice in terms of the Christian doctrine of repentance.[12]

Black Christians who supported the Manifesto, in other words, agreed with Forman that white churches had especially good reasons for paying reparations. On the one hand, they had played a unique role in the oppression of Black people. On the other hand, as Wilmore suggested, white Christians had uniquely *theological* reasons for practicing reparations.

While churches largely ignored or rejected the Manifesto's demands,[13] ongoing advocacy for reparations confronts Christians today with a question: *Do* churches have unique reasons for supporting reparations for Black Americans? If so, what does that mean for just discipleship?

In part two of this book, we explored practices and pedagogies oriented toward acquiring just character. In part three, we consider how the *politics* of the

---

[6]Martin Luther King Jr., *Where Do We Go from Here?* (Boston: Beacon Press, 2010), 84.

[7]See the survey in Darity and Mullen, *Here to Equality*, 9-14.

[8]Foreman, "Black Manifesto," 31.

[9]See James F. Findlay, Jr., *Church People in the Struggle: The National Council of Churches and the Black Freedom Movement, 1950-1870* (New York, NY: Oxford University Press, 1997), 207.

[10]Quoted in Findlay, *Church People*, 207-8. Emphasis added.

[11]Gayraud, S. Wilmore, "A Black Churchman's Response to the Black Manifesto," in *Black Theology*, 96.

[12]Wilmore, "Black Churchman's Response," 98, emphasis added.

[13]See Jennifer Harvey, *Dear White Christians: For Those Still Longing for Racial Reconciliation* (Grand Rapids, MI: Eerdmans, 2014), 121-40.

community might facilitate just discipleship. When I use the language of politics in part three, I am referring to the way the community of faith organizes and arranges its common life, rather than to how Christians engage local and national politics. In other words, what sorts of corporate structures does Scripture call the people of God to embrace? And how do these structures shape the life of the whole people for the work of justice? In this chapter and the next, we will explore the communal politics of the people of God in light of the claim that churches have especially good reasons for embracing reparations.

DO CHRISTIANS HAVE GOOD REASONS TO EMBRACE REPARATIONS?

Most people agree that if you take something from someone, you ought to give it back. But Christian communities have particularly good reasons for embracing the concept. "Thou shalt not steal" is one of the Ten Commandments, a commandment repeatedly reaffirmed in the New Testament.[14] The Torah requires those who *do* steal to restore what was stolen, even if they must become a debt slave to do so (Ex 22:1-3).

Leviticus 6:1-7 [5:20-26] outlines a process of reparation for those who have stolen something. A person recognizes that they have done wrong, restores what was taken and adds a fifth to it, offers a sacrificial "guilt offering," and finally, at the end of this process, experiences atonement and forgiveness before God.[15] Whatever else we might wish to say, the Bible is clear: "If you steal something, you have to give it back."[16]

These texts confront us with a two-part, deeply disturbing reality:

1. *White American Christians and churches flagrantly, repeatedly, and despicably broke God's commandment by stealing Black bodies through the slave trade and Black land throughout the Jim Crow era.* In 1855, "ministers of the gospel and members of Protestant churches owned" an estimated "total of 660,563 slaves whose total market value amounted to" 8 billion dollars.[17] Nor was this rampant theft committed only by individual Christians. Churches and seminaries frequently owned slaves.[18] In the Jim Crow era, Christians actively participated in the

---

[14]See Mk 10:19; Lk 18:20; Rom 13:9; Eph 4:28.

[15]See the helpful discussion in Duke L. Kwon and Greg Thompson, *Reparations: A Christian Call for Repentance and Repair* (Grand Rapids, MI: Brazos, 2021), 136-43.

[16]Kwon and Thompson, *Reparations*, 143.

[17]Kwon and Thompson, *Reparations*, 117.

[18]Kwon and Thompson, *Reparations*, 123.

theft of Black land. Most horrifyingly of all, white Americans often combined breaking the command against theft with the breaking of another commandment: "Thou shalt not murder." The "lynching trail was a trail of stolen Black land."[19]

2. *The white American Christians and churches who committed these thefts rarely made any serious attempt to give back what they had stolen.* By and large, in violation of the kind of process outlined in Leviticus, they died with their sins of stealing unconfessed and unrepaired.

But this is where, for many Christians, the case for reparations becomes complicated. All agree that the Bible teaches that a thief should return what they have stolen, perhaps even with interest. Most white American Christians, however, staunchly oppose the idea that later generations ought to try to restore what was stolen or repair the damage that was done through reparations offered to the *descendants* of those whose labor and land was stolen.

Against this backdrop, I want to explore the Black Manifesto's case for ecclesial reparations in dialogue with one biblical institution that potentially addresses the question of restoration and repair *across* generations: Leviticus 25's year of Jubilee.[20] To grapple fully with the depth and richness of the Jubilee, we need to first understand how it fits within the broader context of Leviticus.

THE YEAR OF JUBILEE AND THE POLITICS OF HOLINESS IN LEVITICUS

The vision of Leviticus is that the Holy One might "walk among" his chosen people and be their God (Lev 26:12).[21] Such language likely alludes to God's "walking with the [first] couple in the Garden of Eden."[22] Thus Leviticus

---

[19]William Darity Jr. and Dania Frank, "The Economics of Reparations," *American Economic Review* 93, no. 2 (2003): 327.

[20]I am not claiming that the Old Testament's agrarian, theocratic politics offers a blueprint for contemporary churches or nations, however. There are serious hermeneutical questions about how the church receives Old Testament law in general, and there are equally difficult interpretive questions concerning how economic practices crafted in an agrarian economy relate to economic practices in our very different economic context. In what follows, I will argue that there are resonances between the Jubilee and the Black Manifesto, and then consider what those resonances might mean for us today.

[21]The phrase "politics of holiness" in the heading comes from Nathan Willowby, "Sanctification as Virtue and Mission: The Politics of Holiness" (PhD diss., Marquette University, 2016).

[22]Christopher J. H. Wright, *Old Testament Ethics for the People of God* (Downers Grove, IL: IVP Academic, 2011), 185.

imagines Israel's life with Yahweh in the Promised Land as a partial return to Eden, a recapitulation of God's original intention to dwell with humanity.

The "holiness" (qadosh) of this God who desires to dwell among his people gestures most fundamentally toward Yahweh's own life and being, his overwhelming purity and goodness, the mysterious otherness of God that both attracts and threatens to overwhelm us.[23] The obvious problem facing Leviticus is how such a holy God can dwell in the midst of a sinful people without destroying them or being driven away by them.[24] The answer is that God's people must *become* holy:

> For I am Yahweh your God, and you will make yourselves holy (hitqaddishtem), and you will be holy (qedoshim), because I am holy (qadosh). (Lev 11:44 AT)

The way of life Leviticus offers its readers is a comprehensive vision of "how Israel might organize itself as a community capable of hosting in its midst the radical holiness of God."[25] Israel will only become capable of such hospitality when they submit every aspect of their lives to God, conforming their behavior to his, allowing themselves to be made holy by Yahweh's holiness.

Against this background, the year of Jubilee prescribes a central plank in what we might call the politics of holiness,[26] a central political practice whereby God's holy presence is "made material within the land and people."[27] This political institution has deep roots in the Torah's overall social, economic, and theological vision. When Yahweh brings Israel into the land, he requires them to divide up the land by household (see Num 33:54). By equitably distributing these fundamental socioeconomic assets within Israel's agrarian economy, Yahweh ensured that each household could "sit under their own vines and fig trees" (Mic 4:4). Whereas ancient kings often held the title to all or most of the land in their communities, in Israel, every family could claim a socioeconomic place to stand and portion to steward.

Why? Because from the very beginning God had called *all humanity* to the task of being *royal priestly family members*. Yahweh's intention for Israel is that

---

[23]See Rudolf Otto, *Idea of the Holy: An Inquiry into the Non-Rational Factor in the Idea of the Divine and Its Relation to the Rational*, 2nd ed., trans. John W. Harvey (New York: Oxford University Press, 1950), 1-24.

[24]See Jacob Milgrom, *Leviticus: A Book of Ritual and Ethics* (Minneapolis: Fortress, 2004), 32.

[25]Ellen F. Davis, *Opening Israel's Scriptures* (New York: Oxford University Press, 2019), 72.

[26]On the relationship between Leviticus and politics, see Gordon McConville, "'Fellow Citizens': Israel and Humanity in Leviticus," in *Reading the Law: Studies in Honour of Gordon J. Wenham*, ed. J. G. McConville and Karl Moller (New York: T&T Clark, 2007), 11-14.

[27]Willowby, "Sanctification as Virtue and Mission," 213.

their life in the Promised Land would serve as a sort of recapitulation of God's purposes for creation and all humanity. In his just arrangement of the Promised Land, Yahweh gives every household a place in the land, and invites them to practice justice by exercising responsible stewardship over it in line with their identity as his image bearers.

Against this background, Leviticus 25:8-55 outlines the socioeconomic policies necessary to maintain this way of life, allowing Israel to become a holy people who live alongside their holy God. By clarifying crucial aspects of how the Israelites will faithfully exercise power over the land and within the community, the year of Jubilee represents the very "epitome of 'righteousness and justice' in Israel."[28]

Leviticus 25:8-13 introduces the year of Jubilee as the fiftieth year in Israel's sacred calendar. On the tenth day of the seventh month, the people blow a trumpet throughout the land, and "make holy" the fiftieth year by proclaiming a "release" (*deror*). Any family that had lost their land in the previous fifty years would return to the ancestral "farm" (*akhuzzah*) allotted to them as their portion in the land (Lev 25:10). As in sabbatical years, the Jubilee includes a break from all organized agricultural activity. Once again, all Israel would glean the natural growth of their fields for food (Lev 25:12).

The "four-fold repetition of the phrase 'if your brother becomes poor'" in the rest of the chapter highlights the way the Jubilee legislation provided justice and mercy for the impoverished.[29] The text outlines how the politics of the jubilary return to one's ancestral land would function within the broader economy of Israel and alongside other economic safety nets already in place. For instance, Leviticus 25:14-16 make clear that the Jubilee makes the permanent sale of ancestral land impossible. The Israelites may, however, lease land from one another, essentially buying the harvest of a certain number of years. Leviticus 25:24-55, on the other hand, describes how another economic safety net, the redemption of people and property by a kinsperson, ought to operate between Jubilee years.

To explain the redemption process, the text describes a member of the community involved in a three-stage descent into poverty. In the first stage, they sell a portion of their land. In the second, they lose the title to their land

---

[28]Moshe Weinfeld, *Social Justice in Ancient Israel and in the Ancient Near East* (Minneapolis: Fortress, 2000), 9.

[29]Robin J. DeWitt Knauth, "The Jubilee Transformation: From Social Welfare to Hope of Restoration to Eschatological Salvation" (PhD diss., Harvard Divinity School, 2004), 46.

in its entirety, before finally being forced to sell themselves and their family into debt servitude in the third stage.[30] The text provides guidance for the applicable systems of economic support that should operate in relation to each stage of this descent, as well as for how the Jubilee year is to be integrated with these systems of support.

The power of this jubilary politics to shape the community for justice can be seen more clearly once we recognize that Leviticus takes economic practices that Israel would have been aware of, and then adapts them in substantial, politically potent ways (see fig. 8.1).[31]Examining this dynamic in some detail allows us to glimpse just how countercultural the Jubilee's social and theological vision truly is.

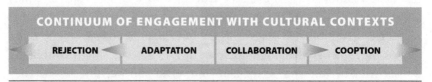

Figure 8.1. Continuum of engagement with cultural contexts

The Jubilee adaptation of ancient royal debt forgiveness edicts. For thousands of years in the ancient Near East, kings announced occasional edicts that forgave debts, liberated slaves, and allowed families to return to lost lands.[32] These edicts allowed newly ascendant kings to gain political power over their rivals by gaining favor from the people.[33] At times, they also freed up labor for religious purposes, since sometimes slaves were liberated from their former masters in order to serve in the temple system.[34]

These edicts were sporadic, and contracts could explicitly state that the land sold or loans extended were *not* to be forgiven in the event of such an

---

[30]See Jacob Milgrom, *Leviticus 23–27*, AB (New Haven, CT: Yale University Press, 2001), 2190-237; David Baker, *Tight Fists or Open Hands? Wealth and Poverty in Old Testament Law* (Grand Rapids, MI: Eerdmans, 2009), 80; Wright, *Old Testament Ethics*, 203-5.

[31]See Joshua Berman, *Created Equal: How the Bible Broke with Ancient Political Thought* (New York, NY: Oxford University Press, 2011), 83.

[32]These are referred to as *andurarum* and *misarum* edicts. See Weinfeld, *Social Justice*, 1-17, 75-93; Milgrom, *Leviticus 23–27*, 2167-69; Baker, *Tight Fists*, 77-86. See also "The Edict of Ammisadqua" (*ANET*, 526-8) and Finkelstein's discussion of the document (J. J. Finkelstein, "Ammisaduqa's Edict and the Babylonian 'Law Codes," *Journal of Cuneiform Studies* 15, no. 3 [1961]: 91-103) for a very thorough example of such an edict.

[33]Weinfeld, *Social Justice*, 10; Raymond Westbrook, *Law from the Tigris to the Tiber: The Writings of Raymond Westbrook*, ed. F. Rachel Magdalene and Bruce Wells (Winona Lake, IN: Eisenbrauns, 2009), 157.

[34]See Milgrom, *Leviticus 23–27*, 2187, 2227; Weinfeld, *Social Justice*, 16.

edict.[35] Because of this, such legislation provided for occasional economic rearrangement and relief *without* affecting the basic economic system in operation between royal decrees.

In contrast to this, the Jubilee is announced and enacted by Yahweh, the divine king who dwells amid his people.[36] Yahweh fixes the Jubilee in time,[37] explicitly rules out the possibility of exceptions,[38] and demands that the Jubilee become the basis for all transactions concerning land (Lev 25:15-16).

The Jubilee adaptation of ancient Near Eastern redemption practices. Second, Leviticus 25 integrates the Jubilee with the practice of land redemption, thus seriously altering that practice. The right of redemption, practiced widely in the ancient world and affirmed in Leviticus 25:24-28, ensured that land a family had lost could be redeemed by a close kinsperson, thus keeping that land within the clan or tribe. The Jubilee, however, ensures that redeemed land ultimately returns to *the individual household*. Without the Jubilee, the right of redemption would easily lead to some families within the clan or tribe becoming a permanently powerful and wealthy class, as they would have benefited from having the first right to purchase any land sold within the clan.[39] In contrast, the Jubilee ensures that no individual household is ever permanently disenfranchised from their family farm.

The Jubilee rejection of ancient Near Eastern lending and debt slavery. Finally, in the ancient Near East, high interest rates on loans often ensured that the borrower would be unable to repay. In fact, one primary economic incentive for making loans was for the lender to gain the collateral on the loan when the borrower inevitably defaulted.[40] Such collateral could include the labor of the borrower (or a member of the borrower's household) through debt slavery.

The Jubilee adaptation of these practices amounts essentially to their rejection. If a family has mortgaged some of their land and still cannot provide

---

[35]Roland Boer, *The Sacred Economy of Ancient Israel*, Library of Ancient Israel (Louisville, KY: Westminster John Knox, 2015), 160; Rudolph Otto, "The Study of Law and Ethics in the Hebrew Bible/Old Testament" in *Hebrew Bible/Old Testament: The History of Its Interpretation*, III/2: *The Twentieth Century*, ed. Magne Saebo (Gottingen: Vandenhoeck & Ruprecht, 2015), 605.

[36]See Weinfeld, *Social Justice*, 10.

[37]Weinfeld, *Social Justice*, 10; Milgrom, *Leviticus 23–27*, 2163.

[38]Milgrom, *Leviticus 23–27*, 2169. The exceptions that prove the rule relate to houses in cities and Levitical lands, both of which are exempted for reasons in accord with the Jubilee's underlying intentions.

[39]Milgrom, *Leviticus 23–27*, 2192-93; Wright, *Old Testament Ethics*, 205; Baruch A. Levine, *Leviticus*, JPS (Philadelphia, PA: JPS, 1989), 168.

[40]See Boer, *Sacred Economy*, 159-60.

for themselves, their Israelite brothers are to lend the family money or food without interest (Lev 25:35-38). Even more radically, if they cannot repay these loans, the defaulting household does indeed enter the household of the lender, but as a "hired hand" or "sojourner," rather than as a debt slave.[41] They cannot be treated harshly or sold at a slave market;[42] instead, they must be treated like paid employees.[43]

This functionally abolishes Israelite debt slavery, transforming that institution into "work for hire" for the destitute.[44] Of course, the Jubilee legislation also requires that the entire household be released in the fiftieth year, allowing them to return to the family farms that offered the best path to economic flourishing in Israel's agricultural economy.

THE SOCIAL AND THEOLOGICAL VISION OF THE JUBILEE

Leviticus 25 offers a breathtaking and innovative socioeconomic and theological vision. Broadly speaking, the Torah envisions an economy in which every family is given a plot in the Promised Land. Families would use these

---

[41]On the relationship between this text and Exodus 21:1-11 see John Sietze Bergsma, *The Jubilee from Leviticus to Qumran: Its Origin, Development, and Interpretation in the Hebrew Scriptures, Second Temple Literature, and Qumran Texts* (Leiden: Brill, 2007), 47-48.

[42]Enrique Nardoni, *Rise Up, O Judge: A Study of Justice in the Biblical World*, trans. Sean Charles Martin (Grand Rapids, MI: Baker Academic, 2001), 87. The language of harsh treatment intentionally echoes Israel's experience of harsh treatment in Egypt. See Ex 1:13-14; Jon D. Levenson, *The Hebrew Bible, the Old Testament, and Historical Criticism: Jews and Christians in Biblical Studies* (Lousiville, KY: Westminster John Knox, 1993), 150.

[43]Leviticus 25 does not, however, prohibit permanent slavery for foreigners (Lev 25:44-46). Fully exploring this difficult dynamic lies outside the scope of the present chapter. However, it ought to be remembered that often law, as a genre, serves to limit pervasive evil rather than eliminate it. See Gordon Wenham, *Story as Torah: Reading the Old Testament Ethically* (Edinburgh: T&T Clark, 2000), 80. In the case of Leviticus 25:44-46, Baker notes that "this law is not designed to encourage" such slavery, but "rather to limit it to those who are outside the covenant community" (Baker, *Tight Fists*, 118). Membership in that covenant community was always porous, as is clear in Israel's laws and stories. Furthermore, whatever Leviticus 25:44-46 permits stands under Leviticus 19:33's command: "When an alien resides with you in your land, you shall not oppress the alien. The alien who resides with you shall be to you as the citizen among you; you shall love the alien as yourself, for you were aliens in the land of Egypt: I am the LORD your God" (Lev 19:33-34). Matt Lynch suggested this admonition not to act like Egyptians is all the more potent given that Pharaoh's harsh oppression in Egypt appears to be alluded to in Leviticus 25:44-46 through the use of the word *prk* here and in the description of Pharaoh's oppression of the Israelites in Exodus (personal communication). Any Israelite who thought Leviticus 25:44-46 gave them license to oppress or offer harsh treatment to non-Israelite slaves would thus be corrected by Leviticus 19:33. Finally, as we will see, the Jubilee trajectory in Ezekiel leads to ever-greater inclusion and justice for outsiders.

[44]Milgrom, *Leviticus 23–27*, 2213.

plots to provide for themselves and care for their neighbors. The politics of
the Jubilee aims to ensure that no family ever permanently loses their family
plot. This is what justice looks like within Leviticus's politics of holiness, not
least because by arranging themselves in this way, Israel would reflect Yahweh's
original purposes for all of humanity to play a royal role in co-ruling his
good world.

It is important to recognize that the Jubilee does not eliminate the regular
functions of an agricultural economy, including some buying, selling, local
trade, and the pursuit of material abundance.[45] Because of this, the legislation
would eliminate neither temporary poverty for some, nor economic growth
for others. Nor does the Jubilee eliminate incentives for economic effort, as is
often suggested. On the one hand, when a kinsperson redeemed their poor
neighbor's land, they would gain the benefit of that land until the Jubilee.[46] On
the other hand, given the fifty-year time horizon, many household heads who
lost their land would die before their children regained the family farm.

What the Jubilee does seek to prevent is the emergence of a *multigenerational, permanently poor class*, in part by undermining the processes whereby
some households could seek to create a *multigenerational, permanently affluent class*.[47] Crucially, the Jubilee would allow families that had fallen into
destitution *for any reason whatsoever* to "resume their place of respect, power,
and dignity in the community."[48] By ensuring that no family could ever permanently lose the farm, the Jubilee legislation aims at a just, radically
countercultural economy based on a relatively equitable distribution of
economic assets.

But the Jubilee also aims at a certain kind of society, one in which economic legislation aimed at economic equity also protects the social *power* of
Israelite families. Unending acquisition of land and labor could have been one
major stop on the road from a village economy toward the emergence of
powerful tribal leaders and, eventually, a monarchy. The establishment of a
monarchy often included the creation of a subservient class on which the
monarch depended, as the prophet Samuel warned the people (1 Sam 8:11-18).
The Jubilee strikes at precisely this point. By eliminating the unending acquisition of *economic* power by any one group over and against the others, the
Jubilee interrupts the unending acquisition of *social* power by any one group

---

[45]Cf. Knauth, "Jubilee Transformation," 204.

[46]Milgrom, *Leviticus 23–27*, 2195.

[47]Cf. Berman, *Created Equal*, 88.

[48]Brueggemann, "Voices," 16.

over and against any of the others. The liberty that the Jubilee declares is political, economic, and social.[49]

The theological foundations of this vision cannot be overstated. Israel celebrates the Jubilee because Yahweh is the divine king who demands they do so. The politics of the Jubilee is one aspect of the politics of holiness inaugurated by the Holy One who dwells in Israel's midst. Thus, when the Israelites announce the Jubilee year, they "make the fiftieth year holy" by implementing the economic policies of their divine king (Lev 25:10). Such policies would allow Israel to give the world a glimpse of God's just purposes for the entire human community and all of creation.

Leviticus 25 repeatedly draws attention to the theological nature of this decidedly political practice. The sabbatical year *belongs* to Yahweh (Lev 25:2, 4). Yahweh has the right to announce the Jubilee because the land *belongs to him* (Lev 25:23). No Israelite family owns their farm; all are merely "tenants" or "sojourners" who work the land of the true King. Similarly, no Israelite can become a slave because, by liberating the Israelites, Yahweh had *enslaved them to himself.* "For they are *my slaves* who I brought out from the land of Egypt" (Lev 25:42 AT).

In the ancient world, the gods gave the *king* the land.[50] Citizens often had the right to what their land yielded, but the king retained the official title, and therefore "[controlled] the means of production."[51] In contrast, in Israel, the divine king bypasses any human ruler and takes each Israelite household as his tenants and servants. Overall human control and autonomy over the land is thereby reduced. But somewhat paradoxically,[52] because these laws do not recognize any human, centralized power as having right to the land, each *individual* household's power and responsibility becomes more important. Because no human being had any ultimate autonomy or absolute power over their land, every single householder gained much greater relative power in the community through their inalienable plot in the Promised Land.[53]

THE BLACK MANIFESTO AND LEVITICUS 25: SIMILARITIES

At this point, we can identify several important points of contact between the Black Manifesto's demand for ecclesial reparations and the politics of the

---

[49]Weinfeld, *Social Justice*, 15.
[50]See Milgrom, *Leviticus 23–27*, 2185; Wright, *Old Testament Ethics*, 89.
[51]Berman, *Created Equal*, 90.
[52]McConville, "Fellow Citizens," 29.
[53]Berman, *Created Equal*, 87.

Jubilee. These connections are not merely interesting from an academic perspective—they suggest the Jubilee might shape the way contemporary faith
communities respond to the case for reparations today.

To be clear, I am not claiming that these points of contact suggest that
Israel's theocratic, agrarian institution provides a prescriptive blueprint for
the church in twenty-first-century America! The Jubilee offers us less of a
political blueprint and more of a moral compass that reflects God's heart.[54]
Deciding how the Jubilee might speak to the church today will require us to
consider exactly how the Torah's economic teaching should shape the church's
contemporary practice. But the first step in this journey is to identify the deep
resonances between the socioeconomic vision of the Jubilee and the socioeconomic vision of the Black Manifesto.

For the Black Manifesto, justice demanded that the Black community receive economic assets to gain both economic standing and social power.
Leviticus 25's legislation directly addresses such concerns about imbalances
of power. Jubilary justice demands that lost economic and social power be
restored by allowing those who had lost family farms to return to their land.
Moreover, by taking the authority for jubilary politics out of the hands of a
king and placing it directly into the hands of Yahweh himself, Leviticus 25
seeks to prevent the formation of a political elite who can use the distribution
of land and practices of credit and debt to amass power for themselves.

There is also a deep connection between the Manifesto and the Jubilee in terms
of acknowledgment.[55] The Manifesto did not demand reparations based on a
generic appeal to the white church's charitable sensibilities. The Manifesto demanded reparations based on the specific claim that wealth had been stolen from
Black people by White people in identifiable ways. The Jubilee also depended on
just this sort of specific acknowledgment. Indeed, the politics of the Jubilee depended on the Israelite community being able to identify when portions of land
ultimately belonging to one family had fallen into the hands of another. While
Brueggemann's definition of justice as "[sorting] out what belongs to whom, and
[returning] it" is reductionistic, he is no doubt right that such specific returning
is central to the work of justice, and nowhere more than in the Jubilee.[56]

---

[54]My thanks to Danny Carroll for suggesting this metaphor.
[55]The idea that any reparations program consists of acknowledgment, redress, and closure comes
from William Darity, Jr. "Forty Acres and a Mule in the 21st Century," *Social Science Quarterly* 89,
no. 3 (2008), 656.
[56]Walter Brueggemann et al., *To Act Justly, Love Tenderly, Walk Humbly: An Agenda for Ministers*
(New York: Paulist Press, 1986), 5.

Does the Jubilee demand repentance? On the issue of acknowledgment, however, some might argue that we begin to see significant differences between the Manifesto and the Jubilee. The Manifesto declares that white churches have the Black community's wealth in their possession due to *theft*. By contrast, the Jubilee does not assume that a transfer of land from a struggling household to a more stable household is illegitimate. Indeed, a struggling household's ability to mortgage their land, receive loans, and even be absorbed into the lender's household as hired workers served as important aspects of Israel's safety net.

In other words, Leviticus 25 suggests that if Household A loses their land to Household B, that may be because Household B was a just, Job-like figure who had been willing to help Household A, rather than evidence that Household B had oppressed Household A. In the Jubilee, then, Household B's restoration of lost land to Household A is not an admission of *guilt*. From this perspective, the fact that the Jubilee is not associated with repentance could be a strong argument *against* a jubilary case for ecclesial reparations.

This is a crucial point; the Jubilee required lost land to be restored *regardless of how the land was lost*. Every jubilary transaction would address socioeconomic disparity, but perhaps many would not be acts of reparation in the sense that they were restoring what had been unjustly taken. But while the Jubilee does not assume that *every* act of land restoration implies guilt on the part of the more powerful party, I suggest it nevertheless envisions the Jubilee as including repentance and repair.

First, the text's repeated admonition that the people not "oppress" (Lev 25:14, 17) one another between Jubilee years makes clear that even supposedly charitable economic transactions could be corrupted. The text suggests oppression could occur through unfair calculations of land-lease prices (Lev 25:14, 17), lending to an impoverished Israelite at interest (Lev 25:36-37), or by treating impoverished Israelite households who had been absorbed into one's own household as slaves rather than as hired workers. The fact that the law prohibits these practices suggests that they were, in reality, widely practiced.[57]

Furthermore, the Old Testament is filled with commands not to steal land and stories that demonstrate land was nevertheless frequently stolen.[58] The Jubilee law does not focus on restoring land lost due to injustice, not least because Leviticus 6:1-7 [5:20-26] outlines the reparations required for those who have

---

[57]Bruce C. Birch, *Let Justice Roll Down* (Louisville, KY: Westminster John Knox, 1991), 182.
[58]See 1 Kings 21:21-26; Ezek 45:8-9; Prov 22:28, 23:10; Deut 19:14, 27:17; Job 24:2.

committed theft.[59] But Israelites with a long history of land-related oppression and exploitation would have known that one of the primary ways land changed hands would be through injustice. They would have known that those who steal land do not always practice the reparation required by Leviticus 6:1-7 [5:20-26]. They would therefore have recognized that Leviticus 25's fixed economic "reset" would, in some cases at least, address land lost due to economic injustices that had not been repented of or repaired at the time of their occurrence.

Second, and of more central theological importance, the fact that the Jubilee year is announced on the Day of Atonement further connects the Jubilee with repentance. On the Day of Atonement, the high priest entered the most holy place and sprinkled the blood of the sacrifices on the atonement cover of the ark of the covenant. The purpose of this unique offering was to purge the holiest place from the impurity, transgressions, and sins of the people so that the tabernacle, the special site of Yahweh's presence, would abide amid the Israelites despite their impurity (Lev 16:16). The Day of Atonement also included the ritual of the scapegoat, when the priest confessed the entire community's sins over the head of a live goat, and then sent that guilt-laden goat into the wilderness. The ritual symbolically purged the community of their transgressions.[60]

But why would this annual Day of Atonement be necessary, given that Leviticus 1–7 already offers guidance for offering sacrifices throughout the year? The text suggests several reasons. For instance, the sacrifices described in Leviticus 4–5 focus on offerings of atonement for "unintentional sin."[61] However we interpret the idea of unintentional sin, it is clear that the category does not cover all transgressions! All year long, sins committed openly and defiantly have infected the holiest place and have gone, likely as not, unaddressed within the community.[62] The Day of Atonement is Yahweh's ritual strategy for providing an annual grand purgation of sin, ensuring that Israel can have a fresh start in their life with God. It is an essential practice whereby this perpetually unholy people can "host the radical holiness of God."[63] And through the fasting associated with this ritual, every single Israelite participates in this practice of repentance and forgiveness.

---

[59]For a discussion of this text in relation to reparations, see Kwon and Thompson, *Reparations*, 139-43.
[60]Levine, *Leviticus*, 103.
[61]The sacrifices for apparently intentional sin against one's neighbors in Leviticus 6:1-7 [5:20-26] are the exceptions.
[62]Milgrom, *Leviticus*, 162.
[63]Davis, *Opening Israel's Scriptures*, 64.

This helps explain why the year of Jubilee would be announced on the Day of Atonement. On the day that Yahweh forgives his people's sins, his people forgive one another their debts. At the same time, just as the Day of Atonement provided a *general purgation for sin* that supplemented and augmented the more specific offerings of purgation for unintentional, confessed sin, so the year of Jubilee provided a *general purgation for economic brokenness and sin* that supplemented and augmented both the specific demands for restitution for wrongdoing and the more ad hoc provisions of other social welfare legislation.[64] "Thus the fiftieth year is assigned the task of atoning for all previous violations and begins a new cycle."[65]

A third association of the Jubilee with repentance occurs in Leviticus 26's outline of blessings for Israel if they obey the law and curses for them if they reject it (Lev 26:1-46).[66] The final curse for disobedience is exile. Leviticus 26:34-35 specifically mentions Israel's failure to practice the sabbatical years, of which the Jubilee was a part, as one reason Israel might be cast out of the Promised Land.[67]

Even if Israel experiences the exile, though, Leviticus 26:40-43 nevertheless provides them with a glimmer of hope. Yahweh will remember his covenant and their land *if*

> they *confess* their iniquity and the iniquity of their fathers in their treachery which they committed against me, and also in walking contrary to me, and . . . if their uncircumcised heart is *humbled* and they *make restitution for* [ratsah] their iniquity. (Lev 26:40 AT)[68]

The solution to Israel's rejection of Yahweh's covenant law, and especially the sabbatical and jubilary legislation that the text uses as a shorthand for that law, includes both *repentance* and *restitution*.

Moreover, what Yahweh demands that they repent of, and make restitution for, is both their own iniquity *and* the iniquities of their fathers (Lev 26:40). This allusion to the idea of corporate or collective responsibility across time suggests that the Israelites' failures included the failure to repent of and make restitution for *the failures of previous generations*.

---

[64]This point is made forcefully and thoroughly in Robert S. Kawashima, "The Jubilee Year and the Return of Cosmic Purity," *CBQ* 65, no. 3 (2003): 371-89.

[65]Yairah Amit, "The Jubilee Law—An Attempt at Instituting Social Justice," in *Justice and Righteousness: Biblical Themes and Their Influence*, ed. H. G. Reventlow and Y. Hoffman (Sheffield: Sheffield Academic, 1992), 56, emphasis added.

[66]On the close literary connection between Leviticus 25 and 26, see Bergsma, *Jubilee*, 82-83.

[67]See Weinfeld, *Social Justice*, 178.

[68]For an argument for this translation of *ratsah*, see Milgrom, *Leviticus*, 323

No doubt such an idea strikes many of us as deeply problematic, and a thorough exploration of the notion lies outside the scope of this chapter.[69] For our purposes, however, it is interesting to note that, under at least some circumstances, repairing the sins of the previous generation is what the Jubilee was all about.

Consider: the average life expectancy of an ancient Israelite male household head was probably somewhat less than forty years.[70] At least in the "case of a three-generation household," the household head would be well into adulthood when they took over decision-making authority.[71] If a household head cheated their neighbor out of their land, it must have often been the case that the following generation would inherit this unjustly acquired land before the next Jubilee came. Given the deceptiveness of oppressive economic practices, it might even be the case that the inheritor of this taken land was not fully aware of the details of its unjust acquisition. Regardless, what the Jubilee requires in this scenario is precisely what Leviticus 26:40 demands: the children *confess* and *make restitution* for the sins of their fathers by restoring the land acquired in their father's generation to the descendants of the family that lost it.[72]

The Old Testament's complex view of individual and corporate guilt and repentance does not suggest that later generations are guilty of their ancestors' sins in the same way they're guilty of their own. The fact that both "their sins" and "the sins of their fathers" are listed in the same breath may suggest that these are theologically related but distinguishable categories. Boda, for instance, speaks of one generation's "solidarity" with the sins of their ancestors.[73] Thinking specifically of the Jubilee, then, people who stole land in the prior generation might be thought of as the original *perpetrators* of economic injustice. However, if later generations ignore the year of Jubilee, they become morally culpable as *perpetuators* of that earlier sin. Indeed, the Jubilee identifies the moment when any *perpetuation* of land loss becomes an unjust act of *perpetration* in its own right. From the perspective of Leviticus, to continually refuse to repair our ancestors' sins is to make them our own.

---

[69]For examples of corporate guilt, see the prayers of repentance in Nehemiah 1:6 and Daniel 9:1-20. For scholarly discussions see Joel S. Kaminsky, *Corporate Responsibility in the Hebrew Bible* (New York: T&T Clark, 1995), 89-94; Milgrom, *Leviticus*, 15, 32; Mark J. Boda, *"Return to Me:" A Biblical Theology of Repentance*, NSBT 35 (Downers Grove, IL: IVP Academic, 2015), 154-59.

[70]See Philip J. King and Lawrence E. Stager, *Life in Biblical Israel*, Library of Ancient Israel (Louisville, KY: 2002), 37.

[71]King and Stager, *Life in Biblical Israel*, 37

[72]Similarly, Numbers 5:8 implies that restitution should be made to a person's next-of-kin if they are deceased. See Kwon and Thompson, *Reparations*, 140-41.

[73]Boda, *Return to Me*, 155.

Again, the Jubilee would have also required faithful, just, wise Israelites to restore land that they had acquired through their own hard work to families that had lost it, even if those families lost it through natural disaster or gross mismanagement. While the text thus calls the people of God to make socio-economic repair central to their overall ethic, participation in the Jubilee does not provide an analogy to the Manifesto's demand for repentance and repair in every jubilary transaction. However, based on the evidence we have explored, the Jubilee institution as a whole *does* provide a powerful analogy to that demand. Indeed, the fact that the Jubilee would in some circumstances require one generation to restore land wrongfully acquired by the *previous* generation to the descendants of the generation that lost it provides a striking example of confession and reparation offered in light of corporate or historic sin.

This dynamic strikes at the heart of one of the strongest arguments against reparations: that while Black slave families deserved reparations from the white families that enslaved them, it is inappropriate to argue for either repentance or reparation from their white descendants. "You cannot repent of a sin you didn't commit," so the argument goes, and without repentance there is no demand for reparation. As Senator Mitch McConnell once said, "I don't think reparations for something 150 years ago for whom none of us currently living are responsible is a good idea."[74]

Against this protest, Leviticus suggests that future generations may well inherit the responsibility for repenting of and repairing the injustices of their forefathers by returning wealth to the descendants of those from whom such wealth was taken. Indeed, precisely such transgenerational repair is required if Israel is to "host in its midst the radical holiness of Yahweh."[75]

THE BLACK MANIFESTO AND LEVITICUS 25: DIFFERENCES

While there are deep resonances between the Jubilee and the Manifesto, we can also identify several significant differences. First, as presented in the canon, the Jubilee *assumes* that Israel *is* and *will remain* a classless society.[76] Each family among God's people is about to inherit a relatively equitable

---

[74]Ted Barrett, "McConnell Opposes Paying Reparations: 'None of Us Currently Living Are Responsible' for Slavery," CNN, June 19, 2019, www.cnn.com/2019/06/18/politics/mitch-mcconnell -opposes-reparations-slavery/index.html.

[75]Davis, *Opening Israel's Scriptures*, 64.

[76]See Walter J. Houston, *Contending for Justice: Ideologies and Theologies of Social Justice in the Old Testament* (New York: T&T Clark, 2006), 196-99.

portion in the Promised Land that will allow them to participate in the economy; the Jubilee is designed to *prevent* the emergence of a class society by ensuring that each family keeps those portions. Because of this, Leviticus subtly implies that any reader of the text might be on either side of a jubilary transaction. For instance, Leviticus 25:14 introduces the section regulating land leasing: "And if you sell anything to your neighbor or buy from the hand of your neighbor" (Lev 25:14 AT). This form of address implies that any hearer could, down the road, be in the position of *possessing their neighbor's land* and needing to give it back, or in the position of having *lost their land to their neighbor* and needing to be allowed to return to it.

By contrast, justice talk elsewhere in Scripture and in our world today often addresses an affluent or powerful class and calls that class to act on behalf of another impoverished or oppressed class. When food stamps are debated in Congress, for instance, we do not expect that the representatives debating the matter might themselves need such social welfare programs. By and large, congressional representatives are not members of the class that depends on food stamps.[77]

Because the Jubilee assumes a community without class, it presents a policy designed to be embraced by all, not least because it could be a benefit to *anyone* who suffered through tragedy or injustice.[78] By contrast, the Manifesto makes its demands in light of America's racial class system. Forman and his supporters stood amid the rubble of hundreds of years of *anti*-jubilary politics, and as such, their demands are made strongly on behalf of one group over and against another. While the Jubilee imagines a unified, classless community living as neighbors, the Manifesto addresses a society dominated by an unjust racial class system.[79]

---

[77]Even if they have been members of this class in the past, their ability to win a seat in Congress makes it unlikely that they would fall back into the class that does depend on food stamps.

[78]Nobuyoshi Kiuchi, *Leviticus*, AOTC (Downers Grove, IL: InterVarsity Press, 2007), 451.

[79]In the prologue to the Manifesto, Forman offered a "rather straightforward Marxist analysis" (Findlay, *Church People*, 201), including the claim that Black people ought to assume "total control" over economic life, including "by use of force and power of the gun" ("Black Manifesto," 27-30). Forman maintained that Black leadership would restructure society for the good of all. This obviously contributed to the white church's rejection of the Manifesto, and certainly the church has very good reasons for rejecting aspects of the underlying worldview of the document. It's worth noting, however, that Black Christian supporters called the white church to focus on the *substance* of the body of the Manifesto, even if they continued to disagree with Forman's "politics and tactics" in the prologue (Wilmore, "Black Churchman's Response," 96). Regardless, my goal in engaging with the Manifesto is to raise the question whether there are good theological reasons for thinking that the church ought to embrace a program of reparations.

Second, Forman demanded reparations from the church because Christians were culprits in Black oppression. By contrast, while jubilary politics certainly required Israelite households to repent and repair economic injustices when they occurred, the primary ground of the Jubilee is the community's identity as a holy people called to a vocation of holiness by the Holy One in their midst.

This must be stated as clearly as possible: the Jubilee is theological all the way down. If we try to preserve the economics while discarding the theology, we do violence to the institution. The economics of the Jubilee are tied directly to the theological claim that both *land* and *people* belong fundamentally to Yahweh, that the Israelites are Yahweh's tenants indentured on Yahweh's land. To unjustly deprive an Israelite household of their land was also and at the same time to unjustly deprive Yahweh of the service that the deprived household owed to him as his subjects. Given that Yahweh's way with Israel offered the world a glimpse of his intentions for all of creation, the theological heart of the Jubilee does not reduce its potential to speak to God's vision of society more generally. But it does remind us that the Bible's vision for human society and economy is always a robustly and intrinsically theological one.

Moreover, the text makes clear that it is Yahweh's *promises* that make the Jubilee possible. Israel can only leave the land fallow or lend freely without interest because Yahweh promises to actively reward his people for their obedience (Lev 25:20-22). These theological foundations for jubilary politics stand in stark contrast to the Manifesto's vision of a self-determining, revolutionary movement.

Third, and less obviously, Leviticus highlights the need for *moral* formation for the people to *become* the kind of just community capable of practicing the Jubilee. The fact that the Manifesto lacks the Jubilee's emphasis on formation is not necessarily a weakness, since it was presumably the white church's job to identify forms of discipleship that would confront the church's complicity with white supremacy. For our purposes, however, it is well worth exploring Leviticus's strategy of just discipleship. Indeed, identifying the Jubilee's distinctive strategies of moral formation will help the church consider *how* to respond to the case for reparations today.

Just discipleship in the shadow of the Jubilee. We can identify two ways Leviticus offers a program of discipleship that would enable the community to implement the Jubilee. First, if Israel's embrace of the Jubilee depended in part on their fostering a just disposition to identify, confess, and repent of sin, the Day of Atonement's rituals would serve to foster this virtuous disposition.

Second, the Jubilee depends on the formation of a people who embrace a vulnerable dependency on God and neighbor and reject the grasping quest for security and control. Leviticus suggests that living within the politics of the Jubilee, including the festival calendar of which it is a part, would habituate the community into this kind of vulnerable dependency.

For instance, the Sabbath and Jubilee years' prohibition of organized agriculture means each Israelite must depend directly on Yahweh's provision and embrace an interruption of socioeconomic hierarchies. In these sabbatical years, everyone, from household head to newly arrived immigrant, becomes a *vulnerable gleaner* in God's abundant fields.[80] We might imagine the formative power of a year in which every employee of a major corporation, including the CEO and board of directors, worked together on the assembly line. But this does not capture it, because the gleaning allows the people to experience God's generosity in providing *apart from* the normal operations of economic life. It is, in other words, a break from the assembly line altogether. In some ways the fallow years are like a recapitulation of the provision of manna in the wilderness.[81] Such a practice would require Israelite household heads to practice the kind of vulnerable dependence that their power and position would normally allow them to avoid. If they embraced it, this practice would shape them for the kind of generous justice required by the Jubilee.

This dynamic can also be seen if we imagine an Israelite household's experience of returning to their lost land during the Jubilee. This return would shape them for vulnerable dependence and a recognition of Yahweh as the ultimate owner of their newly reacquired land. Consider the hypothetical example of an Israelite family participating in this ritual of return. On the tenth day of the seventh month, the entire community participates in the Day of Atonement and its ritual purgation of sin. On this very same day, possibly at the conclusion of the fast,[82] the trumpet is blown and the Jubilee is announced. The family that had been forced to live and work in another's household for decades regains possession of their land. This would be an

---

[80]See Michael Rhodes and Robby Holt, *Practicing the King's Economy: Honoring Jesus in How We Work, Earn, Spend, Save, and Give* (Grand Rapids, MI: Baker, 2018), 135-38, 251-53. Much of the remainder of this section first appeared in Michael Rhodes, "Jubilee Formation: Cultivating Desire and Dependence in Leviticus 25," Cateclesia Institute, October 28, 2020, https://cateclesia.com/2020/10/28/jubilee-formation-cultivating-desire-and-dependence-in-leviticus-25.

[81]See Rhodes and Holt, *Practicing the King's Economy*, 164-73.

[82]Michael LeFebvre, "Theology and Economics in the Biblical Year of Jubilee," *BET* 2, no. 1 (2015): 34-45.

altogether joyous moment. After serving as hired hands for a generation, they are finally restored to a position of social and economic strength.

However, they return to their land at the very end of harvest season *in the midst of a fallow year*.[83] So the moment they regain "control" of the land, the sabbatical system forces them to renounce that control, and instead simply receive the bounty of the land's provision apart from organized harvesting. Then, just five days after their return to their ancestral land, the entire community celebrates the final, most joyful festival of the whole year: the Festival of Booths. This festival lasts for a full week, during which the entire community feasts on the harvest. In the jubilary fallow year, however, this feast would foster a deep sense of dependency among festal participants, because what was feasted *on* would be the results of Yahweh's abundant provision in previous years, Yahweh's provision through the fallow fields' natural growth, and the livestock that Yahweh had fed in those fallow fields all year long.

Moreover, the Israelites spent the entirety of this festival living in huts. Yahweh gives the community a clear explanation for why he has given them this ritual: "You shall dwell in huts for seven days . . . so that your generations may know that I made the people of Israel dwell in huts when I brought them out of the land of Egypt" (Lev 23:42-43 AT). At the very height of the Israelites' celebration of prosperity at the end of a successful agricultural season in the Promised Land, Yahweh asks them to celebrate the year's agricultural success by ritually reenacting their vulnerability as *landless people* led by God in the wilderness. For the family returning to their land in the year of Jubilee, the moment they regain "possession" of "their" land, the feast requires them to ritually surrender that land by reenacting Israel's wilderness wanderings.

Israel would only be able to practice the Jubilee if the people acquired the virtues of acknowledged dependence,[84] humility, and trust, rather than the vices of greed, control, acquisition, and ambition oriented toward self-security. Without these virtues, the Israelites would never be willing to surrender lands they had gained from their neighbors at the Jubilee. Leviticus recognizes this, and, like Deuteronomy, offers a morally formative program of discipleship

---

[83]The dating of the Jubilee and its relationship to the sabbatical year is hotly contested, but thankfully does not significantly impact my argument here. For discussion see Knauth, "Jubilee Transformation," 185-88; Milgrom, *Leviticus 23–27*, 2249; LeFebvre, "Theology and Economics," 34; LeFebvre, *The Liturgy of Creation: Understanding Calendars in Old Testament Context* (Downers Grove, IL: IVP Academic, 2019), 21-23.

[84]See Alasdair MacIntyre, *Dependent Rational Animals: Why Human Beings Need the Virtues* (Peru, IL: Open Court, 2001), 119.

designed to shape Israel's moral life. While it is understandable that this emphasis is missing in the Manifesto, Christian ethics must fill this gap if we
want contemporary Christian communities to live into the Jubilee's vision of
just discipleship.

A JUBILEE CASE FOR ECCLESIAL REPARATIONS?

In this chapter, I've brought James Forman's claim that the white church ought
to pay reparations to Black Americans into conversation with the year of
Jubilee in Leviticus 25. We have seen that the Manifesto and the Jubilee share
concerns about large disparities in wealth and power within the community,
and that both recognize the importance of repentance and repair. Indeed, the
Manifesto envisions, and the Jubilee creates space for, practices of *multigenerational* repentance and repair.

At a deeper level, I have argued that the Jubilee plays a central role in the
politics of holiness within Leviticus's overall vision. Indeed, it offers the
people of God an important practice whereby they seek to host the Holy One
in their midst, becoming holy as Yahweh himself is holy. Christian communities today are likewise called to be holy because the Lord is holy (1 Pet 1:16).
The Levitical invitation to holiness is part of the Old Testament's broader understanding that the community of faith participates in God's mission as a
vehicle of blessing to the nations, in part by living out Yahweh's just and righteous way. How much more, then, should ecclesial communities, called to live
as cities on a hill (Mt 5:14), allow their imaginations to be shaped by Scripture's
jubilary vision? While understanding *how* to receive the Jubilee's word to us
as Christians in the twenty-first century will require us to consider the way
Israel's agrarian, economic laws address the church in a modern economy,
that it must do so *in some way* seems clear.

Yet despite all of this, there is at least one inevitable challenge to making a
jubilary case for ecclesial reparations. If left unaddressed, this challenge will
likely lead even sympathetic readers to resist embracing any serious implications that the Jubilee might have on our lives. Before we can even begin to ask
what the Jubilee might look like in our world, we must address this question:
Did the Jubilee ever even happen?

JUSTICE ON THE WAY

Jubilary Improvisation in
Ever-Changing Circumstances

"But the Jubilee never happened!"

This response seems to be inevitable whenever American Christians talk about the Jubilee. "The question of historicity is endlessly posed," Brueggemann writes, "and, in my experience, no other teaching in the Bible is questioned as this one is about its historicity."[1] This historical challenge is one of the primary barriers to drawing on the Jubilee as a guide for the people of God. If God's people couldn't pull off a Jubilee year in their own day, the argument goes, it's dubious to draw too heavily on the Jubilee in the way we arrange our own socioeconomic life.

The two-sided claim that (a) the Jubilee never happened, and (b) that this means it cannot be a reliable guide for the contemporary church is widespread in both academic and popular conversations.[2] Addressing this challenge is important for this reason alone, but also because the *plausibility* question has plagued the reparations debate in this country for decades.[3] Despite the fact that the United States has engaged in several reparations programs,[4] and in some cases *paid reparations to slaveowners to compensate*

---

[1]Walter Brueggemann, *Reverberations of Faith: A Theological Handbook of Old Testament Themes* (Louisville, KY: Westminster John Knox, 2003), 114-15.

[2]See Robin J. DeWitt Knauth, "The Jubilee Transformation: From Social Welfare to Hope of Restoration to Eschatological Salvation" (PhD diss., Harvard Divinity School, 2004), 12-13.

[3]Jennifer Harvey, *Dear White Christians: For Those Still Longing for Racial Reconciliation* (Grand Rapids, MI: Eerdmans, 2014), 142.

[4]See William Darity Jr. and Dania Frank, "The Economics of Reparations," *American Economic Review* 93, no. 2 (2003): 326.

them for the loss of their slaves,[5] the claim that a program of reparations is simply unfeasible continues to loom large in contemporary debates. For both the Jubilee and reparations, the alleged difficulty of implementation serves as a defeater for the attempt. Thus, receiving the Jubilee's vision for just discipleship requires us to address this question head on. Remarkably, doing so will reveal the power of the Jubilee to shape the politics of ecclesial communities—their corporate structures, practices, and policies—for the work of justice in our world.

DID THE JUBILEE EVER HAPPEN? *COULD* IT HAVE?

What can we say about the widely cited absence of evidence for the Jubilee? I want to first make two brief, preliminary points before turning in the next section to the decisive shift we need to make in thinking about the historicity, and therefore contemporary ethical plausibility, of the Jubilee.

First, it is completely unclear to me why the Israelites' failure to implement the Jubilee would suggest that contemporary faith communities take the demands of the text less seriously. The people of God constantly fell short of Scripture's command not to commit adultery, but at least among Christians with a strong sense of the Bible's authority, I know of no movement to argue that this means we should ignore the seventh commandment. Surely Israel's failure to live up to their vocation to be holy is no grounds for the contemporary church to reject the attempt! Especially given that, according to the New Testament, the *Holy Spirit* dwells in us!

Indeed, Leviticus recognizes that Israel may struggle to implement the Jubilee. The way the book responds to this potential struggle is to *threaten widespread judgment and exile if they do in fact fail.* Scripture does not see the difficulty of the demands of discipleship as getting the community of faith off the hook for becoming a community of disciples. If Western Christians find it easier to believe in the historicity of the bodily resurrection of Jesus than they do the people of God's willing, regular reallocation of economic assets, that may say more about our idolatry than it does the ethical demands of Scripture.

Second, the argument that we have no evidence the Jubilee happened has been seriously challenged. On the one hand, while we do not have any narrative, biblical evidence for an exact celebration of the year of Jubilee, Wright

---

[5]See Tera W. Hunter, "When Slaveowners Got Reparations," *New York Times*, April 16, 2019, www .nytimes.com/2019/04/16/opinion/when-slaveowners-got-reparations.html.

points out that we do not have "any historical record of the Day of Atonement, either. Silence in the narratives proves almost nothing."[6]

On the other hand, what we *do* have is conclusive evidence that ancient communities around Israel practiced debt relief and land return for a thousand years before Israel's entry into the land of Canaan.[7] Because the evidence for these edicts includes contracts of actual land sales,[8] as well as letters discussing the economic impacts of these edicts,[9] we know that these announcements of liberty were not simply royal propaganda, but actual occurrences. Whereas an older scholarly argument suggested the Jubilee was too "sophisticated" for its setting in pre-monarchial Israel, scholars have demonstrated conclusively that pre-monarchial Israel could have implemented precisely what Leviticus 25 describes. Indeed, there is good evidence the Israelite community would have been aware of contemporary examples of similar practices in neighboring communities for much, if not all, of the biblical period.

All this evidence suggests Israel may well have practiced the Jubilee. More importantly, though, such data makes clear that they *could have*. They would have understood the year of Jubilee as a plausible political practice for the Israelite community within the context that Leviticus itself describes: Israel in the wilderness preparing to inherit the Promised Land.[10] Indeed, any Israelite encountering the content of Leviticus 25 at any point in the Old Testament period prior to the exile would recognize the Jubilee as a genuine possibility and the failure to implement it as a genuine failure.

LEVITICAL "LAW" AND THE FORMATION OF A JUBILARY IMAGINATION

The more important point to make related to the historicity and plausibility of the Jubilee, though, is connected to our understanding of Old Testament

---

[6]Christopher J. H. Wright, *The Mission of God: Unlocking the Bible's Grand Narrative* (Downers Gove, IL: IVP Academic, 2006), 295.

[7]Moshe Weinfeld, *Social Justice in Ancient Israel and in the Ancient Near East* (Minneapolis: Fortress, 2000), 77-212; Jacob Milgrom, *Leviticus 23–27*, AB (New Haven, CT: Yale University Press, 2001), 2168; Eckart Otto, "Programme der sozialen Gerechtigkeit: Die neuassyrische (an-)durāru-Institution sozialen Ausgleichs und das deuteronomische Erlaßjahr in Dtn 15," *Journal for Ancient Near Eastern and Biblical Law* 3 (1997): 45-6.

[8]See Knauth, "Jubilee Transformation," 204; Weinfeld, *Social Justice*, 78; J. J. Finkelstein, "Ammisaduqa's Edict and the Babylonian 'Law Codes,'" *Journal of Cuneiform Studies* 15, no. 3 (1961): 91-92.

[9]Otto, "Programme," 47.

[10]See further Jonathan Kaplan, "The Credibility of Liberty: The Plausibility of the Jubilee Legislation of Leviticus 25 in Ancient Israel and Judah," *CBQ* 81 no. 2 (2019): 183-203; Knauth, "Jubilee Transformation," 62.

law more broadly. This may seem like an arcane point; in reality, it is central to our understanding of how a text like Leviticus 25 might shape contemporary Christians for just discipleship.

The claim that there is no evidence that Israel practiced the Jubilee is based on the fact that we have *no exact replication of the Jubilee as it is described in Leviticus 25*. Recent research on the nature of Old Testament and ancient Near Eastern law, however, problematizes the assumptions involved in such a claim.[11] To understand why this is so, we need to recognize that Western readers often approach the law codes of the Old Testament assuming that these law codes function as "statutory law."[12] Statutory law is the typical approach to law codes in our own day. Under statutory law, judges refer to specific statutes within the community's law codes when rendering decisions. The judge and other judicial actors are bound to follow the statutory codes to the letter.

For instance, I once attended the trial of a friend in our neighborhood who had been arrested for selling cocaine. The defense attorney, the judge, and the prosecuting attorney all appeared to want to work out a way for my friend to be released from jail that day. But when the defense attorney twice asked the judge to make a specific ruling to release my friend, the judge replied, "Tennessee law does not permit me to do that." After a recess, the defense attorney tried again with slightly different wording. Same response. Finally, another lawyer in the courtroom shouted out an alternatively worded legal petition that amounted to the same desired outcome. After pondering for a minute, the judge said, "Yes, I can do that." This is a vivid example of how, under statutory law, all legal parties are bound to follow the identified prescriptions of the legal code.

Recent scholarship suggests that ancient law codes did not work this way. Scholars have identified numerous law codes published by ancient monarchs. They have also identified ample evidence of actual judicial decisions rendered by ancient judges.[13] Based on available evidence, these judges did not cite the law codes in their actual decision-making, and often directly deviated from what appear to be their precise legal demands.[14]

---

[11]Michael LeFebvre, "Theology and Economics in the Biblical Year of Jubilee," *BET* 2, no. 1 (2015): 34-45.

[12]For the inadequacy of a "statutory law" conception, see Joshua Berman, *Inconsistency in the Torah: Ancient Literary Convention and the Limits of Source Criticism* (New York: Oxford University Press, 2017), 107-17.

[13]Bernard S. Jackson, *Studies in the Semiotics of Biblical Law* (Sheffield: Sheffield Academic Press, 2000), 115.

[14]Berman, *Created Equal*, 84; Jackson, *Semiotics*, 115.

What then is the function of these law codes?[15] A growing number of scholars suggest that they are a form of "common law,"[16] or perhaps even a form of *Wisdom literature.*[17] Such law codes present the community's understanding of what wise, just communal policy and practice might look like in a given time and place.[18] They thus offer later generations a kind of nonbinding precedent. Judges likely knew these codes and were guided by their wisdom but were not bound to apply them literally or legalistically.

These insights about the nature of the law codes provide historical grounding for the paradigmatic approach to Old Testament ethics championed by Christopher J. H. Wright. Wright raises the question of how Christian ethicists get from the "there" in the ancient world to the "here" of the present.[19] This move from there to here is complicated for a variety of reasons. On the one hand, the economy back "there" was far different from the one "here." On the other hand, there are significant differences between participating in the life of God's people as the church and participating in the life of God's people as a citizen in Israel's earthly theocracy.

Wright's solution is for contemporary Christian readers to explore Israel in the Old Testament, and especially her laws and institutions, as a *paradigm*, "a model or pattern" that allows us to "work by analogy from a specific known reality (the paradigm) to a wider or different context in which there are problems to be solved, or answers to be found, or choices to be made."[20] Understanding Leviticus's politics of holiness as a paradigm *would not* require us to replicate the Jubilee institution in every time and place. It *would* mean allowing the Jubilee institution to catalyze and transform our ethical imaginations, enabling us to evaluate our own ecclesial politics and to imaginatively improvise a politics more in line with God's kingdom.[21]

---

[15]For an overview of options, see Jackson, *Semiotics*, 115-16; Raymond Westbrook, *Law from the Tigris to the Tiber: The Writings of Raymond Westbrook*, ed. F. Rachel Magdalene and Bruce Wells (Winona Lake, IN: Eisenbrauns, 2009), 1-16.

[16]Berman, *Inconsistency*, 145-47.

[17]Jackson, *Semiotics*, 70-92; John Barton, *Ethics in Ancient Israel* (New York: Oxford University Press, 2017), 145-48.

[18]For our purposes, we do not need to render a decision about the exact background of the law codes, and in any case, Jackson is right that it would be foolish to argue for a single model for all ancient Near Eastern legal codes and texts. Jackson, *Semiotics*, 116.

[19]Wright, *Old Testament Ethics*, 63-64.

[20]Wright, Old Testament Ethics, 63-64.

[21]See also Walter J. Houston, *Contending for Justice: Ideologies and Theologies of Social Justice in the Old Testament* (New York: T&T Clark, 2006), 193.

But this should also change the way we answer the question whether the people of God actually practiced the Jubilee. Based on the nature of Old Testament law, we ought to expand our search from strict replications of the institution to a search for evidence that Israel saw the Jubilee as a paradigm and imaginatively improvised the Jubilee's paradigmatic politics elsewhere in the canon.[22]

When we do so, we discover that the Jubilee paradigm in Leviticus encouraged a whole host of politics and practices across the Old and New Testaments. Scripture itself thus models the way the Jubilee paradigm ought to inspire creative, improvisational, jubilary activity in later times and places, including our own. Exploring this dynamic will deepen our dialogue between the Black Manifesto and the jubilary thread in Scripture. It will also open our eyes to new ways that Scripture's politics might inspire contemporary faith communities to respond to the case for ecclesial reparations today.

The Jubilee has roots in God's creative purposes for humanity and all creation. It also flows out of Yahweh's specific commands concerning the Sabbath day (Ex 20:8-11; 23:12; Deut 5:12-15) and the sabbatical system of years (Ex 23:10-11). Because of this, our search will frequently reveal that the Jubilee itself is only one plank in a larger paradigm within the Torah. The rest of the Bible, in other words, drew from both the Jubilee in Leviticus 25 and an array of related Torah texts, especially Deuteronomy 15:1-18.[23] Given the connections between these texts, and the way the Jubilee stands as the Torah's most extensive reflection on matters of land, debt, and slave release, I will refer to this collection of texts as representing a "jubilary politics." Let's explore a few echoes of this jubilary politics in the Bible.

Jubilary politics in Jeremiah 34:8-22. Jeremiah 34:8-11 recounts King Zedekiah's covenant with the people in Jerusalem to free their Hebrew slaves during a Babylonian siege. Initially, the people obeyed. Later, the powerful repented of this manumission and returned their liberated slaves to

---

[22]See LeFebvre, "Theology and Economics," 37, 46; Knauth, "Jubilee Transformation," 62.

[23]This is despite some difficulties in a literal reconciliation of the two legal texts. (The former makes no mention of the Jubilee and the latter no mention of slave release in the sabbatical year.) Because of what I've argued in terms of the nature of the law, there is a connection between the two texts even if Deuteronomy 15:12-18 presents a law that in some ways conflicts with the law as presented in Leviticus 25. Some, however, see each law as applying to somewhat different circumstances. See David Baker, *Tight Fists or Open Hands? Wealth and Poverty in Old Testament Law* (Grand Rapids, MI: Eerdmans, 2009), 170-73; Gregory Chirichigno, *Debt-Slavery in Israel and the Ancient Near East* (Sheffield: Sheffield Academic Press, 2009), 223, 342-43.

slave-service. Jeremiah 34:12-22 offers Yahweh's judgment on this reversal; God interprets their actions as a rejection of the law's regulations concerning slavery, and thus as grounds for God's judgment.

At first glance, the text does not seem to stand in strong continuity with the jubilary politics of either Deuteronomy 15 or Leviticus 25.[24] In Jeremiah 34, the king declares a release for slaves, whereas in Deuteronomy and Leviticus that prerogative belongs only to God. King Zedekiah's pronouncement lacks both the cyclical aspect emphasized in Deuteronomy 15:1-11 and Leviticus 25:8-55, and the reference to limits on the duration of debt slavery that characterize Deuteronomy 15:12-18.

Yet a closer look at the text suggests that both Zedekiah's practice and the prophetic interpretation of it have been definitively shaped by both Deuteronomy 15 and Leviticus 25. The language of male and female Hebrew slaves (Jer 34:9), the reference to sending out one's slaves freely (Jer 34:10), and the phrase "from the end of seven years" (Jer 34:14 AT) are just three of the most obvious linguistic links with Deuteronomy 15.[25] While some reject or downplay similar connections to Leviticus 25,[26] the language of "declaring a release [*deror*]" (Jer 34:8, 15, 17) only occurs elsewhere in texts speaking explicitly about the year of Jubilee (Lev 25:10; Is 61:1; Ezek 46:17).[27] Some claim that this reference to a "release" is derived directly from ancient Near Eastern royal edicts.[28] But those ancient edicts never make the claim that Zedekiah makes that "no one should hold another Judean in salvery" (Jer 34:9). Where then does that idea come from? The only biblical legal text that makes that claim is Leviticus 25:39-54.[29] Moreover, the only biblical, legal text that announces a universal release of slaves, rather than a release based on the years of service, is the Jubilee.[30]

---

[24]See John Sietze Bergsma, *The Jubilee from Leviticus to Qumran: Its Origin, Development, and Interpretation in the Hebrew Scriptures, Second Temple Literature, and Qumran Texts* (Leiden: Brill, 2007), 161; Milgrom, *Leviticus 23–27*, 2257; Weinfeld, *Social Justice*, 153.

[25]See Bergsma, *Jubilee*, 163; Gerald L. Keown, Pamela J. Scalise, and Thomas G. Smothers, *Jeremiah 26–52*, WBC 27 (Nashville, TN: Thomas Nelson, 1995), 185.

[26]For instance, Sharon H. Ringe, *Jesus, Liberation, and the Biblical Jubilee: Images of Ethics and Christology* (Eugene, OR: Wipf & Stock, 2004), 23.

[27]Jeremiah Unterman, *Justice for All: How the Jewish Bible Revolutionized Ethics* (Lincoln, NE: University of Nebraska Press, 2017), 80; Bergsma, *Jubilee*, 164; Keown, Scalise, and Smothers, *Jeremiah*, 188.

[28]See Mark Leuchter, "The Manumission Laws in Leviticus and Deuteronomy: The Jeremiah Connection," *JBL* 127, no. 4 (2008), 648-51.

[29]Bergsma, *Jubilee*, 165.

[30]See Keown, Scalise, and Smothers, *Jeremiah*, 184-85, 188.

Even more importantly, Yahweh himself *affirms* that the decision to inaugurate a covenant of release stood in continuity with the earlier covenantal requirement for a regular release of slaves. While their ancestors refused to follow Yahweh's covenant by practicing debt forgiveness at fixed intervals, Yahweh says, "You yourselves recently repented and did what was right in my sight by proclaiming liberty to one another, and you made a covenant before me in the house that is called by my name" (Jer 34:15).

Don't miss how remarkable this is. Yahweh depicts Zedekiah's slave release as a faithful enactment of the Torah's jubilary laws, *even though Zedekiah's actions obviously differ from the specifics of those laws.*[31] Yahweh *commends* Zedekiah's actions and affirms them as actions faithful to the law, even though they do not perfectly match the laws that Yahweh himself refers to in Jeremiah 34:14. From Yahweh's perspective, at least, Zedekiah was absolutely right to improvise in his application of the jubilary laws in his new time and place.[32] On the other hand, Yahweh declares that their failure to follow through with this covenantal "release" (*deror*) will cause Yahweh to declare his own "release" (*deror*)—a "release" of his people to "sword, pestilence, and famine."

Jeremiah 34:8-22 offers us an example of the Torah's jubilary politics serving as a paradigm that shaped the politics of God's people in a later place and time. The community creatively appropriated both Deuteronomy 15 and Leviticus 25 for a situation in which a direct, one-for-one replication was either impossible, undesirable, or both.[33] They improvised how to live jubilary lives in a situation that the Torah itself does not envision, namely a monarchy under siege. This is true even if the final failure of Zedekiah to enact long-term justice reminds the covenant community of the dangers of depending on a king for jubilary justice.[34]

Jubilary politics in Nehemiah 5:1-13 and 10:31[32]. Nehemiah 5:1-13 recounts another economic crisis, this time after the return from exile. The cries of economically oppressed Judahite families interrupt the book's story of communal triumph in rebuilding Jerusalem. These cries come from three different groups:

1. Those in desperate need of food due to the size of their families (Neh 5:2),

---

[31]Keown, Scalise, and Smothers, *Jeremiah*, 187; Weinfeld, *Social Justice*, 10.
[32]Bruce C. Birch, *Let Justice Roll Down* (Louisville, KY: Westminster John Knox, 1991), 182.
[33]Bergsma, *Jubilee*, 162.
[34]Wright, *Old Testament Ethics*, 325.

2. Those who have lost their livelihood due to mortgaging their fields, vineyards, and houses to get grain during a famine (Neh 5:3), and

3. Those who, after borrowing money to pay the oppressive taxes imposed by the Persians, had lost their fields and vineyards.

This last group had been forced to sell their sons and daughters as debt slaves to their fellow-Judeans (Lev 5:4-5).

Crop failure and high taxes seem to have contributed to the current crisis. But much of the people's suffering is due to debt. This was especially the case when people were forced to offer up fields or family members as collateral,[35] or to pay interest on their loans. After hearing their outcry, getting angry, and considering how to proceed, Nehemiah offers a three-part public response.

First, he *confronts* the powerful for what he sees as a deep moral failure and violation of the fear of God (Neh 5:7-9).[36] Second, Nehemiah tells the people, "Even I and my brothers and servants are lending them silver and grain" (Neh 5:10 AT). If Nehemiah means that he has been lending to the poor *but not* charging them interest, then, in line with Deuteronomy 15 and Leviticus 25, he is calling the community to embrace forms of lending to the poor that are not exploitative.[37] If, as I think more likely, Nehemiah and his men have themselves been involved in exploitative lending, then Nehemiah here confesses that he himself has been part of the problem.[38]

Third, Nehemiah *calls the people* to join him in obeying God by (a) immediately canceling debts and returning interest or collateral they had already taken, and (b) giving up the practice of lending on interest going forward (Neh 5:10-11).[39] Miraculously, in an "extraordinary event without parallel in the ancient world,"[40] the money-lending class *agrees*, *repents* of their actions, *returns* the collateral and interest they had taken, and *forgives* the loans they

[35]See Peter Altmann, *Economics in Persian Period Biblical Texts: Their Interactions with Economic Developments in the Persian Period and Earlier Biblical Traditions* (Tubingen: Mohr Seibeck, 2016), 253.

[36]See J. David Pleins, *The Social Visions of the Hebrew Bible: A Theological Introduction* (Louisville, KY: Westminster John Knox, 2001),183.

[37]See Joseph Blenkinsopp, *Ezra-Nehemiah*, OTL (Louisville, KY: Westminster John Knox, 1998), 260.

[38]See especially Altmann, *Economics*, 256-57, 266; Walter Brueggemann, *Money and Possessions*, Interpretation (Louisville, KY: Westminster John Knox, 2016), 94-95; H. G. M. Williamson, *Ezra-Nehemiah*, WBC 16 (Waco, TX: Word Books, 1987), 240. Note that Nehemiah has already shown a propensity to confess his sin and his community's sin in Nehemiah 1:6.

[39]See Williamson, *Ezra-Nehemiah*, 241.

[40]Unterman, *Justice for All*, 81.

had offered (Neh 5:12). The entire section ends with all the people "praising Yahweh" and following through on their commitments (Neh 5:13).

Some argue Nehemiah's actions neither conform to nor allude to the Torah's jubilary politics.[41] Nehemiah's proclamation is, like Zedekiah's, a one-off proclamation rather than a cyclical reform. Moreover, it's not altogether clear that the behavior of the powerful was technically illegal,[42] and in his response to it, Nehemiah goes *beyond* what either Leviticus 25 or Deuteronomy 15 requires.[43]

Nevertheless, the entire passage has been shaped by numerous allusions to both texts:

- The appeal to the "fear of Yahweh" as a motivation for obedience in Nehemiah 5:9 echoes the same appeal in Leviticus 25:17, 36, and 43.
- The language of returning land (and other "collateral") using various forms of the verb *shuv*, which is ubiquitous in Leviticus 25, also occurs in Nehemiah 5:10-11.
- The prohibition of interest occurs in both Leviticus 25:36 and Nehemiah 5:11.
- The language of "pressing claims" in Nehemiah 5:7 may well be drawn from Leviticus 25:46.[44]
- The reference to the impoverished "brother" Judeans not having "power in [their] hands" (Neh 5:5 AT) resonates with Leviticus 25:35's use of a similar idiom to describe one's impoverished "brother."

At a deeper level, Nehemiah appears to draw on Leviticus 25's attempt to eliminate debt slavery *even as* he goes beyond what that text requires in seeking to accomplish that goal. As we have argued, legal texts offer paradigms of wise, just practice intended to inspire creative and contextual applications in new situations. In light of this, it is notable that Nehemiah's later appropriation of an earlier law leads to a *more rigorous* application. Like Jesus in the Sermon on the Mount, Nehemiah appears to have drawn on the law even as he intensified its demands in line with the heart and spirit of that law.

---

[41]Bergsma, *Jubilee*, 207.
[42]Williamson, *Ezra-Nehemiah*, 238-39.
[43]See Bergsma, *Jubilee*, 206; Milgrom, *Leviticus 23–27*, 2238.
[44]On the similarities between the Jubilee and Nehemiah 5 described in the previous bullet points, see especially Berman, *Inconsistency*, 151-53, as well as Blenkinsop, *Ezra-Nehemiah*, 259; Williamson, *Ezra-Nehemiah*, 239-40; Altmann, *Economics*, 258; Unterman, *Justice for All*, 82; Baruch A. Levine, *Leviticus*, JPS (Philadelphia: JPS, 1989), 273; Milgrom, *Leviticus 23–27*, 2228, 2267.

Like Jeremiah 34:8-22, Nehemiah 5:1-13 offers us an example of God's people pursuing justice in their economic lives by faithfully exercising power in ways that appear to have been inspired, at least in part, by the original jubilary legislation. What then does Nehemiah 5:1-13 add to our understanding of jubilary politics?

First, the text demonstrates that later authors drew on texts like Leviticus 25 and Deuteronomy 15 to figure out how to respond to and repair situations of injustice. In the last chapter, I argued that while Leviticus 25 does not suggest that *every* jubilary return would constitute an act of repentance, there were hints that the practice of the Jubilee would *include* such acts of repentance. Here we have further evidence: the people of God drew on texts like Deuteronomy 15 and Leviticus 25 to address unjust economic practices and to summon perpetrators of injustice to repentance and repair.

Second, Nehemiah 5:1-13 demonstrates both the need for and the difficulty of jubilary politics *once a class society has emerged*. While Deuteronomy 15 and Leviticus 25 envision a society without an established elite, Nehemiah works in a world dominated by clear divisions between the "nobles and the officials" (Neh 5:7) and those further down the rungs of society's ladder. This new context demands a creative implementation of jubilary politics rather than a slavish replication of them. Yet the text also bears witness to the possibility that genuine solidarity might be possible, even in a society divided by class.

The problems facing this now class-segregated society are not only about economics. They're also about *power*.[45] This is why power is such an essential part of the complaint of the poor in Nehemiah 5:3. Because they have lost their land, they are *powerless* to protect themselves and their families from humiliating social and economic degradation. It is deeply instructive that in such a society, the drive toward a jubilary politics does not begin with the good intentions of the powerful, but with the *outcry of the poor against their fellow citizens*. Life lived in a society with deep social and economic divisions makes those divisions, and the economic practices that reinforce them, seem natural and necessary, at least to those who benefit from them. The outcry of the oppressed, which echoes the outcry of the slaves in Egypt,[46] is unapologetically aimed at their Jewish brothers and sisters. It is the suffering poor who insist that they are being denied the treatment that their status as citizens of

---

[45]Wright, *Old Testament Ethics*, 356.
[46]Brueggemann, *Money and Possessions*, 92.

the community demands. They insist that the powerful recognize the essential equality between them.[47]

This outcry is a wake-up call for Nehemiah. At a minimum, it forces him to take dramatic action in confronting others. If we interpret Nehemiah 5:10 as a form of confession, then the outcry also forces him to reexamine his own behavior. The accusation of the poor, combined with his awareness of the jubilary texts of the Pentateuch, ultimately leads Nehemiah and his fellow "nobles and officials" to *repent* of their behavior, and *repair* the damage that had been done.

Yet Nehemiah goes well beyond the literal requirements of the Jubilee in his pursuit of its social vision in his own context.[48] Leviticus 25 envisions a "redeemer" who "redeems" an impoverished member of the community, but who benefits from their labor until the Jubilee. Nehemiah appears to reject any kind of bonded labor, even among fellow Jews. Instead, he advocates that the Jews "ransom" their fellow citizens who have fallen into debt servitude, with no suggestion that the "ransomer" gain any benefit from having done so.[49]

Nehemiah recognizes that the community's moral failures demand an immediate, radical response. This response is inspired by the Torah's jubilary politics, even as it goes beyond the specific demands of any one text. But Nehemiah recognizes that this one-off overhaul is not enough to accomplish economic justice within the community. The economic reforms do not end in Nehemiah 5:1-13, but are picked up in the covenant-renewal of Nehemiah 10, in which the people recommit themselves to practicing a fallow year and debt forgiveness every seventh year (Neh 10:31[32]).[50] Thus Nehemiah's one-off, creative appropriation of jubilary texts leads to and is supplemented by a necessary commitment to a regular practice of debt release. While neither would likely be enough to *erase* class distinctions within the community, it would dramatically reduce the divisions between classes and create the possibility of genuine solidarity between them. Thus the outcry of the poor and the response of the nobles concludes with the *entire assembly* praising Yahweh together (Neh 5:13). In summary, then, Nehemiah presents us with a powerful example of the community embracing jubilary politics in a very different socioeconomic context.

---

[47]Unterman, *Justice for All*, 82.
[48]See Altmann, *Economics*, 269.
[49]Altmann, *Economics*, 269.
[50]On the kind of blending of legal texts at work here, see Berman, *Inconsistency*, 149.

Jubilary politics in Ezekiel. Yet another set of jubilary texts occurs in Ezekiel. If Leviticus presents a holistic way of life that allows the community to host "in [their] midst the radical holiness of God,"[51] Ezekiel prophesies in the aftermath of Israel's failure to do just that. Indeed, a central moment in the book is Ezekiel's vision of the glory of Yahweh departing the temple in response to Israel's idolatry and injustice (see Ezek 10–11).[52]

Against this background, Ezekiel's prophecies of hope for the future in Ezekiel 34–48 include the reestablishment of God's generous kingdom in the Promised Land. Just as Leviticus offered the Jubilee as a central plank in the community's politics of holiness once they entered the land, Ezekiel envisions a renewed and adapted Jubilee practice as an essential component of the new community where Yahweh will once again take up residence among his people.[53] For our purposes, we can identify three distinctive aspects of Ezekiel's vision.

Limits on royal power. First, the Jubilee plays an important role in Ezekiel's vision of a restored, but significantly constrained royal house.[54] The prophet envisions a royal figure from the line of David who himself lives *under* Yahweh's Jubilee. Thus, after several chapters outlining the architecture of the restored temple, Ezekiel turns to the question of how the land shall be divided (Ezek 45). Ezekiel describes a recapitulation of the original division of the land. However, now, the prince will also receive an "ancestral portion" (*akhuzzah*; Ezek 45:7-8).[55] The point of giving the prince his own family plot is immediately made clear in Ezekiel 45:8-9:

> My princes will no longer oppress my people, but they will give the land to the house of Israel for their tribes. Thus says the Lord Yahweh: "Enough, princes of Israel! Turn aside from violence and havoc, and do justice and righteousness! Stop stealing land from my people," declares the Lord Yahweh. (AT)

After further outlining both the economic justice demanded of the prince, and the role that he must play in providing offerings to Yahweh, Ezekiel 46:16-18 returns to the issue of the prince's relationship to the broader community in terms of land.

---

[51]Ellen F. Davis, *Opening Israel's Scriptures* (New York: Oxford University Press, 2019), 72.

[52]On the relationship between Leviticus and Ezekiel see Bergsma, *Jubilee*, 177-80.

[53]Christopher J. H. Wright, *The Message of Ezekiel: A New Heart and a New Spirit* (Downers Grove, IL: IVP Academic, 2002), 363.

[54]See Pleins, *Social Visions*, 322; Leslie C. Allen, *Ezekiel 20–48*, WBC 29 (Nashville: Thomas Nelson, 1990), 270; Houston, *Contending*, 165.

[55]The word *akhuzzah* occurs twelve times in Leviticus 25.

Thus says the Lord Yahweh: "If the prince will give a gift to one of his sons for his inheritance, it will belong to his son as an ancestral possession [*akhuzzah*]. It is his as his inheritance. But if he gives a gift from his inheritance to one of his servants, then it will belong to that servant until the year of release [*deror*].[56] Then it will return to the prince. Surely it is the prince's inheritance. It will belong to his sons. And the prince will not take from the inheritance of the people, to oppress them out of their ancestral possession. From his own ancestral possession he will pass on an inheritance to his sons in order that my people will not be scattered, each away from his ancestral possession." (AT)

All of this amounts to a radical subordination of the prince to the rule of Yahweh as the divine king. Not only is the Jubilee cycle enacted by God rather than by the prince's command, the prince himself is subject to the Jubilee. This will ensure that the people can maintain their plots in the Promised Land.

As both Ezekiel and much of the Old Testament make clear, kings often oppressed the people out of their land, both for their own use and to buy the allegiance of those elites who helped enable and enforce their rule (see 1 Sam 8:14; 1 Kings 21).[57] Ezekiel envisions a political community in which the prince has no more right to the land he possesses than any other Israelite, and therefore no greater ability to dispose of it than any other Israelite. Everyone, from the prince on down, receives their land as a gift, and are obligated to manage it in line with the *divine* monarch's jubilary land policy. The result is a community in which every family can dwell securely.[58] Once again, the jubilary community is concerned with both economic viability and social *power*. If in Leviticus 25 the emphasis is on distributing power broadly in the community, Ezekiel's vision recognizes that this requires placing *limits* on the power of the prince.

Permanent inclusion of outsiders. Second, though, Ezekiel envisions a *radically inclusive* community that goes far beyond Leviticus 25. When Yahweh restores his people to the Promised Land, the land will be allotted as an inheritance not only "for yourselves," but also for the "aliens who reside among you and have begotten children among you" (Ezek 47:22). Presumably, these sojourners' land would also be subject to the Jubilee; the sojourner who chooses to reside among the people of God, then, will have

---

[56]That is, the year of Jubilee.
[57]Barrera, *Biblical Economic Ethics*, 34-37.
[58]See Wright, *Message of Ezekiel*, 363-64.

the opportunity to obtain a permanent socioeconomic place to stand and portion to steward in the Promised Land.[59] No longer will sojourners be kept in a "perpetual state of dependence."[60]

This is a bold reinterpretation of Leviticus 25.[61] Not only were outsiders barred from permanent possession of land in the community, Leviticus 25:45-46 explicitly permits them to be bought as permanent slaves. Ezekiel's jubilary politics of holiness, on the other hand, makes explicit space for a politics of *inclusion* for outsiders who join themselves to the community that belongs to the Lord.[62] "Aliens will be transformed into fellow heirs."[63]

Here we see the Jubilee's deep roots in God's purposes in creation and re-demption driving the community to go beyond even what the Jubilee itself envisioned. Yahweh is the God who calls Israel to be a vehicle of his blessing to the nations, as well as the God that liberated Israel from their harsh en-slavement when they were sojourners in Egypt. In Ezekiel, sojourners from other nations find blessing in Israel by discovering that Yahweh cares so much for them that he gives them a plot in his people's Promised Land.

Vision of the future just kingdom. Third, while Jeremiah and Nehemiah describe historical instances of the people embracing aspects of the Jubilee, Ezekiel is somewhat different. Living in an exilic context far from the land of Israel, he envisions the Jubilee as one aspect of Yahweh's future decisive inter-vention in the lives of his people. Davis argues that Ezekiel's final visions are an act of "world-creating." The prophet invites his hearers to "an imaginative participation in alternative modes of reality."[64] Ezekiel recognizes that this "alternative mode" of reality is utterly dependent on Yahweh's gracious action; indeed, what Israel needs is akin to heart surgery (Ezek 36:26), even resur-rection (Ezek 37:1-14)! Only Yahweh can take his recalcitrant people and rec-reate them into a community capable of permanently hosting Yahweh in their

---

[59]As far as I can tell, commentators do not address the question whether the sojourner would par-ticipate in the Jubilee. Nevertheless, the text seems to presume it. In personal correspondence, Bergsma stated his agreement with this position, and drew my attention to the comparable lan-guage in Numbers 36:4 as evidence.

[60]Daniel I. Block, *The Book of Ezekiel: Chapters 25–48*, NICOT (Grand Rapids, MI: Eerdmans, 2009), 718.

[61]See Jacob Milgrom, *Ezekiel's Hope: A Commentary on Ezekiel 38–48* (Eugene, OR: Cascade Books, 2012), 243-44.

[62]See Walter Eichrodt, *Ezekiel* (London: SCM Press, 1970), 592; Stephen L. Cook, *Ezekiel 38–48*, AB (New Haven, CT: Yale University Press, 2019), 280.

[63]Wright, *Message of Ezekiel*, 365.

[64]Ellen Davis, *Swallowing the Scroll: Textuality and the Dynamics of Discourse in Ezekiel's Prophecy* (Sheffield, UK: Sheffield Academic Press, 2009), 122.

midst, a people for whom Yahweh will be their God, and they will be his people (Ezek 37:27-28).

At the same time, by presenting such an alternative vision in lengthy detail, and in ways that touch very pragmatic, real-world concerns, Ezekiel also invites his audience to live into this vision of the future world in the present. In other words, Ezekiel's "world-creating" is one more way Scripture shapes the imaginations and character of disciples for the practical work of justice. Taken together, then, Ezekiel's jubilary vision serves simultaneously to:

1. Comfort the people with the hope of a future miraculous act of salvation that would include both sociopolitical liberation *and* complete moral and spiritual transformation.

2. Summon the leaders to repent in the present by turning *from* an oppressive economic way of life characterized by unjust land acquisition *toward* a just, jubilary politics lived under the lordship of Yahweh.

3. Embrace the ethnic outsider as a potential insider, a future citizen in the just kingdom that Yahweh will one day bring in all its fullness.

In all these ways, Ezekiel demonstrates the power of the Torah's jubilary politics to inspire both prophetic hope in Yahweh's kingdom-intervention *and* imaginative attempts at living toward that jubilary politics in the present.

The jubilary politics of Jesus and the early church. Jubilary politics and theology do not end in the Old Testament; they find their way into the New Testament as well, most notably in Jesus' first sermon.[65]

> And he came into Nazareth, where he had been raised, and he entered the synagogue on the sabbath, as was his custom. And he rose up to read, and the scroll of the prophet Isaiah was given to him. And unrolling the scroll, he found the place where it is written: "The Spirit of the Lord is upon me, who has anointed me to declare good news to the poor, he has sent me to proclaim liberty to the captives and sight to the blind, to send the oppressed free in liberty, to proclaim the Year of the Lord's Favor." And rolling up the scroll he returned it to the attendant and sat down. The eyes of all in the synagogue were staring at him. And he began to say to them, "Today, this scripture has been fulfilled in your hearing." (Lk 4:16-21 AT)

The "Year of the Lord's Favor" refers to the Jubilee. While a few scholars insist Jesus intended to implement the Jubilee as a literal institution, the majority

---

[65]See Joel B. Green, *The Gospel of Luke*, NICNT (Grand Rapids, MI: Eerdmans, 1997), 197.

recognize that nothing else in Jesus' life and ministry suggests such a literal enactment.[66] What then are we to make of the way Jesus picks up the jubilary thread?

In Jesus' day, the Jubilee had come to be interpreted *eschatologically*. Such eschatological interpretations begin in the Old Testament. Isaiah 61:1-3 envisions the Servant of Yahweh declaring a future Jubilee that appears to be spiritual, political, social, and economic.[67] In an intertestamental text like 11QMelchizedek, jubilary texts from the Old Testament have been combined to describe an eschatological Jubilee that is almost exclusively spiritual: one day, God's people will be liberated "from the [debt] of all their *iniquities*."[68] While in Leviticus 25 the fact that the Jubilee belonged to Yahweh placed the responsibility for its implementation on Israelite families, during the intertestamental period the Jubilee came to be seen increasingly as "God's responsibility."[69]

Some suggest we should understand Jesus' inaugural sermon similarly, with the Levitical Jubilee playing very little role in his ministry and the quotations from Isaiah serving to emphasize the text's spiritual and eschatological message of hope for the forgiveness of sins.[70] But the picture painted in Luke–Acts is far more complex—and far more compelling. On the one hand, Jesus does indeed speak of an eschatological Jubilee in line with Isaiah 61:1-3. But for Jesus, the eschaton, the "last days," have already arrived in his own life and ministry. "Today," Jesus declares, "this Scripture has been fulfilled in your hearing." The end-time jubilary promises are now exploding in the present through the Spirit-anointed ministry of Jesus.

On the other hand, while Jesus certainly uses jubilary language to refer to the forgiveness of sins, for Jesus, the Jubilee provides a paradigm for a liberation that is both spiritual *and* social.[71] We see this dynamic at work in the

---

[66]See N. T. Wright, *Jesus and the Victory of God* (London: SPCK, 2015), 294.

[67]See Sharon H. Ringe, *Jesus, Liberation, and the Biblical Jubilee: Images for Ethics and Christology* (Eugene, OR: Wipf & Stock, 2004), 29-32. Note that in Luke 4:18-19, Jesus appears to be drawing on Isaiah 42:7; 58:6; 61:1-3.

[68]Florentino Garcia Martinez and Eibert J.C. Tigchelaar, *The Dead Sea Scrolls: Study Edition* (Grand Rapids, MI: Eerdmans, 1999), 1207, emphasis added. On the combination of jubilary texts in 11QMelchizekek, see Bergsma, *Jubilee*, 294.

[69]Donald Blosser, "Jesus and the Jubilee: Luke 4:16-30, the Significance of the Year of the Jubilee in the Gospel of Luke" (PhD diss., University of St. Andrews, 1979), 117.

[70]See Robert Willoughby, "The Concept of Jubilee and Luke 4:18-30," in *Mission and Meaning: Essays Presented to Peter Cotterell*, ed. Antony Billington et al. (Carlisle: Paternoster Press, 1995), 51.

[71]See Green, *Luke*, 203.

way Jesus associates the forgiveness of *sins* with the forgiveness of *debts*,[72] one of the primary social evils of his day. The majority of occurrences of Luke 4:18's language of "release" (*aphesis*) in the LXX are found in in Leviticus 25 (21 times) and Deuteronomy 15 (6 times).[73] Luke uses similar language to call disciples to forgive sins *and* forgive debts.[74] Thus the Lukan version of the Lord's Prayer combines the forgiveness of sins the disciples request from the Father with the forgiveness of debts they extend to one another (Lk 11:4).[75] Luke 7:36-50 similarly draws a tight connection between sins and debts. Moreover, Jesus' command that his disciples lend without expecting return, and his promise to bless them if they do so, draws directly on Deuteronomy 15 (Lk 6:34-36).[76]

Indeed, as Green argues, Jesus' subversion of the system of reciprocity required disciples to practice metaphorical debt forgiveness in relation to the *social* obligations that proved so oppressive to both the economically destitute and the socially marginalized.[77] Jesus' jubilary message announced good news to all sorts of marginalized groups, including the physically disabled and the demonically oppressed.[78] We have seen that the Old Testament Jubilee aimed not only at economic viability but social cohesion and solidarity. Jesus' jubilary vision emphasizes the kind of "release" that leads to the marginalized being restored to community.[79]

One final example of jubilary politics and practice comes in Luke's summaries of the economics of the early Christian community in Acts 2:42-47 and 4:32-37. In these passages, the church embraces the "eschatological lifestyle of the kingdom."[80] The signs of such a life include devotion to apostolic teaching, communal prayer, daily meals, and a sustained willingness to share possessions to provide for the well-being of those in the community.

These texts have often been understood in terms of a kind of protocommunism; the community foolishly liquidated their possessions and ate up the proceeds until the money ran out. In her remarkable book *Of Widows and*

---

[72]See Blosser, "Jesus and the Jubilee," 182. See also Ringe, *Jesus, Liberation, and the Jubilee*, 38-90.

[73]See Blosser, "Jesus and the Jubilee," 180-85; Ringe, *Jesus, Liberation, and the Jubilee*, 65-66.

[74]See Green, *Luke*, 212-13; Ringe, *Jesus, Liberation, and the Jubilee*, 34-35.

[75]See Green, *Luke*, 443; Sanders, "Jubilee in the Bible," 6; Blosser, "Jesus and the Jubilee," 271; Ringe, *Jesus, Liberation, and the Jubilee*, 79.

[76]See Blosser, "Jesus and the Jubilee," 264-66.

[77]See Green, *Luke*, 311-12, 443.

[78]Joel Green, "Good News to the Poor: A Lukan Leitmotif," *Review & Expositor* 111, no. 2 (2014): 173-79.

[79]Green, "Good News to the Poor," 173-79; Ringe, *Jesus, Liberation, and the Jubilee*, 71.

[80]Craig S. Keener, *Acts I: Introduction and 1:1–2:47* (Grand Rapids, MI: Baker Academic, 2012), 991.

Meals, Reta Haltman Finger paints a different picture.[81] These texts portray a group of people made up of representatives "from every nation under heaven" (Acts 2:5) becoming *family.*[82]

> *Families* in the ancient world didn't just consume together, they also produced together. Men might have gone out together to tend flocks, work as fishermen, or try to get hired as day laborers. Women might have tended small kitchen gardens and run home-based businesses, spinning wool or making tents. Children contributed to the work of preparing meals and much else. The revenue, tools, social connections, and even living and work spaces required to pull all this off were shared within large family networks like the one the early church became.
>
> So the picture we should have is probably not of Christians selling their homes and eating off the proceeds, but of Christians doing whatever it took to get everybody in the family contributing so everybody in the family could eat. We should picture them, perhaps, liquidating Barnabas's farm to purchase livestock in Jerusalem or tools for a new olive oil–press operation in the city. We should picture children working together in gardens and men working together in trades they shared through their connection to Christ. And we should picture all these nearly impoverished Christians coming home hot and sweaty at the end of the day to share in a little potluck meal called the Lord's Supper.[83]

Is it any wonder, then, that Luke identifies this little community as the fulfillment of Deuteronomy 15's vision, declaring that through the early church's economic practices there "were not a needy person among them" (Acts 4:34; see Deut 15:4)? Is it any wonder that Luke connects this fulfillment to a Jubilee-esque willingness to release their lands and houses for the sake of the well-being of the community as a whole?[84] And given the centrality of the Jubilee to the political, social, economic, and spiritual vision of Scripture, is it any surprise that Luke depicts a community embodying a kind of jubilary politics as the climax of his narrative's concern for the poor?[85]

Of course, part of the need for creativity in applying the Jubilee is driven by the fact that this early cell of Jesus-followers applies the Torah's jubilary politics as a paradigm for their own life and practice, rather than as a piece of

[81]Reta Halteman Finger, *Of Widows and Meals: Communal Meals in the Book of Acts* (Grand Rapids, MI: Eerdmans, 2007), 111-44, 225-44.
[82]Finger, *Of Widows and Meals,* 130.
[83]Michael Rhodes and Robby Holt, *Practicing the King's Economy: Honoring Jesus in How We Work, Earn, Spend, Save, and Give* (Grand Rapids, MI: Baker, 2018), 172.
[84]See Sanders, "Jubilee in the Bible," 6.
[85]See Keener, *Acts I,* 1013.

national political legislation. While Jesus apparently did not expect to persuade "Israel as a whole to keep the Jubilee year, *he expected his followers to live by the Jubilee principle among themselves.*"[86] The book of Acts suggests that the earliest believers got the message, forming a jubilary "contrast society" within the Roman Empire.

In short, Luke–Acts presents the Jubilee as part of an Old Testament paradigm that both shaped Jesus' holistic ministry of forgiveness, liberation, deliverance, and release, *and* guided the early church's attempt to embrace and embody that eschatological kingdom ministry in their common life together.[87] The proclamation of liberty in Leviticus echoed across the pages of Scripture, inspiring imaginations and catalyzing creative, jubilary improvisations among God's people in diverse times and places.

EMBRACING A JUBILARY IMAGINATION TODAY

Can the theology and politics of the Jubilee serve as a guide for our ecclesial politics today—remembering that by "politics" I mean community structures, institutions, and practices of ecclesial communities? Might we even speak of a Jubilee case for ecclesial reparations? Our study thus far suggests the answer is yes, it and offers at least four themes for such a jubilary argument.

First, the Jubilee remains a powerful paradigm for the life of the contemporary church, and thus a resource for thinking about how the church should respond to the case for reparations. The Levitical Jubilee testifies to the centrality of socioeconomic justice and repair in Israel's politics of holiness. In the New Testament, the church is identified as a community that is both *made holy* through the work of Jesus and *given the task* of being holy as God is holy. The way the Torah's jubilary politics echo across the canon strongly suggests that the church must embrace a jubilary politics and practice in its own life, and before the watching world, if it is to fulfill its mandate to "[host] in its midst the radical holiness of God."[88]

Moreover, time and again, we've seen that the Jubilee paradigm inspired later faith communities to embrace *innovative* and *expansive* efforts for economic justice and social solidarity, efforts that often went beyond what the original legislation required. Nehemiah's efforts go beyond what Leviticus or Deuteronomy demand, and Ezekiel offers jubilary portions in the Promised

---

[86]Wright, *Jesus and the Victory of God*, 294-95.
[87]See similarly Sanders, "Jubilee in the Bible," 5; Wright, *Jesus and the Victory of God*, 295.
[88]Davis, *Opening Israel's Scriptures*, 72.

Land to the very outsiders denied access in the Torah. Luke draws on Deuteronomy 15:1-13 to describe a way of life characterized by outlandish sacrificial generosity in pursuit of a community of belonging to which all and sundry were welcomed. There is every reason for the contemporary church to follow in the footsteps of Nehemiah, Ezekiel, and the early church in drawing on ancient texts to think creatively about how to respond to the political and economic issues of our day, including the case for reparations.

Second, just as contemporary demands for reparations highlight the need for *acknowledgment*, *repentance*, and *repair*, the Jubilee can inspire us to embrace a politics of acknowledgment, repentance, and repair in the face of socioeconomic injustice. As with the Black Manifesto, at least under some circumstances, the year of Jubilee required later generations to acknowledge, repent of, and repair the injustice created by their forefathers in previous generations. Later, Nehemiah draws on the Pentateuch's jubilary texts in his command that the people repent of their oppressive economic practices, repair the damage done, and embrace a regular practice of debt forgiveness to ensure that such oppression did not occur again. Likewise, contemporary believers should allow the Jubilee to shape us for the work of acknowledging, repenting, and repairing socioeconomic injustice in our own day, even if that requires us to address damage done in previous generations.

Third, the paradigm of the Jubilee places issues of *power* front and center. What texts like Leviticus 25, Nehemiah 5:1-13, and Ezekiel 45:7-9 aim at is not simply economic viability for all, but a relatively equitable distribution of *socioeconomic power*. The reason for this is not only practical, but theological; people are created to be co-rulers under the divine king. The practice of justice through the faithful exercise of power in community is essential to who we are as humans. Israel was meant to give the world a glimpse of God's purposes for humanity by dividing the land equitably among households and embracing the Jubilee's ongoing protection of that relatively equitable division. The politics of the Jubilee therefore offer contemporary Christians a tremendous resource for thinking creatively about how to respond to unjust and inequitable distributions of power. As we have seen, the Black Manifesto explicitly challenged the church to recognize the unjust distribution of power between Black and white Americans as an inequitable arrangement for which the church bore enormous responsibility.

Fourth, we have seen that the faith community's embrace of jubilary politics depends on *moral formation* oriented toward *economic justice*. Nehemiah offers us a negative example of this. In that text, the emergence of a class-divided society allowed the powerful to be lulled into a deeply anti-jubilary practice. But their lack of just discipleship was overcome by the power of the outcry of the oppressed themselves. Positively, Leviticus suggests that participation in the Day of Atonement and the sacred calendar would shape people to embrace the ongoing practice of a jubilary politics. In Acts, the church's jubilary innovation emerges from their devotion to apostolic teaching and practices of prayer, table fellowship, and the sacraments.[89] Moreover, the very fact that Jeremiah, Ezekiel, Nehemiah, Jesus, and Luke all drew so freely and naturally on texts like Deuteronomy 15 and Leviticus 25 suggests that these economic laws had gotten down deep in their bones. Their imaginations and their ethical character had been shaped by regular reflection on the Bible's jubilary politics.

JUBILARY POLITICS AND THE CASE FOR REPARATIONS

These four themes related to the biblical Jubilee ought to inspire us to pursue just discipleship in all sorts of ways, including in response to the Manifesto's demand for ecclesial reparations. Ultimately, the church has not embraced the Manifesto in any widespread way, either in 1969 or since. But the demand for reparations has continued, and nowhere more fervently than in relation to the wealth gap between Black and white households.

Black households hold a mere one-tenth the net worth of white households.[90] This statistic is quoted so often that it's easy to miss the enormity of the injustice that lies behind it. In 1865, Black people owned a mere 0.5 percent "of the total worth of the United States."[91] Given the legacy of slavery, this is unsurprising. What *is* surprising is that 135 years later, in 1990, Black Americans still owned "a meager 1% of total wealth."[92]

This wealth disparity persists despite the fact that Black Americans save just as much as white Americans at every income level.[93] This wealth disparity persists whether or not Black individuals make the choices in family

---

[89]Based on the clear reference to baptism in Acts 2:41 and assuming that the reference to "the breaking of the bread" includes the Eucharist.

[90]William Darity Jr. and Kirsten Mullen, *From Here to Equality: Reparations for Black Americans in the Twenty-First Century* (Chapel Hill: University of North Carolina Press, 2020), 31.

[91]Dalton Conley, *Being Black, Living in the Red: Race, Wealth, and Social Policy in America* (Berkeley: University of California Press, 2010), 25.

[92]Conley, *Being Black*, 25.

[93]Darity and Mullen, *From Here to Equality*, 33.

life and education that we often associate with economic success. On average, single white parents have twice the wealth of married Black parents and Black household heads with a college degree have "about $10,000 less in median net worth than white household heads" who dropped out of high school."[94] Indeed, Black people "who are working full-time have a lower median net worth than whites who are unemployed."[95]

This wealth disparity persists, in other words, primarily because of past and present racism.[96] On the one hand, white wealth gained through oppression in the past directly contributes to white wealth in the present, because the "major sources of wealth for most" people in the United States comes through inheritances and gifts living parents give to their adult children.[97] On the other hand, Black families were repeatedly denied the opportunity to build wealth well into the twentieth century. Indeed, the US government persistently blocked Black people from participating in America's largest wealth-building initiatives:

- The Homestead Act enabled pioneer families to purchase up to 160 acres of public land for a nominal fee. Nearly a quarter of the US adult population's ancestors received such land. Blacks were largely excluded from the program.[98]

- Black Americans were systematically denied access to the FHA-backed mortgages that dramatically increased homeownership among white Americans. This occurred primarily through redlining,[99] a practice whereby banks would not make home loans in majority Black neighborhoods.

- The GI Bill allowed southern states to exclude Black veterans from the benefits of the wealth-building provisions in the legislation.[100] For instance, out of 3,229 "guaranteed home, business, and farm loans made in 1947 in Mississippi," only two went to Black veterans.[101]

---

[94]Darity and Mullen, *From Here to Equality*, 33.

[95]Darity and Mullen, *From Here to Equality*, 33.

[96]See Jonathan Tran, *Asian Americans and the Spirit of Racial Capitalism* (New York: Oxford University Press, 2022), 225-27; Thomas Pikketty, "About Capital in the Twenty-First Century," *American Economic Review* 105, no. 5 (2015): 48-53.

[97]Darity, "Forty Acres," 661.

[98]See Rhodes and Holt, *Practicing the King's Economy*, 178-79; Darity and Mullen, *From Here to Equality*, 37.

[99]Ta-Nehisi Coates, "The Case for Reparations," *Atlantic*, June 2014, www.theatlantic.com/magazine/archive/2014/06/the-case-for-reparations/361631.

[100]Ira Katznelson, "When Affirmative Action Was White," *History & Policy*, November 10, 2005, http://historyandpolicy.org/policy-papers/papers/when-affirmative-action-was-white.

[101]Katznelson, "When Affirmative Action Was White."

Nor has systemic economic exploitation come to an end. Between 2000 and 2013, both Wells Fargo and Bancorp South were found guilty of race-based predatory lending and race-based redlining in my hometown of Memphis.[102] One recent study demonstrated that Black-owned businesses were twice as likely to have loan applications rejected as whites with "otherwise similar financial backgrounds." When Black firms did get approved for loans, they were "more likely to pay higher interest rates."[103]

How should churches respond to this racial wealth gap, which has created both enormous economic suffering and a dramatic monopolization of social power in American society? First, the Jubilee should inspire contemporary churches to see addressing socioeconomic injustice, in the church and beyond it, as central to its mission. Indeed, Scripture's jubilary politics should inspire Christians to "spend themselves" sacrificially and innovatively in redressing the socioeconomic injustice of our society.

This is all the more crucial because, drawing on our second theme, applying the Jubilee to our context requires us to *acknowledge* the role white churches and Christians played in perpetrating and perpetuating theft, *repent* of that history, and commit ourselves to *repairing* it. Given both the history of white supremacy in the church and the persistent, enormous wealth disparity that continues into our own day, we white Christians are confronted with Isaiah's searing indictment: *the "spoil of the poor is in your houses"* (Is 3:14). According to Scripture's jubilary politics, the fact that we do not belong to the generation that originally put that plunder there does not change the moral fact. The Jubilee summons contemporary Christian communities to *confess* intergenerational economic sins, in part by *repairing* them through costly social action.

What might this look like today? Without giving enormous energy toward the task, we can only guess! But I think the Jubilee might inspire a generation of Christians to think creatively about how to practice reparations. Congregations or denominations could study the history of economic theft in their own communities as a way of seeking to identify the scope of the theft that occurred and what it might look like to repair it. In some instances, that history might become quite specific. Virginia Theological Seminary's efforts

---

[102]James O'Toole, "Wells Fargo Pledges $432.5 Million in Lending, Payments to Settle Lawsuit," CNN Money, May 31, 2012, http://money.cnn.com/2012/05/30/news/companies/wells-fargo -memphis/index.htm; Ken Sweet, "Regulators Fine BancorpSouth $10.6 Million for Redlining," *The Washington Times*, June 29, 2016, https://www.washingtontimes.com/news/2016/jun/29 /regulators-fine-bancorpsouth-106-million-for-redli/.

[103]Darity and Mullen, *From Here to Equality*, 41.

to uncover the institution's complicity in white supremacy led to the establishment of a $1.7 million endowment fund to be used in part to support known "descendants of enslaved persons that worked at the seminary."[104] Such an effort, the school says, is part of a later generation of Christians' attempt to "repair the material consequences of our sin in the past."[105]

Exploring my family's and my community's history and seeking to repent of my sins and the sins of my ancestors has been an important part of my own struggle with just discipleship. I opened this book by telling the story of my church's historic failures. More personally, acknowledging and repenting of the sins of my ancestors includes confessing my family tree includes Robert E. Lee—a nineteenth-century Confederate general who oversaw the massacre of Black Union soldiers and used torture to "discipline" slaves—and a twentieth-century newspaper man who used the power of the pen to advocate for the establishment of the Stone Mountain Confederate Memorial that valorized Lee and others like him.[106] It includes confessing that I have inherited the kind of economic legacy granted to white veterans like my beloved grandfathers, but denied to their Black veteran colleagues.[107] Such repentance, the Jubilee suggests, must lead beyond mere acknowledgment, and toward genuine effort at repair.

In light of our third theme, the Jubilee could inspire churches to connect reparation money with a redistribution of power. This means placing money designated for reparations *outside* the control of the communities paying such reparations.[108] Schoonmaker suggests churches could practice such reparations by giving substantial freewill offerings to historically Black congregations with no strings attached.[109] The idea makes enormous sense, given that

---

[104]See "Reparations" on the Virginia Theological Seminary's website: www.vts.edu/about/multicultural-ministries-/reparations.

[105]P. R. Lockhart, "A Virginia Seminary Is the First School to Create a Reparations Fund," *Vox*, September 10, 2019, www.vox.com/identities/2019/9/10/20859407/virginia-theological-seminary-reparations-slavery-segregation.

[106]On Robert E. Lee, see Adam Serwer, "The Myth of the Kindly General Lee," *Atlantic*, June 4, 2017, www.theatlantic.com/politics/archive/2017/06/the-myth-of-the-kindly-general-lee/529038.

[107]It also includes confessing the ways my own heart and mind have been deformed by life lived within these histories. See Michael Rhodes, "Should We Repent of Our Grandparents' Racism? Scripture on Intergenerational Sin," *The Biblical Mind*, June 19, 2020, https://hebraicthought.org/repenting-intergenerational-racist-ideology-scripture-intergenerational-sin.

[108]This idea should raise questions, for instance, about historically white theological institutions using all or most of any reparation funds for scholarships at their own institution, given the way that such repair leaves the power dynamics relatively unchanged.

[109]Geoffrey Schoonmaker, "Preaching About Race: A Homiletic for Racial Reconciliation" (PhD diss., Vanderbilt University, 2012), 118.

the white church served as the "moral cement" of America's racist society, and often forced Black Christians *out* of white churches and denominations. At the same time, arguably no institution in America has done more for Black empowerment than the Black church!

But churches and denominations could also establish reparations funds that are overseen by Black leadership and distributed however they determined would best serve the goal of repairing the damage done by white supremacy, and especially the racial wealth gap. To address that gap, William Darity and Kirsten Mullen suggest a diverse "portfolio of reparations" that could include "direct payments"; the establishment of a trust fund to which Black people could apply for funds to buy a home, go to school, start a small business, or purchase financial assets; and investing in Black institutions.[110] The church could create such funds, understanding that work as one way of declaring a Jubilee in response to centuries of anti-jubilary politics and practice.

Given that I have argued for the Jubilee as a paradigm for the politics of the church, it makes sense that Christian efforts at reparations begin within each faith community's *own* politics, their institutional structures and corporate practices.[111] The church's self-understanding as an outpost of the kingdom suggests that the church's politics begin with its own life.

But this ecclesial embrace of a jubilary politics would also have implications for the church's engagement with national conversations around reparations. If the church embraced the work of learning its history and seeking to repent of and repair the damage done by that history through innovative efforts at jubilary reparations, it would have more to offer the public debate about reparations. Darity and Mullen, for instance, recognize that reparations will not occur unless there is a dramatic shift in public sentiment; ecclesial reparations could participate in fostering such a shift. Moreover, if the funding for a national reparations program took the form of a "super fund" into which both the federal government and other institutions in civil society could contribute, a movement of ecclesial, jubilary reparations might prepare the way for that national program.[112]

---

[110]Darity and Mullen, *From Here to Equality*, 264-65.

[111]Darity and Mullen oppose such piecemeal efforts at reparations, arguing that the federal government is the institution that bears direct responsibility for enabling white supremacist violence and theft at a national level, and the only institution capable of footing the entire bill. See Darity and Mullen, *From Here to Equality*, 269.

[112]On such super funds, see Darity and Mullen, *From Here to Equality*, 266.

Finally, though, in line with our fourth theme, for the church to embrace a jubilary politics would require the church to embrace whole-life discipleship oriented toward justice, inspired by the Jubilee. The liturgy and worshiping life of the church would have to shape Christians not only to identify their personal sins for which they receive forgiveness, but also to name the "sins of the fathers" and commit to address them. Discipleship would welcome believers to listen to the cries of the poor and would replace our grasping tendency for self-preservation with a cultivated disposition toward open-handed generosity. The preaching, teaching, and worshiping life of the church would become saturated with Scripture's intoxicating jubilary vision of a world in which Jesus' generous reign means that everyone can "sit under their own vine and fig tree" and "none shall be made afraid."

The good news is that *seeking* to embody a jubilary politics is itself an act of just discipleship. The road is made by walking; we become Jubilee disciples by seeking to arrange our corporate lives in line with the Jubilee. We don't have to have all our reparations questions answered to begin living toward a jubilary way of life.

Few issues are more controversial than reparations. But few visions of Jesus' kingdom are as all-encompassing, intoxicating, and joy-inducing as the year of Jubilee. It's time to bring that glorious, joyful vision to the messy, painful task of seeking justice in our world today. It's time to embrace a Jubilee case for ecclesial reparations.

REARRANGING THE CHAIRS
IN THE BELOVED COMMUNITY

Just Discipleship and the Politics
of the Multiethnic Church
in 1 Corinthians and Today

THE WAY JESUS AND THE EARLY CHURCH creatively drew on the Old Testament in arranging their corporate life together reminds us that, for Christians, just discipleship is received and embraced first and foremost within the church.[1] By the power of the Spirit, the people of God are gathered into ecclesial communities that serve as outposts of the kingdom. The church thus exists as a "form of down payment, a guarantee that the age of justice, peace, and joy is not a pipe dream but a future reality that can be known, imperfectly and incompletely but really, in the present."[2] The life of the people of God makes the coming kingdom proclaimed in Scripture *habitable* to a hurting world.[3]

---

[1]Much of the material for this chapter first appeared in Michael J. Rhodes, "Arranging the Chairs in the Beloved Community: The Politics, Problems, and Prospects of Multi-Racial Congregations in 1 Corinthians and Today," *SCE* 33, no. 4 (2019), and is used here with permission. For theological and ethical accounts that likewise prioritize the church, see Stanley Hauerwas and Samuel Wells, eds., *The Blackwell Companion to Christian Ethics*, Blackwell Companions to Religion (Malden, MA: Blackwell, 2004), 6-7; Oliver O'Donovan, *The Desire of the Nations: Rediscovering the Roots of Political Theology* (Cambridge: Cambridge University Press, 1996), 158-62; James K. A. Smith, *Awaiting the King: Reforming Public Theology*, Cultural Liturgies vol. 3 (Grand Rapids, MI: Baker Academic, 2017), 1-90.

[2]Michael Gorman, *Becoming the Gospel: Paul, Participation, and Mission* (Grand Rapids, MI: Eerdmans, 2015), 47.

[3]Stanley Hauerwas, *With the Grain of the Universe* (Grand Rapids, MI: Brazos Press, 2001), 214.

This focus on the church does not mean the people of God withdraw from their broader cultural contexts. The church's experience of God's transforming power within the community equips believers for the church's outward mission, sending believers to live all of life under the reign of Christ. Living as citizens of God's kingdom in every space to which we have been sent is itself a form of just discipleship, part of the way that God invites us to become more and more the people he has given to us to become. In light of all this, a primary place where Christians ought to find themselves becoming just, not least in relation to the racial and economic injustices we have explored in this book, is within the local church.

Yet this theological claim runs up against the reality of church failure that we have encountered again and again. In relation to racism, we continue to be confronted with Dr. King's assertion that "eleven o'clock on Sunday is the most segregated hour of the week."[4] Indeed, fifty years after his prophetic condemnation of church segregation, the "typical church in America" lacks even a single person from a different racial group among their membership.[5] If we understand racial segregation as unjust, it's hard to see how segregated churches could shape God's people for the work of racial justice.

Jennings further complicates the picture by arguing that the church's discipleship practices have often contributed to racial injustice in the past. In the early days of colonialism, the missionary impulse of the church demonically embraced and was embraced by a colonialist logic that placed people on racial hierarchies for the purposes of both would-be Christian formation *and* economic exploitation.[6] Christian discipleship sought to shape people for life with God *and* life in a white supremacist racial hierarchy that profited off them, at the same time and in the same space.

This unjust, anti-discipleship was embraced in the church's life and liturgy. When some of the earliest slave traders arrived in Portugal in 1444, Prince Henry received 235 slaves, and then ordered that two slaves be given to the

[4]Martin Luther King Jr., "Meet the Press" interview, April 17, 1960, www.youtube.com/watch?v=1q88lg1L_d8. At the same time, the politics of the black church has fueled transformation inside black congregations and beyond. See Katie G. Cannon, *Black Womanist Ethics* (Eugene, OR: Wipf & Stock, 2006), 19; Charles Marsh, *The Beloved Community: How Faith Shapes Social Justice from the Civil Rights Movement to Today* (Grand Rapids, MI: Baker, 2006); James H. Cone, *The Cross and the Lynching Tree* (Ossining, NY: Orbis Books, 2011), 1-29.
[5]Korie L. Edwards, *The Elusive Dream: The Power of Race in Interracial Churches* (New York: Oxford University Press, 2008), 15.
[6]See Edwards, *Elusive Dream*, 27, 35.

church as a tithe, an offering of worship to God.[7] Slave catechisms in the New World were created to teach baptized slaves that "everybody is best, just where God has placed them," and to force slaves to answer "God gave them to me" in response to the question "Who gave you a master and mistress?"[8] Black and white church members worshiped in segregated seating sections.[9] Even the giving of new names to the baptized could be used to dislocate Black people from their historic identities in order to claim those identities for use by white slave masters.[10] Tithing, catechesis, worship, baptism, Eucharist . . . all were rendered powerless to address racial injustice and indeed actually shaped people *for* racial injustice.

Grimes argues that under these circumstances, churches became "habitat[s] for vice."[11] When ecclesial formation is infected with white supremacy, life lived in the church too often forms white people to become "inept at the practice of racial justice and skillfully adept at the pursuit of racial injustice."[12] While explicitly segregated churches and slave catechisms are a thing of the past, our ongoing residential and ecclesial segregation means that today, far too often, "neither baptism nor the Eucharist [bring] parochially segregated Black and white" Christians together.[13]

MULTIETHNIC CHURCHES: A POTENTIAL SOLUTION?

Perhaps, however, intentionally multiethnic congregations provide a bright spot amid a depressing racialized landscape. Such churches see the reform of the church itself as key to racial justice in society more broadly. Indeed, many see themselves as responding to Dr. King's challenge by pursuing the "beloved community" within a congregation. Maybe in this way they play a special role in living out an ecclesial politics that makes the just kingdom of God habitable in the world.

That's certainly what has drawn me to multiethnic congregations in my own life and ministry. I served as a worship leader at New City Fellowship Nairobi, a deeply multiethnic congregation that sang in six different languages and brought people together across racial, national, and tribal lines. I was

---

[7] William James Jennings, *The Christian Imagination: Theology and the Origins of Race* (New Haven, CT: Yale University Press, 2010), 16.

[8] Jennings, *Christian Imagination*, 239.

[9] Grimes, *Christ Divided*, 115.

[10] Grimes, *Christ Divided*, 190-92.

[11] Grimes, *Christ Divided*, 87.

[12] Grimes, *Christ Divided*, 93.

[13] Grimes, *Christ Divided*, 200-201.

ordained as a pastor at Downtown Church, a multiethnic congregation in our Memphis neighborhood that had a special focus on reconciliation between Black and white Christians. I have been deeply blessed and transformed by my experience in these congregations. I believe in them.

Along the way, though, it has become increasingly clear that the experience of many people of color within multiethnic churches is more conflicted than we might have hoped. In her important book *The Elusive Dream: The Power of Race in Interracial Churches,* Edwards explores this dynamic with a special focus on the relationship between Black and white Christians within multiethnic congregations. She argues that the conflicted experience of Black participants in such churches has a simple explanation: multiethnic congregations often simply reproduce white norms and power structures.[14] Drawing on data from the National Congregations Study and an in-depth case study of a predominantly Black multiethnic congregation with a Black pastor, Edwards argues that interracial churches "work, that is remain racially integrated, to the extent that they are *first* comfortable places for whites to attend."[15]

What this means is that multiethnic churches often require people of color to assimilate to white norms. In doing so, they simultaneously reinforce those norms for white attendees.[16] Edwards describes how this dynamic plays out in some detail. Her analysis of the way white, Black, and multiethnic congregations worship,[17] talk about (or fail to talk about) race,[18] and engage (or fail to engage) sociopolitical issues in their communities demonstrates that the average multiethnic church essentially acts just like a white church.[19] Thus even as multiethnic churches attempt to embody King's "beloved community" by bringing everyone "to the table," white norms often continue to "arrange the chairs."

In terms of just discipleship, this is deeply problematic. On the one hand, Black congregants can pay a heavy price for attending such multiethnic congregations. As Canon eloquently argues, the Black church has historically served as "the community's sole institution of power . . . the only place

---

[14]This is not to say that every multiethnic congregation is the same. The arguments presented here may primarily apply to efforts at multiethnic church planting led by predominantly white denominations.

[15]Edwards, *Elusive Dream*, 6.

[16]Edwards, *Elusive Dream*, 4-13.

[17]Edwards, *Elusive Dream*, 26-32.

[18]Edwards, *Elusive Dream*, 41-68.

[19]Edwards, *Elusive Dream*, 40-42.

outside the home where Blacks could express themselves freely and take independent action . . . the heart, center, and basic organization of Black life . . .
the citadel of hope."[20] "It is only when we are within the walls of our churches,"
Richard Wright declares concerning the Black church experience, "that we
can wholly be ourselves."[21] Black people in multiethnic churches may face
significant losses in joining churches that are *ethnically* diverse but that require a high degree of *cultural* homogeneity.

On the other hand, the fact that white norms are maintained *implicitly*
allows white members to learn *not* to identify and confront ongoing white
norms and power structures. The *illusion* that these have been overcome in
the congregation contributes to the possibility that multiethnic congregations
serve as habitats for racial vice. In such cases, multiethnic churches risk miti-
gating the problem of the segregated Sunday morning while making the
problem of a racially oppressive Christianity worse. Edwards's research suggests that if multiethnic churches want to embrace genuine justice and reconciliation, they must "rearrange the chairs" so that their ecclesial life undermines,
rather than reinforces, oppressive racist norms.

Paul's criticism of the Corinthian's practice of the Lord's Supper offers multiethnic churches tools for doing just that. This book began with a story from
the church that raised me. My reading of 1 Corinthians emerges from my
more recent experience as a white person attending and leading within a
multiethnic congregation of the sort described, and critiqued, by Edwards.
Her critiques force readers like me to reckon with our "moral kinship with
the Corinthians"[22] whom Paul confronts for their behavior at the Lord's
Supper. While the present chapter focuses on relationships between Black and
white congregants within multiethnic congregations,[23] Paul's assault on division at the Eucharist applies to all sorts of divisions within the church,
ethnic and otherwise. Crucially, Paul does not simply criticize multiethnic
churches; he offers them a hope-filled invitation to rearrange their lives together as outposts of God's just kingdom.

---

[20]Cannon, *Black Womanist Ethics*, 19.

[21]Quoted in James H. Cone, *The Cross and the Lynching Tree* (Ossining, NY: Orbis Books, 2011), 18.

[22]See Brian Brock and Bernd Wannenwetsch, *The Malady of the Christian Body: A Theological Exposition of Paul's First Letter to the Corinthians*, vol. 1 (Eugene, OR: Wipf & Stock, 2016), xx-xi.

[23]Note that while my focus on Black people within multiethnic congregations is driven primarily by my own context (on which, see chapter 1), it is also the case that Black people are by far and away the largest nonwhite racial group involved in interracial congregations in North America. See Edwards, *Elusive Dream*, 154.

ARRANGING THE CHAIRS AT CORINTH

Paul opens his letter to the Corinthians by declaring the world-restructuring reality that their lives are now lived in fellowship (*koinonia*) with the Messiah (1 Cor 1:9). Every Corinthian would presumably consider this mutual fellowship with Jesus good news. What some may have preferred to forget is the intrinsically political nature of such *koinonia*.

The Roman society within which the Corinthians lived "was a steep-sided pyramid, with carefully defined grades and an insistence on the natural, immutable place each person was to occupy in the hierarchy."[24] Within this hierarchy, social capital consisting of wisdom, power, and station could be used to gain social status and economic advantage. In this context, Paul argues that the Triune God is establishing a community in Corinth that is grounded in the cross. The crucified Messiah has unleashed the "power of God and wisdom of God" in Corinth.

Indeed, the cross serves as a guiding political principle in Christ's formation of the Corinthian community. God has chosen to build his church with the foolish and weak in order to shame the wise and strong. God has chosen to build his church with those who are "low and despised" so that he might "reduce to nothing" (*katargēsē*) the "things that are" (1 Cor 1:27-28).

God thus overturns the Corinthian socioeconomic pyramid in his construction of the church. In the context of the letter, the language of bringing to nothing (*katargeō*) is unmistakably political. In the next chapter, for instance, Paul describes the cruciform wisdom of God as standing in stark contrast to the "rulers of this age" who are "doomed to perish" (*tōn katargoumenōn*; 1 Cor 2:6). In 1 Corinthians 15:24, Paul uses the same verb to describe Christ's abolishment of *every* rule and authority and power, culminating in the destruction of death itself (1 Cor 15:26). Read together, these references to the rulers of this age seem to encompass both worldly human political powers and the "false powers" of Sin and Death that stand behind them and which are in some sense the source of injustice and oppression.[25] Both are inextricably bound up with the "wisdom of this age" condemned at the cross, including that worldly wisdom's way of dividing people up into "haves" and "have nots." The cross has "not only broken the back of the powers who would

---

[24]Dale Martin, *The Corinthian Body* (New Haven, CT: Yale University Press), 30.
[25]See Lisa Bowens, "Spirit-Shift: Paul, the Poor, and the Holy Spirit's Ethic of Love and Impartiality in the Eucharist Celebration," in *The Spirit and Social Justice: Interdisciplinary Global Perspectives,* ed. Antipas L. Harris and Michael D. Palmer (Lanham, MD: Seymour Press, 2019).

keep humans separate from God; it has decimated the boundaries they set up to divide humans from each other."[26]

In her work on African American readings of Paul, Lisa Bowens offers a relatively modern example of the explosive power of Paul's logic in the story of Zilpha Elaw, an early Black woman preacher born in the eighteenth century. Called by God to preach under the most hostile circumstances, Elaw wrote about the shock it was to white slave owners to see a Black woman teaching and preaching. "Many of the slave holders . . . thought it surpassingly strange that a person and a female belonging to the same family stock with their poor debased, uneducated, coloured slaves, should come into their territories and teach the enlightened proprietors the *knowledge of God. . . . But God hath chosen the weak things of the world to confound the mighty.*"[27]

Elaw recognized that the church's life constitutes the irruption in the present age of a community embodying the politics of God's coming kingdom. Christ has not only provided liberation from the "rulers of this age," he has fleshed out what that liberation looks like among his people by overturning the Corinthian socioeconomic pyramid *in his arrangement of the church*.

The church's participation in this missional vocation is both a gift to be received *and* a task to be embraced. Paul emphasizes the giftedness in 1 Corinthians 1:18-31, which presents God's work in the church as a fact that God has already accomplished. In the next chapter, however, he makes clear that embracing the task requires the Corinthians to *become* wise in the way of the cross (1 Cor 2:6-7). Such cruciform wisdom will require the Corinthians, and particularly those who could claim to be "wise" in the logic of the world, to become worldly fools (1 Cor 3:18) in their practice of cross-shaped love and service (1 Cor 4:9-16).[28] It is the failure of the Corinthian church to gather in ways that fit this task that draws Paul's ire in 1 Corinthians 11:17-34.

GATHERING FOR THE WORSE

Paul opens his attack on the Corinthians' would-be eucharistic meals by declaring that, when they gather, they gather for the worse rather than for the better (1 Cor 11:17). Why? Because their feasts "shame the have nots" and

---

[26]Brian K. Blount, *Then the Whisper Put on Flesh: New Testament Ethics in an African American Context* (Nashville: Abingdon, 2001), 130.

[27]Lisa M. Bowens, *African American Readings of Paul: Reception, Resistance, and Transformation* (Grand Rapids, MI: Eerdmans, 2020), 90.

[28]See Michael Rhodes, *Formative Feasting: Practices and Virtue Ethics in the Deuteronomic Tithe Meal and Corinthian Lord's Supper*, Studies in Biblical Literature 176 (New York: Peter Lang, 2022), 170-86.

"contempt for the church of God" (1 Cor 11:22). Because the Eucharist stood at the center of early Christian worship, this amounts to Paul saying that going to church was making the people worse! The church had become a "habitat of vice," rather than an outpost of God's kingdom that shaped its members for the work of just discipleship. How exactly were they shaming the poor and despising God's church? Scholars debate the details, but for our purposes we can identify two essential background elements.

First, both Paul's rhetoric and scholarly research on the socioeconomic location of Paul's congregations suggests that the Corinthian church had significant economic diversity. The vast majority of the church's members were almost certainly from the poorer classes. But the church also likely included a much smaller group of congregants who regularly had a modest economic surplus.[29]

Second, within the Greco-Roman world, and especially among associations, meals provided a primary space for claiming one's spot within the socioeconomic and political hierarchy. Associations could include individuals from across the socioeconomic spectrum, including the "lower" classes.[30] Because such associations were simultaneously "autonomous in their structure" and "part of the urban structure of Roman society," their meals provided the community with a politically and morally formative space that could either support or undermine the broader political realities within which the community found itself.[31]

At such meals, decisions about who presided over and provisioned the food, where and how guests sat at the table, and the quantity and quality of the portions guests received all served a political purpose. On the one hand, meals created a sense of solidarity and equality among members.[32] On the

---

[29]For debate about poverty levels and stratification in Pauline churches, see Gerd Theissen, *The Social Setting of Pauline Christianity: Essays on Corinth*, ed. and trans. John H. Schutz (Philadelphia: Fortress, 1982), 164; Steven J. Friesen, "Poverty in Pauline Studies: Beyond the So-Called New Consensus," *JSNT* 26, no. 3 (2004): 363-66; Bruce W. Longenecker, *Remember the Poor: Paul, Poverty, and the Greco-Roman World* (Grand Rapids, MI: Eerdmans, 2010), 53; Timothy A. Brookins, "Economic Profiling of Early Christian Communities," in *Paul and Economics: A Handbook*, ed. Thomas R. Blanton IV and Raymond Pickett (Minneapolis: Fortress, 2017), 81.

[30]See, among others, Richard S. Ascough, "Social and Political Characteristics of Greco-Roman Association Meals," in *Meals in the Early Christian World: Social Formation, Experimentation, and Conflict at the Table*, ed. Dennis E. Smith and Hal Taussig (New York: Palgrave MacMillan, 2012), 59.

[31]Ascough, "Social and Political," 60.

[32]See R. Alan Streett, *Subversive Meals: An Analysis of the Lord's Super Under Roman Domination During the First Century* (Eugene, OR: Wipf & Stock, 2013), 23-25; John S. Kloppenborg,

other hand, meals recognized and reinforced social and economic divisions between participants. Banquets gave associations opportunities "to pay tribute to merited members"[33] or honored guests. Guests further up the social hierarchy could receive larger portions or higher quality food or wine, a practice attested in both the elite literature and in the inscriptions and bylaws of some associations.[34] Seating arrangements recognized and reinforced social hierarchies to such an extent that some associations had to fine members who competitively tried to "move up" the social hierarchy—quite literally—by taking the "better" seat of another.[35]

The awarding of titles, the creation of dedications and inscriptions listing members' gifts to the group, the invitation to elite outsiders to join the meal, and more all participated in a moral economy in which honor was created, competed for, earned, and distributed at the table.[36] In short, if banquets created a certain sense of equality, they also made it clear to all that "some were more equal than others."[37]

In Corinth, then, the *literal* arrangement of the chairs at a meal allowed participants to earn, receive, distribute, share, and compete for honor and status. Such status constituted the primary social capital needed to participate in the politics of the city and pursue economic advantage in the marketplace. Apparently, this behavior had found its way into the eucharistic meals of the Corinthian church.

For instance, Paul's language in 1 Corinthians 11:17-34 likely alludes to the competitive, status-seeking politics that occurred at association meals.

"Precedence at the Communal Meal in Corinth," *Novum Testamentum* 58, no. 2 (2016): 171; Dennis E. Smith, *From Symposium to Eucharist: The Banquet in the Early Christian World* (Minneapolis: Augsburg Fortress, 2003), 111.

[33]Matthias Klinghardt, "A Typology of the Communal Meal," in Smith and Taussig, *Meals in the Early Christian World*, 15.

[34]See Martial, *Epigrams*, I.20, 3.60 [LCL Bailey]; Pliny, *Ep.* II.vi [LCL Melmoth]; Theissen, *Social Setting*, 158; IDelos 1520, trans. Philip Harland, http://philipharland.com/greco-roman -associations/224-honors-by-berytian-immigrants-for-a-roman-banker; Ascough, "Social and Political Characteristics," 59.

[35]See Dennis E. Smith, "Meals and Morality in Paul and his World," *Society of Biblical Literature Seminar Papers* 20 (1981), 324; John K. Chow, *Patronage and Power: A Study of Social Networks in Corinth* (Sheffield: Sheffield Academic Press, 1992), 68; Rachel M. McRae, "Eating with Honor: The Corinthian Lord's Supper in Light of Voluntary Association Meal Practices," *JBL* 130, no. 1 (2011): 167; Jerome Murphy-O'Connor, *Keys to First Corinthians: Revisiting the Major Issues* (Oxford: Oxford University Press, 2009), 182.

[36]See Kloppenborg, "Precedence," 192-93.

[37]Dennis E. Smith, "The Greco-Roman Banquet as a Social Institution," in Smith and Taussig, *Meals in the Early Christian World*, 29.

Twice he uses the verb "praise" (*epaineō*) to declare that he has none for those who are behaving this way in church. But Kloppenborg points out that *epaineō* is one of the most common verbs used by Greco-Roman associations when they made decrees celebrating and honoring specific members of their group.[38] If those shaming the have nots did so by claiming honor and prerogatives they believed were due to them because of their praiseworthy status, Paul's refusal to give them praise is an ironic slap in the face.

Moreover, Paul's deeply ironic statement that their divisions reveal those who are *hoi dokimoi* among them gestures in a similar direction. *Hoi dokimoi* can refer to those "considered worthy of high regard, respect, or esteemed,"[39] and is often used, along with its verbal form, to describe the testing and approval of new members who wanted to join an association.[40] "Consequently, the term *genuine* (*dokimoi*) . . . derives its primary meaning from the politics of the table whereby rankings are to be assigned to those of higher status"[41] and demonstrated or approved character. Against this backdrop, Paul declares to the powerful that their actions, which they "thought merely marked them as social elites, in fact ironically marked them as standing under divine judgment."[42]

Paul criticizes the Corinthians for exalting the "haves" against the "have nots" in the way they gathered. At the very least, they probably offered better seats and more and better food to believers with a higher status in Corinthian society. We need to be clear, though: most Corinthians probably saw this as culturally appropriate business as usual. The more powerful Corinthians likely contributed more to the community's meal than others. What harm could there possibly be in providing some sign of honor and status to them for their service?

Every harm imaginable, at least according to Paul. Standing in a long tradition of prophets who condemned the worship of God's people because of their oppression of the socioeconomically poor (see Is 1:11-17; Amos 5:18-24),

---

[38]John S. Kloppenborg, "Associations, Christ Groups, and Their Place in the *Polis*," *ZNW* 108, no. 1 (2017): 39.

[39]Roy E. Ciampa and Brian Rosner, *The First Letter to the Corinthians*, PNTC (Grand Rapids, MI: Eerdmans, 2010), 544.

[40]John S. Kloppenborg, "The Moralizing of Discourse in Greco-Roman Associations," in *"The One Who Sows Bountifully": Essays in Honor of Stanley K. Stowers*, ed. Caroline Johnson Hodge et al. (Providence, RI: Brown Judaic Studies, 2013), 218-19.

[41]Smith, *Symposium to Eucharist*, 197; see also McRae, "Eating with Honor," 179.

[42]Ciampa and Rosner, *Corinthians*, 544.

the apostle declares that their behavior makes it utterly impossible to call the meal they are eating a genuine Lord's Supper.

Given Paul's vision of the church as designed to embody the upside-down politics of God's kingdom, it is easy to see why. *Their meals are more Corinthian than Christian.* Like the multiethnic churches Edwards studies, the way they arrange the chairs may communicate that everyone belongs at the table. But that arrangement simultaneously reinforces the broader culture's understanding of who at the table matters more and who matters less. The congregation in Corinth, like many multiethnic congregations today, fails to embrace the politics of God's kingdom in their common life together.[43]

Note that Paul can only confront the church in this way because of a report that he has *heard* (1 Cor 11:18). The most likely candidates to have spoken up to Paul about this issue are themselves lower status believers within the congregation, perhaps those servants from the house of Chloe referred to in 1 Corinthians 1:11. As in Nehemiah's day, the healing of social stratification and oppression within the community of faith requires leaders to listen to the outcry of the community's victims, and then throw their weight behind them (1 Cor 11:34).

But Paul does not merely point out that their meetings currently reflect the politics of Corinth more than the politics of Christ. He calls the Corinthians to "rearrange their chairs." Thus, after rebuking "the community for a meal that is *not* Christlike," Paul reminds them of the story of Jesus' own Last Supper.

> For I received from the Lord what I passed on to you, that the Lord Jesus, on the night that he was handed over, he took bread, and after giving thanks, he broke it and said: "This is my body, which is for you. Do this in remembrance of me." In the same way, after supper, he took the cup, saying: "This cup is the new covenant in my blood. Do this, as often as you drink it, in remembrance of me." For as often as you eat this bread and drink this cup, you proclaim the Lord's death until he comes. (1 Cor 11:23-26 AT)

Paul reminds the Corinthians of the story-shaped roots of their feast in order to draw their attention to Jesus and his sacrificial self-offering on the cross for their sake. This story is an openly political story, the story of a crucified king who gave his body and blood in order to establish a new covenant community. In line with our model of moral formation, Paul expects this story to shape the character of the community.

---

[43]Brock and Wannenwetsch, *Malady,* 12.

But Paul does not simply remind them of the story of Jesus' death for their sakes. He reminds them of Jesus' command to *practice* that story, to ritually reenact it through the eucharistic feast itself. This meal ought to play a major role in their moral discipleship, shaping them "for the better" by forming in them a kind of embodied memory of Jesus' death. Their feast should serve as a morally formative practice that fosters in them a holistic, virtuous disposition to remember Christ's loving self-sacrifice and to enter a community founded on and committed to such loving self-sacrifice in the world.

Having reminded them of the story of the Lord's Supper and the Lord's instruction to *practice* that story in their meal, Paul goes on to claim that their meal practice has been coopted to such an extent that they now stand guilty of the body and blood of Jesus. Their abuse of the "have nots" amounts to an attack on Jesus himself.[44] As a result, they are currently experiencing the Lord's judgment, precisely because they eat "without discerning the body" (1 Cor 11:27-29).[45] Because Paul's focus in this passage is on the way their meals shame the "have nots," eating without "discerning the body" most likely refers primarily to their failure to discern the entire Corinthian congregation as the body of Christ.[46] In other words, their eating and drinking represents a failure to recognize the church as God's community in which those the world considers "have nots" have a privileged place at the table.

The solution, then, is twofold. On the one hand, the Corinthians must embrace a practice of *self-examination*: "Let a person examine themselves and thus eat from the bread and drink from the cup" (1 Cor 11:28 AT). Once we recognize that the "body" (1 Cor 11:29) is a reference to the congregation, this self-examination "is not [an] invitation for the Corinthians to probe the inner recesses of their consciences but [a] call to consider how their actions at the supper are affecting brothers and sisters in the church."[47]

Second, having examined themselves and their actions through the lens of the cross, the Corinthians must *allēlous ekdechesthe*. While most translations render this phrase "wait for one another," given the hospitality context, it is

---

[44]Anthony C. Thiselton, *The First Epistle to the Corinthians: A Commentary on the Greek Text*, NIGTC (Grand Rapids, MI: Eerdmans, 2000), 890.

[45]So also Martin, *Corinthian Body*, 194.

[46]See Gordon Fee, *The First Epistle to the Corinthians*, rev. ed., NICNT (Grand Rapids, MI: Eerdmans, 2014), 623; David G. Horrell, *The Social Ethos of the Corinthian Correspondence: Interests and Ideology from 1 Corinthians to 1 Clement* (New York: T&T Clark, 2000), 153; Richard Hays, *First Corinthians*, Interpretation (Lexington, KY: Westminster John Knox, 1997), 200.

[47]Hays, *First Corinthians*, 200.

probably better to translate "receive" or even "welcome one another."[48] This meaning is well-attested in the LXX, Second Temple Jewish literature, and Greek writing.[49] Paul thus exhorts the church to truly "welcome one another" by sharing in a meal at which status competition has no place and in which the "have nots" receive physical as well as spiritual nourishment.

WHAT DOES WELCOMING ONE ANOTHER LOOK LIKE IN THE BODY OF CHRIST?

1 Corinthians 12 sheds further light on what this "mutual welcome" should look like. In 1 Corinthians 12:12-13, Paul draws on a "long rhetorical tradition that portrayed the [city] as a body"[50] to describe the Christian community as a body made up of Jews and Gentiles, enslaved and free persons. When Greco-Roman thinkers used this body image, they often suggested that the "physical givenness of the human body mandates the hierarchy of the social body."[51] In a famous example from Livy, for instance, a senator convinces a group of commoners who have gone on strike to go back to work by telling them a story about a body. As Martin summarizes it, once upon a time,

> the members of the body went on strike against the belly, complaining that they did all the work, only to turn over all the produce to the belly, which simply stuffed itself with the fruits of their labors. Of course, their strike eventually led to the death of all the members.

The story convinces the commoners to end their strike and get back to work. Harmony is restored. "Naturally, everyone lives happily ever after."[52]

Paul's initial argument that, analogous to the physical body, the congregational body depends on the very diversity of its members (1 Cor 12:14-21), appears to fit nicely with this Greco-Roman technique. "Yes, that's right," powerful Corinthian Christians might have replied. "Everyone has their role to play. Our hierarchical seating arrangements and differing portion sizes simply recognize that truth." Appearances can be deceiving, however, and Paul has intentionally laid a trap for those in his audience who would quickly assent to such a hierarchical understanding of the community.

---

[48]See Bruce W. Winter, "Lord's Supper at Corinth: An Alternative Reconstruction," *Reformed Theological Review* 37, no. 3 (1978): 74-78.

[49]See Ps 118:122; 3 Macc 5:26; Sir 6:23, 33; 18:14; 32:14; James H. Moulton and George Milligan, *Vocabulary of the Greek New Testament* (Grand Rapids, MI: Baker Academic, 1995), 192.

[50]Martin, *Corinthian Body*, 30.

[51]Martin, *Corinthian Body*, 93.

[52]Martin, *Corinthian Body*, 93.

Thus in 1 Corinthians 12:22-24, Paul takes this conservative metaphor in a radically different direction, arguing that God himself has established the one body so as to give *greater* honor and dignity to those members who *appear* to be weaker or lacking in honor and dignity. The language, which refers euphemistically to genitals,[53] suggests that such parts not only play an essential role within the body, but also that their "unpresentableness" is socially constructed.[54] Paul depicts God as actively choosing to organize his church so as to give "greater honor" to those parts of the body that have been *socially conceived of* as inferior outside the church (1 Cor 12:24).[55] God has indeed arranged the church in a specific way, but not in the way the Corinthians had. God acknowledges social standing within the church, but only in order to privilege those at the bottom of the social pyramid.

This "application of the critique of Christ and the cross to the church"[56] reinforces and applies what Paul argued in 1 Corinthians 1:27-28: God has chosen the foolish and weak in the world's eyes to destroy the world's very notion of strength, wisdom, and status. The Corinthian meals should reflect this work of God's by affording *greater honor* to the members of the community *denied honor* in Corinthian society.

This theological insight clarifies the close analogy between Paul's attack on social stratification in Corinth and the socially oppressive stratification along racial lines at work in many American churches today. What the more powerful Corinthians must learn is that "God pays no regard to their preexisting [social and economic] capital."[57] While they might seek to arrange their gatherings in hierarchies determined by the preexisting social capital of wisdom, power, good breeding, wealth, station, or ethnicity (see 1 Cor 12:12-13),[58] God himself has arranged his community so as to afford special honor in the church to those at the bottom rung of the culture's social ladder. As Blount

---

[53]Martin, *Corinthian Body*, 95.

[54]Horrell, *Social Ethos*, 180-81.

[55]See also Fee, *Corinthians*, 678-79.

[56]Thiselton, *Corinthians*, 1007.

[57]John M. G. Barclay, *Paul and the Gift* (Grand Rapids, MI: Eerdmans, 2015), 539.

[58]For discussions of Paul's view of ethnicity, see Margaret M. Mitchell, *Paul and the Rhetoric of Reconciliation: An Exegetical Investigation of the Language and Composition of 1 Corinthians* (Louisville, KY: Westminster John Knox, 1993), 94n174; Cavan W. Concannon, *"When You Were Gentiles": Specters of Ethnicity in Roman Corinth and Paul's Corinthian Correspondence* (New Haven, CT: Yale University, 2014), xii; Love Sechrest, *A Former Jew: Paul and the Dialectics of Race* (New York: T&T Clark, 2010); Love Sechrest, "Identity and the Embodiment of Privilege," in *1 and 2 Corinthians*, ed. Yung Suk Kim (Minneapolis: Fortress, 2013), 27.

argues, Paul thus challenges "the ideology of privilege" wherever it may be found.[59]

Paul's solution does not merely require *refraining from* privileging the socially powerful; it requires *actively according special honor and worth to the socially disenfranchised*. One surprising purpose of this Pauline "preferential option" for the socioeconomically marginalized, however, is the *unity of a church* in which there "are no schisms in the body." The result of their countercultural gatherings will be an ecclesial body in which each member shares in the sufferings and glory of the rest (1 Cor 12:26). Their "'redistribution of honor'" is aimed at a "form of equality."[60] Moreover, because this discussion occurs in the context of Paul's teaching on spiritual gifts, the cumulative effect is this: every congregant, including the most powerful patron, depends for their well-being on the gifts the Spirit gives through every other member, including the poorest and least powerful congregant.[61]

Paul therefore calls the Corinthians to "rearrange" the metaphorical chairs in their gatherings so that their life together reflects the upside-down reality of God's kingdom. The politics of that kingdom must be received, embraced, and embodied by the Corinthians if they are to participate in God's mission, proclaiming the Lord's death until he comes.

REARRANGING THE CHAIRS IN MULTIETHNIC CHURCHES TODAY

There is a powerful analogy between the Corinthians' preservation of social disparity and the typical multiethnic church's preservation of racial disparity. In both cases, the church "arranges the chairs" in line with oppressive social hierarchies, rather than deconstructing them within the church. Just as the Corinthians' social life was inappropriately arranged in line with hierarchies related to the cultural capital of wisdom, power, wealth, ethnicity, and station, contemporary North American multiethnic churches are too often arranged in line with our society's elevation of white norms. This threatens the church's missional identity encapsulated in its life together and impoverishes the church's ability to participate in an outward mission of love and justice to the world around it.

---

[59]Blount, *Whisper*, 141.

[60]Horrell, *Social Ethos*, 182.

[61]Brian Brock and Bernd Wannenwetsch, *The Therapy of the Christian Body: A Theological Exposition of Paul's First Letter to the Corinthians*, vol. 2 (Eugene, OR: Wipf & Stock), 72.

But if the problems are similar, so also the solutions: white Christians in multiracial churches must learn to *discern* their Black and brown brothers and sisters as full members of the body of Christ and *examine* the way their own behavior in the congregation and outside of it constitutes a failure to treat them as such. This requires church leaders and white Christians generally, like Paul, to listen to the voice from below (1 Cor 11:18). Such voices can name the way our gatherings shame the socially marginalized and, as a result, despise the church of God (1 Cor 11:22).

Practically speaking, such listening, discerning, and examining requires multiethnic congregations to create and affirm safe spaces for "people-of-color-only" discussions.[62] This will help our brothers and sisters identify where the chairs need rearranging. Moreover, such churches must pursue genuine racial diversity in leadership at the highest level. Indeed, in light of 1 Corinthians 12:22-24, what Edwards refers to as "spiritual affirmative action"[63] in church leadership is not an ecclesial capitulation to a vision of diversity driven by democratic ideals or the alleged influence of Critical Race Theory. It is the church's reception of the triune God's strategy for according greater honor within the church to the members most likely to lack it outside of it. If many multiethnic churches are not *led by* Black leaders who are fully supported in their role, then the multiethnic church movement in the United States will fail to confront racism against Black people. Indeed, it will *reinforce* it by mirroring rather than dismantling the reality that white people "disproportionately fill positions of power in nearly every arena of American life, including politics, education, and business."[64]

In a similar vein, the success of multiethnic churches may, in the end, depend on these churches' ability to cultivate strong relationships with historically Black congregations. As McCaulley puts it, Black churches "got something to say,"[65] and the entire church would be well served by listening. This is not to suggest that any church tradition is perfect. But given their

---

[62]Glen Kehrein testified to the power of such spaces in multiracial churches in the original Christian Community Development Association handbook (John M. Perkins, ed., *Restoring At-Risk Communities: Doing It Together & Doing It Right* [Grand Rapids, MI: Baker, 1996], 168). In 2015, the CCDA held a women-of-color only conference designed to create safe spaces for pastors, community development workers, and others to process their experiences working within multiracial spaces that nevertheless often conform to white norms.

[63]Edwards, *Elusive Dream*, 76.

[64]Edwards, *Elusive Dream*, 79.

[65]Esau McCaulley, *Reading While Black: African American Biblical Interpretation as an Exercise in Hope* (Downers Grove, IL: IVP Academic, 2020), 1.

history, Black churches carry gifts of worship, social engagement, preaching, evangelism, and discipleship that could strengthen the church more broadly. This is true not least because, as Lloyd argues, the experience of oppression that has shaped the theologizing of the Black church makes Black theology particularly adept at identifying the idols of our day, including the idolatry of white supremacy.[66]

Indeed, the Black church has long experience in dismantling idolatrous hierarchies within its own ecclesial politics. Cone argues that the Spirit's eschatological presence in the Black church allows worshipers to experience "a rupture in time":

> The janitor becomes the chairperson of the Deacon Board; the maid becomes the president of Stewardess Board Number I. Everybody becomes Mr. and Mrs., or Brother and Sister. The last becomes first, making a radical change in the perception of self and one's calling in the society. . . . It is this experience of being radically transformed by the power of the Spirit that defines the primary style of black worship.[67]

Clearly such a description captures an "arranging of the chairs" that accords greater honor within the church to the parts of the body that lack it outside. But white Christians will never be blessed by the Black church's gifts nor confronted with their prophetic unmasking of idolatry if we are not willing to learn with, from, alongside, and under such churches and their leaders.

As multiethnic churches begin to uncover racial injustice in our communities, we must also learn to "rearrange the chairs" within our congregations to *privilege* those who the broader culture assigns lesser value. Such an assertion goes beyond the typical understanding of multiethnic churches as places where people "meet in the middle" in terms of racial norms and expectations within the church. Paul's argument, it seems to me, goes further, declaring that the *unity* of the church requires *privileging* the socially marginalized. By actively subverting cultural hierarchies within the church, white members can begin to learn, by the power of the Spirit, to "speak in the mother tongues of others,"[68] and thereby participate in genuine solidarity with Black members of the body of Christ.

---

[66]Vince Lloyd, "The Political Theology of Martin Luther King, Jr.," presented at Fuller Seminary, October 2018, https://fullerstudio.fuller.edu/fuller-dialogues-black-public-theology.

[67]James H. Cone, "Sanctification, Liberation, and Black Worship," *Theology Today* 35, no. 2 (1978), 140-41.

[68]Willie James Jennings, *Acts*, Belief (Louisville, KY: Westminster John Knox, 2017), 27-33.

This is the missional shape of mutual welcome that Paul offers us: a way of ecclesial life that privileges the gifts, viewpoints, and preferences of members from groups marginalized by the broader culture, and, by extension, denies some of the privileges the dominant culture takes for granted in the church and beyond it. And while my own context has led me to focus primarily on Black and white Christians in multiethnic churches, Paul's vision is by no means limited to these two groups.[69] Wherever social hierarchies are created along any lines that divide us, whether lines of race, class, ethnicity, ability, language, social status, gender, education, or otherwise, Paul offers us an explosive vision of a church that dismantles those hierarchies in the way they gather together as the body of Christ.

As churches practice cruciform, mutual welcome, the diverse members of the congregation become the channels through which the Spirit gives good gifts to all, as together we journey toward just discipleship. Moreover, by embodying this countercultural ecclesiology, the church itself proclaims the good news of our crucified king as we await his return. A eucharistic community arranged in line with the logic of the cross is, *by its very public existence*, a proclamation of the gospel. "For as often as you eat this bread and drink this cup, *you proclaim the Lord's death until he comes.*"

Some may question whether such a vision is realistic. But as Jennings declares, such a way of life is "not an unattainable goal. It is the reality that surrounds the Christian. Our goal must be to embrace it."[70] Moreover, if we attend to Paul's own rhetoric, the danger of continuing to "gather for the worse" through our implicit support of racist hegemony is deadly. Such gatherings risk becoming gatherings unto judgment (1 Cor 11:29).

Yet even here there is reason for hope. For Paul, such judgment is itself a sign of Christ's ongoing presence with his people. "But when we are judged by the Lord, we are disciplined so that we may not be condemned along with the world" (1 Cor 11:32). The church in Paul's day, and perhaps in ours, is judged by Jesus precisely as a gracious act of our Lord's disciplining activity in our midst and on our behalf, so that we might not stand condemned

---

[69]As a reminder, by focusing on relationships between Black and white Christians, I am not intending to promote a problematic Black/white binary, nor to downplay the suffering experienced by and contributions of other communities of color. For a powerful exploration of what the whole church can learn about theology and justice from the Latina/o church, for instance, see Robert Chao Romero, *Brown Church: Five Centuries of Latina/o Social Justice, Theology, and Identity* (Downers Grove, IL: IVP Academic, 2020).

[70]Jennings, *Acts*, 27-33.

with a world that refuses to be shattered and renewed by the "logic of the cross."

FEASTING FOR THE LIFE OF THE WORLD

But does this emphasis on the life of the church subtly fund a sectarian withdrawal, a refusal to confront the injustices of the broader communities in which we live? Does this text leave us without guidance for engaging, or even an excuse for refusing to engage racism outside the church?

Scholarship has sometimes interpreted Paul in ways that might lead in this direction. When Paul writes that those who are hungry should simply eat in their own homes (1 Cor 11:34), Theissen interprets this as a compromise with the elite.[71] From such a perspective, it's as if Paul is saying, "Quit getting the church dirty at the Lord's Supper, marginalize the poor on your own time."

In response to such an interpretation, I suspect Paul would have declared: "May it never be!" Instead of seeing his words about the hungry eating in their own homes as a compromise, Fee declares, "As with the issue of slavery in Philemon, Paul attacks the system indirectly to be sure, but at its very core. Be a true Christian at the table, and the care for the needy, a matter that is always close to Paul's heart . . . will likewise become part and parcel of one's life."[72]

From Fee's perspective, and in line with the model of character ethics we've been exploring, Paul sees the Lord's Supper as a practice that should shape the moral and political character of God's people *for the better*. The character of those who are being shaped "for the better" by these rearranged Lord's Supper meals will do justice by faithfully exercising power in the way they treat different members of the body of Christ within the church. But this "for the better" will not simply remain at the eucharistic table. After all, "how long could those of high status continue to serve" those lower down society's ladder "meager meatless portions and watered-down wine in their own homes when, the evening before, they had both shared in the one meal, the one bread, the one cup given to them equally by the *Lord himself*?"[73] How long could individual homes, themselves political and economic units in the Greco-Roman political economy, embody a social world dominated by the "haves" against the "have nots" once both parties had shared a meal at which greater honor was given to the dishonorable parts and the foolishness of God overturned

---

[71]Theissen, *Social Setting*, 164.
[72]Fee, *Corinthians*, 603, emphasis added.
[73]Rhodes, *Formative Feasting*, 228.

the wisdom of the world?[74] Against Theissen's argument that Paul here presents a "compromise" with socioeconomic marginalization, I suggest Paul invested in a Lord's Supper practice that he believed had the power to reshape the Corinthians' world around the logic of the cross, both at the table, and beyond it.

This insight, I suggest, stands at the heart of just discipleship. The discipleship that occurs through our participation in the politics of ecclesial communities does not stay put. A church that receives the politics of God's kingdom in its own life—practicing the eucharistic feast to which Jesus himself invites us and mutually welcoming one another by privileging the gifts of those marginalized outside the church—will send transformed Christians equipped with cruciform love and service into the world around them. In their life together, and not least as an outpost of God's kingdom, they will "proclaim the Lord's death until he comes."

---

[74]See similarly Blount, *Whisper*, 141.

PART 4

DISCIPLING POLITICS

JUST DISCIPLESHIP
AMID THE NATIONS

INTO EGYPT

Contemporary Evangelical Politics and
"The Joseph Option"

AMERICAN EVANGELICALS love a Good Samaritan story.[1] But by our own admission, our fellow Americans shouldn't expect us to act like Good Samaritans in the voting booth. At least that's how the executive director of Lifeway Research summarized polling conducted just before the hotly contested 2020 presidential election.[2] When white evangelicals-by-belief were asked "Who do you hope your presidential vote *benefits the most*?," 61% said their primary goal was either to benefit "people nationwide who are like me" or "me and my family." Non-evangelicals were 11% less likely to identify these as their primary goals, and 9% more likely to identify "people who our country has failed" as those they most hoped to benefit.

Evangelicals might argue that self-interest is a legitimate and appropriate concern within a democracy. True enough. But that doesn't explain why self-interest, and interest for "*people like me* nationwide," would be significantly *stronger* among evangelicals than among other Americans. Indeed, one might expect Jesus' call to love our neighbors as ourselves to push us in the opposite direction.

---

[1]Portions of chapter 11 and 12 first appeared in Michael Rhodes, "Instead of Fearing Loss of Political Power, Christians Should Consider the Daniel Option," *Center for Hebraic Thought* (2020), available at: https://hebraicthought.org/politics-and-religion-evangelicals-daniel-joseph/. Use of the term *evangelical* can be controversial, and casting aspersion on evangelicals is common. For the most part, I have tried to limit my references to evangelicals to sections of the book where I draw on specific research on evangelicals as a named subgroup.

[2]Lifeway Research, "Most Evangelicals Choose Trump over Biden, but Clear Divides Exist," September 29, 2020, https://lifewayresearch.com/2020/09/29/most-evangelicals-choose-trump-over-biden-but-clear-divides-exist.

Alternatively, we might argue that by pursuing a world that's good for evangelicals, we're also pursuing the kind of society that's best for everyone. By honestly advocating for our specific vision of the good in the public square, we're pursuing the *common good*.

There's definitely something to that argument. Unfortunately, at least some data suggests many of us are quite happy to fight for privileges for ourselves while denying similar privileges to others. For instance, evangelicals are more likely than other voters to identify religious freedom as a political priority.[3] But as a group, white evangelicals strongly supported the Trump administration's ban on Muslim immigration,[4] and largely backed the dramatic reduction in the resettlement of refugees fleeing religious persecution.[5] That reduction in refugee resettlement meant the United States welcomed roughly 90 percent fewer *Christians* fleeing religious persecution.[6] Again, evangelicals might argue that there's a difference between religious liberty and immigration policy. Fair enough. But given the openly self-focused goals of evangelical voters, perhaps we can understand why, when we say we're concerned about "religious freedom," critics accuse us of meaning "religious freedom for people like us."

In parts one and two of this book, I argued that the Bible offers us a path of moral discipleship oriented toward justice. The biblical stories, practices, virtues, and community politics we explored all help disciples *become* just. In part three, we explored the church's politics, understood as the way the people of God arrange their common life together. The biblical Jubilee and the Corinthian Lord's Supper demonstrate the way the countercultural political life of God's people bears witness to God's own justice in our unjust word.

But the just discipleship to which Scripture calls us in our political lives is not limited to the way we live as a countercultural community. Indeed, one critical aspect of just discipleship is our participation in the broader political processes of the communities in which we find ourselves. In part four, we consider the way just disciples ought to engage the politics of the nations and places within which we find ourselves.

---

[3]Lifeway Research, "Most Evangelicals Choose Trump."

[4]See Dalia Mogahed and Azka Mahmood, "American Muslim Poll 2019: Predicting and Preventing Islamophobia," May 1, 2019, www.ispu.org/american-muslim-poll-2019-predicting-and -preventing-islamophobia.

[5]Griffin Paul Jackson, "Persecuted Christians Resettled in US Drop Dramatically Under Trump," *Christianity Today*, July 10, 2020, www.christianitytoday.com/news/2020/july/persecuted-christian -refugees-trump-open-doors-world-relief.html.

[6]Jackson, "Persecuted Christians Resettled."

The political stats with which this chapter opened, however—and we could cite troubling statistics from across the political spectrum—suggest all may not be well in our political witness. While that may seem obvious, I suggest that many of our failures are not primarily failures of political agendas or policy platforms, issues of strategy or legislative tactics. They are not failures to pick the right political "team," whether we identify the "right" team as Republican or Democrat. They are primarily failures of political *discipleship*. And as is so often the case, this discipleship failure stems from a failure to be shaped by Scripture. What might it look like for the Bible to shape us to do justice in our engagement with the politics of the nations and communities where God has placed us?

MOVING BEYOND THE "ROMANS 13 ONLY" POLITICAL OPTION

We might start by moving beyond the curiously small selection of biblical passages Christians rely on when thinking about local and national politics. For many of us, Scripture's political witness begins and ends with Romans 13:

> Let every person be subject to the governing authorities; for there is no au-
> thority except from God, and those authorities that exist have been instituted
> by God. Therefore whoever resists authority resists what God has appointed,
> and those who resist will incur judgment.

Many Christians hear Paul calling the church to an entirely submissive rela-
tionship with political leaders. From this perspective, being a political disciple simply means submitting to the powers-that-be.

Of course, the exegetical and theological traditions that constitute American Christianity offer much more nuanced interpretations of Romans 13:1-7, and much more complex accounts of political theology. To identify my own Calvinist tradition with this flat-footed "Romans 13 Only" approach to politics would be a distorting caricature. But I fear that this distorting caricature shapes the practical political theology of many Christians in the pews.

The problem with basing our entire approach to politics on Romans 13:1-7 is not the passage itself,[7] which is an essential text for a fully biblical account of political discipleship. The problem is that Romans was written to Christians

---

[7]Properly interpreted, at least. For interpreters who read Romans 13:1-7 as far more than a simple endorsement of the status quo, see Allan A. Boesak, *Black and Reformed: Apartheid, Liberation, and the Calvinist Tradition* (Eugene, OR: Wipf & Stock, 2015), 37-8; Esau McCaulley, *Reading While Black: African American Biblical Interpretation as an Exercise in Hope* (Downers Grove, IL: IVP Academic, 2020), 25-46.

who had little to no *direct* influence over the type of political system in which they lived, or the specific political players involved. When Paul wrote about the authorities who wielded the sword, he was talking about a group to which none of his Christian audience belonged.

By contrast, American Christians *do* have the opportunity to influence local and national politics in all sorts of ways, including by seeking to *become* one of the authorities who wields the sword. "Romans 13 Only" Christians have often taken the text's apparently "simple statement of God's authorization of the state"[8] as an invitation to do just that, seeking to gain and use political power as they see fit. Again, the problem is that Romans 13:1-7 does not directly address a situation in which Christians can become leaders within, or even have any substantial direct influence on the politics of the community in which they find themselves.

If we want Scripture to help us become just disciples in our contemporary political context, to inform *whether* and *how* we seek the welfare of the society to which we've been sent by voting, running for office, lobbying, or marching in protest, we need to be formed by Scripture beyond Romans 13:1-7.

EXPLORING THE "JOSEPH OPTION"

If we're looking for examples of God's people gaining direct political power among the nations, the Joseph narrative is our first stop.[9] At first glance, Joseph seems like the perfect model for wise, faithful action. The narrator describes Yahweh's presence with Joseph as the source of his success under hostile circumstances (Gen 39:2, 21). When Joseph's promotion in Potiphar's house puts him in the way of sexual temptation, he resists (Gen 39:6-20). When his political promotion gives him the opportunity to exact revenge on his brothers, he forgives. Indeed, he describes himself to his brothers as a pro-life, political figure that God uses to "save many lives" (Gen 50:20). Wenham goes so far as to call Joseph "the model ruler in Genesis, the ideal king."[10]

Perhaps Joseph even recognizes that his use of life-saving political power is part of his missional responsibility as a member of Abraham's family. After

---

[8]Nicholas Wolterstorff, *Hearing the Call: Liturgy, Justice, Church, and World* (Grand Rapids, MI: Eerdmans, 2011), 309.

[9]The seed for this chapter and the next was planted by a deeply pastoral, brilliant response by Walter Brueggemann to a question I raised in a Q&A session about how to work within broken systems without getting sucked into them.

[10]Gordon Wenham, *Story as Torah: Reading the Old Testament Ethically* (Edinburgh: T&T Clark, 2000), 26.

all, Yahweh promised that Abraham's family would be a vehicle of blessing to all the families of the earth (Gen 12:2). It is through Joseph that Jacob, the wandering sojourner, stands before the most powerful ruler on the planet, and blesses him (Gen 47:7).

Yet before we go all in on the "Joseph Option" for Christian political engagement, we need to take another look at his famine relief program. The story of Joseph in office shows us both the possibilities *and the pitfalls* God's people face when they participate in the politics of the nations.

EXPLORING JOSEPH'S FAMINE RELIEF PROGRAM

In Genesis 41:48, Joseph gathers "all"[11] the food of the seven good years and stores it up in cities. But it isn't till Genesis 47:13-26 that Genesis describes how Joseph distributes this food during the famine that follows.[12] First, because Joseph gathered "all" the food of the good years, he is able to gather "all" the Egyptians' money into Pharaoh's house as payment for the food the Egyptians desperately need once the famine begins (Gen 47:14). When the famine outlasts the Egyptians' cash, they plead with Joseph: "Give us food! Why should we die before your eyes? For our money is gone" (Gen 47:15).

If the Egyptians' request that Joseph *give* them food was a plea for charity, his response promptly places them back in the realm of economic transaction: "Give me your livestock, and I will give food to you in exchange for your livestock, if your money is gone" (Gen 47:16). The Egyptians comply, and their horses, flocks, herds, and donkeys are enough for them to buy their way out of starvation that year.

But in the next year, they're forced to return. This time, they propose the solution: because their money and livestock now belong to Pharaoh, Pharaoh could give them grain in exchange for the only things they have left: their bodies and their land (Gen 47:18). Joseph agrees, and buys "all the land" of Egypt and the Egyptians themselves as slaves for Pharaoh (Gen 47:19-20).[13] In exchange, Joseph gives the Egyptians seed to plant, on the understanding

---

[11]The term *all* here cannot be literal, not least because Joseph outlines this policy in terms of collecting a fifth of all the Egyptians' produce during the good years (Gen 41:34). But the frequent use of *all* may be intended by the narrator to draw our attention to the extent of Joseph's acquisition.

[12]See Ellen Davis, *Scripture, Culture, and Agriculture: An Agrarian Reading of the Bible* (New York: Cambridge University Press, 2009), 73.

[13]On the important text critical issue in Gen 47:21, see Gordon Wenham, *Genesis 16–50*, WBC (Nashville: Thomas Nelson, 2003), 449; Mark G. Brett, *Genesis: Procreation and the Politics of Identity* (London: Routledge, 2005), 130.

that 20 percent of their future yield will go to the crown (Gen 47:24). The passage ends with the Egyptians expressing gratitude to Joseph for saving them by enslaving them, and with the narrator telling the reader that the land tenure agreement Joseph designed during the famine "stands to this day" (Gen 47:26).

Modern readers will almost certainly find aspects of Joseph's behavior disconcerting. But many scholarly defenders of Joseph argue that to criticize him would be to ignore the desperate nature of Egypt's circumstances and anachronistically impose our modern values on a premodern text.[14] I agree with their concern that we read the text within its own context. But I also suggest that a closer look demonstrates that *Scripture itself* raises concerns about Joseph's deployment of political power.[15]

First, the Pentateuch's socioeconomic legislation shares Joseph's concern for saving life. But this legislation is relentlessly opposed both to the concentration of land ownership and the permanency of debt servitude that Joseph accomplishes for Pharaoh. Joseph's establishment of Egyptian indebtedness as a "statute until this day" provides a stunning contrast with the limits on debt celebrated in the Torah.[16] Milgrom even argues that the description in Leviticus 25:25-55 of an Israelite's descent into poverty intentionally alludes to, and implicitly condemns Joseph's enslavement of the Egyptians in their similar three-stage descent into bondage.[17]

Some commentators point out that 20 percent is a relatively low tax rate based on ancient parallels.[18] But surely it is more relevant that Leviticus 25:36-37 prohibits lending money to the poor on interest or giving food for profit at all. Samuel offered a withering critique of landgrabbing royalty based on a tax rate half of that which Joseph lays on the people (1 Sam 8:17).[19]

---

[14]For one of the most thorough defenses of Joseph's politics, see Lindsay Wilson, *Joseph, Wise and Otherwise: The Intersection of Wisdom and Covenant in Genesis 37–50* (Eugene, OR: Wipf & Stock, 2007).

[15]Another option would be to see Joseph as a trickster hero, one of Israel's "own" getting ahead against the people who would become Israel's paradigmatic enemy: see Ellen F. Davis, *Opening Israel's Scriptures* (New York: Oxford University Press, 2019), 37. I find this unlikely for a variety of reasons, not least the fact that the ordering of Genesis and Exodus would make the "joke" on Joseph/Israel.

[16]On this contrast, see Shira Weiss, *Ethical Ambiguity in the Hebrew Bible: Philosophical Analysis of Scriptural Narrative* (Cambridge: Cambridge University Press, 2018), 179.

[17]Jacob Milgrom, *Leviticus 23–27*, AB (New Haven, CT: Yale University Press, 2001), 2192, 2228.

[18]Wilson, *Joseph, Wise and Otherwise*, 193; Weiss, *Ethical Ambiguity*, 116.

[19]Weiss, *Ethical Ambiguity*, 181.

But why should we read Genesis 47:13-26 in dialogue with Israel's later laws and stories, rather than simply within its own narrative? Because I think that's what Genesis's readers would have done. Genesis was not published in the newspapers during the Egyptian famine to tell the people about Joseph's new policy. The "implied audience" of Genesis is not the people of God prior to the exodus at all, but rather the people of God looking *back* to the stories of their ancestors long after their community had been liberated from Egypt.[20] From that perspective, it seems only logical to ask how Joseph's political behavior in Egypt stacks up against Israel's long reflection on political behavior in their own community.

At this point, however, some might raise an objection. Might not the Egyptians' gratitude at being allowed to become slaves to Pharaoh suggest that desperate times call for desperate measures? Perhaps Joseph demonstrates precisely that difficult political wisdom we need when forced to choose between bad options and worse ones.

The problem is that Genesis repeatedly reminds us that Joseph *does* have options. The immediate prelude to the story of Egypt's austerity measures in Genesis 47:13-26 is the record of Joseph's quite different approach to his own people. Only twelve verses after Joseph provides for his family's "little ones" by *giving* them land grants in the "best of the land" of Egypt, Joseph provides for Egyptian "little ones" by *taking* the land from their parents. Only after ensuring that his own family will have land for their flocks, and only after ensuring that some of his own brothers will get hired as caretakers of Pharaoh's livestock (Gen 47:4-6), does Joseph dramatically increase Pharaoh's flocks and herds by getting for him all the livestock of the Egyptians (Gen 47:17). Perhaps most tellingly of all, the narrator makes clear that the only Egyptian families that get an exception to Joseph's land acquisition policies are the priestly families, including, presumably, the powerful priestly family into which Joseph himself had married.[21]

Again, I am not arguing that contemporary readers should have a problem with Joseph's behavior in Genesis 47:13-26. I am arguing that the narrator of Genesis does, and that the narrator presents the story in such a way that the

---

[20]Evidence that Genesis expects the readers to be aware of the later law comes from passages like Genesis 26:5, which describes Abraham's obedience using language that appears to draw directly from Israel's later legal texts.

[21]See Nahum M. Sarna, *Understanding Genesis* (New York: Jewish Theological Seminary Press, 2015), 288; and J. Gerald Janzen, *Abraham and All the Families of the Earth: A Commentary on the Book of Genesis 12–50* (Grand Rapids, MI: Eerdmans, 1993), 179-81.

original readers would get the message. That's why the story of Joseph's treatment of the Egyptians is bookended on *both* sides by a reminder that while the Egyptians are saved through slavery, Joseph's family is saved through generous, royal gifts (Gen 47:11-12; 47:27).

We need to linger for a moment at this point. Joseph acquires Pharaoh-like power in Egypt. He uses that power to save both his family and the Egyptians, but in a way that dramatically enriches his own people while seriously and permanently reducing the socioeconomic standing of the Egyptians. If biblical justice focuses on the faithful exercise of power, here, at least, we've got good reasons to suspect that Joseph has not gotten an A+ on the justice test. At the same time, the "Joseph Option" is starting to sound eerily familiar. Joseph stands squarely with those whose primary political goal is to improve the plight of their own family and others "like them."

The problem is, Scripture knows that the "Joseph Option" does not end well. Joseph's success at helping Pharaoh gain power comes back to haunt his descendants. Whoever the original readers of this story were, they were readers who knew that soon after Joseph enslaved the Egyptians, the Pharaoh "who knew not Joseph" enslaved Joseph's family.

This dynamic explains the curious name given to the good land Joseph gets for his family in Genesis 47:11. On eight previous occasions, Genesis calls this good land Goshen. But in Genesis 47:11, just before describing Joseph's treatment of the Egyptians, the narrator describes it as the "land of Rameses," an apparent reference to a city that hadn't been built yet in Joseph's time. Why?

Because the narrator wants to remind us that one day the political tables will turn. Instead of receiving the best of the land as a reward for the skillful manipulation of food surpluses, Joseph's enslaved descendants will be forced to build bigger and better storage cities for Pharaoh, *including the city of Rameses* (Ex 1:11).[22] While Joseph manages to get his brothers jobs as "chiefs" in Pharaoh's bureaucracy, the next time we hear about such "chiefs," the Pharaoh of Exodus 1:11 is setting them over the "forced labor" imposed on the Israelites.[23]

---

[22]Leon R. Kass, *The Beginning of Wisdom: Reading Genesis* (Chicago: University of Chicago Press, 2006), 630; Kenneth Matthews, *Genesis 11:27–50:26*, NAC (Nashville: Holman, 2005), 848.

[23]If we follow the MT of Genesis 47:21, which describes Joseph moving the Egyptians to cities, rather than the LXX and most English translations, which describe Joseph enslaving all the Egyptians, then this action too foreshadows the way Joseph's descendants would suffer under the Pharaoh of Exodus and his similar relocation project.

The overall message is clear: live by the political sword, die by the political sword.[24] Build your tribe's kingdom in the land of Goshen through self-serving politics, end up as slave labor building somebody else's kingdom in that same land later on.

This is all the more dramatic when we remember what the original readers of this story knew about Egypt's economy. Ancient readers likely knew that in Egypt, Pharaoh owned essentially everything. They knew that the Israelites had suffered tremendously under such a centralized political economy. They knew that God had brought the Israelites *out* of Egypt and *into* the Promised Land. They knew that God had given Israel specific directives to establish a political economy completely different from Egypt's. How surprising it must have been to those readers to have learned that it was an Israelite, one of their own, who first established Egypt's well-known political system! It would be like an American discovering, at the height of the Cold War, that Thomas Jefferson had helped write the Communist Manifesto.

Despite this dark side to Joseph's politics, I don't think Scripture vilifies Joseph, and neither should we. All biblical characters are mixed bags, morally speaking, and there's a lot to like about Joseph. We should celebrate his willingness to reconcile with his brothers, his resistance to sexual temptation in Potiphar's house, and the commitment to the future of God's people beyond Egypt that he demonstrates on his death bed.

Then again, Scripture invites us to appreciate David's commitment to God, while expecting us to condemn his abuse of Bathsheba. Scripture invites us to marvel at Solomon's wisdom, while expecting us to condemn his later idolatry and subsequent oppression of the people. Scripture surely invites us to appreciate many aspects of Joseph's character. But it seems to me it also invites us to critique his use of political and economic power.

On the other hand, though, we shouldn't overlook the suffering Joseph experienced in Egypt. He was well acquainted with the injustice faced by immigrants the world over.[25] We see this especially in the way Potiphar's wife draws attention to his ethnic otherness in her successful attempt to get him unjustly thrown in jail. Even with hindsight, this political story is more tragic than tyrannical. But arguably Scripture has offered us this story to help us *avoid* some of those tragedies.

---

[24]Daniel R. Shevitz, "Joseph: A Study in Assimilation and Power," *Tikkun* 8 (1993): 52; Walter Brueggemann, *Genesis*, Interpretation (Louisville, KY: 2010), 356.

[25]See M. Daniel Carroll R., *The Bible and Borders: Hearing God's Word on Immigration* (Grand Rapids, MI: Brazos, 2020), 21.

Avoiding the political tragedies we encounter in the Joseph story and in our own contemporary politics requires us to think more deeply about political *discipleship*. What kind of formation is required for the people of God to engage political power justly, *without* getting coopted or corrupted? To help us answer these questions, it's worth examining political *discipleship* in the Joseph story.

POLITICAL DISCIPLESHIP IN THE "JOSEPH OPTION"

Potiphar's wife uses Joseph's ethnic otherness against him (Gen 39:14, 17). When the chief butler suggests Joseph might be able to help Pharaoh interpret his dream, he remembers Joseph as an ethnic outsider (Gen 41:12). After Joseph interprets Pharaoh's dream and gets promoted to power in the royal administration, however, he becomes increasingly assimilated to Egyptian culture and practice. Among other dynamics, then, his story stands toward the beginning of a long venerable tradition of Jewish reflection on the "ambivalence" of "power and assimilation."[26] As such, the narrative offers a warning about the way pagan political power exerts formative influence on the people of God. The Egyptians, it turns out, have their own patterns of political discipleship, patterns that will seek to shape anybody who gets involved in Egyptian politics.

And that's the problem. God's people may seek political power to do justice. If we often want to secure justice first and foremost for ourselves, at our best, we want to secure it for others as well. But when God's people gain power in the politics of the nations, they quickly face new temptations to assimilate into unjust patterns and practices. Such politically de-forming discipleship undermines the ability of God's people to be vehicles of God's justice to the world (see Gen 18:19).

One early warning sign Joseph may be susceptible to these temptations comes in his initial reaction to Pharaoh's request that he interpret his dream.[27] Joseph rightly responds that it is God, not him, who can interpret dreams. But then Joseph confidently declares that "God will give Pharaoh a favorable answer"—literally, God will answer *shalom* for Pharaoh (Gen 41:16).[28]

---

[26]Shevitz, "Joseph," 51.

[27]Indeed, while the narrator tells us that Yahweh was with Joseph at the first two stages of Joseph's ascent, that expression is absent at the beginning of Joseph's ascent into a powerful position in Egypt. This raises some ambiguity for us as readers as to the precise nature of Yahweh's actions in relation to Joseph's success in Pharaoh's house. God is at work, but this does not vindicate every aspect of Joseph's own actions in Pharaoh's court.

[28]A point noted by Brett, *Genesis*, 117-18.

Why would Joseph assume God's dream would offer peace to this powerful Egyptian ruler? Surely he has experienced enough injustice in Egyptian society to know that Egypt might well have come under God's judgment! In Genesis 20:3-7, another foreign ruler, Abimelech, had received a dream from God warning that he was as good as dead because he had taken Sarah into his harem. Even though Abimelech acted in ignorance, God still made it clear that he needed to change his behavior, and that he depended on the prayerful intercession of Yahweh's prophet, Abraham, to survive (Gen 20:7). As we will see in the next chapter, at least one other Israelite also interpreted dreams for foreign rulers. Rarely, however, did he offer an interpretation that did not require some sort of moral change from the ruler, and never did he assume that Yahweh's message to the monarch would be a peaceful or pleasant one.

Might this hint that Joseph has become *too* ready to be useful to Pharaoh's regime? If so, it's no more than a hint. But that hint does serve to set readers on alert as to how Joseph will navigate the necessarily tricky task of working in the Egyptian court without losing his identity.

In any case, we cannot fail to miss the "Egyptianization" Joseph undergoes after he wins Pharaoh's favor. The king promotes him over "all the land of Egypt," and then gives him a ring, fine garments, and a gold chain (Gen 41:41-42). These changes emphasize the enormous power now placed into Joseph's hands, so that "apart from [his] consent none should lift his hand or his foot in all the land of Egypt" (Gen 41:44 AT). But they also point to an identity transformation associated with this promotion to power. Whereas the first garment that gave Joseph an elevated status was given to him by Israel, these garments come from Pharaoh.[29]

Later, Joseph will mimic some of Pharaoh's actions, giving his brothers new clothes before they go to Pharaoh to ask for special favor in his land. Clearly, Joseph has learned that securing influence in the political economies of the nations requires adaptation. But how then do the people of God know where to draw the line? How do they faithfully maintain their identity as the family of Abraham, a family uniquely called to embody God's justice amid the nations, even as they seek to influence and wield secular political power? The

---

[29] As noted by Calum M. Carmichael, *Law, Legend, and Incest in the Bible: Leviticus 18–20* (Ithaca, NY: Cornell University Press, 1997), 99. Indeed, the powerful Pharaoh seems to impose quite a bit of this Egyptianization on Joseph. If this makes Joseph's embrace of this new identity more understandable, it makes that embrace no less dangerous. See Safwat Marzouk, "Migration in the Joseph Narrative: Integration, Separation, and Transnationalism," *Hebrew Studies* 60 (2019): 80.

ambiguities in Joseph's story seem designed to raise these questions in our minds.

The warnings continue immediately after Joseph's promotion. Pharaoh gives Joseph a new name, likely naming him after one of his gods.[30] He also gives him Asenath, daughter of one of Egypt's most powerful priests (Gen 41:45), as a wife.[31] While the Bible does not always raise concerns about marriage to women from foreign religious communities, it's worth noting that Joseph's marriage did cause serious consternation among early interpreters. Some of the rabbinic texts call Asenath's father a "master" rather than a priest, while others argued, without further evidence, that she "was the daughter of Dinah and Shechem," and therefore of "Jewish heritage."[32] The Greek text *Joseph and Asenath* solves the problem by having Joseph refuse marriage until Asenath rejects the gods of Egypt and converts to Israel's God.

Moreover, since Joseph offers us an early example of the people of God in power, we should also note Scripture's many warnings about the danger *political* marriages pose to a ruler's *faithfulness*. From Deuteronomy's law of the king (Deut 17:14-20) to the story of Solomon's many wives (see 1 Kings 11:1-4), Scripture suggests power alliances formed through marriage offer enormous temptations.

Indeed, if the fact that Joseph creates a loophole allowing priests to keep their land raises questions as to whether he may have aligned himself politically with the priests, his claim that "a man like" him practices "divination" raises questions as to whether Joseph adopted at least some of his in-laws' pagan worship practices as well (Gen 44:15).[33] After all, divination is explicitly condemned elsewhere in the Pentateuch (see Lev 19:26; Deut 18:10).

Finally, while Joseph gives his first child with Asenath a Hebrew name, that name means "God has made me forget all my hardship and *all my father's house*" (Gen 41:51). But how can Joseph participate in Yahweh's mission of blessing the nations through the family of Abraham if Joseph forgets Abraham's house?[34]

---

[30]Gerhard Von Rad, *Genesis: A Commentary*, OTL (London: SCM Press, 1972), 378.

[31]Sarna, *Understanding Genesis*, 288; Wenham, *Genesis*, 397; Matthews, *Genesis*, 763.

[32]Matthews, *Genesis*, 764.

[33]Some commentators think this is just a part of the ruse (Sarna, *Understanding Genesis*, 304-5; Matthews, *Genesis*, 799), but I think Janzen is right that the narrative raises a question whether Joseph has begun to "think of himself in terms that threaten to betray his vocation" (Janzen, *Abraham*, 182).

[34]Carroll suggests the fact that these are Israelite names indicate Joseph has not forgotten his God or his home (Carroll, *Bible and Borders*, 22), while Matthews suggests that they indicate Joseph is

In short, I suggest that Joseph's rise to power has offered him ample opportunity to be discipled by Egypt in problematic ways. He struggles to maintain the countercultural identity and covenantal memory necessary to avoid political cooption. As a result, when his brothers show up, Joseph is *unrecognizable as a member of Abraham's family.* He looks like an Egyptian (Gen 42:8), talks like an Egyptian (Gen 42:23), and eats like an Egyptian (Gen 43:32).[35] This last dynamic is particularly interesting, because by eating like an Egyptian, Joseph embraces a practice based on Egyptian stereotypes about the "Hebrews" (Gen 43:32)[36]—Egyptian stereotypes that may well have been at work in getting him unjustly thrown into prison! Small wonder, then, that when he first speaks with his brothers, although he *recognizes* them, the Hebrew who has become like Pharaoh (Gen 44:18) "acted like a foreigner towards them" (Gen 42:7 AT).[37]

Even simply within the book of Genesis, Joseph's Egyptianization raises troubling questions for us. Read with the warnings from the Law and the Prophets ringing in our ears—"*Don't go back to Egypt!*" (see Deut 17:16; Is 31:1), "*Do not do as they did in the land of Egypt!*" (see Lev 18:3; Ezek 20:7)—his Egyptianization appears downright alarming.

The story doesn't end there, of course. The portrayal of Joseph's ever-softening heart toward his siblings, and his eventual forgiveness of their deep betrayal suggest that he does not finally forget his identity as a member of God's people. His desire both to reconcile and rescue his brothers suggests Joseph has begun to realize that his Egyptian power is best used in "responsible service of others."[38] Nevertheless, even after his heart change toward his brothers, the narrative hints that Joseph's use of power to help his family gain special favor is not only unjust to the Egyptians, but dangerous for the Israelites.

The "Joseph Option" and the dangers of settling down. The promise that Abraham's family would participate in Yahweh's mission of blessing to the

---

"trying to forget his past life" and *may* suggest that he has "neglected the promises made to the Fathers" (Matthews, *Genesis*, 766). It may be that the tension is intentionally ambiguous.

[35]See Carolyn J. Sharp, *Irony and Meaning in the Hebrew Bible* (Bloomington: Indiana University Press, 2008), 60.

[36]Sarna, *Understanding Genesis*, 302; Carroll, *Bible and Borders*, 22. See also Marzouk, "Migration," 75.

[37]The verse offers a wordplay using various forms of the verb *nakhar*, which in the hiphil means something like "recognize," but in the hithpael something like "make oneself a stranger to" (see Holladay, 5551; TWOT, 1368).

[38]Walter Moberly, *The Theology of the Book of Genesis* (New York: Cambridge University Press, 2013), 245.

nations is bound to the promise that God would establish his family in the land of Canaan (see Gen 12:1-7). This did not keep Abraham or his descendants from "sojourning" or "staying as foreigners"[39] in the land of Egypt (Gen 12:10). For that matter, the patriarchs "sojourned" even in the land of Canaan (Ex 6:4), and Jacob tells Pharaoh that his life, like the lives of his fathers, was characterized by constant "sojourning" (Gen 47:9). Small wonder, then, that the brothers tell Pharaoh they have come to Egypt in order to "sojourn there" (Gen 47:4-5 AT).

But in Genesis 47:11, Joseph goes beyond their request for a place to sojourn by giving them an *akhuzzah*, a "possession," in the land of Egypt. Every other place Genesis applies this word to the people of God, it is to describe their gaining a settled possession in the Promised Land.[40] For instance, Abraham purchases a semipermanent possession in the land of Canaan while sojourning there, as a burial plot (Gen 23:4-20). This plot serves as something of a down payment for the people of God's future possession of the land. Across the Pentateuch, *akhuzzah* consistently refers to the Promised Land, both as a reference to the land in its entirety and as a reference to the inalienable plots belonging to each Israelite family. Indeed, Leviticus 25's discussion of the year of Jubilee uses the term thirteen times.[41]

Against this backdrop, it's hard not to see Joseph's use of Egyptian power to get his family a "possession" in the land of Egypt as deeply problematic. If Joseph helps Israel "gain a possession" in Goshen at the Egyptians' expense, it is also, in many ways, at their own. After all, the last time a foreign nation had invited Israel to "gain a possession" in their midst, it had been with the explicit purpose of assimilating them in order to gain their "livestock, their property, and all their animals" (Gen 34:10, 23). Yet in Genesis 47:27 it is one of Israel's own who helps the people gain a possession in the land of Egypt.

"From sojourners whose sole security was reliance on God's promise, Israel's ancestors now become dwellers reliant for security on their own landholdings and the powerful position of Joseph."[42] But those who participate in power politics not only find that such power can be used against them; they also find that it is hard to release one's grasp from the culture of power if one

---

[39]See Holladay, 1494; TWOT, 330.

[40]Gen 17:8; 48:4 generally, and specifically in relation to the burial plot Abraham buys from the Hittites in Gen 23:4, 9, 20; 49:30; and 50:13.

[41]See Calum Carmichael, *Illuminating Leviticus: A Study of Its Laws and Institutions in Light of Biblical Narratives* (Baltimore: Johns Hopkins University Press, 2006), 129.

[42]Bruce C. Birch, *Let Justice Roll Down* (Louisville, KY: Westminster John Knox, 1991), 113.

begins to lose it. Even after they've been rescued from slavery, Joseph's descendants sometimes wondered if they hadn't been better off in Egypt.

The "Joseph Option" as political tragedy. Joseph's story is filled with nuance and ambiguity, and I by no means intend to paint his political actions in an entirely negative light. Scholars who explore his story from a migrant perspective emphasize that Joseph never fully loses his Israelite identity, and that he embodies a kind of cultural bilingualism.[43] The narrative positively portrays Joseph ultimately remembering God's promises to his people, and indeed dying with them on his lips (Gen 50:25).

Moreover, Joseph is only the first of several biblical reflections in the Old Testament on the possibilities and pressures facing God's people when they get involved with pagan power politics. But that comparison also reveals that Joseph, through no fault of his own, uniquely lacks two essential resources for resisting de-forming Egyptian political discipleship.

First, he lacks community. Yahweh entrusted his mission of blessing to Abraham's *family*. It was this family that would keep the way of Yahweh "by doing righteousness and justice" (Gen 18:19), and thus serve as vehicles of Yahweh's blessing to the nations. But Joseph's isolation in Egypt—created by the traumatic *injustice* he experienced at the hands of his brothers—surely left him more vulnerable to the kind of Egyptian cooption that could prevent him from fully embracing a missional vocation of justice and blessing to the nations.

Second, Joseph does not have access to the law. While we can assume he had some knowledge of his family's vocation to be a community of justice and righteousness, unlike every member of that family after Sinai, he lacks the Torah's wise guidance as to what that righteousness and justice looked like in practice. The righteous law of God gave future generations an invaluable resource for living wise, just lives amid and in the sight of the nations (see Deut 4:6). If the original readers of Genesis would have heard Joseph's actions in chapter 47 with the laws of the Torah in the background, they might also have recognized that Joseph himself did not have access to such a resource.[44]

Joseph tragically lacks both the countercultural community and the countercultural law to guide his political discipleship and practice. Even if he does offer an example of what wisdom oriented toward political success looks like,

---

[43]Marzouk, "Migration," 75; Carroll, *Bible and Borders*, 22.
[44]See the discussion in Sharp, *Irony*, 60.

the wisdom he offers is, at best, a wisdom separated somewhat from the fear of Yahweh that is the beginning of Israel's wisdom, and a political success separated from the relentless pursuit of justice that constituted Israel's primary political ethos.

Even if Joseph had the best of intentions, his exercise of "worldly wisdom" fell short of the wise justice Yahweh expects of his people.[45] But this only underscores the warning to ancient and modern readers who read this text as the people of God and with the law as a resource. Scripture offers us the tragedy of Joseph's politics to help us avoid repeating such tragedies in our own political engagement with the nations.[46]

EMBRACING THE "JOSEPH OPTION" . . . AND THEN SOME: CHRISTIAN NATIONALISM AND EVANGELICAL POLITICS

Unfortunately, we American Christians have often far exceeded the failures of the "Joseph Option." Rather than seeing ourselves as citizens of the just and righteous countercultural kingdom of God, a vehicle of God's blessing to the nation to which we've been sent, we have frequently fought to gain political power for ourselves. The statistics we explored at the beginning of this chapter suggest as much. But exploring American politics further reveals an even darker side to the story.

Historically, far too many of our white Christian forbears used their political power to pursue their own prosperity at the expense of their neighbors. White Christian pastors participated in the theft of indigenous land and wrote the majority of all written defenses of slavery.[47] Like Joseph, they sought the best of the land for themselves. Unlike Joseph, those they fought to enslave were often their own brothers and sisters in the faith.

After the Civil War, many white Christians continued to embrace and defend the kind of white supremacy that claimed the best of the land for "us and ours," while subjecting Black, brown, and indigenous people to displacement, dispossession, and the terrorist violence of lynching. White churches largely failed to support their Black brothers and sisters in the civil rights movement, and indeed often actively opposed them.

---

[45]See Janzen, *Genesis*, 180; Kass, *Beginning*, 633-4.
[46]While Von Rad suggests the narrative reflects a "naïve pleasure in the possibilities of human wisdom" (Von Rad, *Genesis*, 410-11), I argue the narrative is anything but naïve.
[47]Elizabeth Jemison, *Christian Citizens: Reading the Bible in Black and White in the Postemancipation South* (Chapel Hill: University of North Carolina Press: 2020), 20.

Today, the underlying theological fuel for much political action among Christians is a commitment to Christian nationalism. Indeed, as of 2013, nearly two-thirds of *all* Americans "either mostly or completely agreed with the statement, 'God has granted America a special role in human history.'"[48] Many Christians describe this "special role" in ways that apply "references to biblical Israel to the contemporary American polity,"[49] believing that the nation is somehow the heir of promises made only to the people of God.

Christian nationalism claims promises God made to his people for a contemporary nation-state. Such nationalism needs to be named for what it is: idolatrous heresy. The coming kingdom of God relativizes the importance and role of all temporary political structures and authorities.[50] While such temporary structures and authorities are important for the common good, and the object of Christian mission and concern, when they become the source of Christian hope, they have become idols.

This idolatry of Christian nationalism has infected both political parties. Former President Barack Obama called America the "last best hope on earth."[51] Former Secretary of State Hilary Clinton declared that "The United States is an exceptional nation . . . [a] shining city on a hill . . . the indispensable nation."[52] In his presidential acceptance speech, President Joe Biden spoke of a "faith" that "sustains America." Then, after quoting a hymn filled with Scriptural allusions, Biden called the people to "embark on the work that God and history have called us to do . . . with faith in America and in each other."[53]

On the Republican side, President George W. Bush called the "ideal of America" the "hope of all mankind." Then, applying Scripture describing the incarnate Christ to America he declared: "And the light shines in the darkness,

---

[48]Samuel L. Perry and Andrew L. Whitehead, *Taking America Back for God: Christian Nationalism in the United States* (New York: Oxford University Press, 2020), 6.

[49]David T. Koyzis, *Political Visions and Illusions: A Survey and Christian Critique of Contemporary Ideologies* (Downers Grove, IL: IVP Academic, 2003), 120. See also Perry and Whitehead, *Taking America Back*, 11.

[50]D. Stephen Long, *Augustinian and Ecclesial Christian Ethics: On Loving Enemies* (Lanham, MD: Lexington Books, 2018), 191-92.

[51]Nico Pitney, "Obama's Nomination Victory Speech in St. Paul," *HuffPost*, November 5, 2008, www.huffpost.com/entry/obamas-nomination-victory_n_105028.

[52]Daniel White, "Read Hillary Clinton's Speech Touting 'American Exceptionalism,'" *Time*, August 31, 2016, https://time.com/4474619/read-hillary-clinton-american-legion-speech.

[53]Andrew Harnik, "Read the Full Text of Joe Biden's Speech After Historic Election," *ABC News*, November 7, 2020, https://abcnews.go.com/Politics/read-full-text-joe-bidens-speech-historic-election/story?id=74084462.

and the darkness has not overcome it."[54] At his inauguration, Trump called
the American people a "righteous public" that was "defended by God."[55] Vice
President Mike Pence borrowed words from the epistle to the Hebrews to call
an audience to "run the race marked out for us." "Let us fix our eyes on Old
Glory and all she represents," he said. "Let's fix our eyes on this land of heroes
and let their courage inspire." Clearly, Christian nationalist idolatry infects
Americans on both sides of the political aisle.

The thing about idols is that because they are gods made in *our* image, they
tend to look like us and promise to give us what we want. This, I believe, is
why much of the Christian nationalism that has infected evangelicalism is
better understood as *white* Christian nationalism. Whitehead and Perry argue
that Christian nationalism, especially when held strongly by white Americans,
generates "antipathy and mistrust toward those who do not meet the membership requirements of *native-born, Christian, and white*—namely, racial
minorities, nonwhite immigrants, and Muslims."[56] Their research, for instance, shows that a strong commitment to Christian nationalism serves as a
strong predictor that a person will downplay racial discrimination in policing
or that they will endorse dramatic reductions in immigration.[57]

Such deformed discipleship may help explain, at least in part, the events of
January 6, 2021. After months of continuously claiming that the election had
been stolen from him, Trump told a crowd of supporters that they should go
to the Capitol and protest the process by which Congress was certifying the
results of the election. Just before Trump took the stage, his personal lawyer,
Rudy Giuliani, had called for "trial by combat" against the Democrats.[58] After
Trump's speech, the crowd of supporters became a mob that forcefully took
over the Capitol.

The prevalence of Christian nationalism among the mob helps explain why
the insurrectionists carried "Jesus Saves" and "Jesus2020" banners alongside
Confederate flags; prayed to Jesus Christ, thanking the heavenly Father for
their "God-given opportunity to stand up for" their "God-given rights" and

---

[54]George W. Bush, "President's Remarks to the Nation," George W. Bush White House
Archives, https://georgewbush-whitehouse.archives.gov/news/releases/2002/09/20020911-3.html.

[55]NPR, "President Trump's Inaugural Address, Annotated," January 20, 2017, www.npr.org
/2017/01/20/510629447/watch-live-president-trumps-inauguration-ceremony.

[56]Whitehead and Perry, *Taking America Back*, 16.

[57]Whitehead and Perry, *Taking America Back*, 21.

[58]Maggie Haberman, "Trump Told Crowd 'You Will Never Take Back Our Country with Weakness,'"
New York Times, January 6, 2021, www.nytimes.com/2021/01/06/us/politics/trump-speech-capitol
.html.

allowing them to send the message to those they opposed that "this is our nation, not theirs"; thanked God for filling the Capitol "with the white light of your love . . . filling this chamber with patriots that love you, that love Christ"; and praised God for allowing the United States of America "to be reborn."[59] If America is God's country, and Trump is God's president, then those who stand against him are not only enemies of America, they are enemies of God.

Many Christians condemned the insurrection itself. But the problem is that the extremes on display at the Capitol have emerged out of a deformed political discipleship that infects white American Christians much more broadly. Instead of living as countercultural sojourners whose community serves as a vehicle of blessing to the nation to which we've been sent, we have too often fought for power so that we could gain for ourselves a "possession" in the land. Like Joseph, we have succeeded.

But like Joseph, our success has come at a cost. It has required us to embrace deeply de-forming patterns of political discipleship. If Joseph's Egyptianization left him unrecognizable to his brothers, the Americanization of white evangelicals has left us unrecognizable to Black and brown evangelicals-by-belief in the United States, to say nothing of our brothers and sisters in the faith around the world. Indeed, like Joseph, our Americanization has led us to treat many of our Black and brown brothers and sisters in Christ like strangers, or worse. As the insurrectionists said, "this is our nation, not theirs."

Earlier I argued that the "Joseph Option" eventually discovers that those who live by the political sword, die by the political sword.[60] Build your tribe's kingdom in the land of Goshen through self-serving politics, end up as slave labor building somebody else's kingdom in that same land later. If white evangelical political discipleship continues to be oriented primarily toward grabbing power to secure our own perceived good, we will discover this same truth.

This future fallout might well include the erosion of religious liberty that many Christians worry about, myself included. But I have in mind primarily a far worse enslavement: the enslavement of our political lives to the idolatrous effort to build a "Christian America" through political control, and the enslavement of our gospel witness as the result of those idolatrous efforts.

---

[59]"A Reporter's Footage from the Inside the Capitol Siege," *New Yorker*, www.youtube.com/watch?v=270F8s5TEKY.
[60]Shevitz, "Joseph," 52; Walter Brueggemann, *Genesis*, Interpretation (Louisville, KY: Westminster John Knox, 2010), 356.

Indeed, I believe that our embrace of Christian nationalism has already done untold damage to the witness of the gospel in this country. Because of our failures, too many of our neighbors associate Jesus with a violent mob carrying both crosses and Confederate flags.

Make no mistake: our political idolatries do not put God's kingdom at risk. But they do put our *participation* in God's kingdom mission of bringing blessing to the world at risk, not least as those idolatries continue to disciple us toward *injustice*. The stakes are high. Christians, and especially evangelical Christians tempted toward some form of Christian nationalism, should learn from the "Joseph Option," rather than embracing it in an unnuanced way. But how? What is the shape of a more faithful political witness? And what forms of political discipleship might shape us for that witness?

EMBRACING THE "DANIEL OPTION"

*Moral Discipleship and the
Exercise of Political Power*

IN THE PREVIOUS CHAPTER, I argued that much of the American church suffers from impoverished political discipleship in relation to national and local politics. A "Romans 13 Only" approach has led many Christians to advocate for a straightforward submission to the political powers-that-be, on the one hand, and to seek to become part of the powers-that-be in order to use political power for our own purposes, on the other. The former emphasis has often undermined Christian attempts to confront or resist the state. The latter emphasis has generated all sorts of questionable behavior and belief, including Christian nationalism.

What's the solution? One option is to exchange a "Romans 13 Only" Option for a "Revelation Only" Alternative. John's apocalyptic vision of imperial Rome as a monstrous dragon or seductive prostitute reminds some Christians of our own American society. From this perspective, being a political disciple means identifying the idolatry of political powers and refusing to get involved with them. If "Romans 13 Only" folks find political power natural, benign, and very easy to use, "Revelation Only" folks find political power to be an unnatural, dangerous idol to be utterly rejected.

Political theology offers a much more robust, nuanced account of this kind of politics than my brief summary implies. To identify neo-Anabaptist political theology with this flat-footed "Revelation Only" alternative would be a distorting caricature, for instance. The problem is that I suspect this caricature strongly shapes the practical political theology of many Christians.

Revelation, like Romans, provides an essential, irreplaceable resource for Christian political theology. But a political theology that relies almost exclusively on Revelation for understanding how to relate to the state finds itself facing the exact same problem we encountered in the previous chapter. Despite their differences, Revelation, like Romans, was written to Christians who had little to no *direct* influence over the type of political system in which they lived or the specific political players involved. John's summons to resist the *seductions* of the empire was written to a people who had little to no ability to *change* it, at least through direct political activism.

Some have interpreted both Romans and Revelation to suggest that this powerlessness is *normative*. The mission of God's people simply does not include getting involved with power politics. To do so is to exchange the way of Jesus for the way of worldly violence. The posture of the church is a posture of dispossession.[1]

I am grateful for the contributions such theology has made to my own thought. As a result, in reaction to the "Romans 13 Only" approach, many of us have embraced a political theology that emphasizes

1. the church's work as a counterculture that prophetically protests the injustice of our world and embodies a kingdom alternative, and

2. the church's need to resist de-forming discipleship that tempts us to try to run the world through power politics.

But should political theology end there? Is secular political power simply to be critiqued and rejected? If not, how should the church engage secular political power without falling into the trap of the "Joseph Option"? If the "Joseph Option" cautioned us against the dangers of deploying political power for our own purposes, another Old Testament figure reveals the shortcomings of *both* the "Joseph Option" and any "Revelation Only" alternative. The figure I refer to is Daniel.

THE "DANIEL OPTION"

There are good reasons for reading the stories of Daniel and Joseph in conversation with one another.[2] Both are taken from their homes through injustice,

---

[1] See D. Stephen Long, *Augustinian and Ecclesial Christian Ethics: On Loving Enemies* (Lanham, MD: Lexington Books, 2018), 225.
[2] See Carol Newsom, *Daniel*, OTL (Louisville, KY: Westminster John Knox, 2014), 64-65; Matthew Rindge, "Jewish Identity Under Foreign Rule: Daniel 2 as a Reconfiguration of Genesis 41," *JBL* 129,

and rise to positions of prominence by interpreting dreams in the court of a foreign king (Gen 41; Dan 2). Both are strongly associated with wisdom.[3] Both face the challenge of maintaining the sort of bicultural identity necessary to survive as a member of God's people living in a foreign land. Both have a significant influence on the rulers they work for and the political community those rulers oversee.

Yet there are also significant differences between their political witness, not least in the way Daniel's community finds itself constantly at odds with their imperial overlords. Joseph's promotion is the end of his political problems; Daniel and his friends' promotions set them up to get thrown into furnaces and fed to lions.

It's worth exploring the differences between the "Daniel Option" and the "Joseph Option" more carefully. Might Daniel offer us an example of "seeking the welfare of the city" to which we've been sent when we find ourselves in positions of power and influence there?[4] To answer this question, let's compare Joseph and Daniel in terms of their moral discipleship, their priorities in political advocacy, and the results of that advocacy.

MORAL DISCIPLESHIP AND THE "DANIEL OPTION"

Faithful Christian witness requires moral discipleship oriented toward justice. For ancient Israel, such moral formation was deeply intertwined with the need to maintain their identity as children of Abraham, even as they necessarily embraced a multicultural identity in their interactions with the nations. Comparing Joseph's and Daniel's approaches to such formation reveals several differences between these two political options.

Formation and food in Daniel 1. The imperial court gave both Joseph and Daniel new names, names likely related to pagan gods (Gen 41:45; Dan 1:7).[5] Joseph's naming occurs amid a robust process of Egyptianization. But when the chief of the eunuchs "set" a new name on Daniel, Daniel's immediate

---

no. 1 (2010): 88; W. Lee Humphreys, "A Life Style for Diaspora: A Study of the Tales of Esther and Daniel," *JBL* 92, no. 2 (1973): 217.

[3]See Tim Meadowcroft, *Like Stars Forever: Narrative Theology in the Book of Daniel* (Sheffield: Phoenix Press, 2020), 2.

[4]See Justin L. Pannkuk, *King of Kings: God and the Foreign Emperor in the Hebrew Bible* (Waco, TX: Baylor, 2021), 97; Meadowcroft, *Like Stars*, 54.

[5]For discussion, see Carolyn J. Sharp, *Irony and Meaning in the Hebrew Bible* (Bloomington: Indiana University Press, 2008), 56; Newsom, *Daniel*, 47; Daniel L. Smith-Christopher, "Daniel," in *The New Interpreter's Bible*, vol. 2, *Introduction Apocalyptic Literature, Daniel, the Twelve Prophets* (Nashville: Abingdon Press, 1996), 39.

response is to "set" his heart against being "defiled" through eating the royal food and wine (Dan 1:7-8).

Such royal fare served a critical role in imperial displays of power and grandeur throughout the ancient world.[6] To refuse it would be to resist some of the power and prosperity the empire offered to those willing to play by their rules.[7] The narrator thus highlights the way Daniel actively embraced a bodily act of counter-discipleship when subjected to the imperial formation associated with naming.[8]

The specific reasons why Daniel and his friends decide to refuse the royal fare have never been fully explained.[9] Commentators agree their decision relates in some way to Jewish food laws.[10] The problem is that their specific decision to refuse both the king's portion and the king's wine doesn't correspond completely to any particular set of Jewish food laws. Their decision apparently depended on their own discerning contextualization of the food laws in this specific and, no doubt, highly debatable way.[11]

But this apparent arbitrariness is part of the point. If disciples are going to resist assimilation, they've got to draw the line somewhere,[12] and the process of determining where to draw the line, and sticking to it, is a critical task of moral formation. Nor was the decision to resist the king's food simply "a simple determination" to "settle on and sustain a point of difference."[13] These young exiles are offered food by an empire seeking to shape them for its use through a specific training regimen. That regimen included rich fare stolen from the empire's victims,[14] but also training in the "literature and language of the Chaldeans" so that they would be able to serve the king (Dan 1:4). The intended outcome of such training included their physical appearance. For Nebuchadnezzar, their usability depended both on their being "without blemish, handsome" *and* "skillful in all wisdom, endowed with knowledge, understanding learning" (Dan 1:4 RSV). Indeed,

---

[6]See Newsom, *Daniel*, 45.

[7]See Smith-Christopher, "Daniel," 40-42.

[8]See Carroll, *Bible and Borders*, 25; Brennan Breed, "A Divided Tongue: The Moral Tastebuds of the Book of Daniel," *JSOT* 40, no. 1 (2015): 123; Pannkuk, *King of Kings*, 171.

[9]Carroll, *Bible and Borders*, 25.

[10]Anathea Portier-Young, *Apocalypse Against Empire: Theologies of Resistance in Early Judaism* (Grand Rapids, MI: Eerdmans, 2011), 259; Carroll, *Bible and Borders*, 25.

[11]See Newsom, *Daniel*, 48.

[12]Newsom, *Daniel*, 48.

[13]Meadowcroft, *Like Stars*, 38.

[14]Smith-Christopher, "Daniel," 40.

Nebuchadnezzar likely understood their being good in appearance and their being skillful in wisdom as related.

This explains why the chief of the eunuchs is afraid that the Daniel diet will leave him looking worse than the others (Dan 1:10). The food practices Daniel proposes require that he and his friends risk "failure in the very terms set by the Babylonians," and in the "most obviously observable way."[15]

God's vindication of Daniel and his friends' choices sets the tone for the stories that follow.[16] These Jewish exiles seek to maintain their moral and cultural identity, while also adapting to and navigating the exilic court to which they've been sent. The result of their counter-formation is a God-given triumph in that court; instead of appearing worse, they appear *better* than those who ate the king's food (Dan 1:15). Instead of simply assimilating to the wisdom of the Babylonians, God *gave them* "knowledge and skill in *every aspect* of literature and wisdom" (Dan 1:17). Through their faithful formative discipleship, they not only maintain their identity, but become "ten times better" than anybody else in court (Dan 1:20).

This first story shows us that moral formation, especially when facing the possibility of political cooption, *starts small*. The stakes are high in Daniel 1, but not nearly as high as they become in the chapters that follow. Faithfulness in small things, including faithful resistance to the emperor's food at the emperor's table, prepares one for faithfulness in greater things.

But it is not only resistance on display here. These Jews apparently accept both their pagan names and the opportunity to serve the king (Dan 1:19). Indeed, the text subtly suggests that the universal wisdom God gives to his faithful, countercultural disciples *includes* the "literature and language of the Chaldeans" (Dan 1:4). Formation in God's wisdom apparently requires identifying areas of commonality with the culture; indeed, such areas of commonality provide important resources for seeking the welfare of the city to which one has been sent.[17] Daniel neither accepts nor rejects the Babylonian wisdom tradition. Instead, he *masters* it, discerning how it might be both "used and refused."[18]

The story makes clear that pagan wisdom and formation always have to be redirected and reframed. Sometimes, as elsewhere in Daniel, they will have

---

[15]Meadowcroft, *Like Stars*, 38.

[16]Meadowcroft, *Like Stars*, 36.

[17]Meadowcroft, *Like Stars*, 39-40. Smith-Christopher does not adequately engage these aspects of the text in his claim that Daniel operates from a theology of "Christ against culture" (Smith-Christopher, "Daniel," 34).

[18]Portier-Young, *Against Empire*, 226.

to be rejected outright. But there can be no doubt that the text also makes clear the possibility that God's people might discover, even in the shadow of empire, what Reformed theologians refer to as "common grace insights." Identifying such areas of commonality is one way the "Daniel Option" faithfully pursues a multicultural identity.

Of course, the fact that political witness includes both "using and refusing" only makes the "Daniel Option" *more* dangerous, and *more* dependent on counter-formation oriented toward just participation.[19] Only genuine disciples can navigate these dangers. Daniel 1 models how the community both participated in the broader culture and created a "particular subculture within that host culture."[20] Their process of just discipleship and discernment enabled them to identify the difference between seeking the good of the city and idolatrously selling out.

Formation through prayer and fasting in Daniel. Prayer and fasting also serve as important disciplines of moral discipleship. Here again, the differences between Joseph and Daniel are instructive.[21] In Genesis, Joseph regularly talks *about* God, but, unlike Abraham, Isaac, and Jacob, Joseph never talks *to* God.[22] Daniel, on the other hand, models a life of prayer. Having practiced resisting Nebuchadnezzar through counter-formative food practices in Daniel 1, in Daniel 2, he resists Nebuchadnezzar through the weapon of prayer.[23] When King Nebuchadnezzar threatens to kill all the wise men of his court, Daniel calls on his companions to join him in prayer for mercy (Dan 2:5-18). God's answer to Daniel's prayer, which allows him to interpret Nebuchadnezzar's dream and save the lives of the wise men, leads Daniel into further prayers of praise and thanksgiving (Dan 2:20-23). Through such prayer, Daniel and his friends learn to orient their entire lives toward God as the true emperor over all the earth.[24]

In Daniel 6, Daniel is willing to die rather than give up his practice of ritual prayer. This ritual practice includes praying at specific times, kneeling, facing Jerusalem, and both praising God and seeking mercy from him. Such physical

---

[19]See Daniel L. Smith-Christopher, *A Biblical Theology of Exile* (Minneapolis: Fortress, 2002), 190.

[20]Meadowcroft, *Like Stars*, 41.

[21]Rindge, "Jewish Identity," 92-93.

[22]Bruce C. Birch, *Let Justice Roll Down* (Louisville, KY: Westminster John Knox, 1991), 113.

[23]Birch, *Let Justice Roll Down*, 52.

[24]See Stephen B. Reid, "The Theology of the Book of Daniel and the Political Theory of W. E. B. DuBois," in *The Recovery of Black Presence: An Interdisciplinary Exploration*, ed. Charles B. Copher, Jacquelyn Grant, and Randall C. Bailey (Nashville: Abingdon, 1995), 41.

postures are part of the process of moral formation; "the act of kneeling does not so much communicate a message about subordination as it generates a body identified with subordination."[25] That is why Daniel's prayer rituals should be understood as, among other things, an act of moral formation oriented toward just discipleship in exile. Kneeling in prayer shapes Daniel for a kind of bodily remembering of where his true allegiance and ultimate subordination lie. Such a body shaped by prayer, Daniel demonstrates, is willing to risk the lions rather than be found faithless to one's true Lord.

In Daniel 9, Daniel prays and fasts during a time of political transition and in response to the word of Yahweh to Jeremiah (Dan 9:1-2). Remarkably, Daniel not only acknowledges Yahweh's sovereign power, but also confesses his sin and the sins of his ancestors in rejecting Yahweh's law (Dan 9:11). Through such prayer and fasting, Daniel names both his community's and his own moral failures, and bodily enacts a complete dependence on Yahweh for rescue. The angelic messenger describes such prayer as giving one's heart to understanding and humility before God (Dan 10:12). By giving his heart to prayer and fasting, Daniel embraces a bodily, disciplined disposition of confession, dependence, and reverence toward Yahweh.[26]

Liturgical practices both express political virtues and *form them*. The book of Daniel shows us the centrality of prayer and fasting in forming the virtuous dispositions we will require if we are to become just disciples capable of participating in the political arena.

Of course, the power of Daniel's formative discipleship in relation to food and prayer depends in part on the fact that Daniel often practices these disciplines in *community*. If Joseph's Egyptianization occurs in part because of his (unjust) separation from the community of promise, Daniel and his friends model what it looks like to create a countercultural community of disciples in exile.

Formation and biblical law in Daniel. Daniel 9 reveals yet another source for moral discipleship oriented toward political justice within the "Daniel Option": Scripture. We have already noted the centrality of the Mosaic law and the prophet Jeremiah to Daniel's prayer and fasting in Daniel 9, as well as the probable influence of the Mosaic law on their food choices in Daniel 1. But it's telling that even Daniel's critics recognize the centrality of God's law to his moral discipleship.

---

[25]Catherine Bell, *Ritual Theory, Ritual Practice* (New York: Oxford University Press, 2009), 100.
[26]Portier-Young, *Against Empire*, 243.

Thus the court conspirators who trick King Darius into writing an unalterable law that gets Daniel thrown into the lion's den recognize that they cannot find "any ground for complaint against this Daniel *unless [they] find it in connection with the law of his God*" (Dan 6:5). The text thus sets up an instructive conflict. On the one side, there's the "law of the Medes and Persians." Such law may be unalterable, but it is easily manipulated for injustice. Standing alongside this unalterable, unjust law is King Darius, who is neither powerful nor intelligent enough to work justice through this law. On the other side stands the law of Daniel's God, through which Daniel triumphs over his enemies and remains faithful, not least through the divine king's power to rescue those who keep his commands (see Dan 6:22).

Apocalyptic wisdom and formation for just discernment. Finally, the "Daniel Option" depends on Daniel's willingness to *receive, accept,* and *live into* the apocalyptic visions, dreams, and angelic interactions that dominate large portions of the book. Such visions, dreams, and angelic revelations are political apocalypses in this sense: they reveal the truth of the world *as it is,* rather than as it merely *appears* to be. They allow Daniel to see past the political propaganda, identify the idolatrous tendencies of every politician and regime he encounters,[27] recognize Yahweh's *own* rule as the dominant and enduring political reality, and discern what wise, just action looks like at a given time and place. In other words, Daniel's just political participation requires him to receive and respond to revealed wisdom about human empire, the empire of Yahweh, and human political agency under Yahweh rule.

Apocalyptic wisdom and human empire. On the one hand, the book of Daniel makes the startling claim that Gentile empires have received their political sovereignty from Yahweh. It is Israel's God who gives the king of Judah to Nebuchadnezzar (Dan 1:2). It is Israel's God who "has sovereignty over the kingdom of mortals, and [he] gives it to whom he will" (Dan 4:25[22]). While defeated peoples could see themselves as abandoned by their local god, the book of Daniel claims that even in Judah's defeat at the hands of Gentile kings, it is Yahweh who is truly sovereign. Yahweh "actively works in, through, and over the conquering king(dom)."[28]

This reality makes it possible for Daniel and his friends to participate in imperial politics, critically and creatively seeking the good of the community

---

[27]See Smith-Christopher, "Daniel," 34.
[28]Pannkuk, *King of Kings*, 235.

to which they have been sent *through* their work within the court of foreign kings. But it also completely transforms the way they see these Gentile kingdoms, and indeed the way these Gentile kingdoms are forced to see themselves. For example, while Nebuchadnezzar looks like the unshakable king of the universe, in Daniel 2, God sends Nebuchadnezzar a dream that reveals an entirely different political reality. Nebuchadnezzar sees a statue made of "fine gold, its chest and arms of silver, its middle and thighs of bronze, its legs of iron, its feet partly of iron and partly of clay" (Dan 2:31-33). For Jewish readers, such a statue would most likely be seen as an idol.[29]

So while God reveals to Daniel that Nebuchadnezzar is indeed the head of gold (Dan 2:37), Daniel makes clear to Nebuchadnezzar that this makes him no more than a slightly shinier piece of idol statue that will soon be smashed to pieces and blown away by the wind (Dan 2:34-35, 44-45).

> As you looked on, a stone was cut out, not by human hands, and it struck the statue on its feet of iron and clay and broke them in pieces. . . . [They] became like the chaff of the summer threshing floors; and the wind carried them away, so that not a trace of them could be found. (Dan 2:34-35)

The God-given dream makes it clear: empires come, empires go. Some are better, some worse. But the final fate of all human empires is the same: they will be smashed to pieces and brought to an end (Dan 2:44).

If the God-given dream of Daniel 2 shows that Nebuchadnezzar is a shiny gold statue slated for destruction *at best,* Daniel's apocalyptic dream interpretation in Daniel 4 shows the king that, at worst, he's an idolatrous tyrant. Nebuchadnezzar learns that if he acts like a beast long enough, God just might turn him into one. Nebuchadnezzar's outrageous pride and injustice (see Dan 4:27[24]; 5:20) lead to his being "chopped down," driven out from among humans, and forced to live like a beast of the field until he learns to praise and honor Israel's God as the true, sovereign ruler of all things (Dan 4:34[31]).

The idolatry and violence of Gentile empires only intensifies in Daniel 7–12. In these later apocalyptic visions, the gloves are off. These chapters portray future regimes as monstrous beasts that wage violent war against one another and the people of God. The visions are the stuff of nightmare, alarming Daniel himself and contemporary readers alike (see Dan 7:15).[30]

---

[29]Carol Newsom, "'Resistance Is Futile!' The Ironies of Danielic Resistance to Empire," *Interpretation: A Journal of Bible and Theology* 71, no. 2 (2017): 176.

[30]These visions may well describe the devastating oppression the people of God faced under Antiochus IV in the second century BCE (Portier-Young, *Against Empire*, 227).

These visions reveal pagan political powers as they really are, rather than as their pomp and propaganda portray them: beasts that "devour the whole earth," challenge the Most High (Dan 7:23, 25) and exalt themselves over every god (Dan 11:36). They cast truth down to the ground (Dan 8:12), destroy saints (Dan 8:24), prosper by deceit, and destroy many (Dan 8:25). The worst of them will seduce some of God's people even as they profane the temple with abominations (Dan 11:31-32).

In a world filled with abusive, idolatrous political power, just political participation requires the willingness to adopt God's perspective on the *moral* and *theological* reality of human empires. Where human empires claim permanency, God's apocalyptic wisdom reveals they are fleeting and temporary. Where human empires describe themselves as benevolent authorities essential for human flourishing, God's apocalyptic wisdom reveals the relentless propensity to idolatry that dogs every human political regime. This is the truth that political disciples pursuing the "Daniel Option" must *receive* and *embrace*.

Apocalyptic wisdom and the empire of Yahweh. The "Daniel Option" also depends, however, on an equally apocalyptic vision of Yahweh's own imperial rule. The stone that smashes Nebuchadnezzar's statue, and with it every human empire, is *God's own kingdom.* This kingdom, which will fill the whole earth and stand forever, depends solely on God's action—the rock of God's kingdom is not cut out by any human hand (Dan 2:44-45; cf. Dan 8:25). It is Israel's God who brings judgment on even the most destructive of human kingdoms, replaces them with his own, and entrusts his everlasting kingdom to his faithful saints (Dan 7:26-27). Indeed, Yahweh's sovereignty extends even to the dead, many of whom "shall awake, some to everlasting life, and some to shame and everlasting contempt" at the "time of the end" (Dan 12:2-4). Here, in the clearest reference to resurrection in the Old Testament, Yahweh declares that his kingdom cannot be overcome even by death, the "last weapon of the tyrant."[31]

Nor is Yahweh's reign only a future phenomenon. Heaven rules even in the present (Dan 4:23[26]). It is Yahweh who gave Judah's king into Nebuchadnezzar's hand (Dan 1:2), Yahweh who rescues his faithful ones from death by fiery furnace or lion's den (Dan 3:28; 6:22), and Yahweh who sets whoever he wants over the "kingdom of mortals" (Dan 4:25[22]). Nor is *being*

---

[31]N. T. Wright, *Surprised by Hope: Rethinking Heaven, the Resurrection, and the Mission of the Church* (Grand Rapids, MI: Zondervan, 2010), 20, 50.

set over such a kingdom any sign of moral or political superiority; Yahweh sets over such kingdoms whoever he wills (Dan 4:25[22]), even "the lowliest of human beings" (4:17[14]).

Daniel's visions, dreams, and angelic revelations reveal the true wisdom easily missed in a world swimming with human imperial pretension and propaganda: Yahweh is bringing a future kingdom to replace all others. Even in the present, Yahweh regularly weighs human regimes in the balance, casting down those he finds wanting (Dan 5:25-29). "The LORD reigns" is the central confession of all biblical politics. Just, faithful political participation requires Daniel to recognize this vision of Yahweh's rule as the defining political reality in the present and in the future.

Apocalyptic wisdom and human political agency under Yahweh's rule. Finally, the dreams, visions, and angelic encounters offer the "Daniel Option" a vision of what the faithful exercise of political agency looks like in a world that is simultaneously overrun with problematic human political powers *and* definitively ruled by the divine king.

The vision in Daniel 7 that launches the second half of the book portrays an intensification of imperial violence and idolatry, followed by the sudden intervention of the Ancient of Days (Dan 7:9-10). God's victory over these political powers in Daniel 7:13-14 is connected to the arrival of "one like a Son of Man," to whom is given dominion

> and glory and kingship,
> that all peoples, nations, and languages
>   should serve him.
> His dominion is an everlasting kingdom
>   that shall not pass away,
> and his kingship is one
>   that shall never be destroyed. (Dan 7:14)

Such a vision echoes the vision Daniel received in Daniel 2.

But this later vision leaves plenty to wonder over. While Daniel 7:13-14 was interpreted early on as a messianic prophecy, and adopted as such by Jesus himself, it's clear from Daniel 7:18, 22, and 27 that this "one like a Son of Man" is also associated with the holy ones, who are themselves said to receive this everlasting kingdom.

Tim Meadowcroft argues the ambiguity between the individual "one like a son of man" and the people of God more generally is part of the theological point. The vision points to the people of God's participation in the divine life through the "Son of Man." The phrase "Son of Man" offers an intentionally multivalent and complex image that points to God's own work to enable his people to participate in his victorious installment of his kingdom over and against all the kingdoms of the world through the work of the Messiah.[32] This is just what we'd expect in light of Scripture's justice story explored in chapter two (see fig. 2.3).

This means that God will rule the world through his saints in the future, *and* that God enables his saints to participate in his rule partially in the present, even amid the empires and cultures of their world. This is, in fact, what the reader witnesses in Daniel 1–6, as Daniel and his friends creatively criticize and resist, but also often collaborate with the political rulers of their day. The apocalyptic visions thus reveal the way the community of faith's political vocation to share in the reign of God in the future determines how they begin to share in the reign of God in the present: empowered by God's presence and wisdom, and in line with his coming kingdom.

That doesn't mean, however, that political collaboration with earthly empires is *always* a faithful option. Daniel refuses to work with Belshazzar at all, and if this outright rejection is the exception in the first half of the book,[33] it becomes the norm in the second half. The apocalyptic visions of Daniel 7–12 depict times when God's people would participate in his kingdom, not by collaborating with the kingdoms of the world, but by *refusing* any collaborative engagement with them at all. Indeed, the second half of the book seems to call the people of God to forsake political collaboration and embrace instead a posture of total resistance.[34]

This dynamic forces us to deal with the relationship between the visions of Daniel 7–12 and the stories in Daniel 1–6. In some ways, the difference between these two sections mirrors the differences between the "Romans 13 Only" Option and the "Revelation Only" Alternative. What does the posture of resistance and rejection in the latter half of Daniel mean for the earlier depiction of God's people participating in imperial politics in the first half?

Some argue the two halves of the book come from two different contexts and represent two different and mutually exclusive responses to Gentile rule.[35] From this perspective, the book of Daniel forces readers to choose how to engage political power; *either* participate *or* refuse. Yet the final form

---

[32]See Meadowcroft, *Like Stars*, 90-107.
[33]Humphreys, "Life Style," 221.
[34]Portier-Young, *Against Empire*, 228.
[35]Humphreys, "Life Style," 223.

of the book maintains a close link between the two sections,[36] not least by describing the more negative visions of the second half of the book as occurring *during* Daniel's service to pagan rulers described in the first half (see Dan 7:1; 8:1; 9:1).

Others argue the stories in Daniel 1–6 operate like a "hidden transcript." The oppressed speak about their pagan overlords in what *appears* to be a relatively positive way, while actually revealing a deeper, more subversive message.[37] Positive portrayals of pagan leaders are simply "official correspondence;" they do not suggest any "positive and working relations with the regime."[38] If Daniel 1–6 occasionally appears to "[endorse] imperial rule," the text hides a more revolutionary meaning under the surface.[39]

This interpretation allows the overtly negative portrayal of empire in the apocalyptic visions of Daniel 7–12 to overwhelm completely the apparently more positive possibilities of the first half of the book.[40] This interpretation sides with the "Revelation Only" Alternative; participating in secular political power may *look* possible, but the deeper truth is that all political power must be resisted and rejected.

But if the "hidden transcript" concept has provoked important discussion, its application to Daniel 1–6 is misleading. Daniel and his friends go toe-to-toe with the empire again and again in these tales, and bear witness again and again to the imperial reign of Yahweh. There is, in fact, no "apparent hesitancy on the part of the author to be entirely explicit about the true nature of God's power over empire."[41] There is nothing particularly "hidden" about Daniel and his friends' witness to Gentile political rulers. Indeed, they repeatedly, openly, and defiantly risk martyrdom through that witness.[42]

Rather than setting the two halves of the book against each other, or interpreting the entire book primarily in light of the more negative visions in the second half, I suggest the final form of the text invites us into the messy tension of political *discernment* in an apocalyptic key. Just political participation

---

[36]Meadowcroft, *Like Stars*, 2.

[37]The language of "hidden transcript" is drawn from James Scott, but has been deployed widely within biblical studies.

[38]Smith-Christopher, *Exile*, 83.

[39]Alexandra Frisch, *The Danielic Discourse on Empire in Second Temple Literature* (Leiden: Brill, 2017), 103.

[40]This seems to be a fair characterization of the position taken by Smith-Christopher (see Smith-Christopher, "Daniel," 21, 34).

[41]Frisch, *Danielic Discourse*, 123.

[42]See Portier-Young, *Against Empire*, 34-39.

requires God's people to decide, in light of God's revealed wisdom, when and how we can participate with worldly politics and when and how worldly politics must simply be resisted. The tension "between the accommodationist impulses of the court tales and the adversarial cast of the vision narratives"[43] is maintained precisely because such a tension forces the *reader* to practice the kind of wise discernment the "Daniel Option" requires.

Daniel's own wise, just political participation depends in part on his willingness to live in line with these visions of the world *as it is,* rather than in the world as it merely *appears* to be. The visions allow Daniel and his friends to discern *when* they can participate in seeking the good of the city by working with their Gentile political overlords, when they must refuse to follow a specific command, and when they must refuse to cooperate with the regime at all. This kind of apocalyptic political discernment is crucial for just disciples seeking the good of the city to which they have been sent.

WHAT'S THE GOAL OF POLITICAL POWER?

Daniel and Joseph differ in their moral discipleship, but they also differ in the way they exercise political power. While both use their political influence to save lives, their stories subtly suggest different approaches to political participation. We see this most clearly in Daniel's interpretation of Nebuchadnezzar's vision of himself as the cosmic tree about to be chopped down (Dan 4:1-36[3:31-34]). After interpreting the dream, Daniel offers advice to the king on how to prolong his "prosperity" (Dan 4:27[24]).

Like Joseph, Daniel interprets a dream of impending disaster given by God to an imperial ruler, and like Joseph, Daniel seeks to help the empire avoid that disaster. Yet Joseph's response to Pharaoh's dream is entirely technocratic: a famine will come; therefore precautions must be taken. Far from costing Pharaoh anything, Joseph's recommendations help Pharaoh acquire significant economic and political power through the famine relief program.

Daniel's advice to Nebuchadnezzar goes in a startlingly different direction:

> But, your majesty, be pleased to accept my counsel: break with your sins by doing justice, break with your errors by showing favor to the [oppressed], in case there might be a prolonging of your success. (Dan 4:27[24])[44]

---

[43]Meadowcroft, *Like Stars*, 86.

[44]This is Goldingay's translation (John Goldingay, *Daniel*, WBC 30 [Grand Rapids, MI: Zondervan, 1996], 79), except that I have followed the NRSV in translating *anayin* as "oppressed" rather than "needy." Such language often refers not simply to those who are materially poor, but to those who have been afflicted (see HALOT, 852, 856-57, 1951).

Daniel's "advice" on how to Make Babylon Great Again amounts to an accusation that Nebuchadnezzar is currently committing sins that need to be "broken off"[45] to avoid God's imminent judgment. What is required is not simply for Nebuchadnezzar to *stop* sinning. He must proactively do justice and mercy for the oppressed.[46] If he does, Daniel suggests, the God of heaven may well relent from the judgment that Nebuchadnezzar has glimpsed in the dream.

But why would Daniel seek to help Nebuchadnezzar prolong his reign in the first place? The regime Daniel seeks to extend is the very regime that devastated Jerusalem and exiled God's people! Surprisingly, though, Daniel has already demonstrated a measure of "genuine affection"[47] for Nebuchadnezzar in his expressed wish that the judgment prophesied in the dream might fall on Nebuchadnezzar's enemies (Dan 4:19[16]).[48] Small wonder that some rabbinic interpreters argued that Daniel was later punished for wickedly offering Nebuchadnezzar advice.[49] Even for some of Daniel's earliest interpreters, his willingness to seek the prosperity of the Babylonian regime suggested a far too cozy relationship with oppressive imperial forces.

If the reason why Daniel sought to help Nebuchadnezzar prolong his prosperity is confusing, his recommendation for doing so may also strike us as strange. It does not appear to be "directly correlated with Nebuchadnezzar's failure to recognize the sovereignty of the Most High."[50] The failure to acknowledge God's sovereignty seems to be the reason Daniel himself gives for the impending judgment (Dan 4:26[23]), and the reason the narrator gives for the judgment actually falling on Nebuchadnezzar (Dan 4:30[27]). Nebuchadnezzar implies that his sanity is restored to him because he finally acknowledges God's sovereignty (Dan 4:34[31]). Why then does Daniel, in the middle of all of this, offer *justice toward oppressed humans* as the solution for Nebuchadnezzar's sinful refusal to acknowledge God's sovereignty?

---

[45]HALOT, 1959; Goldingay, *Daniel*, 81.

[46]The LXX and some modern commentators understand *tsidqah* as referring exclusively to "almsgiving" (Newsom, *Daniel*, 145; HALOT, 1963), as it no doubt came to mean in later periods. But because Nebuchadnezzar is "addressed as *king*," the more comprehensive language of justice is more appropriate here (Goldingay, *Daniel*, 81).

[47]Newsom, *Daniel*, 143.

[48]This might be understood as court rhetoric, but that is much less likely given that Daniel actually offers Nebuchadnezzar advice.

[49]Bava Batra 4a; see also Newsom, "Resistance Is Futile!," 173. On the history of interpretation generally, see the excellent summary by Breed in Newsom, *Daniel*, 150-56.

[50]Newsom, *Daniel*, 145.

Because Daniel stands in a long line of prophets who know that the way human rulers acknowledge Yahweh's sovereignty is precisely by doing justice for the poor. Jeremiah condemned King Jehoiakim for building his luxurious "house" through unrighteousness and injustice, making "his neighbors work for nothing" (Jer 22:13). For oppressed Israel, as for all of those living on the underside of empire, the kind of imperial affluence Nebuchadnezzar celebrates when he boasts of building Babylon as a royal "house" for his own glory and majesty (Dan 4:30[27]) always depends on the oppression of the poor. But Jeremiah contrasts Jehoiakim's behavior with King Josiah's, for whom all went well, *because* he did "justice and righteousness" (Jer 22:15). "Is this not," Yahweh asks, "*what it means to know me?*" (Jer 22:16 AT).

Daniel, whom we see pondering Jeremiah's prophecies concerning Jehoiakim in Daniel 9, has learned that the way rulers recognize Yahweh's sovereignty is by doing justice for the poor. Nebuchadnezzar can only acknowledge God's sovereign kingship by reflecting the kingdom of God's priorities.[51] Prioritizing justice for the poor is the only sure path Daniel knows toward promoting the peace and prosperity of any kingdom.[52] Daniel's advocacy on behalf of the poor embodies the kind of political wisdom that does not merely accomplish prudentially preferable outcomes, but exercises wisdom oriented toward justice.

God created people in his image as royal priestly family members. Because justice and righteousness are at the center of God's character and job description, they are to be at the center of *humanity's*. The special emphasis on the king's justice and righteousness in Israel is simply a function of his greater power and influence in the society at large; the king has exponentially greater responsibility to do justice because he wields exponentially greater power. Furthermore, the special emphasis in the Old Testament on God's people doing justice and righteousness is not due to their having a special code of ethics distinct from the ethics of the world, but rather because they have been called by Yahweh to embody in their own life the justice and righteousness that Yahweh intends for all humanity.

Because of this, doing justice and taking action on behalf of the needy stand at the center of the Old Testament's political vision for both Israel *and* the nations. In both cases, that responsibility falls especially to the rulers.

---

[51]John Goldingay, "The Stories in Daniel: A Narrative Politics," *JSOT* 12, no. 37 (1987): 105.
[52]Goldingay, *Daniel*, 95.

"Even pagan kings are called to be the means of God's caring kingship being implemented," and so "Daniel assumes that" even a pagan "regime that puts justice first will [prosper]."[53]

Both the "Daniel Option" and the "Joseph Option" recognize that God's people can, at least on some occasions, use political power to seek the good of the communities to which they have been sent. Both agree with Jeremiah that, on such occasions, God's people find their "welfare" in seeking the broader community's "welfare" (Jer 29:7). But in other ways, they differ substantially in terms of their overall approach to political advocacy.

Joseph pursues his political goals without ever confronting the regime. Daniel, on the other hand, recognizes that you *cannot* seek the welfare of the empire without confronting the rampant injustice of the empire. Advocating for justice requires Daniel to advocate for the common good of all, and especially the poor and oppressed. Joseph, on the other hand, uses his relationship with imperial power to give infinitely preferable treatment to his own family. Joseph enables Pharaoh to prosper by the kind of economic practice the law could only label, at least in retrospect, injustice. Daniel offers Nebuchadnezzar the path to true prosperity: justice and mercy for all, and particularly the marginalized.

Daniel's political advocacy also achieves dramatically different results from Joseph's. While Pharaoh acknowledges that God has given Joseph the ability to interpret his dream, that acknowledgment is a brief prelude to his emphasis on Joseph's own wisdom. By contrast, Daniel's consistent faithfulness leads Nebuchadnezzar to accept Daniel's view of *God*.[54] Indeed, the portrait of Nebuchadnezzar here is, according to Newsom, a humanizing one, presenting him as a "redeemed sinner."[55] So while "God's role elevates the status of Joseph in Pharaoh's eyes," Daniel "elevates the status of God in the eyes of Nebuchadnezzar."[56]

Indeed, Nebuchadnezzar's humanizing transformation may well include his implementation of the kind of justice for which Daniel advocated. The fact that the story is told *by* Nebuchadnezzar *to* the nations suggests that Nebuchadnezzar is well aware of Daniel's wise counsel that justice and mercy to the poor is the path to recognizing the sovereignty of the "King of heaven." Nebuchadnezzar's final praise to the king of heaven extols him precisely for

---

[53]Goldingay, *Daniel*, 95.
[54]Rindge, "Jewish Identity," 94.
[55]The culmination of a narrative trajectory begun in Daniel 1 (Newsom, *Daniel*, 149).
[56]Rindge, "Jewish Identity," 94.

the fact that "his works are truth, and his ways are justice" (Dan 4:37[34]).[57]
Presumably, one way Nebuchadnezzar will honor this divine king is by conforming his own ways to God's, including by imitating the kind of righteousness and justice for which Daniel has advocated.

Indeed, Daniel 7:4 probably alludes to Nebuchadnezzar's humanizing
transformation. Here, at the beginning of the much darker apocalyptic depictions of empire that dominate the second half of the book, a beast that looks
like a lion but with wings like an eagle emerges from the sea. This creature,
representing a political kingdom, has its wings removed and is given a "heart"[58]
like a human being. The language alludes to Nebuchadnezzar, whose descent
into madness was described as being given the "heart" of a beast (Dan
4:16[13]). Given that Daniel 7 draws a stark contrast between monstrous
Gentile empires and the coming kingdom of Yahweh, whose rule will be expressed through one "like a Son of Man," the "humanization of the first beast"
representing Nebuchadnezzar is a "startlingly positive image."[59] It suggests
that Nebuchadnezzar's punishment has been, as Ephrem the Syrian put it, a
"careful administration of *pedagogical* pain."[60]

The medicine apparently took. For Nebuchadnezzar's reign to be divinely
depicted as a beastly regime transformed into a more humane one, in a
chapter celebrating the vindication of one like a Son of Man, suggests that
Nebuchadnezzar may have begun to conform his rule toward the character of
the divine king and coming kingdom. *This does not mean that Nebuchadnezzar's
kingdom becomes the kingdom of God.* The head of gold is still a part of the
imperial statue that will be smashed by the arrival of Yahweh's reign. But
neither does that make the humanizing of Nebuchadnezzar's penultimate
kingdom meaningless. Indeed, for those who suffer under oppressive imperial
power, the humanization of oppressive rulers could be very meaningful
indeed, even if those oppressed sufferers continued to pray and long for that
final ruler who would inherit, and share with his saints, a kingdom that would
have no end.

In conclusion, then, the "Joseph Option" and the "Daniel Option" embrace
different practices of moral discipleship. Out of that moral discipleship, they
pursue distinct approaches to exercising political power, and achieve different

---

[57]On which, see Caio Peres, "A Lion Ate Grass Like an Ox: Nebuchadnezzar and Empire
Transformation in Daniel 4," *Scandinavian Journal of the Old Testament* 35, no. 2 (2021).
[58]While the NRSV translates "mind," the word *levav* is regularly translated as "heart."
[59]Newsom, *Daniel*, 223. See also Goldingay, *Daniel*, 162.
[60]Quoted in Newsom, *Daniel*, 156.

results. Whereas Joseph's Egyptianizing discipleship leads to a kind of political advocacy that enslaves the Egyptians, concentrates power for Pharaoh, and privileges his own family, Daniel's moral discipleship allows him both to collaborate with the regime *and* confront it, condemning Nebuchadnezzar for his oppression, and inviting him to pursue prosperity through justice and mercy for the oppressed. Joseph's efforts won short-term gains for his own family but may well have contributed to their future enslavement. Daniel participates in the transformation of Nebuchadnezzar's violent regime, with life-saving results for all.

THE "DANIEL OPTION" BEYOND
ROMANS AND REVELATION

The "Daniel Option" offers a serious challenge to both the "Romans 13 Only" Option and the "Revelation Only" Alternative. On the one hand, Daniel challenges the "Romans 13 Only" Option's comfort with acknowledging, celebrating, and submitting to the power of the state. Even the *best* regime in the book of Daniel tends toward the monstrous and must be regularly resisted and confronted. Because of a relatively rosy view of political power, "Romans 13 Only" Christians may see seeking, gaining, and using political power as a relatively benign process that is always a faithful option for the believing community. By contrast, Daniel depicts participation in pagan political processes as often deeply dangerous to the community's integrity and even their lives. Because political power tends toward the idolatrous, participation requires constant vigilance, deep discipleship oriented toward allegiance to God, a primary identification with God's countercultural people, and a habituated commitment to justice. Such discipleship is necessary if the people of God are to gain the wisdom necessary to know *when* and *how* they can collaborate with secular political powers, and *when* and *how* they must reject such collaboration.

In all of this, the "Daniel Option" affirms "Revelation Only" Christians' sense that secular politics can tempt the people of God to the idolatry of trying to run the world. The "Daniel Option" agrees that the people of God must learn to live *first and foremost* as "resident aliens,"[61] a "peculiar people" whose primary allegiance is offered to God alone, and whose life together fosters the kind of character that allows them to embody a prophetic alternative to the status quo.

---

[61] As argued in Stanley Hauerwas and William H. Willimon, *Resident Aliens: Life in the Christian Colony* (Nashville: Abingdon Press, 2014).

But the "Daniel Option" *rejects* the idea that these commitments require God's people to refuse political participation in the nations and places in which they find themselves. The Danielic counterculture is *suspicious* of political power, but unlike the "Revelation Only" Alternative, it is not *allergic* to it. Indeed, while the book often depicts such power as thrust on Daniel, on at least one occasion, he actively seeks to promote his friends to political offices within the imperial court (Dan 2:49). The "Daniel Option" believes we can, at least sometimes, be both a "resident alien and invested in the state, in all of its glorious failing."[62] Indeed, we can and should seek to transform the state whenever we can faithfully do so.

The "Daniel Option" therefore agrees with the "Romans 13 Only" crowd that the community of faith's involvement cannot be limited to living as a countercultural community or to prophetic protest. Daniel's political discipleship depends on the kind of moral formation and countercultural witness celebrated by the "Revelation Only" Alternative. But out of that moral formation and witness, Daniel engages in power politics. Indeed, faithful discipleship requires him to do so.

Moreover, through that engagement, Daniel demonstrates that idolatrous political powers can *change,* can move toward justice and the common good. Daniel demonstrates, in other words, that the state can indeed function as "God's servant for" the people's "good" (Rom 13:3). This remains true even though Daniel recognizes that change remains temporary and that the state's justice and goodness fall far short of the fullness of God's own kingdom.

Perhaps we can even say that Daniel holds together in one book, and indeed in one human life, the political theologies of both Romans 13 and the book of Revelation. If so, such a reading gives support to Alan Boesak's claim, articulated in the shadow of South African apartheid, that Romans 13:1-7 offers a depiction of the state as God intended it, whereas Revelation depicts the kind of state that has so rejected God's intention that it can only be resisted.[63] Daniel would then offer us a model of someone who lived under both sorts of political regimes, and demonstrates for us the difference in political practice that each demanded.[64]

---

[62]James K. A. Smith, *Awaiting the King: Reforming Public Theology*, Cultural Liturgies vol. 3 (Grand Rapids, MI: Baker Academic, 2017), xiii.

[63]Allan A. Boesak, *Black and Reformed: Apartheid, Liberation, and the Calvinist Tradition* (Eugene, OR: Wipf & Stock, 2015), 54.

[64]A similar point is made in Nicholas Wolterstorff, *Hearing the Call: Liturgy, Justice, Church, and World* (Grand Rapids, MI: Eerdmans, 2011), 364.

THE "DANIEL OPTION" AND CONTEMPORARY POLITICAL THEOLOGY

The "Daniel Option" reveals the problematic tendency of some American Christians to choose between a shallow "Romans 13 Only" Option and a shallow "Revelation Only" Alternative. But it must be said that part of the reason for our shortcomings is that political theology is *complicated*. Figuring out how to live out our sole allegiance to God in a complex world we're called to love and serve is a messy business. The "Daniel Option" makes our political theology more complicated because it invites us to hold in tension commitments and positions that seem, at first glance, to be mutually exclusive.

Earlier I suggested that the "Romans 13 Only" Option and "Revelation Only" Alternative are distorted caricatures of serious political theology. It is an enormous gift, then, that theologians working in a variety of traditions are seeking to craft political theologies that move beyond the reductionist problems that lurk *within* their respective traditions.

For instance, D. Stephen Long offers a masterful exploration of the argument between "Augustinian" and "ecclesial" approaches to Christian ethics. Writing from within the ecclesial approach,[65] Long makes a strong case that each of these two camps have undergone enormous revision under the influence of the other's criticism. He advocates for a political theology that maintains an emphasis on the church's embodiment of its own "unique form of politics," while also advocating that this ecclesial approach recognize that Revelation's vision of the new Jerusalem creates a place for the good of nations that "endures."[66] He thus conceives of an ecclesial or neo-Anabaptist political theology that is open to engaging secular politics, because nations are not "demonic," but rather "dethroned authorities who nonetheless have 'glory and honor' to bring to the city set on the hill (Rev 21:26)."[67]

James K. A. Smith, in a sort of mirror reflection of Long's project, offers a political theology rooted in my own Calvinist, neo-Kuyperian tradition, but informed by the ecclesial approach. As such, he argues that Christians can and should pursue cultural transformation, not least in the secular political realm, recognizing that the Spirit can and occasionally does "bend . . .

---

[65]While also offering a thorough and important critique of Yoder's devastating sexual abuse and its implications for the ecclesial approach. See D. Stephen Long, *Augustinian and Ecclesial Christian Ethics: On Loving Enemies* (Lanham, MD: Lexington Books, 2018), 105-12.

[66]Long, *Augustinian*, 216.

[67]Long, *Augustinian*, 276.

political orders" toward the just and righteous character of God's kingdom.[68] At the same time, however, Smith draws on the insights of the ecclesial tradition, and especially the work of Stanley Hauerwas.[69] He thus summons neo-Kuyperian political theology to recognize the way life lived in *any* political society, whether the nation-state or the political society that is the church, is deeply *formative,* even liturgical.[70] The fact that political disciples are "made, not born" means that "political theologies" must "carefully consider the ways that political life is bound up with the formation of habits and desires that make us who we are."[71]

Such an insight guides Smith toward a chastened neo-Kuyperian theology of participation in secular politics, one that recognizes the idolatrous, religious tendencies of the state and the political reality of the church, *without* treating these insights as requiring "mutual exclusivity or total antithesis" between the politics of the church and the politics of the nations.[72] Holding these claims together allows Smith to offer a nuanced account of political discipleship. The body of Christ can and should pursue discipleship oriented toward exclusive allegiance to Jesus, but living that discipleship out includes, at least when possible, the messy work of using political power to bend political institutions, even "if ever so slightly, toward the coming kingdom of love."[73]

My hope is that my interpretation of Daniel might contribute to the articulation and practice of this kind of political theology, in the academy and in the pews. Indeed, the "Daniel Option" offers at least five crucial insights for such a lived political theology.

First. The "Daniel Option" makes clear that *justice,* and especially justice for the poor, is a primary political virtue for political agents and a primary political metric for evaluating any political institution. This is true for the church as a political entity in its own right, because the church is an outpost of the kingdom of God.

But it is also true for any secular political system with which the people of God are engaged. Thus, in its immediate context, the book of Daniel's

---

[68]Smith, *Awaiting the King,* xiii.

[69]Smith, *Awaiting the King,* xii-xiii.

[70]Smith, *Awaiting the King,* 9.

[71]Smith, *Awaiting the King,* 9-10.

[72]Smith, *Awaiting the King,* 16.

[73]Smith, *Awaiting the King,* 17. Calvinist political thought attempts to guard these endeavors from turning into religious coercion through a commitment to "principled pluralism" (see 131-50).

description of the wise as those who will cause "righteousness" or "justice" among the "many" primarily refers to the role the wise play in fostering righteousness and justice among God's oppressed, countercultural people (Dan 12:3). But the language of "causing righteousness" (*matsdiqe*) among this oppressed counterculture finds a clear echo in Daniel's earlier attempt to cause even the tyrant Nebuchadnezzar to embrace such "righteousness" or "justice" (*tsidqah*; Dan 4:27[24]).[74] In other words, God's unique vision for justice and righteousness guides his people's politics in the church and outside of it. This is true regardless of whether the political moment requires the people of God to participate, resist, or withdraw from the broader political community. Faithful politics, in Daniel and in the rest of Scripture, demands the just, faithful exercise of power on behalf of the oppressed.

Second. The "Daniel Option" relentlessly reminds political theology that the *way* we engage secular political powers depends on our discernment of the unique possibilities of our particular moment. Daniel does not fit neatly into a "for" or "against" approach to secular politics, because he works hard for Nebuchadnezzar, refuses to work for Belteshazzar, and glimpses a future day when any collaboration with a future regime would be nothing short of apostasy. As a result, those claiming that faithful participation in the power politics of the empire can be a godly way to pursue real change for justice and the common good can claim the Daniel of Daniel 1–6 for their team, but will struggle to understand the Daniel of Daniel 7–12. Alternatively, those who see all power politics as complicity in oppression, and who therefore counsel either straightforward resistance or withdrawal as the only faithful postures, have the *exact same problem with the book,* only in reverse.

The Daniel we encounter in the canonical form of the book holds these apparently contradictory positions together. He embodies, in his own life, both outright resistance and cautious, constructive engagement with empire. The shifts in his behavior, I suggest, are best understood as "ad hoc"[75] determinations *based on wise discernment of his context*, rather than as evidence of a changing theological perspective. Such discernment depends on

- A countercultural community whose formative discipleship includes spiritual disciplines of prayer, fasting, corporate repentance, and calculated resistance to the contemporary equivalent of the king's food and imperial pedagogy.

---

[74]See Breed, "Divided Tongue," 129.
[75]See Smith, *Awaiting the King,* xiv.

- A countercultural community whose formative discipleship includes receiving and embracing the distinctive account of justice, righteousness, and holiness encountered in Scripture.
- A countercultural community whose formative discipleship shapes its members to embrace God's own perspective on their contemporary political realities.

This last point demands further explanation. The apocalyptic political wisdom that shapes Daniel's politics reveals the relentless propensity to idolatry and oppression of all political power. Every single regime Daniel encounters, those he works with and those he refuses to work with, demonstrates this tendency toward the idolatrous. Indeed, the end of Daniel 2 intentionally leads us to believe Nebuchadnezzar has learned his lesson, only to spend the following two chapters recounting his repeated "relapses."[76] At the same time, this universal idolatrous tendency does *not mean* that every political regime is equally problematic. Daniel's God-given visions depict Nebuchadnezzar as a head of gold, while describing future rulers as hideous monsters. God's people must make serious moral distinctions *between* various contemporary political options.

By contrast, scholars sometimes speak about empire in a way that suggests every "empire" is equally problematic. At the popular-level, Christians sometimes suggest a sort of broad moral equivalency between all the supposedly equally corrupt political parties or platforms on offer. But while the book of Daniel recognizes continuity between empires, it *also* distinguishes between better and worse regimes. Indeed, it is the community's discernment of these very differences that determines whether the appropriate response is creative collaboration, constructive confrontation, or outright resistance.

Political discernment for the "Daniel Option" thus rejects any kind of political false equivalencies, against pretending that each politician or political group proves equally amenable to Christians with a good head on their shoulders. The Daniel Option's depiction of monstrous, beastly regimes confronts us with the task of identifying when rejection and resistance are the appropriate course. Daniel's political discipleship shaped him to seek God's kingdom in secular politics whenever possible. But it also prepared him to recognize when political regimes had become so corrupt that participation was no longer a faithful option.

---

[76]Pannkuk, *King of Kings*, 170.

Third. Because justice stands at the heart of biblical politics, and because every political power tends toward idolatry and injustice, Christians must practice prophetic confrontation with political powers, *even and especially the ones with whom they collaborate.* For instance, it is remarkable that Daniel decides that he can work with Nebuchadnezzar, the tyrant who sacked Jerusalem and ransacked the temple. That reality challenges any kind of political purism that would put narrow constraints on the faith community's ability to make partnerships with those with whom they have deep disagreements. But just discipleship also requires Daniel to put his boss in his place, prophetically confronting Nebuchadnezzar's idolatrous view of his own regime and his unjust treatment of the poor.

Perhaps the greatest temptation facing Christians who get deeply involved with secular politics is to allow their partnerships with political powers to blunt their ability to prophetically critique the unjust and idolatrous tendencies of those powers. But from the perspective of the "Daniel Option," faithful political witness includes criticizing the hell—literally—out of our own political team. Indeed, based on the corporate prayer of repentance in Daniel 9, the "Daniel Option" requires us to criticize the hell out of our own political selves!

To return to the example of contemporary evangelical politics, if Christians discern that they can work with the Republican Party in the Trump era, they must, for instance, confront their party's dehumanizing attacks on immigrants and refugees. If Christians discern that they can work with the Democrats, they must, for instance, confront their party's refusal to defend the lives of the unborn. In either case, Christians must confront idolatrous nationalism whenever they encounter it in any political party or movement.

But of course, maintaining a political posture that is both *prudent* and *prophetic* is extremely difficult.[77] That difficulty drives us back to the importance of moral formation oriented toward just discipleship. Christians who can practice the "Daniel Option" in the halls of power will only emerge from countercultural communities that shape their members for deep allegiance to Jesus and his just kingdom, on the one hand, and toward a relative, "calculated ambivalence"[78] toward secular political power on the other.

I say *relative* ambivalence because Daniel is truly invested in the well-being of his people, and indeed, the well-being of Babylon. That, after all, is

---

[77]The language is Goldingay's.
[78]Smith, *Awaiting the King*, xiv.

just what Jeremiah instructed when he wrote to the exiles that they should "seek the welfare of the city" to which they'd been sent (Jer 29:7). The challenge is to embrace the kind of ecclesial life that relativizes such commitment to the nation in light of the church's fundamental identity and allegiance as an outpost of the kingdom of God, under the reign of Jesus, and guided by Scripture. It is this kind of just, morally formative, Scripture-soaked political discipleship that we so desperately need. In a world in which idolatries and injustices lurk on both sides of the political aisle, political discipleship under the reign of Jesus is the only avenue for faithful political participation.

Fourth. The "Daniel Option" offers Christians a peculiar form of political hope. On the one hand, even Nebuchadnezzar can change. He can even learn a thing or two about the kingdom of God, and that is good news for everybody. At the same time, such political success is short-term and provisional at best. Even when the empire learns something (Dan 2), it soon forgets it (Dan 3). Should the Nebuchadnezzars of our world finally learn their lesson (Dan 4), this will not usher in the kingdom of God. More likely, it will usher in the election of another round of oppressive politicians (Dan 5)! This reality counterbalances the kind of political theology that tends toward an overly optimistic view of political structures or processes.

The "Daniel Option" therefore calls the people of God to work and hope for short-term political change whenever possible, while also relentlessly reminding us that our final political hope is tied exclusively to God's ultimate triumph over every human kingdom. This victory comes solely from God and is outside the control of any human power: the stone of God's kingdom is cut by no human hand (Dan 2:45)![79] That central theological claim stands at the center of Christian political discipleship, chastening our hopes, but also relieving us of the burden of trying to bring the kingdom ourselves through our own political efforts.

Fifth. The "Daniel Option" requires God's people to embrace *suffering* in our political lives. While the regimes in the book of Daniel change, the countercultural community's willingness to suffer for their allegiance to God stays the same. While the "Daniel Option" does not seek this suffering out, it does offer contemporary faith communities an important question: Where does our political practice require us to suffer for the sake of faithfulness to God and for the sake of justice for our neighbors?

---

[79]See the helpful reflections in Smith-Christopher, "Daniel," 56.

THE "DANIEL OPTION" EMBODIED

I hope that these five insights, along with my larger interpretation of Joseph and Daniel, help the kind of nuanced political theology represented by Long and Smith take root in the pews of American churches. To that end, I want to close by suggesting a modern day figure whose political life echoes aspects of the "Daniel Option": the late Reverend Dr. James Netters Sr.[80]

Reverend Netters was, at the time of his death in 2020, the "longest serving pastor of a single church in the City of Memphis."[81] Installed at Mt. Vernon Baptist Church in 1955, Netters' engagement with the community led him to participate in Dr. King's civil rights movement. He was on the stage during King's "I Have a Dream Speech," and inspired by King's example, he and six others were the "first arrested during the bus sit-in demonstrations" in Memphis.[82] Those demonstrations led to the integration of the Memphis city buses, but they also paved the way for Dr. Netters to be elected as one of the first Black city councilors in Memphis.

Netters saw his involvement in politics as an extension of his ministry. His willingness to engage politically both outside and inside the system placed him in a unique position. During his first year in office, the sanitation workers' strike began. Netters worked on the streets as a protestor and was teargassed during the infamous strike on March 28, 1968. But he also worked behind the scenes in his role as a council member. His efforts contributed to the victory for sanitation workers, albeit not before King's assassination.

Netters continued to pastor Mt. Vernon, lead local community outreach efforts, and participate in local government and civic institutions. He served as an assistant to Mayor Wyeth Chandler and used his influence to open doors for Black Memphians to get involved in local government. Like Daniel, this no doubt required constant discernment, negotiation, an ongoing commitment to spiritual formation, and a willingness to stand up to power. Trying to hold together his prophetic voice with the need to participate in politics required Netters to walk something of a tightrope. But perhaps because he remained grounded in the daily life of the poor through his service as a pastor, Netters walked that tightrope with integrity.

---

[80]My thanks to my friend Rev. Dr. Melvin Watkins for offering me insight into Pastor Netters' political theology and practice.

[81]"Pastor Emeritus—Dr. James L. Netters Sr.," Mt. Vernon Westwood, accessed November 15, 2022, https://mt-vernon.org/dr-james-l-netters-sr.

[82]Mt. Vernon Westwood, "Pastor Emeritus—Dr. James L. Netters Sr."

Netters' legacy lives on in the continued witness of Mt. Vernon under the leadership of my friend, the Reverend Dr. Melvin Watkins. Rev. Netters' life reminds us of the power of the "Daniel Option" and the kind of lived political theology that takes that option out into the world, both in the streets and in the halls of power. Such a lived political theology depends on the kind of just discipleship exemplified by the "Daniel Option." May we embrace it!

"FOR THE JOY SET BEFORE US"

Concluding Reflections on Just Discipleship

JESUS BRINGS JUSTICE TO VICTORY (Mt 12:20). Tracing the story of that triumph in Scripture introduces us to a God who loves justice, weaves his just way into the fabric of the world, rules by justice, and welcomes his royal priestly sons and daughters to share in his just rule by faithfully exercising power in imitation of their just God and king.

Following the justice thread in the Bible also confronts us with the tragic rejection of God's just way by those human image bearers. Adam and Eve rebel against God, Cain kills his brother, humanity fills Yahweh's good world with violence . . . and that's all in the first six chapters! When God calls Israel to participate in his plan to reclaim his rebellious world, justice stands simultaneously at the center of their job description and as the summary of God's indictment: Israel, like all humanity, failed dramatically. Israel and humanity's history is dominated by the story of humans unfaithfully exercising power in rebellion against God's good, just way.

The good news of the gospel is that our just God *reigns* and *will not give up* on his plan to rule his world through human image bearers. When humanity and Israel reject their identity and job description as his royal priestly sons and daughters, God sends Jesus as *the* Human, *the* faithful Israelite, *the* King, *the* High Priest, *the* Son of God.

Nor does Jesus exercise his royal power by wiping unjust people off the map, or even by demoting them to a smaller role in his world. In Jesus, the Triune God makes atonement and offers forgiveness to us for our injustice; liberates us from our enslavement to Sin, Death, and the Devil; unites us to himself; invites us to walk his just way in the newness of life; and gives us his Spirit to ensure that we do.

Figure 13.1. Jesus brings justice to victory by establishing a people who do justice

The result? Jesus establishes the church as a community of people empowered by the Spirit and called by God to make King Jesus' just reign *encounterable* in the world. Because the Just King is present among God's people, they serve as witnesses, drawing others to come to Jesus, to be forgiven of their sins and recommissioned as his royal priestly family members. And one day, our Just King will return. The Risen One will raise his people from the dead and reclaim his world in full. The triune God's risen, rescued people will share in God's just rule in a world resurrected and remade forever and ever, world without end. Amen!

Discipleship is the journey of becoming the people God has created us to be within this grand story, guided by Scripture and empowered by the Holy Spirit. Discipleship is a gift we receive freely from God. But God's *gift* of discipleship transforms us for the daily, joyful, Spirit-filled *task* of discipleship. Standing at the center of that gift and task is the calling to *become just*.

Justice does not exhaust the Scriptural story or the disciples' identity and job description. But justice, understood as the faithful exercise of power in community, does stand at the center of the Scriptural story and the disciples' identity and job description. The Bible gives us exhilarating, empowering, explosive guidance for creatively seeking to become *just disciples* in an unjust world.

BECOMING JUST DISCIPLES: THE ROAD BEHIND

In part two, we focused on *becoming just disciples* in terms of our character. Getting a taste of Deuteronomy's feasts invited us to imagine how our life together might foster the kind of just, God-fearing habits that include generous justice in a society deeply divided by class. Hearing the Psalms' justice songs suggested a way of singing that could shape God's people to stand in solidarity with the victims of society's injustice. Listening to the proverbial father's provocative pedagogy fostered in us a desire for the kind of just wisdom that strives for an economy that works for the poor. Gazing on Jesus in 1 John inspired us to open our hearts to the cries of our siblings suffering under economies and cultures deeply corrupted by the devil's influence, and to imitate our Lord through acts of self-sacrificial love in response.

In part three, we focused on the people of God *becoming a just people* through our "in house" politics, the structures, institutions, and norms that guide our common life together. Reflecting on the year of Jubilee forced us to reckon with God's design for his people's socioeconomic life. The Jubilee offered us both a vision of God's just, "every vine and fig tree" economy. It also offered us a just practice whereby God's people could preserve that economy, even if later generations had to acknowledge and repair the injustice of their forefathers to do so. Exploring the way later generations of saints drew on the politics of the Jubilee to discern how to arrange their lives together in later times and places suggested a similar path to us. The Jubilee can inspire the contemporary church to reimagine our life together. It may even inspire American Christians to embrace ecclesial reparations as a jubilary response to our ancestors' failures.

Hearing Paul's words to the Corinthians concerning their struggle to arrange the congregation's politics in line with Christ's invited us to audit the way our own churches often arrange themselves in ways that reinforce unjust hierarchies. But Paul also inspired us to imagine how to "rearrange the chairs" of our congregations so that we might live into our identity as a community that, by its very existence, "proclaims the Lord's death until he comes."

Finally, in part four, we explored how just disciples and just ecclesial communities might seek justice amid the nations, places, and politics of the world around us. Watching Joseph's rise to power prompted us to reflect on both the possibilities and the problems of participation in politics. The "Joseph Option" forced us to consider the way that American Christians, like Joseph, have often used power to claim a place for ourselves in "Egypt," only to discover that, in doing so, we have embraced a problematic "Egyptianization" and risked enslaving our political witness. But by tracking Daniel's rise to power, and the similarities and differences between the "Daniel Option" and the "Joseph Option," we were inspired to imagine a way of just, political discipleship that allows us to seek the good of the places to which we've been sent without being coopted by political idolatry.

JUST DISCIPLESHIP: THE ROAD AHEAD

We've covered quite a bit of ground on our quest to explore what Scripture says about just discipleship. What remains on the road ahead?

Here at the end of what has turned out to be a longish book, I find myself wanting to shout "What remains!? *Nearly everything!*" We've only explored the very tip of the Bible's justice iceberg,[1] and I've brought everything I've said about just discipleship in the Bible to bear on a remarkably narrow range of contemporary issues. I'm convinced the American church *must* grapple with matters of racial and economic justice, and I haven't said nearly all that can or should be said even about those issues. Even if I had, though, God calls just disciples to pursue justice *in every area of life!* If we want the church to truly embrace a vision of *just discipleship* we will have to imagine how Scripture shapes us to live in light of a whole host of contemporary challenges, opportunities, contexts, and callings.

This has come home to me personally, because just as I finished writing this book, my family found ourselves called away from our beloved Memphis neighborhood to Aotearoa/New Zealand[2] on the other side of the planet. The Bible calls God's church to become a community of just disciples here, too. But embracing that call here requires an awareness of histories and contexts far different from the ones we left behind in the United States!

This book does not offer a comprehensive map to just discipleship. But I hope it *has* offered a compelling invitation to the *journey* of just discipleship. The biblical interpretation offered ought to give God's people plenty of ideas for driving a bit further down the road on this journey. Ultimately, though, the church must put plumbing the depths of just discipleship on our long-term agenda. What might that look like?

Embrace the agenda. In *Just Discipleship* I do not offer a blueprint. But I do seek to model a method. That method involves:

- Exploring what the Bible says about justice-oriented discipleship, while
- equipped with the insights of theologians exploring moral formation, and
- desperate to discover what it will mean to live the text creatively in our own context.

I hope that readers of the book have been like the Bereans, eagerly wrestling with the texts we've explored to see if my account truly reflects God's

---

[1]Note the lack of a single chapter devoted to either the Prophets or the Gospels!
[2]Aotearoa is the Māori-language name for New Zealand.

Word (Acts 17:11). For readers who have found my interpretation and method compelling, *Just Discipleship* opens up an entire agenda for biblical interpretation, an agenda that I hope will be taken up by scholars, pastors, students, and Jesus-people in the pews. Assuming our map of moral discipleship in chapter three has paid off in the exegesis that followed, I invite Christians to use that map to explore God's vision for just discipleship in the Bible and in our world in relation to the refugee crisis, the plight of the unborn, religious persecution, the climate crisis, homelessness, end-of-life issues, violence, addiction, injustice against indigenous peoples, legal reform, technology, and *so much more.*

If this agenda is taken up with any seriousness, it will lead Christians both to *revise* and *improve* my map of moral formation, as well as to discover vistas in Scripture's vision of just discipleship that I cannot even imagine. Indeed, from a scholarly perspective, it seems to me we have only begun to see the fruit of bringing the riches of theological ethics into genuine, interdisciplinary dialogue with the task of theological interpretation. I hope *Just Discipleship* encourages others to embrace this agenda.

Engage new dialogue partners. Wrestling with just discipleship in the Bible and in our world has also led me to engage new, and for me somewhat unexpected, dialogue partners. This has included grappling with other disciplines. We have considered the work of economists, historians, social scientists, psychologists, and cognitive scientists. While I fall short of even an amateur understanding of these fields, occasionally listening in to try to understand what they're saying in relation to minimum wage legislation, American religious history, the shape of American neighborhoods, the power of disclosure among trauma victims, or the way imitation appears to be hardwired into our brains has proved enormously fruitful. If just discipleship requires us to read our Bibles carefully, it also invites us to engage others seeking truth in God's world to imagine what it would look like to live the Bible today.

Engaging unlikely dialogue partners has also led me to listen to voices from outside my theological tradition. I'm a cradle Presbyterian, went to a Presbyterian college, and am an ordained minister in a Presbyterian denomination. But my exploration of just discipleship has been deeply enriched by moral theologians from the Roman Catholic tradition, Anabaptist-leaning ethicists, Anglican theologians, Baptist colleagues, and more. While I remain rooted in my theological tradition, learning from the church more broadly has proved deeply enriching.

Most importantly, though, just discipleship has required me to engage dialogue partners from very different social locations than my own, and especially those from the Black church. These voices have deeply affected the way I read the Bible and see the world. This is *not* because truth is relative. It is *not* because nonwhite or economically marginalized interpreters are automatically better or more virtuous than white interpreters from more affluent backgrounds. It is *not* due to my commitment to some hidden critical theory or agenda. It is simply due to the common-sense observation that our experiences make it easier for us to see some things in Scripture and our world, and easier for us to miss others. I *see* different things in Scripture's texts about fatherhood now that I'm a father. Spending time with small-scale farmers in Kenya opened my eyes to teachings about farms and fields. My new Māori colleagues and students are helping me discover new depths in Scripture's ecological vision. And Black Christians engaged in the fight for justice have again and again helped me see aspects of God's heart for justice that I would otherwise have overlooked.

Listening to voices from other social locations or theological traditions may feel alarming for some. In the face of those concerns, I'd just remind you of my own story at Second Presbyterian Church. We had the same Bible John Perkins had in the 1990s. For that matter, we had the same Bible as those praying protestors in the 1960s. Indeed, among those barred from the church during the kneel-ins was *a Black Presbyterian elder!* Scripture is the final authority for Christians. But my church's story suggests we struggle to hear Scripture's authoritative voice alone or isolated in homogeneous groups. Reading Scripture in community with others, and especially with those who have suffered oppression and exclusion, has proven crucial for us in *hearing* Scripture as God's address to us today. Engaging new dialogue partners will prove crucial for the church in our quest to become *just disciples*.

Get started somewhere. God's vision for justice in an unjust world can be overwhelming, but just discipleship cannot afford to be paralyzed by the immensity of the task. No one Christian or church can do it all, but we can all take the next step toward becoming the just individuals and communities God has called us to be. So, to borrow an adage from the community development world, start small and start soon!

As you consider how to begin, gather others together and listen to the Spirit's guidance. If you feel your heart drawn toward Deuteronomy's vision of feasting on the road to justice, start asking how your community can build proximity to the poor and overcome economic segregation in your life to-gether. Look for ways to put feasting at the center of that work! If you're sur-rounded by people suffering due to structural injustice in your city, gather friends, meditate on Joseph and Daniel's story, and consider what it might look like to embrace the "Daniel Option" in *your* community. If you love music or lead people in prayer, lean into the Psalms' justice songs and imagine how they might transform the communities where you have influence. If you exercise power in your workplace, or feel called to speak up for the working poor, return to Proverbs with eyes attuned to that book's justice talk. Ask yourself what that pedagogy might lead you to do as you seek to faithfully exercise power at work, advocate for new policies for the working poor, or protest their plight on the streets. If you feel called to the faithful exercise of power in an area to which the texts I've explored seem inapplicable, go search out the Scriptures for how they might shape God's people for the justice God is calling you to work for in his world. Regardless, get started somewhere . . . and soon!

Expect joy. Justice talk can feel exhausting, not least in relation to matters of race and class. This isn't just because the contemporary church is currently raging about these issues. It's also because the path of just discipleship is a costly, cross-shaped path. We may wonder whether it's worth the effort, espe-cially when the church's interests so often seem fixed elsewhere.

Maybe that's why the Bible repeatedly reminds us that the cruciform journey of justice is drenched with God's generous joy. Just disciples follow a Just King who "for the sake of the joy that was set before him endured the cross, disregarding its shame" (Heb 12:2). That same king calls us to take up our crosses and discover the joy that only he can deliver. That's why pursuing justice in the Bible has brought us to a feast with an over-the-top, whatever-you-deeply-desire menu; opened our eyes to a world in which doing justice is a *joy* to disciples; and given us songs to shout about the happy, just life of God's people. God's jubilary, reparative politics cost God's people farms and fields, but it came with two-year vacations and a new family characterized by daily fellowship with God and one another. Because God wrote justice into the song creation sings, when we embrace just discipleship, we find ourselves humming along with that creational tune. Just discipleship brings *joy* because through just discipleship we live the lives our God created us for.

To refuse just discipleship, to ignore God's demand that we faithfully ex-ercise power in his world, isn't just sinful . . . it's stupid. When we reject God's just way, we turn away from the only path that provides the joy we deeply desire. So let's embrace just discipleship instead! And as we do, let's expect to experience the joy of the Just King who brings "justice to victory."

Embody the invitation. Finally, when the church lives out God's just way in the world, we embody an invitation. A church that lives in line with God's justice *proclaims the kingdom of God by its very life*. Many of our neighbors find the biblical story unbelievable, not least because of the way we so often fail to reflect the character of our Just King. But when we live out our calling as just disciples, God's kingdom becomes *encounterable* in our broken, unbelieving world. We not only tell people *about* the kingdom; we embody in our ecclesial life "the presence of the kingdom."[3] By embodying that kingdom, by making God's reign encounterable, we offer our neighbors a compelling invitation to *join* the kingdom by giving their lives to the king.

Scripture isn't just a story. But it is a justice story. Just disciples learn to *live* that story, for the glory of God, for the good of their neighbors, and for the sheer joy of living life with our Just King. What are we waiting for?

---

[3]Leslie Newbigin, *The Open Secret: An Introduction to the Theology of Mission* (Grand Rapids, MI: Eerdmans, 1995), 48-49, emphasis added.

SCRIPTURE INDEX